Pius XIV

Pius XIV

The Smoke of Satan and the Man of God

A NOVEL
by
Don Giuseppe Pace
(Originally published under the pseudonym Walter Martìn)

TRANSLATED BY
Brian Welter

AROUCA PRESS

Copyright © Arouca Press 2024
Translation © Brian Welter 2024

Originally published under the pseudonym Walter Martìn in 1978 with the title *Pio XIV Pontefice di transizione*. This English edition, which retains part of the original title, is based on the Italian edition published as *Habemus Papam* by Fede & Cultura in 2011.

Special acknowledgements extended to Luca Fumagalli who helped in reviewing the English translation and to Jonathan Arrington who provided greater context for many of the Latin phrases which he also ensured were translated accurately.

All rights reserved.

No part of this book may be reproduced or transmitted, in any form or by any means, without permission.

ISBN: 978-1-990685-92-7 (pbk)
ISBN: 978-1-990685-93-4 (hc)

Arouca Press
PO Box 55003
Bridgeport PO
Waterloo, ON N2J 0A5
Canada
www.aroucapress.com
Send inquiries to info@aroucapress.com

Cover design by
Julian Kwasniewski

Contents

Translator's Foreword ix
Preface to the Italian Edition (2011) xiv
Historical Note xvii

1. The Revenge of Car Wreckers 3
2. Life is a Dream 8
3. Senile Tenderness. 16
4. Power of Seclusion 21
5. The Age of the Disuse of Reason 25
6. Ah, those doves 30
7. Plans 36
8. The Window on the Seminarians 40
9. Father Gregorio, Former Prophet of Ill Omen 49
10. The "Sub-Conditione" Lie 59
11. Monsignor Gabriel Wong 64
12. The Canon Lawyer's Response 71
13. To the Correspondence Office 77
14. To the Parish of the Three Holy Brothers 82
15. Refined Surgery 92
16. François René Visconte de Chateaubriand 100

Interlude 111

17. Father Aurelio's Ten Points 118
18. "Auri sacra fames" 127
19. Catholic News 140
20. The Great Sorcerer 146
21. The Catholic School 158
22. Without the Church there is no Holy Scripture . . 164

23	Introibo ad altare Dei	174
24	Every Promise is a Debt	180
25	"Principiis Obsta!"	189
26	Father Medina and his Page	197
27	Not Westernizing the Church?	209
28	Romolo Gives Himself Away	225
29	"Tischreden"	234
30	Stravinsky's "Fireworks"	244
31	Broadcasting	251
32	"Ludwig and Friedrich"	259
33	The Prodigal Son	264
34	A Lesson in Aesthetics	270
35	Legitimate Defense	276
36	Lateran VI	291
37	"Traditionis restauratio"	308
38	"Felix culpa"	319
39	A Mountain of People Twice Murdered	328
40	English Attitude	336
41	Thomas Morgenröte Searches for the Rock	348
42	"Nomen meum Legio"	354
43	From Wellhausen to Maternalism	367
44	Sermons	380
45	Petty Sociology in the Sacristy	387
46	Before and After Treatment	393
47	Drugs are a Serious Problem	406
48	At the Olive Wood Cross	413

Translator's Foreword

IN *PIUS XIV*, AUTHOR WALTER MARTÌN, PEN name for the Italian priest, Don Giuseppe Pace, provides welcome clarity for our ambivalent and uncertain era. In a simple and straightforward style, he appeals for the full and uncompromising restoration of the Traditional Latin Mass and, in fact, the complete liturgical life of the pre-Vatican II Catholic Church. He premises this call on his observation that the Council has been disastrous for individual believers and the Church. The novel's articulate and authentic dialogues on the Council, covering its famous spirit and revolutionary impact on Catholicism, strongly suggest that the author as a priest witnessed or even participated in such conversations among Church leaders.

Alongside his strong advocacy for the Traditionalist position, Martìn provides insight into the proponents of reform and revolution. He reveals the clericalism behind the zeal for Vatican II. The stubborn ideology, love of power, and tendency to acquiesce to the world brook no dissent from the faithful, who are expected to obey all revolutionary ideas. Unsurprisingly, it often seems that the novel's characters are referring to current events in the Church. Martìn also reveals the impact of the Council on priests and bishops at the psychological and spiritual levels after they traded the Catholic tradition for the spirit of the world. They replaced metaphysics with evolution, St. Thomas with Teilhard de Chardin, and the Person of Jesus Christ with the abstraction of *humanity*. Martìn memorably depicts the resulting sharp decline in spiritual life and moral virtue in such individuals and the Church as a whole.

The fact that the adoption of a pro- or antitraditional stance leads to grave spiritual, psychological, and moral consequences reflects the reality that this spiritual battle offers no neutral position. This is because of the nature of the Tradition of the Church. Tradition fosters certain virtues, such as humility, acceptance of God's will, and dependence on God through prayer. The rejection of this makes the heart restless. This restlessness works to turn the Church into a social service agency and advocate for perpetual revolution. The mentality of the reformers of Vatican II involves the spirit of protest and the attempt to build something of substance from the ruins that are left behind. But what they end up building reflects the utilitarian, pragmatic, and anti-metaphysical mentality of the twentieth century:

> They changed the Mass as one changes attire. The most dismayed faithful were comforted by being told, "Here is finally a clean shirt, lighter, if you like, but functional."

These men of restless and proud protest, as depicted in *Pius XIV*, possess an unreasonable hostility towards the Latin liturgy. Their revolution has become the new normal, the new tradition, that regards the Latin Church as something to be overcome and left behind. Conversion triggers a return to Tradition, as Martìn demonstrates, with certain characters undergoing spiritual and psychological changes brought on by their interactions with Pope Pius XIV.

The dialogues between traditionalists and Vatican II enthusiasts revolve around the organic development of the Mass versus the notion that the liturgy can be changed at will in order to fit into the spirit of the world. The Church no longer informs the world, but is informed by the world. This is the Protestant spirit: The Church does not change the believer; the believer changes the Church. One can even say that Martìn wrote an anti-woke novel *avant la lettre*, before wokism existed in its current form. The author would likely be unsurprised by the nonsense we are currently living through. The novel reveals how the Council allowed the Church to turn from a pillar against revolution into a pillar of wokism itself. The Church became subversive against itself, against its own tradition.

Much of the Church is therefore enemy-occupied territory. The reader gets the impression that the Pope and his few supporters have sequestered themselves off from the Vatican's notorious intrigues. These intrigues are not of the Spirit, but of the world, particularly in the past few decades. Even in the Vatican itself, then, it is the world, it is modernity, that holds sway. The author notably avoids directly depicting the intimidating Vatican machine aside from an episode with the Vatican post office when the Pope decides to see what has happened to all his mail and finds that a hidden hand has been misdirecting all but the most harmless of correspondence. Soon after his election, Pope Pius XIV leaves his Vatican apartments for a simple cell in the monastery of a humble order, where he eats his meals and becomes part of the community.

As the dialogues, intrigues, events, and works of restoration unfold over the course of the novel, the author successfully conveys a sense of what was lost and how worldly banalities, such as jazz and other contemporary music, replaced the previous majesty. Jazz is the least of it, as ecumenism, evolutionism, and liberation theology characterize the new Catholic Church. In opposition to this, the author develops an ecclesiology that traditionalists will welcome: The Church is here to proclaim the Good News and provide the sacraments. It is not here to push for social and political revolution or act as a social service agency. Yet the warmth of the traditionalist characters refutes the accusation of indifference to the poor. They are not rejecting the needy, but the Marxist abstractions of *humanity* and *sinful structures*, neither of which have anything to do with the Gospel or with real humans. The guiding philosophy in the novel is realism, which Martìn portrays well.

If Vatican II was a rupture that overturned the spiritual lives of the vast majority of priests, religious, and the laity, Latin offers the key to restoration. *Romanitas* includes all the treasures that the outsider Osiris Market has purloined from indifferent priests and other parish leaders who operate in the Vatican II spirit. Interestingly, this dishonest and greedy entrepreneur knows more about the true value of these sacramentals and other items than the churchmen do. He is aghast when the traditionalist Pope means to put an end to his sacrilegious selling off of these articles—candlestick holders, chalices, old missals—and wants the Church to put them back into their rightful places. He is as viciously dead set against the Pope as the liberal churchmen are. Like them, he has a worldly agenda.

Market and the liberal clerics recognize that the traditionalists are about to ruin their common agenda. This is a significant insight of the author. Agendas tend to run and ruin certain aspects of Church life. Hardly any sunlight exists between the agendas of the churchmen and that of Osiris Market. The latter's worldliness is obvious. But the anti-traditionalists are just as worldly by adopting the materialist ideologies of the twentieth century. The author covers this horizontal spirit exceptionally well. He shows the revolutionary agenda, the revolutionary spirit, of the anti-traditionalists. Market wants to sell off the material patrimony of the Church, the physical traces of its tradition, while the anti-traditionalists resolutely oppose many elements of the spiritual and moral patrimony of the Church.

Despite all this, *Pius XIV* offers hope because it is a book of faith. The love and perseverance of Pius XIV and his supporters easily triumph over the agendas and treachery of their opponents. Pius and his supporters rely on prayer and their love for the Church and its Tradition. They rely on Christ. They are not easily moved to action, but when they do act, it is with singleness of purpose, peace of mind, and a focus that is unswayed by all the maneuvering and hostility of their adversaries. They are confident of their future victory because they are serving Christ, not the world and its ideologies. The laity's active participation in this, largely through devotion to the Latin liturgy, is an invitation to the reader to lend tangible support to Tradition. This is the book's call to action. The author does not see the Catholic layperson as a passive observer of this spiritual battle, but as closely involved. Perhaps it is not too much to say that the reader will come away from this book with the sense that we are all playing a role in some cosmic drama.

Brian Welter

Preface to the Italian Edition (2011)

AT THE DAWN OF THE THIRD MILLENNIUM, the genre *Vatican-fantasy* means little more than Dan Brown and the *Da Vinci Code*, *Angels and Demons*. Apart from rare jewels of doctrine and narrative such as Michael O'Brien's *Father Elijah: An Apocalypse*, the genre refers to anti-Catholic nonsense at the bookstore that readers with middling literary and theological tastes might make into a success as they participate in a sort of common ownership of bad taste, bad culture, and bad faith.

The genre has had other ancestors. In 1914, André Gide tried his hand at it with the nihilistic and irreverent *The Vatican Cellars* that was, at least, produced by a future Nobel Prize winner. But the genealogical tree of this genre can be traced back in another direction Over the centuries it is not far-fetched to find the archetype in the so-called Gnostic gospels, of which the most emblematic example is the *Gospel of Judas*, discovered every two or three hundred years by anti-Christian propaganda.

All this is to say that *Vatican-fantasy* normally means hatred for the Roman Catholic Church, with certain exceptions, but an old and never-eclipsed editorial law teaches that there are no exceptions in the history of the printed word. However, from time to time an isolated case comes along, a gold nugget that reveals a precious vein to which only the good have access. It didn't take much, therefore, to convince the Italian editor Fede & Cultura to publish *Habemus Papam*, which is a real and authentic nugget of Catholic *Vatican-fantasy*.

This wasn't the publisher's first step in this direction. In a way, it took its first step with Rosa Alberoni's *Intrigo al Vaticano II* (2010). But Alberoni's novel, as a fictional reconstruction of a real event, is a reflection on the past. In contrast, *Habemus Papam* depicts a fictional present and future.

Let us turn to the history of this book, which technically was never published even after some had already read it. Carlo Rasellis, long-term president of the Turin section of "Una Voce" and a protagonist in this little literary case, reveals the mystery in his notes. In the late 1970s and early 1980s, *Una Voce* of Turin printed the novel, then entitled *Pius XIV*,[1] for non-commercial purposes in "pro manuscripto" form. The author, the Salesian Don Giuseppe Pace, chose the pen name Walter Martin.

After that, *Editiones Sancte Michaelis* released three currently out-of-print, four-hundred page editions that recount the history of Pope Pius XIV after his election without much deep support as a way to end an interminable conclave. Pius is a transitional pope, as the subtitle of the 1979 manuscript declares. The electoral cardinals expect him to be as dull as he is old, to be a meek man who is to ferry the Church from one progressive papacy to the succeeding, more progressive papacy. But Pius XIV is so old and so enamored of the Church that he combines his own eternally young love for the Mystical Body of Christ with his own old age and restores the honor of Tradition.

To understand what is reserved for the reader of this novel, built with skillful narrative, suspense, sound theology, and good doctrine requires an explanation of who Don Giuseppe Pace was. When he died in 2000 at 89, he left behind a great quantity of writings on a wide variety of subjects, all chiseled with expertise and depth. But it is not for his erudition that his readers have come to love him. What aroused the veneration that only certain priests know how to inspire, was his

---

[1] As mentioned earlier, we have decided to use this title for the English edition.

attachment to Tradition, in a Church that was boldly marching towards the abyss of progressivism. It was his fidelity to the traditional Mass that his brothers made him pay bitterly. It was the ability to read the future that distinguishes those who do not forget the past and, indeed, love it. It was that goodness hidden in the heart of those who know how to combine Truth and Charity.

Habemus Papam contains all of this, embodied in *Pope Pius XIV*. This is a man who, step by step, puts back in their places of honor all that had been hidden in the previous few decades: the Mass, prayer, devotion, doctrine, theology, morality, and even good manners. It is a stainless repertoire of the fundamentals of the Catholic faith that, in certain pages, almost seems to be a prose version of *Iota unum*.[2]

Written at the end of the 1970s, *Habemus Papam* has not lost any of its freshness. Quite the contrary. It has more to say today than when it was published. It would be a shame if it were not put back into circulation, if only to explain what the hermeneutic of continuity is to the tin soldiers who, antagonistic to progressive tendencies only on the surface, still confuse this hermeneutic with the obligation to continually justify the current disorder. Armed with doctrine and the facts, Pius XIV explains that the hermeneutic of continuity is as simple as one can imagine: Not only can everyone see all the errors that were committed, but the truth must be restored for each of those errors.

At this point, who still has the courage to call it a *Vatican-fantasy*?

Alessandro Gnocchi *and* Mario Palmaro

---

[2] *Iota unum*, by Romano Amerio, critiques Vatican II and asserts that the Council caused a rupture with Tradition.

Historical Note

IN 1978, THE YEAR OF THREE POPES, A BOOK entitled *Pio XIV Pontefice di transizione*[1] was published. Its author, Walter Martìn (the pen name for Don Giuseppe Pace), wanted it to be known as a novel, though in reality its fictional narrative contained an ample display of the logic and hopes of Catholic Tradition, which the liturgical reform of the post-Vatican II period had put to a harsh test.

Readers of this reissue of the third edition of the work might want to know the now-distant events of the era that led to its writing, since it contains brief hints to the direct participants of those events.

The promulgation of the *Novus Ordo Missae* in 1969 sparked a widespread movement of protest of the clergy and faithful as represented by the *Brief Critical Examination* of Cardinals Ottaviani and Bacci and by the *International Association "Una Voce,"* organized by the faithful.

In Italy, Rome, Bologna, and then Turin each saw an *Una Voce* group organized, in the latter city welcomed in the Church of the St. Trinity. There, the brave Monsignor Attilio Vaudagnotti, indifferent to the obvious and harsh hostility of the local Church, continued to publicly celebrate the only Holy Tridentine Mass in the city.

Very soon a Salesian, a man of great faith and inextinguishable literary streak, Don Giuseppe Pace, joined the *Una Voce* group. He also continued to celebrate the old rite, but was restricted to the catacombs. He began to collaborate with

---

[1] *Pius XIV: Transitional Pontiff*

Monsignor Vaudagnotti in the celebrations at St. Trinity. When the small journal *Notizie* appeared next to that of *Una Voce*, he became the principal collaborator under the pen name Fra Galdino da Pescarenico. His articles defending Tradition and the Holy Mass brought great comfort to the readers.

The idea of bringing his thoughts on the subject together into a single work developed while he was collaborating with *Notizie*. The first edition of *Habemus Papam* was immediately followed by a second and then, at the beginning of the 1980s, a third one revised and with a new title.

May those who read these pages find spiritual comfort, consolation, courage, and perseverance in sustaining and defending the cause of the Traditional Holy Mass, the true fulcrum of our faith, for the greater glory of God and of His Church. One, Holy, Catholic, and Apostolic.

Turin, 2011
Carlo Raselli

Pius XIV

*The Smoke of Satan
and the Man of God*

I

The Revenge of Car Wreckers

Faithful to the motto, *INSTAUrare omnia in Christo*, to lead everything back to the path of Tradition, he was prematurely worn out. How much opposition had he not met? Open opposition apart from declared enemies, underhanded but no less merciless opposition from unfaithful ministers. After the swift transition and the meteoric passing away of such a pontiff, progressivism had boldly returned on the crest of a wave. The attacks of the "self-destroyers of the Church" had reconquered the command positions, from which they had already been removed. Priests' cassocks once again disappeared, as if by magic, and once again the apostolic Mass was driven back into the catacombs. The weak were giving up, but then many of the strongest types appeared lost and contradicted themselves.

Conversely, the Roman October did not deny itself. The sun's light and color filled the Villa Borghese, the Pincio, the Gianicolo, and the other gardens of Rome. It warmed and cheered up the hearts of those who crowded these places. Satisfied, red-faced, and enormous, they now descended to the west, behind the dome of St. Peter's Basilica, in a triumphant procession of golden clouds, while vast storms of birds circled in the sky in surprise, making their terrific maneuvers before starting off as one on their flight across the Mediterranean to Africa. Thousands of birds. They appeared as soft strips of black veils at the mercy of a strange wind.

Only the paths of the Vatican Gardens remained deserted. It was already too cool for the Pope's weary legs. His eyes were too mournful despite the tremendous display of vibrant foliage and flowers. The Pope preferred to be locked up in his studio, in its tropical warmth which to the Camerlengo, in fact, felt muggy. This was why the Camerlengo always kept his visits to the Pope so brief and rare. But this was not the only reason. Additionally, the Pope was no longer capable of following a conversation all the way through, even ones that were not so long, in spite of all the vitamin and hormone drinks that the pontifical chief physician had prescribed him and that he meticulously made sure to take on time.

On this night the Camerlengo had found the Pope bent over his desk, as if reading. But he had not been reading at all, although he had spread out in front of him a newspaper that still smelled of fresh ink. After recapturing the Pope's attention with the usual courtesies, the Camerlengo placed in front of him a huge protocol sheet, and suddenly entered into the heart of the argument:

"Here you are, Holiness, the list of prelates who, in my humble opinion, should become part of the college of electors. All are young, if not in years, then in mentality. And these three, the oldest, are in tune with the times."

The Pope quickly glanced at the sheet, then pointed to a name and asked:

"Even this seventy-nine year old?" But not expecting an answer, he continued: "He will still be in time to attend the next conclave that will make you my successor."

"Who says, Holiness?"

"That my days are numbered... And these, who are they?"

"Those excluded from the conclave according to the *motu proprio Praelati sine cura*. They are all from the ancien regime, no less than these others, who will cease to be valid in two months due to the *motu proprio*."

"They will therefore not participate in the next conclave. Because even if I die this very night, you will easily delay things until then. You can then count on a mathematically certain majority in your favor, Eminence."

"Oh Holiness, in a conclave, whoever enters Pope exits cardinal!"

"This will not happen to you, Eminence. In any case, let's leave this to Providence, who will miraculously remove the last obstacles to the renewal of the face of the Church...Yet look, Eminence, at the things that are published by this monthly magazine that claims to be Catholic. Look at this here: 'I am not an observant Catholic, thank goodness! Because I would not know how to reconcile obedience as my duty and respect towards the hierarchy, the Pope at the top—understand? The Pope at the top!—who seems committed to destroy the Church, or at least to make it hated in the eyes of the whole world, depleting the acquired wisdom of two millennia in order to look up-to-date. It looks like an undiscriminating girl who flirts with everyone and who ends up not being taken seriously by anyone.' Do you understand, Eminence, what these people dare to write?"

"Cassandras, Holiness, short-sighted and cheeky Cassandras!"

"While they misunderstand the ecumenical springtime, due to which the old Mass, which had been reappearing everywhere, had to be banned once again. How many enthusiastic reports..."

"Enthusiastic reports? How many times did we receive some glowing report on the progress of the Church's bold leap onward and upward that we had stubbornly desired for the people's progress and the process of universal evolution? How many times, did we use to say, were we suddenly taken hold of by giddiness? Yes, it was really like that! It happened right in front of that dense curtain of smoke that sometimes blocked from our view the radiant vision of this whole immense ocean of new lights that were burning like flames and expanding in every direction. And it's strange to say, although spanning such boundless and glowing horizons, suddenly it became dark all around. We felt an icy chill numbed our bones, and inside us resonated, restrained and insistent, the voice,...the voice of Cassandra? The voice of this cricket?"

"Really, I hadn't thought of Pinocchio's cricket, Holiness. I heard this expression repeatedly here in the Vatican. It's used here all the time. I heard it just an hour ago again from one of the prelates that I made up the list with and showed you."

But the Pope was no longer listening. His head had fallen towards his chest, as if he were reflecting on something. His hands, though resting on the desk, were trembling.

"Take a rest, Holiness, take a rest! Rome's autumn is beautiful. Did you see how magnificent it was today too? Winter is short. Next spring will restore all of Your Holiness's strength that is necessary to lead from the bridge of command, the prow, the world's holy ark."

Seeing no sign of response from the Pope, who stayed unmoving, dozing rather than absorbed in anything, the Camerlengo began speaking softly again:

"Take a rest, take a rest, so you can recover," he said. He took back his protocol sheet and slowly left the room.

In fact, the next day, the bells of St. Peter's Basilica spread the sad news around the city, and, around the world, the communique of the *Ecumenical Press* reported on the "Pope's peaceful death, as his health failed, in his role as an ancient patriarch, at his place of work." In fact, he was found that morning sunk in his armchair, in front of the television. He had been there for some time, as his body was cold when he was found, with his chin on his chest, his pen in his right hand, and a picture of the Crucifix in his left. At the bottom of the picture he had scribbled in shaky letters his last three words: *Miserere mei, Deus!*

As normally happens in such situations, the craziest hypotheses about the Pope's death, which were turned into crime novels, were spread. No shortage of suspects was suggested. The Vatican's agency, *Ecumenical Press*, despite the understandable insistence of the world's other leading news agencies, added nothing to the first and only bulletin in which, in succinct and laconic terms, it had given notice of the Pontiff's death. No further photos were provided after the first one, which had been authorized by the cardinal Camerlengo. It portrayed the august body of the Pontiff as already prepared for burial, almost hidden by the garments. As well, this "historical sobriety," as defined by the same Vatican agency, wanted to avoid giving any misplaced impressions. This had the opposite effect, which only grew.

"The braying of donkeys doesn't get to heaven," declared someone simply in the Vatican. "Tomorrow, as soon as the Plasma N-jet spacecraft enters orbit around Mars, and the video shows Mars from only a few kilometers high, the thoughts of people will turn elsewhere, and they will start talking of other things."

However, both at the Vatican and elsewhere, in countless Christian families and religious institutions, many said in their hearts or sometimes even out loud, "The Lord has called to Himself the Pope of the Reformation. The Pontiff kept implementing this reform. Who knows why? The Church's self-destruction. Peace to his soul! They say that he had a holy death. Now, however, may the Lord finally grant us the Pope who can make things balanced again."

There was no speculation or gossip. But prayers and penance multiplied with renewed faith. Many had been doing so for some time already to obtain such a grace. In fact, as the cobblestones themselves might have said, the Holy Spirit would have equal reason to select such a Pontiff among the prelates who were reunited at the conclave.

2

Life is a Dream

IT HAD BEEN SNOWING ENDLESSLY. In all that snow that had made Rome ever more silent and white, the cardinals and other prelates, heading towards the bronze doorway in order to enter into the conclave after three months of a vacant pontifical see saw an auspicious sign: The conclave would be concluded in a few days. For Christmas, only a few days away, the Church needed a new Pontiff. But Christmas had come and gone, as had New Year's and Epiphany. The faithful, the curious, and the journalists who had gathered under Bernini's portico, or remained cooped up in their own cars in the Piazza San Pietro, did not spot the white smoke that signified that an election had taken place.

All of January had passed after Epiphany. Then February and March. And still no new Pontiff. The situation, serious enough at any time, had now become rather dramatic. Were there too many political groups among the conclave fathers? Were the leaders of each group too hardliner? The fact was that in the conclave the supporters of ever-new movements and ever-new combinations had multiplied. Each was convinced, in turn, that he had found the formula of compromise that would bring the impasse to an end and would proceed to collect the required *quorum*. But each was badly disappointed by the inevitable response of the urn.

By this time, the Piazza San Pietro, inundated everywhere with the sun of the approaching spring, was nearly deserted.

The Roman populace, so demanding in earlier times with their desire for a Pope fast and good, had disappeared. They seemed to have forgotten everything related to what was happening on the other side of the bronze doors. Even rumors, snatched by journalists (who every now and then, out of sheer professional scrupulosity, had returned to their offices) and reported by one of the dailies with the most sensational titles possible, were of less interest than the visit to Rome of the president of the Hot International Club.

This lack of interest was so dehumanizing! The conclave prelates suffered profoundly as a result. They felt humbled, like undisciplined schoolchildren, in their failure to choose a new master. They were like a group of fighting roosters, divided into different ranks, without any followers or glory. They sighed, complained among themselves, and repeated, "What an example we're giving the faithful!" "What an example we're giving all of humanity!" "And what a torpedo in the ammunition depot of transatlantic ecumenism!" Transatlantic ecumenism? Actually, there were those who thought it was a ghost ship rather than an ocean liner, its sails kept puffed up by the arsenal's mighty fans. Although it was only made of papier-mâché, it did not sink, because it was still held in the slipway by the hull. But it was so close to the water that it seemed to be already there, moving solemnly and safely towards the high seas.

But many conclave prelates were worried thin by another issue, which was the denial of universal, ceaseless, and irreversible progress. The conclave should have recognized the implementation and historical verification of this dogma. Instead, this belief seemed to be in a state of regression in contrast to the preceding papal election.

Things had now reached the point that tremendous sacrifices and the greatest renunciations were imposed on everyone in order to reach the earliest possible conclusion. With this very purpose, the same cardinal Camerlengo, having entered into the conclave mathematically certain to come out as Pope, was now willing to renounce his own candidature *ad interim*, all things considered. A transitional Pope was needed. During such a short pontificate, and with the help of his loyalists, he could assure himself of a more secure majority at the next conclave than at the current endless one.

In truth it had to be said that the Camerlengo was an excellent man, with an artistic temperament, excellent taste, and vast erudition. He felt at complete ease among artists. There, he couldn't help but have his own needs. There, at times he couldn't help but appear intransigent. Otherwise, he was docile, the most docile. Because of this, the Pope had raised him so high, secure of his docility. The Pope had entrusted him with the task of carrying on the work of aggiornamento in the ecumenical-universal Church. Certainly, the Camerlengo was not unaware of the adulation bestowed by those expecting to find in him a reforming Pope according to their own expectations, and by those who intended to gain certain personal advantages. But now the cold slap in the face from the conclave liberated them from almost all of this excitement.

From among other prelates a project gradually emerged that, if not identical to and having the same aims, was at least similar. Indeed, to bring this prolix and inconclusive conclave to an end, what was needed was the expediency of a transitional papacy, a brief and colorless pontificate. This Pope would soon be followed by the hoped-for but still immature pontiff, a pontiff open to the world who would have to open yet another window to the world.

One can easily see that there is in the human brain something far more perfect than a battery of thermionic valves and fleshly transistors because in the very morning during this conviction became a common belief among the conclave fathers, on Pasquino's bust a cartoon appeared which depicted a figure repeatedly swinging an ax at the deepest part of the keel of the ark of St. Peter. From the saint's mouth came out cartoonishly the words, "Air, air. I'm suffocating in here!" and the verses in the Roman dialect:

> May the new Pope not think
> To enlarge the window a bit;
> For the windows above the world,
> Give the impression that the ark is already hitting
>   the bottom.
> If the Church needs fresh air,
> Do not kick it down into that dark sewer
> Of the world; For all of that stench
> Cannot come from the Holy Spirit.

So the name of Father Pio da Briletri began to be passed from mouth to ear among the prelates of the conclave during breaks. Father Briletri was already a missionary bishop in the Middle East, and had now returned as simply Father Pio, as the spiritual father of the cloistered Sisters of the Passion. Well-advanced in years, far from imposing, good-natured and friendly, appreciated by all, certainly harmless, and lacking any capacity at taking the initiative to govern, he therefore would leave everything as it was. He would have left people free to continue doing their thing. He produced only one original work in his life, a small book with the inoffensive title *Winter Flowers on the Island of Cyprus*. He gave away a copy of his omnibus work to a friend with the modified title, *Winter Flowers on the Island of Cyprus in Light of the Second Vatican Council*. They shared a good laugh. There was no question: Considering Vatican II to be outmoded, he was exactly the man who was wanted. Even more, a rumor circulated among the people that he was a saint of miracles. A long-dead sister had appeared to him and saved his life.

Well, that fact was true: He had confided it: himself—though who knew why, in fact He almost immediately felt regret—to the community of cloistered nuns. But it had been as if he had declared it to a group of journalists at a press conference. Thank goodness he was personally known to only a very few, and could therefore go around unnoticed. Besides, by now he seldom got around, totally intent as he was on writing a *Sacred History* to be filled with personal insights which had come to maturity during his stays at holy sites.

As for that extraordinary event, things had gone in the following way.

Father Pio was then an adolescent of no more than sixteen years. While waiting to enter an apostolic school, he took up Latin with the help of a venerable priest who had set him on the right path. In summers, he occasionally went cycling—an old-fashioned and rather heavy two-wheeled racer—in the surrounding valleys. On that day, it could have been three o'clock in the afternoon. He sped out of a tunnel, and was flying down a street unpaved at that time, but made of smooth earth. At the end, a further three hundred meters, the road turned at a right angle onto a bridge, whereupon it once again straightened out before disappearing into another tunnel. Under the bridge, at a good fifty meters lower down, flowed the white rapids of a river between rocks and crags. The road was flanked on the right by the side of the mountain. The side was as regular as a wall cut artfully into the living rock, without any sort of opening, and on the left by a small wall, less than a meter high. Just beyond that was the abyss with the thundering river at the bottom.

Not a soul was on this little road at this hour.

"Great!," Pio exclaimed, before increasing his already high speed.

A few meters from the bridge he planned to pull hard on the brake lever and make the ninety-degree turn, pass over the bridge, and enter the other tunnel. He knew every inch of the route and could therefore continue at this speed secure in his knowledge of his path. Suddenly, a young woman crossed right in the middle of his path, two meters from the handlebars. He braked sharply to avoid running her over. The wheel, suddenly blocked, skidded on the road for a meter.

"Complete idiot!" After passing the woman, he turned to look back to at least give thanks, as a child would do in similar circumstances. But the road was as completely deserted as it had been a few minutes earlier. The young woman was no longer there.

He finally recognized her: "But that was...that was Cecilia!"

Cecilia was his older sister by about ten years, the first of nine children. She had died after catching a deadly illness seven or eight years earlier. She had loved her little brother, the eighth, and had been like a little mother to him.

"Yes, it really was Cecilia! She didn't look at me so I wouldn't recognize her right away. If she hadn't done that, I would have ended up going over that wall. But it was really her!" In the meantime, continuing at times to look back, he had come to the turn near the bridge, and found the road blocked there. The first section of the bridge had collapsed. To cross it, he had to take the bicycle on his shoulders and proceed like a tightrope walker on the planks thrown across the broken bridge. This was why cars and trucks had not been on the road—the route was blocked. Pio had not paid attention to the sign a kilometer before the bridge that warned passers-by. Two wooden slats had been placed two meters before the bridge as a warning. But they could only be seen when they were banged into. Had he arrived at the bridge at his usual speed, he would have been sent on a fifty meter flight, which would have left him at the bottom, among the rocks in the beautiful white, gushing river. To stop this flight, Cecilia had made sure that he arrived at the bridge at a walking pace. She had aspired to become a missionary sister, but had died before achieving her dream. She had thereby saved the life of her Pio, so that at least he could become a missionary.

It is a short step from being miraculously saved to becoming a healer. Pio had become famous as a miracle healer. What was certain, besides the fact of the apparition, was that he was truly pious. He was also rather timid.

"This is why he leads such a retired life," a well-informed source told the Camerlengo: "Now he is totally absorbed by the imminent transition on the final bridge towards the hereafter, which is certainly not going to leave him with enough brains to think about taking dealing with pressure in this world. He is just the man we need!"

No one could now remember who was first inspired to put forward his name as a possible, albeit transitional, Pope. After his election, some said it had been a diabolical inspiration. Their dead-and-buried belief in the existence of the devil took on new life. Conversely, after the fact some of the faithful went so far as to say it had been the work of the Holy Spirit himself. The most enlightened of certain church spheres decisively rejected this, and for many quite valid reasons, foremost among them that, if the Holy Spirit truly existed, and had taken any part in that business, it would have been easier to induce the little friar to accept such a flattering, purely formal office of no consequence that, in any case, would be brief. Instead, it had cost something to get him out of his friary.

When, awkward and hesitant, he was forced to step inside the hall of the conclave, a smile of smug understanding radiated from the faces of many prelates. It was so vivid that it seemed to brighten even the darkest colors of Michaelangelo's Last Judgment, which filled the setting of the chapel. The burst of somewhat forceful and rude applause that followed his "Yes" recalled to his mind the rattling of thunder that, at the approach of winter, announced in Palestine the stormy beginning to the rainy season. This was beneficial rain for many things, as it assured the harvest in the new year. He saw himself on the saddle of a donkey when leaving Bethphage and going down the steep valley of the Mount of Olives towards Gethsemane, among the hosannas of the faithful. He saw himself carrying the Cross as he climbed the last part of the Via Crucis as he spotted the many Crucifixes of the crowd. He saw himself raised between heaven and earth, nailed to the Cross, and mocked by his executioners.

He couldn't help but repeat: "Yes, yes, yes!" But no one heard him, as they were all intent on clapping their hands in applause, as if to impede him from expressing any reservations that would weaken in any way the clear and round fullness of that "yes."

3

Senile Tenderness

FATHER PIO, ALREADY MONSIGNOR Pio, and now Pope Pius XIV, had spent the night in prayer in a Vatican chapel since the day of his papal election. Pius XIV? He had been asked what name he would take. He in turn had asked if it was really necessary to take a different name from his baptismal one, which had been chosen by his father. They had said no, and he had concluded:

"I am very happy with this one, which was given to me in honor of St. Pius V, given that Pius X had not yet been canonized. I will keep it as Pope." Such simplicity had softened the prelate in charge of ceremonies, and he communicated the good news to the other prelates with tears in his eyes. This led to another round of hearty applause. So he became Pius XIV.

Then Pius XIV had spent the whole night in the chapel.

He had wanted to rest alone, but the old assistant who had accompanied him also spent the night there and secretly united his prayers to those of the Pope in adoration before the Blessed Sacrament. It is worth noting that this private chapel still had the Holy Tabernacle with the Holy Eucharist. This was known to only a few. The knowledge was kept secret within the restricted circle of somewhat old-fashioned clergy and laity.

The Pope noticed that he was not alone when, towards dawn, he started to look for a bell to ring for someone to serve at Mass. In fact, he felt fresh and energetic, and therefore well-disposed to saying a beautiful Mass. As it was, there was no need to call for anyone.

"Let's say a beautiful Mass of the Holy Spirit? And now as Pope I'll permit myself to also add the *Oremus* of Our Lady of Good Counsel. What do you say?" The assistant nodded. It was a rather long Mass during which the Pope could not avoid recalling the Mass celebrated on Calvary, at the Altar of Our Lady of Sorrows between the site of the crucifixion and that of the erection of the Cross. Each time that the Pope sobbed a little, his assistant would be unable to hold back a tear. The Mass ended. The Pope knelt down to give thanks while his tired assistant sat on the sidelines, dozing until the Pope's playful voice shocked him:

"Excuse me so much for disturbing your sleep. But I looked around a bit out of the doorway, and also took a few steps around there. But to move around this labyrinth, I really need Ariadne's thread. Papal infallibility is not enough. Take me to the place where, around this time, the Supreme Pontiff should be found."

"At this time, the Supreme Pontiff should still be in bed."

"Well, take me to an office where, with the help of my Guardian Angel, I can begin to be the Pope, even though it is a bit early. Then you're going to go and get a few things, and sleep a bit more comfortably. For now I will take the anxious burden on myself. I feel perfectly in form and ready to face what is awaiting me first."

"But before that, at least a cup of coffee. At your age, Your Holiness, you should take it. If Your Holiness is satisfied with that." The many rooms were completely deserted at the early morning hour. They arrived in a dark little room. In the corner shone the red eye of a coin-operated hot drink dispenser.

"If Your Holiness agrees," repeated the assistant, who added, "You know? This is also good stuff. And at this hour, I think it would be difficult to find anything better." As he was saying that he put two tokens into the machine before bringing back two cups of hot, aromatic coffee.

"Excellent!" exclaimed the Pope. "Thank you so much, good friend."

"Camillo. I'm Camillo, like my uncle who, like me, was cameriere for many years. You know, I know all the corners at the Vatican." They then walked through other parts, just as deserted as the previous ones. Raindrops fell against the window pains, pelting down as was normal for Rome in April. As he opened each door in front of the Pope, Camillo blew his nose and dried a tear. For a while, the Pope tried not to let on that he was aware of this, but after a while it became so obvious that he could not avoid a witty comment.

"Senile tenderness, my friend, the psychologists would say. You must keep in mind that today psychology is more infallible than the Pope when he speaks *ex cathedra*. You are old, Camillo!"

"But it was also Your Holiness who gave me an example. I wouldn't say he's much younger... As for psychologists... But it seems to me rather that—" but something in his throat cut him off. Seeing the Pope expecting the conclusion of his thought, he swallowed hard and, as if speaking to himself, said in a low voice,

"It's been a long time since I served a somewhat Christian Mass here!"

"Do you mean in Latin?"

"It's not a question of Latin, but of what's inside. The Mass can be said in Latin as well as the new and already worn out Masses. But it's like when someone returns your wallet empty after it was stolen when it was full. I always remain a... Does that make sense?"

"I think so." After saying that, the Pope smoothed his white goatee, but did not add anything.

"Here, in this office, someone should come to look for you in due course, though perhaps not so soon." The Pope walked to a window, looked for an instant at the swollen clouds, and repeated to himself:

"An empty wallet!... But where to begin?"

At this very instant, as happens when someone holds his breath to allow others to hear a weak voice, so the rain suspended its tapping on the windows while the Argentine chiming of the ringing for the Angelus happily and cheerfully entered the hall.

"Strange!" exclaimed Camillo. "It has been a long time since the *Angelus* bells have been rung!"

"This is where to start! *Angelus Domini nuntiavit Mariae.*" They recited the *Angelus* together. When the Pope dismissed Camillo, he sat close to the window, and began to watch with a child's curiosity. He was fascinated by the rivulets fed by the drops of rain falling on the glass. They removed the last traces of soot that had settled there for so long because the window, a little out of reach, had never been cleaned.

There was no need to make plans. Planning things required knowing at least the main elements of the things to be programmed, while at this moment he repeated to himself that his head felt as if it was the emptiest in the entire hemisphere. He could not anticipate what awaited him. He did not even try to imagine it. He rather regretted that he had not immediately asked to have some of his trusted brothers with him, as they were a little more familiar with the Vatican than he was.

"Already? But who?" He could not find, then and there, a single name. Everything had happened so quickly and without reflection! He felt as if he had become engulfed in a sudden wave, and was being dragged by a fierce and relentless current. Nothing remained for him to do except humbly recommit himself to Divine Providence. He was the same man who until now had always taken the leadership responsibility! He was unfamiliar with Vatican life and the pontifical bureaucracy. He did not even know the names of the principal ecumenical-ecclesiastical dicasteries, which were brand new. He had only been to the Vatican a few times. The first time, for a few minutes, was the day before his episcopal consecration, so many years before. The most recent time was only a few weeks prior to his election as Supreme Pontiff when he went to a bank, the Istituto per le Opere di Religione, to pick up a check from the cash desk that had been sent from a benefactor in the United States to nuns whose chaplain he was. He knew that there, at the Opere di Religione, they would not withhold a single penny from him, which was true. While waiting in the line, in front of the window of the cash desk, he made the acquaintance of a friar who was employed in the Vatican. After speaking at length, and since it was late, the friar invited him to the nearby refectory of his little religious community, the Laurini Fathers, near the Porta di Sant'Anna. Nearly all of the Vatican experience of the new Supreme Pontiff Pius XIV began and ended there.

4

Power of Seclusion

"These arrangements—may Your Holiness pardon my frankness—are unenforceable because they are not at the same speed as the fast pace of this present history. Forty Hours' Devotion or fasting are venerable practices because of the functions that they exercised in previous times. We no longer have these functions today. If Your Holiness really cares that the faithful obtain heavenly favors that they feel they need, let's say that Your Holiness desires to multiply the scripture-based celebrations in an ecumenical-universalistic climate at all levels."

"All right, Monsignore, all right, but I would like it clearly stated that I would like the Forty Hours'; that those who are of age make a small fast; that the children offer some flowers to the Madonna for the new Pope. Have I made myself clear?"

"Perfectly, Holiness!" But as the Pope had suspected, no one conveyed his instructions to the bishops and parish priests, even though they were his first authoritative instructions as Supreme Pontiff.

"Yesterday evening, also in St. Peter's Basilica, in the Chapel of the Blessed Sacrament, the celebration desired by Your Holiness took place," Camillo informed him a few days later on the phone from an office close to that of the Pope himself.

"Did they have an hour of Eucharistic Adoration?" the Pope asked.

"An hour of adoration? It was not in the program!"

"You didn't think of it?... Come to me now!" That was what Camillo wanted. The way was clear, being under the control of only two attendants who did not even ask him where he was going in such a hurry. Two minutes later he was standing in front of the Pope, who asked him:

"So there was no Eucharistic adoration?"

"You cannot adore who is not there. There is a large Bible there, in front of Bernini's Tabernacle, but the Tabernacle is empty, and it has been so for quite a while. They have repeated to the point of boredom that Christ—that's their hastily-stated name for Our Lord Jesus Christ—they therefore say that Christ would be as much in the book as in the bread. Not only that, but that He is only in the bread while we are eating it—in a dynamic sort of way—while He is permanently in the book. Therefore, they say, the Word must take over, and in fact has taken over to the point that the Bible is always there, while now in the Chapel of the Most Holy, no one is waiting for us. Instead of becoming flesh, the Word, according to them, has made himself paper—" Camillo would have continued for who knows how long, but the Pope interrupted him to ask:

"Were there a lot of people there?"

"Four cats, plus a pastor and the usual rabbi, because of whom nothing was read and commented on except for passages from the Old Testament, including the reading from the prophet Isaiah which says that all the people of the earth would one day ascend the mountain of the Lord. Then they read about Zeru... babbel." But he fell silent because the Pope had started to smooth his goatee, which he interrupted after a few seconds to ask:

"How is it possible to speak through Radio Vaticano?"

"Recently it has been done in this way: a technician goes to the Pope's study, a larger one than this, with a recording device, and records everything. Then he immediately gets the Pope to listen to everything that has been recorded, and then he leaves."

"Very good! Then..."

"But then everything is reviewed by a prelate, usually by the same one who in the past previewed the speeches that the Pope then read at the microphone. This supervisory job fell to various prelates, depending on the subject."

The Pope started stroking his beard again, then added: "Exactly! No one can be an expert in everything... And what if I speak to the public at some of my audiences?"

"Does Your Holiness want so quickly to revoke the directions that you have given? The ink isn't even dry on that."

"What directions?"

"These ones, written here, in this bulletin: 'In view of the tremendous worries and problems that accumulated during the long *vacatio sedis*[1], the Pope's public audiences will remain suspended until further notice.' It was issued only yesterday by the *Ecumenical Press*."

"Do you really see me as so harassed? My only problem is finding a way to communicate one of my wishes to the faithful. I hope that they pray for me. I really don't know how to resolve it."

"Perhaps Your Holiness, who — excuse me! — is a novice, is demanding too much. If I were in your place — excuse me! — if I were Pope, I would begin to express this desire to the cloistered nuns, the ones who had you as chaplain until recently. These religious sisters certainly don't need to be reminded to pray for Your Holiness. But they can communicate this desire to some other community... and one thing will lead to another."

The Pope smiled. That could be the good way to resolve the problem that was so close to his heart, and in the most discreet way.

---

[1] "empty [period of the episcopal] see," whence Sede Vacante, "The See being Empty." A phrase of Canon Law in regard to Episcopal Sees, when they have no legal occupant.

"Yes, Camillo, I believe that you are right: *parva favilla*[2]..."

"...big second flame. By that route there, Your Holiness will see that we will reach all of the parishes of the diocese of Rome and perhaps even the whole of Latium."

Camillo was partly wrong. Before long, through this very discreet route, these papal orders reached the parishes, churches, and chapels of the entire globe without even one exception, not even in the pious mission of Polynesia.

They were not, however, properly carried out everywhere. In certain churches, the faithful, on their own initiative, took their turn in front of the Holy Tabernacle, which nevertheless remained closed and in the shadows where it had been confined. In other churches, after some resistance, even the parish priest ceded ground, and solemnly exposed the Blessed Sacrament. This aroused strong emotions and brought comfort to everyone. Elsewhere, however, the faithful had no other choice but to gather at the foot of the Statue of Our Lady to recite the Holy Rosary in a private shrine or at the foot of the Cross. In such places, only the sorrowful mysteries were recited and meditated upon for hours at a time. Their churches remained closed. Conversely, in these churches, which were already so beautiful and populated by saints and by the real presence of the Holy of Holies, nothing remained except the filth of a meeting hall, and all that was left of the sacred was the muted organ. The festive celebrations held on Saturday evenings, less and less attended, were filled with the din of drums, the electric guitar, and the voices of some unbearable but stubborn singer-songwriters.

---

[2] "small ember" / "glimmering spark"—that could start a forest fire, as in many ancient proverbs.

5

The Age of the Disuse of Reason

THE POPE FIRST HEARD OF THE happy outcome of Camillo's ploy from one of his sisters. It had taken much work to arrange her visit. The date of that special audience was repeatedly put off. She was made to go through endless reception rooms. But she would not be kept away. She was old, but she was an oak! A guest, as in previous times, of the sisters who had had the Pope as a chaplain, she was in no hurry and was willing to repeat her question every day, even for a month, like the widow in the Gospel parable who finally got her way with the unjust judge.

It was in the Convent of the Passion that she learned that her superior had conveyed the Pope's wishes to the superiors of the convents that she knew as well as to the most readily available benefactors. All of these individuals had in turn done the same thing. The oil slick thus spread out, not only reaching the Pope's country of birth but, floating on waves, had with surprising rapidity reached as far as Tierra del Fuego and New Zealand.

It was there, in the Convent of the Passion, that the Pope's sister made the acquaintance of Camillo, and entrusted him with her mission for her brother, Pius XIV. Camillo spoke of this to the Pope. One fine and very early morning, following a carefully-studied itinerary and finding no unforeseen obstacles along the way, he managed to get her all the way to the Holy Father's private chapel. Then the Pope's sister had the joy of seeing her Pio celebrate the Mass with the same devotion with which he had celebrated one of his first Masses in his native village in a chapel of the Friars Minor at the altar of the Sacred Heart. Seeing him from the back—as he celebrated towards God and not towards the pews—he was the same as ever in his composed gestures, deep genuflections, and clear and devoted words. It was enough to forget that he once had brown hair, not white like now. But after the Mass, the hurricane exploded.

"But what kind of pope are you, if you are not able to make yourself heard by those you want, when you want, and how you want?" asked his sister with heartfelt eloquence. "You are cut off from everything. You only see the mail that they give you, as you haven't even received my letters, and you are not familiar with anything. I hope they haven't elected you for this reason! They fear a guide for the faithful and for themselves, miserable for them in itself, but infallible in its being God's gift. They have elected you simply to have a pope in name only! You shouldn't have accepted! But if the Lord permitted things to go as they did, *digitus Dei est hic*[1]! Don Carlo, who is a saint and who doesn't waste his words, told me this and repeated it. So help yourself so that heaven helps you! At least let these three come to you—Fathers Norbert, Gregory, and Aurelius. You will no longer be alone, and you will be able to do something. For the first thing, do you know what you need to do? Since in so many churches the God of the Eucharist is considered last in the class, the first thing you need to do is to announce a Eucharistic Crusade. It was not for nothing that Don Paolino promoted you to head of the Crusaders of the Blessed Sacrament when you were still a boy. Now the time has come for you to show yourself worthy of that promotion, and to engage in battle, like at Lepanto. Yes, this is the first thing that you

---

[1] "This here is the finger of God!" A patent indication of the traces of God's usually miraculous intervention. Famous for how often the early Jesuits said this of the Order's remarkable founding and beginnings.

have to do. As for the second, it is inseparable from the first, because can there be a son where the mother fails? So you have to call for a Marian Crusade, but with the Virgin as *Mater Dei*, because it means hardly anything to me—excuse me, Our Lady, she knows that I love her—because it means hardly anything to me that she is Mother of the Church, Mother of the world, mother of Christ, and so on, if she is not the Mother of God. Council of Ephesus!... Hello!... Ah, I almost forgot... and to say that this is the very reason that I came! Here it is!"

She opened her briefcase, took out and opened a package before showing the contents to the Pope. "Here are a few pairs of stockings, very warm. Can you feel how soft they are?... And here are some fine woolen shirts, neck high here in the front. They'll be good for you, even in the summer. So the day you start talking properly again, you won't lose your voice so soon—because your throat has always bothered you. I plan, God willing, on showing up soon... And now, give me your blessing!"

After that she left by the same way that she had come in, still following the guidance of the faithful Camillo. While going, she passed several people who looked at her with questioning eyes. But besides showing her the way out, what could they do for her? In fact, no one said anything to her. After a few minutes, she boarded the bus for Stazione Termini. Her breathing was easier now that she was free of the burden that had troubled her heart until a few hours before.

"My sister is right," the Pope said to himself in the sacristy of the chapel, as he folded and then arranged the socks and shirts that his sister had spread out in front of him. "But I had figured it out as well, heck! Father Norbert taught Sacred Scripture and dogmatics for so many years, he knows many languages,... and he's a nice guy too! Father Aurelius knows all the bishops of the world, knows by memory the entire Code of Canon Law, and also—well, I don't know if this is more of a vice than a virtue—he is quite diplomatic. As for Father Gregory, he has at his fingertips all of the holy fathers and councils in the entire history of the Church. Those three—yes, all three would have been papabile! I should at least make them cardinals. How will this be done?"

The prelate tasked with helping him in this matter did nothing but cause him difficulties. How many reasons he had! At the very least, the Pope needed postpone a decision with such weighty consequences and that all the members of the episcopal college would judge as rash.

"...*non licet* to pass over collegiality," the prelate told him. "And also, these three reverend fathers, all three, are old. One of them will soon be eighty. According to the decree it is absolutely *non licet* to create them cardinals."

The Pope, who out of pure courtesy forced himself until then to avoid refuting the prelate's thin and only apparent reasons, at this last point, seemed to lose his temper:

"Oh no! You who deemed me papabile at my age, you cannot say those three are not cardinal-material. All three are less old than I am!"

But seeing the prelate squinting his eyes in amazement at this protest, he regained his composure, began stroking his goatee again, and added: "You see? There was a Pope, one of the most recent, who at eighty years called a Council, the same Council that you have repeatedly appealed to in these last few minutes of conversation, almost forgetting all the other councils, which also seem to have concluded with good things. And how old was St. John the Apostle when he wrote the fourth Gospel? You do not mean to say that the Gospel is worthless given the advanced age of the human author, more than eighty, and the age of the divine Author, eternity. Did you mention aggiornamento? Thank-you so much! But update yourself a bit on the history of the Church, update yourself a little in Sacred Scripture! In any case, thank-you for your counsel. I'll think it over."

The prelate came out speechless and worried:

"Did he really lose his temper, or was that just my impression? That impulsiveness, that liveliness, that sudden and unexpected energy. No, that energy is of a totally other nature than the fleeting and purely nervous kind that explodes in a burst of irrational impatience. And if it is really the energy of another kind, things could get complicated really fast. I have to talk to the Camerlengo about this!"

The Camerlengo in turn wanted to speak about this to a few other prelates who were summoned to a small council. All together they took to weighing this news regarding the Pope's behavior and the reactions that this behavior incited in the Vatican and elsewhere, even though this behavior did not add anything significantly different from the see had it remained vacant.

6

AH, THOSE DOVES

THE POPE CONFIRMED CAMILLO AS his private cameriere, and would have liked to approach him even outside of the temporarily-assigned apartment. But until that day, he had avoided doing so in order to prevent showing distrust towards the staff assigned to his work office. Camillo, conversely, had been strongly warned by the Pope about being seen outside of this small apartment, and he knew only too well the delicacy of the situation to avoid even considering disregarding this warning. Now, however, a new fact had arisen, and the matter seemed too urgent to wait until dinner to inform the Pope. Camillo began by informing the superior of the Convent of the Passion of the news over the telephone, and then telephoned the Pope himself to extend to him the superior's wishes for a quick recovery.

"Recovery? What's this about? Come to me at once!" Camillo knew that to get the green light to visit the Pope, he would have to give his reasons for this exceptional visit to the Pope to each of the valets whom he would meet along the way. But he was careful not to say that it was the Pope himself who had called him. He thought it more prudent to invoke one of the many pretexts from his well-stocked repertoire, all of them as likely as ever.

"Sick? Who spread such a rumor?" the Pope asked him.

"The *Ecumenical Press* agency ten minutes ago in a bulletin authorized by the cardinal Camerlengo."

"Perhaps this morning I appeared more sick to you than usual?"

"Not at all! Such news needs to be brought to the attention of Your Holiness as soon as possible, but I could not telephone you without bringing a lot of trouble onto myself if this telephone is tapped, whereas no one would have any reason to attack me if I expressed wishes for Your Holiness's speedy recovery. I therefore phoned the Convent of the Passion. The superior already knew of the illness of Your Holiness. She had just heard at that instant from Radio Vaticana. I did not think it prudent to deny it. If Your Holiness is not ill in one way, he is in another, and prayers never hurt. The Pope smoothed his whiskers, and then asked:

"Do you know how to give injections?"

"If I can say so discreetly to Your Holiness, during the war, I had to do a few months of service in the health department until my exemption came. During these months, we took a nursing course."

"All right, if I am sick, I will need at least a few injections, don't you think? Get everything you need to give injections, if you don't already have them. It will be a good excuse for you to come to me at least once in the middle of the morning and once in the middle of the afternoon and, in the case of an emergency, as often as it seems convenient for you. Have I made myself clear?"

"Of course. You have the right to choose a nurse of your confidence," added Camillo before demanding: "What injections?"

"Whatever type of injections because, thank goodness, I don't need any. I feel as good as a Pope! Well, we could do a series of Heparin-Vit injections. It will be enough for you to make a few vials of it disappear, one after the other, and pour a few drops of denatured alcohol on your fingers," directed the Pope, amused by the comedy he had just concocted. "They will be intentional injections."

"But even for intentional injections, without a precise prescription from the papal physician, I would end up in jail for attempted murder of Your Holiness."

Speaking of the devil, at this very moment the papal physician walked in as the valet hurried to announce his arrival to the Pontiff. The Pontiff moved to greet him, politely asked him to enter, and had him sit close by at his side. Then he was shown the best way to take his pulse, and with interest took the pulse of the physician. He shook his head and concluded:

"Thank-you, dear physician, for your attention, but regarding my illness—*senectus ipsa morbus*![1]—the care of this cameriere and this expert nurse, whom I now have occasion to present to you and who now have the honor to receive from you the due investiture, are enough. You, on the other hand, must stay sheltered from these April rains, much more so given your rapid pulse—did you notice it?—arrhythmic and high, just like hypertension. Are you perhaps suffering from some sort of heart disease? I wouldn't be surprised if your blood pressure was over 200. And then this little jaundice that I see on the sclera, you know, is a sign that you need a detoxifying hepatoprotector, such as, for example, Heparin-Vit. Good-bye, professor! Take Heparin-Vit and a hypotensive, and stay at home and get better!"

When Pius was a theology student in Rome, then known as little brother Pio, he had attended a course in medicine for missionaries, taught with excellence by the Knights of Malta at the Hospital of St. James in Augusta, on Antonio Canova Street. Such concepts, which had made him such a magician among the Arabs, had always stayed with him, and it was a game for him to draw from this memory the four clinical terms thrown at the physician as a way to get rid of him in no time.

As he made his way to the elevator to return to his clinic after having made his report on the Pope's health to the Cardinal Camerlengo, the papal physician had to agree that he was

---

[1] "Old age itself is a malady." Famous quote from Terence's *Phormio*.

hypertensive and, moreover, intoxicated. Everything around him was a jumble, so much so that instead of taking the door that led to the elevator, he went through another that led to the washroom.

In the last office, in which he set foot, the Cardinal Camerlengo, made him understand, diplomatically, that the only thing that remained to do was resign. The doctor replied, with medical jargon, that it was disgraceful on the part of His Eminence to proceed in such a manner, that he would not stand silent before such an affront to his reputation, that he would not hesitate for a moment to hand over to the international media a signed statement in which he would declare that he had not been consulted in any way on the health of the Pope until that very morning, that he had never issued any health bulletin whatsoever, and, moreover, that he had found the Pope that very morning to be in perfect health. The Camerlengo stood up and, with slow, serious steps, began to measure the length of his office. The physician profited from this silent, reflective pause to calm himself and, in the calm, redo his calculations. After five minutes of this very long silence, the Camerlengo stopped, shook his head, and exclaimed:

"A beautiful deception! The whole world knows that the Pope is sick, while the Pope does not want to say that he is sick! I should not have given my *Placet*[2] to this accursed bulletin! It is not convincing to release another one a few hours later saying that the Pope is recovering."

A violent downpour hit the window panes, which put a little hope in the Camerlengo's heart. He continued:

"As long as this storm lasts, the Pope will not come out of his cave. Let's give it some time, and not change anything. Much more that this beautiful storm should last a good while longer."

"That's for sure," added the physician wisely and heartened. "The weather bulletins produced by satellites are infallible

---

2   Agreement.

nowadays, almost as much as my joint pain is. Rain for another two weeks at least."

They shook hands and encouraged each other before parting, still friends as they were before: "Rain for at least fifteen more days. We can sleep soundly. Today the meteorological bulletins are infallible. And so are the joint pains."

Renewed by the washing of so much rain, all of Rome's domes glistened in the April sun that afternoon under a clear sky in which not even the smallest shadow of a cloud could be seen despite the infallibility of meteorological bulletins and the foreknowledge of arthritic pain.

So the Pope, isolated in his apartment since his election, was able to go down to the Vatican Gardens that afternoon with Camillo's guidance. He was renewed by a world of so many beautiful paths and plants and even of flower beds already in bloom despite the rain that had lasted until the morning.

"These are marigolds, very hardy. They resist all temperatures," a gardener ventured to explain. "Those are gigantic tulips, very striking but without any scent. These ones here are hyacinths, very fragrant. They come from Holland."

"Ah, from Holland!" *Deus in adiutorium meum intende!*"[3] intoned the Pope, tugging on the crown of the Holy Rosary. Camillo and the gardiner responded:

"*Domine, ad adiuvandum me festina!*"[4] At the Pope's side, they accompanied him in the recitation of the Rosary as all of them proceeded slowly to the Grotto of Our Lady of Lourdes.

It was there where the event took place that produced an ocean of conjectures and which revealed to the whole world that the Pope was well, at least as well as an old man nearly eighty years old could be, someone who was weak but without any specific illness. Everyone knew this from the photos taken

---

3 "O God, come to my assistance!" (Ps. 69:1)
4 "O Lord, make haste to help me." Ibid. This is the response to the above.

by a lucky amateur who, on that day and at that hour, thanks to the agreement of his uncle who was a gardiner, was in the Vatican Gardens with his camera. In fact, he was only there to have a better vantage point for taking a beautiful photo of the Dome of St. Peter with the spring foliage, still dampened by rain, in the foreground. As could be easily seen, he was no genius when it came to artistic imagination even if he considered such a photo to be unprecedented. Nonetheless, he was able to make a short film, though with sneaky and therefore discontinuous pictures of the Pope's walk in the Vatican Gardens. It was a historical document with very attractive scenes.

The Pope asked Camillo for something to feed the doves which were flying to him. Camillo had nothing, but the gardiner handed the Pontiff a few cookies. A little dove came and landed on the Pope's right palm and began pecking at some crumbs. Another little dove landed on the Pope's right shoulder. The Pope tasted a cookie. Showing that most of his teeth were still in place and still quite firm, he began to take large bites out of a pear, like a child, while with his handkerchief he tried to prevent the juice, which dripped down, from soiling his beard and the beautiful cassock of the whitest wool.

It was that scene with the pear that brought smiles to anyone who saw it. And who didn't see it? Everyone who did see it wanted to see it again, along with the scene with the doves. The old man was so nice, with his heavenly eyes, like a good child, while the sun, low on the horizon, lit a halo around his forehead. The short color film was the beginning of a fortunate time for the author. He felt obliged to send to the Pope half of the proceeds that came to him from everywhere in the world through his uncle.

7

Plans

"I DON'T HAVE ANY ILLNESS other than old age. There is only one cure for that, death. I am preparing myself because I can't delude myself that I can get by any longer. If it were said of one of my predecessors, elected when he was less old than I am, that he was elected only for his presumed short pontificate, that he should consider himself to be a transitional pope, all the more reason should it be said of me. I am nothing but a transitional pope."

"But Leo XIII, after reaching eighty years after twelve years as pontiff, took another thirteen years to transition," observed Camillo. "And he always enjoyed such a lucid mind that he was able to dictate poems even in the last hours of his life."

"It's true. *The strong ray sends out light, while the dying sun is enveloped in a pale shadow*. But he was a lion, while I am only a pious birdie. As soon as things calm down around here, I will have to retire and leave the position to someone who truly knows how to be the Pope. I don't plan to imitate St. Celestine V. The Lord will see to it that He calls me to Himself in due time, which is to say, in the short time, in the short term, as He now so strangely wants me here. So strangely because who among the prelates at the conclave knew me? No one, no one at all! And I would love to be buried here, in this little meadow, with all of these beautiful spring crocuses."

"Your Holiness, for some time now, the popes have had their

tombs in the Vatican Grottoes."

"Under those vaults, so low that they seem to want to crush you, I would not resist. Even if I were dead, I would have the impression of dying a second time from suffocation. Here, on the other hand, under the sun and rain, in the shadow of the Cross. Indeed, I would consider it a distinguished work of mercy toward my predecessors, buried down there, to bring them out and line up their mortal remains. How many faithful, seeing the row of our crosses, would say so many *Requiems* for us, more than if we were down there, hidden and as if twice buried.

As for their monumental tombs, even those in the Basilica, they could be housed in some great museum, along with Bernini's baldaquin and his glory, which were added later. They bring clutter to the Basilica. They're distractions. Instead of the monumental tombs, we could have a devout Stations of the Cross built, preferably developed in a type of *Passio Domini*[1] that begins with the agony in Gethsemane or even before that with the institution of the Eucharist in the Upper Room."

"But what an expense!" Camillo objected. "They say that the new Church of the poor has already spent billions on Pharaonic works, so secular and far from urgent."

"All of these could be sources of revenues for the Holy See, and therefore for the sustenance of seminaries and missions for at least a century. The national or international organization that would take on this task would have to indemnify the Holy See for all of these treasures, and also for those of the present Vatican museums. Saving so many treasures of art from destruction or dispersion was a providential work, and blessed were the popes who accomplished this all! Almost no one else would have been able to accomplish so much. If similar historical circumstances were to be repeated... One never knows! Only time is irreversible! Certainly not what

---

[1] The Lord's Passion.

happens in time. Gian Battista Vico was not the only one who said this, and neither was he the first. Already in *Ecclesiastes* we read *Nihil sub sole novum*.[2]

"We therefore say that if similar historical circumstances were to arise again, everyone who had the means would have to use them to save those priceless treasures once more. Now this task can be accomplished by one of the various institutions which were developed for this very purpose, a purpose that the Lord did not assign to His Church and that therefore the Holy See can only exercise in case of emergency and *ad interim*. Such a case does not exist today. Meanwhile, all priests, from the chaplains of nuns to the pope, must roll up their sleeves for specific, direct, and exclusively supernatural activities." At this point, the Pope began coughing, which broke off his sentence.

"You have spoken a bit long, Your Holiness. The air is still cool and humid, and can give you a sore throat. Remember the recommendations of your sister," Camillo told him, and then added: "Though you have spoken true words, Your Holiness!"

"Do you think so?"

"And how many people without an ounce of faith would not have any reason to set foot in here and meddle in Church affairs, and spoil them," chimed in the gardener, who was surprised when the Pope offered no rebuke for his impertinence. For good measure, he asked for the Pope's excuse. He asked permission to leave, pointing out that he still had several things to put in order before the evening, and then left.

"True and holy words," Camillo continued, "and such as Your Holiness uttered a moment ago might constitute a speech to make *Urbi et Orbi*."

"When they let me do it. For now, I can only say it to you and this good gardener. Oh, before I make any speeches, I need someone to help me see clearly, to find the key to the solution, which to me seems rather knotty at the moment." The

---

[2] "Nothing is new under the sun." (Eccles. 1:9)

Pope looked all around, as if to find his bearings, and saw a beautiful little chapel among the foliage of the bush that they were walking through.

"What is that chapel?" he asked Camillo.

"It is the Chapel of Our Lady of the Guard, put up by Benedict XV. He was Genoese, and could not be without his Lady. As for that knot, you need someone to give you a hand, Holiness—some prelate you can trust, one of those three fathers whose names your sister reminded you."

It was not that the Pope's sister had any particular knowledge in the ecclesiastical domain, much less any divinatory virtues. She only knew of these three because her own brother had mentioned them to her several times and with much enthusiasm.

"You should bring them here so I can see them in the afternoon walk which, weather permitting, I think would be good to include in our daily schedule. All three of them together, or one at a time, it makes no difference. If one at a time, the first should be Father Aurelius Meyerbeer."

But Father Aurelius Meyerbeer, the jurist, had left very recently for Germany, while Father Gregory was still in Rome, but ill. The Pope had the Vatican correspondence office send Father Aurelius a registered letter from him. Meanwhile, Camillo made it known in the most discreet way possible that the Pope wished to see Father Norbert, the theological and Biblical scholar. A few days later, as agreed, Father Norbert was able to meet with the Pope right there, under the protection of Our Lady of the Guard.

8

The Window on the Seminarians

"That's right, mio caro," the Pope responded. "You have to help me as you helped me that time when I had to prepare for the academic disputation of the thesis *Divus Thomas unicum magistrum habuit Jesum Christum*. Then, in addition to the *a priori*, *a posteriori*, and *a simultaneo* arguments, you also prepared the stumbling points and the objections. As for multiplying these both, there are those who are already doing it: you should simply help me to dodge the rocks and dissolve the objections."

Father Norbert was roughly the same age as the Pope, but did not show it at all. He had already been Brother Pio's fellow student, though a few years ahead in his studies. And now he declared himself happy to be at the complete disposal of the Pope, much more so because he had retired some time ago and no longer spent even an hour in the classroom. This was not due to any age- or health-related incapacity, but because his classroom approaches had been repudiated as outdated due to method or content. He had been slowly squeezed out from his teaching duties under the most specious pretexts. He had not resisted. That would have been a waste of time. Those who maneuvered against him had the determination of the accomplices of Brutus. They wanted to get rid of all of the closed-off, retrograde old school teachers and replace them with open-minded ones who were in tune with the times.

First of all, Father Norbert had been dropped from teaching a course of philosophy that he offered in a diocesan seminary because he opposed Cartesian methodological skepticism, had reservations about evolution as the fundamental law of the universe, and had demonstrated, data in hand, that the *Sinanthropus pekinensis* business, concocted by Father Teilhard de Chardin, was nothing but a gross historical forgery. Then he was dropped from teaching his course on Sacred Scripture that he gave in a study house of his own order because he did not accept Bultmann's demythologization of Scripture and underscored repeatedly that extinguishing the Star of the Magi would necessarily lead to extinguishing the Upper Room's tongues of fire. Initially, in lieu of the chair of Sacred Scripture, in view of his merits, with so much gratitude, and so on and so forth, he was given a totally harmless course on Patristics. But he used this to put forth the *apologia* of St. Augustine and St. Thomas, and of all the other Fathers and Doctors of the Church. This was the doctrine of all those thinkers and saints, doctrine that he continued to call traditional, definitive, required, and not subject to reform. This doctrine was the check on the traitors, who were dishonest about God, and on the anthropocentric fashion of theology. He had to be removed from that marginalized and modest chair. Just imagine! One day he had dared to say:

"We know who Thomas Aquinas is: a Saint, a Doctor of the Church. But it is doubtful if someone today can become so. For the doctrine of the faith, definitions of dogma are intelligible without equivocation and are infallible and immutable while the romanticism of the various modernist Schillebeeckx and Küngs are firstly against reason itself and the most basic common sense."

In the end, he was removed together with another eminent monsignor from a course for aspiring teachers of religion. In truth, most of them did it only for the salary. He was let go in a very gracious manner. He was about to begin the first lesson of the new academic year when a female teacher rose to her feet and read an announcement that had been put in her hands a few minutes earlier by the great director of the purge. The announcement thanked the professor, so esteemed and dear, and offered him a medal of merit, a generic decoration. It was said, as one says in passing of something well-known, that to everyone's regret, his course had been suspended for that year due to new timetables and programs and other such ridiculous fables. Father Norberto did not let the student finish the announcement. He rose, took his coat and hat from the coat rack, and without uttering a word, walked out of the same classroom that in earlier times his lectures on religion had been so often followed with the liveliest interest and passion, and filled with applause.

At present, forgotten by all, Norbert prayed, and read and wrote books that would likely not be published. He also heard confessions, but fewer and fewer given the anti-Confession propaganda tenaciously pursued by a not-inefficient group of clergymen. What had happened to Father Norbert had also happened to other teachers, true masters, who were replaced with petty or improvised rhetoricians. The radical and ruthless purge of non-aligned seminary teachers went hand in hand with the rapid decline in student numbers and quality.

"May the wind blow away the dry leaves," the new rector of the seminary of the Marian Institute said to console himself.

Yet others observed: "When the Madonna sent them here to us, they were not dry leaves. They were fresh flowers of innocence and virtue. Where, why, when, and how did they become dry leaves?"

"Our lady? What does our Lady have to do with it? Vocations, like ideologies, are the consequence of the economic situation. They abound in underdeveloped countries. As populations progress, vocations become more rare. It is inevitable due to the dialectics of the universe itself."

The Window on the Seminarians

No reply to this was needed, as who could reason with such Marxists? Moreover, on Vatican Radio, the head of the ecclesiastical and religious institutes responsible for the education of seminarians, Cardinal Geyser replied succinctly, "No one can say today because no one knows how young people will evolve" when asked, "What is the future of the seminaries?"

St. Thomas's *Oportet addiscentem credere*[1] was replaced by the *Oportet magisterium credere discipulo*.[2] This latter was the admirable basic principle of so-called responsible student self-education, with the new professors indulging every spontaneous manifestation of this. This principle was moreover valid in the hypothesis that this self-education be strictly preceded by the appropriate self-generation. This implies the free and natural choice of the unborn for their parents.

The remaining seminarians did not feel like dry leaves at all, as they were filled with hope! Only one thing still bothered them: That there still remained someone who was persuaded that he had something to teach them. Responsible self-education was gradually being fused with a no-less-responsible self-instruction. The results could be easily imagined.

If nothing else, neither diocesan seminaries nor those of religious institutes lacked entertaining environments. Even the excitement of dancing was offered. This was a primary index of impulsive vitality, and a precise thermometer of the unwrapping of the personality. And then... meetings, conferences, debates, motions, majorities, minorities, independent groups, and votes. *Placet! Non placet! Iuxta modum!*[3] Also on offer was an entire, very serious, and picturesque emulation of the last pastoral

---

[1] "It is incumbent on the one who learns to believe/trust / "The learner must believe." Summa Theologiae II-II, q. 2, a. 3 (and in several other places).
[2] "It is incumbent on the teacher/magisterium to believe/trust the student." / "The learned must believe the learner."—a seemingly ridiculous inversion of the normal order of learning!
[3] The three normal responses from the voting members [often bishops] at a council: "it pleases" = I approve; "it does not please [me]" = I do not approve; "it pleases somewhat/with some reservations."

Council, and a no less serious and picturesque preparation for the next Council, provided it be equally pastoral. Such a series of assemblies, so committed, open, conclusive and effective, that to say they were pure and simple parodies, would have been quite out of place and even superfluous.

"Oh yes!" sighed a stubborn, deteriorating, and marginalized die-hard, who was miraculously still left there in those circles, a helpless and sighing spectator: "Self-education, self-instruction, responsible choice, like that made by Adam and Eve in the earthly paradise!" But the élan vital of evolution was inexhaustible and irreversible.

An atmosphere of permanent vacation spread more and more freely in those increasingly spacious dwellings in which each happy inhabitant made up his own schedule, perhaps varying it from one day to the next, and even in the course of the same day, though always in a responsible manner and without any distracting financial worries thanks to the sacrifices and generosity of so many faithful. Though the number of benefactors was slowly declining, the corresponding decrease in the number of beneficiaries, which was providential, meant there was always enough.

Thus, the numerous private rooms of these fortunate seminarians, who continued to give themselves the rather bourgeois title of students, featured a television, though it was small and economical because it was from the Church of the poor! Each room also had a radio or hand-held radio, a recording machine, a record player or record player plus corresponding disco, and a camera for filming documentaries of particular pastoral importance. Plus there was a small cabinet. It was as indispensable as ever for enlightening the mind that was weary from the careful reading of so many pamphlets on social awareness, crowd psychology, third world liberation, and even various weeklies especially for sportsmen and sentimentalists of all colors. This cabinet-bar had a small espresso machine on one side and a mini-fridge on the other. Many seminarian rooms also had an electric guitar hanging in the place of honor, where in previous times an image of the Immaculate Conception had hung. The guitar was an instrument more liturgical and sacred than David›s zither itself; an instrument that could produce any sound effect, even at high volume, after only five very easy lessons of only five minutes each: *Ne impedias musicam!*[4]

Overlooking the multi-sport field and its swimming pool, numerous garages for the many modest and inexpensive personal cars—no more than one for each student—were almost everywhere, though with variations from one seminary to the other. They were very useful, even indispensable, for the owners' frequent tours, always for pastoral purposes, to San Remo, Santa Margherita Ligure, Pozzuoli, Herculaneum, Mount Vesuvius or Mount Etna. Sometimes, though no more than five or six times a year, seminarians even went to some transalpine city or locality, but almost always within the Common Market.

It is true that there was some excess. But is understandable given the exuberance of youth. Some had gone to Calcutta—not by car, of course, but airplane—to bear witness with their presence at an ecumenical congress organized to direct the attention of the North Indian head cutters to true Catholics. Moved by true zeal, they then moved on to give equal witness to their proud yet silent faith as far as Hong Kong and Sydney. They justified this deviation by appealing to the example of a certain Supreme Pontiff, whose footsteps they intended to follow. This was a rather thin reason, much more so because neither in Hong Kong nor in Sydney had anyone been able to recognize them as Catholic priests, not only because they were not yet priests, but also because even if they had been, they gave no sign as such. Yet certain superiors of the various seminaries found the seminarians' reason entirely plausible. Exceptional but plausible.

---

4 "Do not impede / stop the music!"

Of course, having arrived on the eve of priestly ordination, many seminarians would ask for a suspension in order to experience the non-priestly, non-celibate state and then make a responsible choice for the priesthood and celibacy, and they would get married. This was not done lightly, however. Everything had been pre-arranged long before. It was therefore easy for them to find, immediately or almost immediately after their nuptials, a professional arrangement that would help them contribute to the progress of humanity. These nuptials were sometimes celebrated in the seminary itself for the edification of the other seminarians. As for the professional arrangement, it might only be as ticket-takers on the city tram lines. This did not require a great change from their customary uniform, except for the polo shirt, which was strictly forbidden during service hours. Instead, they had to change much of their ordinary behavior, since city streetcars and their passengers absolutely required decent manners. They also sometimes had to make the sacrifice of getting up at a fixed time, even at seven in the morning, to be on duty at eight. In the seminary they had been allowed to get out of bed just before lunch, as long as this did not constitute a surrender to bourgeois life since they were so fiercely opposed to all forms of this. In short, even in the seminaries that famous Vatican II window to the world had opened, and now new air blew in at last!

Father Norbert declared himself as determined as ever to cooperate with the Pope at such a chaotic time. He was convinced that, while the *Salva nos, perimus!* needed to be said, it was also necessary to maneuver the rudder energetically. They had to work with all their might to throw out of the boat all the filthy water that had entered through that window that was open at the bottom of the keel. Otherwise the Lord might have said to them, that is, to the Pope and the bishops:

"First do your part! I have not had you elected so that you may sleep or so that you may let everything drift away, certain that I will decide in one fine moment to intervene with a wonderful miracle. That would be the same as if I had entrusted the Church›s boat to the winds and waves instead of to St. Peter. Even worse is if you secretly plot with all this power in collaboration with the winds and the waves, to bring the faithful together ecumenically even while at the same time you say that you do not want to intervene and are waiting for me to manifest my glory and power."

Father Norbert made the rehabilitation of the seminaries an urgent priority. The Lord kept making vocations bloom, like lilies along the edges of a quagmire. Some parish priests welcomed the best young men in their parishes into the life of the priesthood, but only privately. Both the young men and their parents did not trust the diocesan seminaries. This was the right thing to do! A green sapling should not be grafted onto a moth-eaten trunk.

The solution to the problem of the old seminaries would emerge spontaneously within a few years, for lack of material *circa quam*[5], for lack of aspirants. Instead, it was necessary to bring into new seminaries—"new" above all morally and entirely immune from contagion—the young men who were now being cultivated mostly individually in the ecclesiastical virtues of a few good priests, and to entrust them to the care of virtuous and safe teachers. Certainly, benevolent and willing bishops would be found to foster this revival. As for studies, Father Norbert had no doubts. He condensed his program into a few words:

> Until seminarians have learned to think—I do not say to express themselves, which is the minimum, but to think—in Latin, it is vain to hope to have priests of the Church of Our Lord Jesus Christ, who wanted it Roman. The renunciation of Latin is a suicide for Christendom. It is the murder of Christian civilization,

---

5 "regarding which" material which one could reasonably work on or with.

that is, of civilization without adjectives, since, after the coming of Our Lord, there can be no true civilization among men, which is not in all its institutions saturated with Christian inspiration. Now it was said that Christians are Semites spiritually. I say that they are Romans *a fortiori*.

The sixteenth-century Counter-Reformation had a name, the Council of Trent. The twentieth-century Counter-Reformation must have an even older name, St. Thomas Aquinas. The vacuum caused by the anti-Thomists, who are slavish followers of the mental romanticism of Protestants, has cleared the way for a hot air balloon festival. The balloons soar high and fast. They keep on inflating as the atmospheric pressure decreases until they burst and can no longer be seen. The darkness that succeeded the eclipse of St. Thomas is brightened with fireworks that are reinforced by the firecrackers of the progressive press. They attract attention, seem amazing, fade away, and leave nothing but smoke and darkness. "Either the Summa or the Bible, either man or God,' say the anti-Thomists. They surely do not know that St. Thomas's commentaries contain more Bible than the writings of all their Wellhausens[6] and Bultmanns do."

Father Norbert still had many things to say, though enough had already been said at that first session. While dismissing him, the Pope told him that he also wished to meet with Fathers Gregory and Aurelius. He added his intention to make all three of them cardinals as a way to give them greater authority and the possibility of placing them in ecclesiastical dicasteries.

"And to participate in the future conclave?" Father Norbert asked him, both serious and facetious. The Pope, now pensive, smoothed his beard for a moment, and then answered with his own question, "Will there be any need?"

---

6 Reference to Julius Wellhausen (1844–1918), German biblical scholar and orientalist.

9

Father Gregorio, Former Prophet of Ill Omen

NOT WANTING TO WASTE TIME AND not knowing when, or even if, Father Aurelius would return from Germany, the Pope therefore had to meet with Father Gregory. The latter was at that moment not in a position to go to the Pope for an audience, either at the chapel under the guardianship of Our Lady of the Guard or in some other corner of the Vatican. It was up to the Pope to go to him.

"But how?"

"The Swiss Guard," Camillo replied, "They would die before betraying someone. I'll have a word with the Swiss guard who is scheduled for duty at the door of St. Anne on the day and hour at which Your Holiness has decided to leave. You will need to leave right after the change of guard and return before the next shift, so that we have the same guard at the gate. No one will be surprised to see a taxi enter and then leave, with a priest who paints miniatures. He is a relative of mine, who always comes to the Vatican like that. His build is similar to Your Holiness's. He will be happy to give up his seat in the taxi to Your Holiness, and wait in one of his little studios in the picture gallery until you return. I think Your Holiness will be able to go anywhere in black without being noticed. There are still no pictures of you around here, and the pictures in the newspapers have not been very good."

They were able to execute Camillo's plan the very next day. A minute after 3:00 p.m., a taxi with Camillo and the Pope in a simple friar's getup drove away from St. Anne's door and headed for the clinic of Saints Cosmas and Damian. When they arrived near the entrance of the building, Camillo paid the driver and got out with the Pope. The front door was open, the gatehouse deserted, and the elevator ready, as if everything was waiting for them. They headed up to the third floor, and approached Father Gregory's room. They knocked lightly on the ajar door, pushed it open, and entered.

Father Gregory had not been forewarned of the Pope's incognito visit, but was not surprised. Dressed in his order's black habit, seated in a comfortable chair, and holding the breviary, he gave the impression that, just like the elevator, he had been expecting them. He had undergone a rather delicate surgery, but everything had gone well. He was regaining his energy every day. It was not the time to linger in compliments. After a few witty comments lightened the mood, Father Gregory came straight to the point:

"Pius XII was aware of modernism's deafening and relentless activity. This became frightfully destructive under the form of neo-modernism and progressivism immediately after the last World War ended. Pius XII did not come to terms with the enemy. He also didn't consider dialoging with it. He fought it. The encyclical *Humani generis* of August 12, 1950 especially witnesses this. Pius XII died on October 8, 1958," continued Father Gregory, who had a real passion for dates. "He died bitterly, especially because he had seen himself betrayed. The echo of his words no longer crossed the threshold of his study. Everyone knows that an attempt was even made to tarnish his memory. They made his agony into something morbidly gruesome to be thrown to the general public in order to deconsecrate this memory. Everything was premeditated with satanic hatred. Modernism is unforgiving, and its hour had come, the hour of darkness.

"The modernists hoped for a transitional pope, a brief papacy that would develop a devotion to democracy, socialism, and progressivism. The transitional pope was to pave the way, and then disappear. Nineteen days after Pius XII's death, on October 28, 1958, John XXIII, who was closer to eighty years than seventy, was elected as successor. Ninety-nine days after his election, the new Pope announced the convocation of a Council as something inspired from on high.

"If we take the unanimous statements of the Pope and bishops, at the time of the opening of the Council they believed that the state of the Church was excellent. The faith was intact, not threatened by a single error. The Church was flourishing, solidly united, at a profound internal peace. Its outreach to the world was vast and effective. The alarmism of Pius XII, as well as of Saint Pius X, was pathological or, more precisely, psychiatric.

"They said, 'The essentials of faith, morals, church and ecclesiastical institutions—all of these are perfect and untouchable.' Who would have dared to think, for example, of tampering with the traditional Mass, such as now happens almost universally? They said, 'It is only a matter of dusting off the faith, morals, and Catholic institutions from the wear and tear of time, in order to make it all shine brighter in the eyes of all, believers and unbelievers alike, throughout the world.' From the dust of time. This is the great perpetrator, the great prevaricator—time! Then, instead of time being this perpetrator, they were going to force the Church itself to recognize itself as a sinner. They wanted to get to this point where the Church has to be converted to the world. Therefore, the Church had to recognize that it had sinned by not embracing this conversion until then.

"They said, 'We will rejuvenate the face of the Church. We will make all those wrinkles disappear!' So they started a biblical revival, refuting St. Paul, who had gone so far as to claim that the Church is the bride of the Lord, *non habentem maculam aut rugam*[1], thanks to the almighty gift of His divine Bridegroom.

"Finally, that great, fateful word, 'aggiornamento!,' was uttered. Thanks to the aggiornamento, they said, the separated Christians of East and West will come together in agreement around the Catholic Church, enter into filial dialogue with her, accept her dogmas as they are, without reservation, mitigation, compromise, or any subtext. They will joyfully submit to her discipline, morals, and liturgy, so sublime and perfect.

"'Thus to all men, even to non-Christians, the Church, replenished by the Council with new vigor and impetus, will point the right way to the solution of the problems of justice and peace *in terris*...' and so on and so forth.

"All this was given as certain, thanks to an absolutely unconquerable optimism, based as it was on a heavenly illustration. They said, 'The signs of the times, the new conditions of the spirit of humanity, which is gradually maturing, in this historical hour of world history.' Yes, yes, they were really saying that! 'Everyone will see in the post-conciliar era the springtime of the Church, because we will make this Council the new Pentecost.'

"As a matter of fact, there is only one Pentecost for the Church, that of the Upper Room, and it will accompany her until the consummation of the centuries. That is enough for her! Any other can only be a new Babel!

"In the Cenacle, the apostles were favored with charisms exclusive to them and not transmissible to their successors in the episcopate, who therefore lack them. The apostles enjoyed the charism of revelation. What this means is that they received by divine revelation the patrimony of dogmatic, liturgical, and moral truths that makes up the *Depositum fidei*.[2] However, the bishops, as their successors, do not enjoy such a charism. The *Depositum fidei*, which they receive perfectly

---

1 "not having spot or wrinkle." (Eph. 5:27)
2 "The deposit of the Faith."

and irreformably pre-established, is theirs only to transmit faithfully. As soon as they believe themselves to be favored with the charisms of a new Pentecost, like the apostles were, they abjure *ipso facto* the Church founded by the Lord, in order to found a new one. This new one no longer has anything to do with the Lord Himself. Well, this prejudicial illusion negatively affected even the last Council to a fair degree, and now we can see its fruits.

"A luminary of this Council—and he will be ashamed of it as long as he lives" but Father Gregory didn't finish the sentence, but stood there with his frozen expression. Someone had knocked on the door. He gave the Pope a questioning look, and then answered:

"Come in!" A nun with a well-stocked tray appeared in the doorway. She entered, laid the tray on a table, and said, "I thought you would like a drink, unless Your Holiness prefers coffee or hot tea." The three men—the Pope, Father Gregory, and Camillo—looked at each other questioningly. The nun continued unfazed:

"As soon as I saw Your Holiness get out of the taxi, I sent the concierge away. He's a bit of a songbird. I made the elevator go down. I will remain alone in the concierge's office until Your Holiness has gone out again. However, in half an hour the doctor may come, and he is a doctor with a clinical eye."

"Thank you, sister!" the Pope said before quickly correcting himself, "Thank you, my child!" She was indeed a very thin, little sister who seemed transparent in her all-white dress that would make people say that she was made all of light. "Our Lady will reward you," the Pope concluded.

"Oh, of course! But I would also like a grace from Your Holiness."

"What is it?"

"I would like to attend a Mass of Your Holiness...I know you say the traditional one. I was a novice, when the Mass—our soul!—was replaced by a surrogate. They say that even you are not so fond of the new substitute. Half the novices died of it. They left the novitiate in short order, and went back home. But the first stab in the heart was that Holy Saturday—I was then a postulant—when we no longer heard the Exsultet.

"We waited for it from Holy Saturday to Holy Saturday. We had prepared for that morning with so many Lenten flowers! 'Because we did not understand Latin,' they told us. But it was they who did not understand us! If they had understood us, they would not have tortured us like that, with no possibility of appeal. They were telling us that the liturgy belongs to the people, while they were stealing it from us. Then the ancient Mass reappeared, but only to disappear again...."

"Grace granted!" the Pope said. "In due course, and hopefully also early." The nun knelt down, kissed his left hand, and left. Two glistening tears remained on the Pope's hand. He looked at them and started to make a gesture to wipe them away with his handkerchief. But he quickly changed his mind:

"They cost too much. Why spoil them?" he said, leaving the tears where they were.

Father Gregory cleared his throat, and then resumed:

"So we were saying that this luminary of the Council and the post-conciliar era had the courage to write that the inspiring spirit of the Council itself, from its beginning to its conclusion, had been the spirit of Teilhard de Chardin. And he did not write this to condemn the Council—far from it—but to exalt it! Inspired by an apostate! I believe that the Holy Spirit also had a certain part, albeit modest and discreet, if only in that it prevented the authoritative definition of heretical dogmas. Sure! In the Acts of the Council, with a little good will, even a Teilhardian can find his own thing in it. They called it a crisis of the Church, a crisis of growth, a crisis of development, a crisis of self-demolition—expressions, as we can see, that are perfectly synonymous.

"The Church cannot enter into a crisis. Christendom, yes! So four centuries ago, the Christianity of England, having submitted to its pastors, went into crisis, became almost completely Anglican, and ceased to be Church. There were a few bishops who did not betray the Church, but they had their heads cut off. More distant in time, the Christians of the East, docile to their own bishops, entered a crisis, became Arian, and ceased to be Church. Who opposed the shepherds who betrayed the flock? First and foremost, a deacon, for he was not yet even a priest. Athanasius, when he stood almost alone against hundreds of bishops who denied—and that was not a negligible thing!—the divinity of Our Lord Jesus Christ.

"One leader of the Holy Roman Church exclaimed, 'Crisis of the Church, self-destruction of the Church, which no one could have foreseen then.'

"Only the blind could not foresee it! I sounded the cry of alarm then, in our theologate, among the teachers, but with the outcome you already know. A Council without canons, I said then, can be nothing but an artillery battery without cannons or a field sown with wheat but without watchdogs. *Inimicus homo* can sow all the weeds he wants there, at any hour of the night or day.[3] A Council without canons, I used to say then, is a building of precious stones, but without a roof or a foundation. It will collapse on the builders. It is like fine wine, bottled, but not corked, and left within reach of anyone. Some will let it fade away, others will get drunk on it, and the rest will soon end up souring.

"A pastoral council, not doctrinal? As if there could be anything more pastoral than dogma! Shouldn't shepherds lead the flock to the pastures of dogmatic, theological, and moral truth? Was the dogmatic Council of Trent, the most dogmatic, not pastoral? Was it not made by shepherds of souls? What

---

3 A reference to Mt. 13:28: "And he said to them: An enemy hath done this. And the servants said to him: Wilt thou that we go and gather it up?"

was it? Perhaps a congress of astronomers, or worse, astrologers, scrutinizing the constellations? Without dogma there is no pastoral. There is only subversion in all fields, up to the supreme subversion, which is what is manifested in the liturgical field."

Father Gregory paused to look at Camillo, who had not missed a syllable of the monologue, before asking him, "Do you wonder, you, sir?"

"After so many years of living in the Vatican, what could I still wonder about? And then —" Camillo lingered for a moment before concluding, "— and then I think so too — I, and all of us working in lower positions, think so."

"Let's conclude," said the Pope, "Before the doctor arrives. What do you recommend?"

"Everything has been compromised by the supposedly inoffensive but worst interpreted formulas of Vatican II, and then more so by the so-called post-conciliar logic which imposed in the name of the Council the opposite of what the Council itself had deliberated—just look at the total substitution of vernacular languages for Latin, against Articles 36, 54 and 116 of the Liturgical Constitution, and Article 59 of the correlative Instruction—; What, by appealing to a pastoral and fallible Council, was compromised must therefore be restored by an infallible, and therefore itself profoundly pastoral, dogmatic Council. It is said that it was a cardinal, a very far-sighted one, who inspired John XXIII to convene the Second Vatican Council. Well, I am not a cardinal..."

"But I will make you one," the Pope interrupted.

"Thank you!" replied Father Gregory without flinching. He continued, "Well I, simple cardinal *in pectore*, suggest that you get a Council ready. You can get it ready it, and your successor can carry it out, but—*coram Sanctissimo*[4]! Do you know why

---

4   "In front of the Most Holy [Sacrament]" liturgical shorthand for any ceremony that takes place while the Blessed Sacrament is exposed publicly.

English parliamentarians, passing in front of the president's gallery, still genuflect?"

"Because in more ancient times parliament was carried out in the presence of the Most Holy."

"A Council, I believe, is something more sacred than an assembly of senators. Therefore, *coram Sanctissimo* at the beginning, during all the sessions and until the conclusion. It will be Lateran VI, reconnecting with Trent through Vatican I."

"We must return to the Vatican. We will see each other again. Get well soon.... A Council! I don't even know where to begin to make you a cardinal!"

"Get Father Aurelius to tell you, at least by missive."

The Pope and Camillo went out. Waiting for them at the porter's lodge was the little nun, Sister Rosa, who was in fact the director of the entire clinic. She offered the Pope a carefully wrapped package and said:

"Here, Father, in this package is a precious chalice, purchased for over five million at the auction of Mr. Osiris Market, from one of our benefactors who wanted to prevent its desecration. We know in what hands so many sacred ornaments, which we so revere, have fallen. She has entrusted it to us. I phoned her... and she is happy to offer it to Your... Your Fatherhood."

"How about compensation for this?"

"The lady only requests that she accompany me to the Mass of Your... Fatherhood." Outside the gatehouse they found the taxi that had driven them there an hour and a half earlier ready to go. The trip back ended up being quite an adventure! Zigzagging through back alleys, they arrived fairly quickly at Piazza Leonina, threaded through Via di Porta Angelica, found the gate of St. Anne's door wide open, and reached their point of departure without any surprises. The miniaturist priest took a seat in the taxi. Camillo looked at the taximeter, and put his hand in his wallet. The driver stopped him:

"These are the baiocchi[5] you gave me for the outward journey, including a tip. Here: A small offering for St. Peter's Pence. When you need to pass incognito, go ahead and phone the company, 2242824, and say you want Cincinnatus. Better if you phone at least a day in advance. I'm Cincinnatus. Your Holiness, you have my respect. Please pay attention, have courage, and be well!"

He released the brake, pressed the accelerator, and sped away. The gate closed behind his taxi. The Swiss guard looked at his watch, and then said with satisfaction:

"We still have twenty-seven good seconds at our disposal. Sehr gut!" Meanwhile, the martial steps of the Swiss picket that was coming over for the change of guard out of the Elm courtyard resounded on the porphyry cubes of Belvedere Street.

---

5   Papal States coins.

10

The "Sub-Conditione" Lie

"Father Aurelius has not shown up. If you have time, why wait? I have to fix things myself. I have to start a Council and make two or three cardinals. Let's start by making cardinals. I consider that the easiest preliminary undertaking."

So the Pope once again found himself dealing with the cardinal Camerlengo. Pius XIV needed his collaboration for the appointment of the new cardinals. The Camerlengo first provided the Pope with the list of prelates who hadn't become cardinals due to the sudden death of his predecessor. Pius XIV took the list, assured the Camerlengo that he would carefully examine it, and told him that for now he was anxious to make three cardinals, Fathers Gregory, Norbert, and Aurelius, who were certainly well known to the Camerlengo and as deserving as ever. But it was no use! The Pope found him most courteous, but elusive.

"Your Holiness, many prelates, in collaborating with you, are heedless of their health and any private interests. And I believe I am not the last of these. Now it is my duty to remind you that Your Holiness was elected by the conclave on the condition that he would not do anything out of the ordinary. This act, I am sorry to say, has the appearance of something out of the ordinary. It is my duty to discourage Your Holiness, for the honor of the Apostolic See. I am not speaking to you in a personal capacity. If Your Holiness does not wish to reverse his decision, I would feel obliged to resign, and I would not be the only one to do so. Your Holiness would shortly be isolated, and—forgive me for being blunt. I speak to you from my heart—such isolation would impose on you the duty to convene the conclave and resign."

"How many times have you repeated the word *duty*, Your Eminence!" observed the Pope before they both fell silent. The Camerlengo's words had been truly serious, and they had not been uttered at random, in a moment of uncontrolled outburst. They had been suggested to him, not to say imposed on him, by the participants in that little *conciliabulum*, who were also dismayed by the news, duly verified and confirmed, that Pius XIV, like Father Pio before, celebrated the pre-Reformation Mass every day, and that to the admonitions courteously addressed to him in this regard, he had replied scathingly that no juridically valid provision opposed it, and that if there ever was one, they could consider it clearly abrogated.

If only they had known this earlier! How could they have suspected it? A fundamentalist, chaplain of cloistered nuns, okay, whatever! But a rebel too! This was too much! Fortunately he celebrated the Latin Mass strictly privately, which contained the scandal. Outside the Vatican, no one, they believed, knew anything at all about it. They were certain of that. But how long would such a scandal remain contained? Anything was now possible. It was probable that the guy would one day manage to slip between the barriers of that bureaucratic-diplomatic-protocol network and succeed at celebrating Mass publicly, if not with total solemnity, in St. Peter's itself. Desperate times called for desperate measures. It was necessary to let him know that his election was not absolute, but bound by the collegiality sanctioned by the Second Vatican Council. Put another way, his election was not final and unconditional, but *sub conditione*, that is, conditional on the fact that he considered himself the interpreter and executor of the will of the Apostolic College of

The "Sub-Conditione" Lie

bishops. This was the majority in the College, ultimately the prelates comprising that small *conciliabulum* who had induced the Camerlengo to act as their ambassador.

The Camerlengo had tried to be the best ambassador. At a certain point, he felt pity for the old man in front of him who seemed bewildered, intimidated, a clumsy chick floundering behind mother duck. For a while he looked at the Pope with questioning eyes. Then, as the Pope hesitated to give any reply and, eyes closed, was instinctively shaving off his white beard, the Camerlengo became convinced that he had hit the jackpot. This had gone well for him, though it didn't bring much satisfaction. Finally, the Pope opened his eyes and began speaking:

"In conclusion, according to those who elected you as their ambassador, I am Pope *sub conditione*, right?"

"Evangelically, I will tell you, *Tu dixisti!*" the Camerlengo replied to him while inwardly objecting to something. He did not dare to take full responsibility for the embassy, an embassy that he had agreed to report to the Pope.

"Elected *sub conditione* means that if the condition is not carried out, the effect of the election ceases, and I cease *ipso facto* to be the one and only authentic Pope. I automatically return to being poor Father Pio, or at most poor Monsignor Pio, whom I was until a few days ago. Is that so?"

"I would say so, yes."

"We are certainly operating under such a condition," remarked the Pope as he paused to blow his nose. He resumed with a question. "We are operating in the legal field, and therefore in an intentional field, aren't we, Your Eminence?"

"I would say so," replied the Camerlengo, curious to see what the Pope was getting at.

"Such a condition is certainly operative, but only if it has been openly proposed by one party and formally accepted by the other, and always on the assumption that it's a condition that is harmonious with Christian morality. Otherwise, it would still be inoperative. We are in the intentional field, Your Eminence, in the field of knowledge, and no one can accept a proposal that has not been proposed to him—in this case, proposed by the conclave, and accepted by me. Is it your understanding that this has happened?"

"I distinguish," the Camerlengo took to say, stumbling over a few scraps of minor logic: "*Distinguo: Explicite, transeat, vel etiam concedo, sed implicite* ... It simply lacked the explicit form ... and therefore ... itself of purely formal value ... and, as such, ... superfluous to the effects."

The Pope interrupted him, mostly out of compassion, to prevent him from continuing to fumble so pitifully:

"Dear Sir, that condition, implied, is a lie and remains so even if explicit. Let me prove it to you right now, first of all with an *ad hominem* argument. The majority of the College of Cardinals, stated but not granted that you are its authorized ambassador, recognizes my authority to convene the conclave, before which I should resign, and depose my authority as Vicar of Our Lord. Only on this condition would I cease to be the Vicar of Our Lord. This means that until this condition is fulfilled, I hold my papal authority unconditionally, and I am and remain the Vicar of Our Lord, unique, legitimate, authentic, and according to the unanimous conviction of the majority of the College of Cardinals or Apostolic or Episcopal whatever. Is that clear?"

The Camerlengo did not know what to answer. The Pope continued:

"But there is more. In fact, the other condition, the one placed by me on my resignation, has occurred. You in fact stated a moment ago, in plain words, that if I did not step back from my plan, you would resign. Well, I will not step back from my plan. So you have the condition for your resignation, and it remains. And I am willing to accept it, unless you withdraw this condition immediately. As for the conclave, I will convene it when I deem it opportune—and if I deem it opportune.

May it not pop into anyone's mind to convene another one, and conjure up some anti-pope there! In the current times, it is relatively easy to find those who want to play such a game. But the first ones who would not believe in Him would be his own great electors."

The Pope got up and made out to leave, but having reached the threshold of the door, he turned to the Camerlengo, and said to him:

"I hold no grudge against you whatsoever for your agreement to act as ambassador and tell me the lie of *sub conditione*. That tale did not come out of your mind and heart. In any case, at the tribunal of God, you will receive credit for any righteous intention of yours. There they all submit their resignation in that they all must put down every mask."

Having said that, he left to carry out his own business, leaving the Camerlengo with beads of cold sweat covering his forehead.

II

Monsignor Gabriel Wong

"ALL RIGHT, ALL RIGHT, MONSIgnor, but I feel the need to make an address, if only with a few brief words, *Urbi et Orbi*!" concluded the Pope rather briskly.

"Certainly, Your Holiness! But a certain amount of time must be allowed to elapse—psychological time, the time for the psychology of the crowd that is necessary for the *Urbi et Orbi ex una parte* to recover from the inactivity that they all became accustomed to during the unending conclave. *Et ex alia parte*[1] to recover from the traumatic shock from the conclusion of the conclave. It was so sudden, so surprising, that it had a miraculous quality for many. In any case, *quod differtur non aufertur*.[2] And the words of Your Holiness will be all the more welcome and consequently all the more effective, the more they will have been desired and expected: *Utinam dirumperes coelos et descenderes!*[3]"

"Do you really think so, Monsignor?" the Pope asked skeptically. "I rather believe that not a few will end up saying that the new Pope is a stupid dog who doesn't know how to howl, while the wolves are tearing apart the flock."

---

1 "from one part" "on the one hand" / partially—here, to the City and the World...partially (some exceptions). "and on the other hand" / for the other part.
2 "What is differed or put off is not put aside completely or wholly removed."
3 "Oh that thou wouldst rend the heavens, andcome down." (Isa. 64:1)

"'*Laetare et benefacere*⁴ and let the sparrows sing!'⁵ said the saints. Your Holiness, prepare whatever you feel you need to say. Then let's study it together. I have some practice in this. In the meantime, here is the list of audiences. Quite a few. First this one, then the rest. *Serva ordinem et ordo servabit te.*⁶ *Il faut fixer des priorités.*⁷ It's a matter of establishing priorities. And these hearings must take precedence. Elles sont des priorités.⁸ I will be at your side. I am a polyglot, so your task will be reduced to..."

"...to a mere formality."

"Precisely! Here is the first list for you."

"So many names! Parippileethathottu... but what kind of philosopher is this guy?" exclaimed the Pope.

"He is actually a world-renowned scientist. He won the Libéll Prize for electrophysics, and, more recently, was the first to isolate the positron. He brings Your Holiness the gift of a miniature synchrotron, a micro-synchrotron..."

"...with which I should enjoy isolating the micro-positron.... And as for all the others on the list, what did they isolate?"

"These are eminent personalities in the field of art and philanthropy, people who have tried to get a papal audience since the first news of Your Holiness' election. This is Miss Candy Fluerfluerie, author of the work that won the Banquet prize..."

"And is that not enough for you? Are there any bishops on this list?"

"Actually, for bishops, there are the relevant dicasteries in addition to the bishops' conferences of various national churches."

---

4 "Rejoice and do good."
5 "*Laetare et benefacere* and let the sparrows sing!" A saying of St. Ignazio da Santhià (1686–1770).
6 "Keep order and the order will keep you." Ancient proverb often attributed to St. Augustine (without source).
7 "We need to set our priorities."
8 "They are priorities."

"Various national churches? And as for the *Credo unam ecclesiam*, where did that go?" the Pope asked before his eyes quickly turned to the long list of names. Wouldn't getting closer to all these individuals, even if for a moment, loosen the net around him a little more? So he closed his eyes, and smoothed his goatee, while in his heart he turned to Our Lady of Good Counsel as his holy mother had taught him. Finally, he opened them again and asked:

"Who gave an audience to all these fine gentlemen?"

"Me, Your Holiness," replied the prelate triumphantly.

"And then you will receive them, or any other person you like. It's all the same to me. As you leave, you will see in the reception room a bishop who has come a long way and who has not been received to date by the relevant dicasteries. He's coming by, who knows how, Your Excellency's Audience Office. In fact, he has managed to get there already. I have scheduled a meeting for him this morning. He is waiting there."

The monsignor's mouth gaped wide open, and his eyes even more.

"Yes, yes, Your Excellency!" the Pope continued, "There was some good soul who took it upon himself to wait for him at the bronze door to accompany him here. The Swiss were prohibited personally by me from skewering him with the halberd," the Pope added, smiling. "Have the goodness to introduce him to me. Thank you and goodbye!"

Drapery paintings and ceilings, carpets and chandeliers began to make a jumble around the head of that good prelate who, although he knew the way by heart, struggled for a moment to find the door handle. To receive him while in an audience with all those people? Who on earth could have counted them all? There was nothing left to do but to dump everything on the shoulders of Monsignor Bruno De Gaudenzi, his subordinate, who fortunately had handled everything, and to report the incredible news to the cardinal Camerlengo. He went off immediately to find him.

Shortly thereafter Monsignor Gabriel Wong was on his knees at the Pope's feet, weeping and unwilling to get up. He had been a high school student of Father Pio in one of the many then-flourishing apostolic houses of the Order of Father Pio. Then he had gone to the college *De propaganda Fide*, as it was called when there was still a faith to be propagated. After that, he returned to the Far East for more practical training. He had lost contact with his teacher and spiritual father, but had not forgotten him. Now he saw him standing there before him, with the same simple and benevolent look as before.

Although kneeling at the Pope's feet, he had to stand with his head bowed a little to address the Pope himself, who was sitting before him. Wong was tall and slender, and did not look in the least like his recently-reached sixty years. Indeed, he retained a light and rather quick step. His hair was still black as ebony, as black as the pupils of his sparkling eyes which, like his lips, were ever ready for an intelligent smile. In conversation he never appeared guarded and suspicious, but was calm. Although equipped with a very quick intuition, he had the slow, sententious reply of some ancient sage of the East, accompanied, or, more frequently, preceded, by an almost always unpredictable yet expressive and dignified gesture.

He could also express himself most often in the language of his interlocutors, as he spoke Italian and various other modern languages, including some from the Far East, with the same ease as his mother tongue. Latin was also dear to his heart. In short, Wong was one of those exceptional, aristocratic people, although of modest birth, who, without instilling fear or an embarrassed awe, knew how to immediately capture the respectful confidence of everyone.

He had kept good news for the Pope. To bring it, he had been busy immediately after the announcement of Pius XIV's election as supreme pontiff. The other news that he had, which was less positive, would wait until a later date. All the places were already filled and reserved for many years to come in Wong's enormous, freshly-opened seminary. So many good young men were crowding to get in and were sacrificing so much to deserve such a privilege! Catholic parents considered it a great grace from the Lord to have a son who would give up a future family of his own and consecrate himself wholly to God for his entire life. In fact, Wong would soon have such a large number of priests in his diocese that he would be able to send many of them as missionaries to the people in the interior, alongside the few remaining European missionaries.

"What do you attribute so many vocations to, when elsewhere seminaries are deserted, novitiates empty, religious institutes and dioceses agonizing for lack of vocations?"

"There are many reasons, but I will tell you only the one that touches on them all: we have maintained the discipline of St. Charles Borromeo and St. Pius X. My seminarians are educated by their superiors, both European and Eastern, in prayer, study, silence, the flight of worldly curiosities, not wasting time."

"Have you not opened your windows to the world?"

"Do you mean the world which Tacitus calls *saeculum* in the phrase *Corrumpere et corrumpi saeculum vocatur*?[9] In my seminary, we have few magazines, no radios, and the television under lock and key. A superior records in advance, and duly announces, what will be offered for viewing to the seminarians at an appointed time, and therefore they cannot watch things at any hour of the day or night. I allow absolutely no worldly and irresponsible mass media to influence the seminary schedule or

---

9 The [secular] world is said to corrupt and be corrupted." From Tacitus' on the Origen and placement of the Germans—or "On Germany and its Tribes, 19.3—although the original has a "NOT" in front of the whole sentence, and is usually taken to mean: "it is not called 'the fashion' [saeculum] to corrupt and be corrupted". So, the author is playing with the meaning.

to atrophy the intellectual faculties of the seminarians. If they are to spread the Spirit of God, they must not fill themselves with the spirit of the world."

"The spirit of the world! Dear Gabriel, do you remember the Epistle of the Mass of St. Gabriel of Our Lady of Sorrows?"

"It is taken from the first letter of St. John: 'Beloved, *nolite diligere mundum, neque ea quae sunt in mundo.*[10] Whosoever loves the world does not have the Father's charity in him; for everything that is in the world, is concupiscence of the flesh, concupiscence of the eyes, and pride of life. All those things that do not come from the Father.' I know it entirely by heart, the Mass of my Saint, so—I assure you!—I could rewrite it exactly as it was on the day when the old Missals were destroyed, as the new one doesn't have anything from the old."

"Oh, your memory is not failing you!"

"I think it was the Mass of my Saint and my devotion to Our Lady of Sorrows that preserved me from the storm. I would have wrecked my diocese as soon as I had yielded an inch to the reformist manias since what developed was a tug-of-war type of situation. There comes a certain moment, a critical moment, in which the side that gives up a single millimeter ends up being swept away. Therefore, I could not yield even one inch.

"Ours is a neophyte Christianity. It would not have withstood the post-conciliar logic, with its changes, first in one direction and then the opposite, and often completely arbitrary and illegitimate despite all appearances. This logic implied the repudiation of what our neophytes had recently accepted as sacrosanct and unreformable, and that they loved with all their souls. We defended ourselves as best we could. We are removed from things and a bit out of reach. The post-conciliar troublemakers did not feel like covering all that distance. We immediately sent back the few who dared to wherever they

---

[10] "Love not the world, nor the things that are in the world" (1 John 2:15).

came from. We haven't had any serious trouble from above so far, and I don't think it will start now!"

The Pope smiled. Wong continued, "It was too serious and harsh. I questioned my canon lawyer, who after examining and reviewing all the documents related to the case, and after consulting other canonists, including here in Rome, gave me his response in writing. Here it is!"

Wong handed the Pope a file, containing the response.

12

The Canon Lawyer's Response

THE REFORMED LITURGY OF VATIcan II is centered on a new Mass that is based on a heretical concept, that the Mass or Last Supper is the assembly of the faithful gathered around a presider to commemorate the Lord. This concept had been condemned by the Council of Trent and anathematized. Later the definition from Vatican II was improved on, but the reformed Mass remained as it was, according to the previous definition.

But even if the hypothesis is made that the new Mass was conceived according to Catholic doctrine, it does not follow that the traditional Mass must be dropped. Even if the hypothesis is made that the traditional Mass has been declared abrogated, such a declaration would remain completely ineffective because, in the face of a millenary tradition, there is no valid abrogative law. If St. Pius V himself, instead of repressing liturgical abuses, had intended to establish a new Mass to replace the traditional one, from the point of view of obligation, he would have hit a brick wall.

The formula of the words of consecration in the Traditional Canon when the chalice is elevated is preceded by the expression *et accipiens hunc* (where *hunc* equals *this*) *præclarum calicem*.[1] This *hunc* was removed from the vernacular translation, which left room for the heresy that the chalice of

---

[1] "and taking this wondrous chalice/cup."

the Mass is different from the chalice of the Upper Room, and that the Mass is only commemorative of a fact that happened in the past, and that it is not renewing this fact. The consecratory formula of the chalice says *novi et æterni testamenti, mysterium fidei,*[2] which means, "sacramental sign (*mysterium* means *sign*) of God's faithfulness (which is *fidei*) to the new and eternal covenant."

Every attempt to expunge this expression was condemned until the last decree of the Holy Office (July 24, 1958). The Reformed Canon was deprived of the formula of the words of consecration. Why was this? This expression *mysterium fidei* is placed later in the consecratory formula in order to provoke an acclamation. In this, the attention of the faithful is distracted toward a future coming of the Lord, as if he had not come just then by virtue of the consecratory act. This is accomplished at the cost of destroying the liturgical perspective of the Canon, which is centered on the Father before shifting its perspective to Jesus the Judge on the Last Day. The traditional Canon speaks of blood *qui...effundetur*, "which will be poured out." The priest, in repeating this verb in the future tense, places himself "in" the Upper Room, and represents the consecrating Jesus at the imminent point of the bloody consummation of his sacrifice, therefore "before" this occurs. In the Chinese translation, this verb in the future tense has been translated with the past participle "effused." Thus the celebrant who utters it places himself "outside" the Upper Room, and "after the Lord's bloody passion, so that its celebration, from being an ongoing action, which Jesus" death fixes for eternity, fades into the commemoration of an event that was and is no more. In the expression that precedes the consecratory formula of the chalice, and then in this same formula, we read, "drink from it all: ... poured

---

2 "of the new and everlasting covenant, the mystery of faith."

out for many." Thus we find in this the binomial "all-many," which the Latin becomes *omnes-multi*, in Greek *péntes-polloì*, in Aramaic *kol bistra-saggiˤan*, and in Hebrew *kol bashar-rabbim*. In the Chinese translation of these expressions, "many" has been translated as "all," to insinuate the error that all will be saved. Altered in this way, the consecratory formula causes confusion, which only an *ex cathedra* intervention would be able to dispel totally.

In order to guarantee the "use" of the traditional Canon in the celebration of the Holy Mass, the Council of Trent excommunicates those who consider it reformable. Why would those who, while leaving it more or less intact in theory, but have in practice "disbarred it from use," escape such a sanction? Here's another question, to which we would appreciate an authoritative answer.

A law is repealable if it is deleterious. It can only be repealed by better law. But the traditional liturgy is not deleterious, while that of the current liturgical reform is. Therefore, the latter does not abrogate the former. An appeal was made to the liturgical constitution of the Second Vatican Council to abrogate the traditional Mass, but Article IV of this constitution actually intends to protect this Mass. Therefore, this abrogation is unconstitutional. The diffusion of a complex, confusing, often incoherent, and fundamentally unconstitutional law that was obtained through myriad psychological pressures, lacks the requirements of a legally effective promulgation. These requirements, concealed by a tricky pseudo-promulgation, are therefore void. This is how liturgical reform was spread.

Conclusion: *omnibus accurate perpensis*,[3] the traditional Mass alone still remains the only prescribed Mass with all the chrisms that make it canonically unexceptionable; and therefore

---

3 "after having precisely weighed all things."

at least licit and without the need for special permissions or indulgences, both to all priests and to all the faithful. —Athanasius Yuen-koon-wing.

"Why didn't you let me know you were coming?" the Pope asked Wong, as he put the jurist's response in a drawer of his desk. "You should not have bothered the Sisters of the Passion. Fortunately, Camillo often goes there!"

"I wanted to forewarn you in writing, Your Holiness. Even though the answer was late in coming, I set out anyway. Once here, however, no one would let me in."

"Did you write to me? I didn't receive anything. Nothing more than letters of good wishes, nice words. Nothing else reaches me. I thought the Pope had a more interesting correspondence, that the bishops had things to tell him."

"National councils or bishops' conferences today focus things on themselves, and stop there, even those issues whose knowledge and solution would be up to the pope."

"Would be up to?"

"Certainly! It is a short step to go from national bishops' conferences to national churches. Not only that, but by virtue of national conferences, the bishop himself is no longer the pastor of his diocese, except in exceptional cases. The bishop cannot think about or make his own decision about anything decided and imposed on him by a majority of the bishops of that nation, for all the dioceses of that nation. Majority of bishops? A scattered minority of a few curials, who impose their often corrosive plans on these bishops' conferences, who in turn are confronted with a *fait accompli*. In any case, the pope remains out of the picture, and if any primacy is still accorded to him, it is only a primacy of honor, an honor deserved in other times, when he was recognized for what he is by divine right, bishop of all the faithful, directly.

"Collegiality, which has deprived the Pope of his power, has by extension deprived the very bishops of the power they wanted. When the combustion in the power plant stops—as happens to the engine of my seminary's thermal power plant whenever the oil runs out—how will the engines that are connected to this still run? The disempowered bishop, one can easily understand, is tempted to let things go. He is very aware that, at a certain age, he will retire even though he will still have his full physical strength and the best of his moral powers. The same can be said of parish priests, who are deprived of their power by presbyteral councils, and jolted from their seat by surprise like billiard balls. One certainly does not bother to make economies, sacrifices, expenses, to beautify the room being rented at the hotel for a few days.

"Many elderly parish priests continue unfazed at the frontline battle, though in situations that are as bleak as ever. But very few young priests, and there are already so few of these, aspire to be parish priests, much less as they see the older ones doing things. I recently saw a parish priest of the diocese. He's an old acquaintance. And he told me about his new parish assistant priest. First of all, the new priest demanded that the garage of the rectory house be enlarged to make enough room for his rather large automobile. He demanded one day completely off every week, even a Sunday sometimes. He demanded the elimination of all fares and tariffs. He demanded a monthly payment of four hundred thousand lire. And he declared that he would not provide any service before nine o'clock. That same parish priest also bought a second car to put at the disposal of a friar, his friend, who now collaborates with him. My friend, the older priest, immediately sent that young assistant parish priest back to the person who had sent him. He's probably an activist somewhere now."

"Did we really need someone from East Asia to paint the situation of our poor West in such realistic colors?!"

"Your Holiness, I lead my diocese, but I have not lost sight of anything that concerns the whole Church. Besides, some of my heart has remained in Rome."

"However, you have not been able to get a letter of yours from the East to the West."

"Unless it got lost in the mail," observed Wong, smiling.

"Let's go and see," said the Pope, as he pressed a button.

13

To the Correspondence Office

TWO MINUTES LATER CAMILLO entered with a bowl containing everything needed for the injections. The Pope, smiling, said:

"Let's postpone the injection until tomorrow!"

Then, turning to Wong, he observed, "I have made a habit of it. From the beginning of the treatment, I have been putting off the injection day by day, and plan on doing so until the end of it. I feel that this does me extraordinary good.... And now, Camillo, put down that bowl, and take us to the office where the letters addressed to the Pope arrive and are screened. And listen: you must lead us there in a way that does not allow those in that office to have any forewarning. Are we clear on that?"

Camillo laid his bowl on a small table, pondered for a moment, and then concluded:

"All right!" He nodded to the Pope, and all three of them went out.

When they reached the elevator, Camillo turned to the valet on duty and said in a voice loud enough for the usher sitting at the other end of the short corridor, "Take us up to His Holiness's apartment." But as soon as the elevator was in motion, he added, "Actually, take us down to the Correspondence Office floor." The unsurprised valet understood, performed the U-turn, and let the three out at the prescribed station, five meters from the entrance to the Correspondence office. They entered, much to the astonishment of everyone there.

"Your Holiness, what an honor, what a surprise! It's been so long since a Pontiff set foot in here!"

"Thank you, thank you!" said the Pope: "You can commemorate the event with a plaque, if you want to, but not right away.... You stay here too, Monsignor!" he said abruptly to a ruddy, completely bald clerk in a black cassock and purple belt.

The latter had gotten up in a hurry, picked up a bundle of folders and, with a quick gesture of reverence to the Pontiff, was heading towards the adjacent room.

"Just leave everything here," the Pope added, "Perhaps you too can help me. I have come to find a letter that is so dear to my heart."

But Wong, with his keen eyesight, had already discovered where his letter might be, if it had not already been destroyed.

"Your Holiness, here is the box for the Asian Countries, and here is the folder with the latest arrivals."

While saying this, he bowed graciously, thereby preventing the clerk from interfering, and took the folder, opened it, extracted a letter from it, and showed it to the Pope, declaring, "Here it is, with the caption 'Awaits reply.' Indeed!"

Then the monsignor, who was the office manager and had been trying to get away with all the folders, came forward and said to the Pope:

"Your Holiness, we have been told to minimize the work of Your Holiness...."

"That is, told to send some of the letters addressed to me here and some there," said the Pope, "And others you just put to the side, like the last one from His Excellency, here present."

"Precisely, Your Holiness. The letters asking for an audience go to the Audiences Office; those from the bishops' conferences, depending on the subject, go to the various Roman dicasteries; those asking for alms, go partly to the ad hoc office, and partly to Your Holiness."

"...along with the packets of letters from well-wishers," the Pope interjected, "the packets of newspapers, packets of telegrams requesting the apostolic blessing, like this one," as the Pope pulled one out of his pocket. "Addressed to me by the participants of the annual convention of the societies of tambourine players. In short, in order not to tire me, you were instructed not to let me know anything, and to cover me with streamers."

No one breathed. No one moved. One could hear a page in a book being turned or someone writing with a pen. Everyone sat sullenly, heads bowed at the desk or keyboard. The Pope well knew that none of those present had acted of their own free will, but he wanted his will to resonate, and reach those responsible. He wanted to induce them to milder counsel, without the need for investigations and punishments. He would then treat the wound. But first he had to complete the surgical operation, begun *ex abrupto*[1], but which had been on his mind for some time now. He approached the desk of the nearest clerk, and bent down as if to read the letter that the clerk had before him. The clerk moved it close to him, saying:

"Here, Your Holiness. It's from a benefactor. He's sent five million lira for St. Peter's Pence. He would like a pontifical commendation. I will reply by thanking and informing him that the grace has been granted to him. Tomorrow, Your Holiness will find this letter on Your desk..."

"...so before I would have seen it, the answer would have already been sent with grace already granted!"

"You know, this is a benefactor who is on the list that we, in our slang, call primers. You can see his name here: Mr. Osiris Market."

"Osiris? What a beautiful name for a Christian! Unless he was baptized in the waters of the Nile. Either tonight or

---

[1] "abruptly"

tomorrow, it makes no difference. You can give me his letter right now, so you don't have to bring it."

While talking, the Pope took the letter and put it in his pocket. Then he leaned over the basket full of thrown away letters, took one lying on the top from the Sisters of Misfortune, and then asked, "And in here, what dicastery is this? Judging by the volume of correspondence being diverted to it, I would have to conclude that it is much more important than the Pope's correspondence." He glanced at the letter, and then snapped, "Ah, no! Camillo, we need Cincinnatus here."

The thoughts of the most educated of those present turned to Lucius Quincius Cincinnatus, who was temporary dictator and savior of Rome several times. They thought that the Pope proposed to imitate him. They had no idea that Cincinnatus was a taxi driver, and that the Pope had at that instant decided to go as soon as possible to pay a visit, similar to the one he was paying then and there, to the ancient and venerable parish of the Three Holy Brothers. The letter, in fact, said among other things:

"Our parish priest does not want to hear anyone's confession anymore. He says that collective confession before Mass is sufficient. But even this confession is not done because four noisy hippies play an entrance saraband. The priest gets everyone to go to Communion, even children, without any instruction or preparation whatsoever. He no longer keeps the Holy Eucharist, not even in the sacristy, where he had long since confined it. After Mass, he pours the consecrated particles that were not consumed during Mass into the particle box. He does not give Communion outside of Mass. He has gotten rid of so many of the church's paintings, and he sells the oldest and most precious furnishings to a businessman.

The Pope also put the letter in his pocket, and took out his handkerchief, as if he had to blow his nose. But everyone saw that his eyes were watering with tears. He merely ordered all the employees of the Correspondence office not to throw away any more letters, and not to throw away any of the letters already trashed. He established a timetable, provisional for the time being, for bringing him packages of letters which were to be opened, accompanied with a list of them, and a note as to their contents. Letters of a strictly confidential and reserved character were to be closed. Then he said:

"Thank you all, may Our Lady bless you, and goodbye!" and he made to leave. But the Monsignor in charge barred his way, knelt suddenly at his feet, and said:

"Your Holiness, forgive us! Forgive me. Forgive us, if against our will we were the cause of any displeasure to you. We are subordinates. We must obey orders, even if they are strange and unpleasant."

"Get up, Monsignor, get up! How could I forgive you, all of you, for doing your duty? The fact that you have carried out exactly an order, however strange and unpleasant, is my guarantee that I will have diligent and intelligent collaborators in you. It is I who must thank you. As for a reward, the Lord will give it to you, because the salary you receive is already great if it is enough for this life."

"And then bless us!" They all got down on their knees.

"I bless you wholeheartedly, you and all your loved ones, and with me Our Lady blesses you: *In nomine Patris, et Filii, et Spiritus Sancti.*"

"Amen!" they all replied as a chorus, and began breathing again.

14

To the Parish of the Three Holy Brothers

CAMILLO HURRIED TO PREPARE the Pope's second clandestine exit. He was to phone Cincinnatus and the miniaturist priest, and he was to meet with the Swiss guard. After thinking about it, he concluded:

"The Swiss guard is here—just a stone's throw away. Let's start with him! He's from Grindelwald. I'll ask at the barracks if there's anyone from Grindelwald. Let's hope he's the only one! I'll ask him how much snow falls in winter in his village, if the ski resorts are comfortable and cheap, and then I will ask him when he will be available."

The Swiss guard would be on duty at the gate of St. Anne's from 3 to 5 p.m. the next day. At that time, Cincinnatus would be on hand. The miniaturist priest, Don Ciccio, said he was happy to give the Pope a hand this time too. So the next day just after 3 p.m., Cincinnatus's taxi crossed the threshold of St. Anne's gate, with four passengers on board. The Pope, Wong, and Don Ciccio, all three *in nigris*[1], were cramped together in the back, and Camillo was in the front with the driver. The Pope remarked to Don Ciccio:

"You've come too, Reverend! My heart tells me that a spiritual miniature work awaits us."

---

[1] "in black [vestments]"—indicates a solemn occasion for the clerics thus dressed.

When they reached a small alley beside the parish church of the Three Holy Brothers, they got out of the taxi and entered the church. Inside, in front of the first pews, *in cornu epistolae*, was a young lady, obviously a teacher, instructing about twenty children, boys on the right and girls on the left, on the catechism. No one else was in the church. The unexpected arrivals tried their best to avoid distracting the children by kneeling in the pew closest to the side door, which was all in shadow. They remained there, watching and listening.

The poor church was ancient and desolate! Vanished altarpieces, niches emptied out to resemble eye sockets without eyes, a balustrade encased in a wooden shelf, on which towered a rough tavern table. If the upper part of the ancient consecrated altar had not been so easily seen in the background, the shelf would have looked like a boxing ring. The tabernacle was hidden by the shelf and, of course, no Eucharistic lamp was lit.

"Woman, behold your Son!" said the Master, "And then turning to St. John, he said to him, "Behold your mother! St. John's mother was also at the foot of the Cross. Her name was Salome. But Salome, too, very willingly gave her son, the best son she had, to Our Lady."

All the spellbound children looked at their teacher without blinking. "Well," concluded the teacher, "Confession makes us the same as that, with our souls as beautiful as at baptism, and even more so, like St. John's, without stain, in the grace of God. It makes us brothers of Jesus, who is God, and children of Our Lady, who is the Mother of God. Now you know how to confess well. You know what your sins are and you know what resolutions you have to make. As soon as it is possible, you will go to confession. After the trip to Our Lady of Divine Love, you will return home much richer in grace. For now you must take Communion as the priest says, but do so while asking for God's forgiveness in your heart each time, and promising in your heart never to offend him again, just like St. Dominic Savio, who said... Albert, what did Dominic Savio say?"

"Death, but no sin!" promptly replied little Albert.

"Very good!" continued the teacher, "And like Saint Maria Goretti, who knew how to die, but did not want to sin, and she is now in Heaven in the choir of Virgins. Also she had the intention to confess well at the first opportunity. And now..."
She was about to dismiss her catechumens, when, at a nod from the Pope, Wong came up to her and said:

"Madam teacher, if you think they are prepared, we could hear their confessions. There are three of us, all licensed to hear confessions throughout the diocese."

"In that case, I would first like to make a confession, while you help the boys. Then they can go to confession, and I will help them. Please remember, Reverend: it takes some practice to keep them under control."

So Wong took the teacher's place, and started discussing with the little boys Jesus' deposition from the cross in Our Lady's arms, and then the song of lamentation of the pious women, and perhaps even Our Lady herself, behind Jesus' body, which was carried to the tomb, from which he would gloriously rise, never to die again. Don Ciccio took his place in the pastor's confessional. It was a monumental, artistic confessional, equipped with all the relatively new bells and whistles—an internal lamp, call button, external red light and dimmer internal one. And all full of dust. The priest heard the teacher's confession there. The Pope sat next to it in a pew, had one of those children come up to him, knelt down next to him, made a nice sign of the cross, and began to hear the confession. So all the boys went in turn to the three confessors, who had come to them quite unexpectedly, and quietly made their confessions. They were all well disposed, devout, serene, and quite content.

During the taxi journey, Wong had actually talked about the confession that the little ones must make prior to First Communion.

"It is true," he said, "That below a certain age, it is hardly possible to give a warning which would allow one to appreciate the gravity of the matter, so that even consent, however perfect it may seem, cannot be consent of mortal sin. It must therefore be presumed that under a certain age usually no mortal sin can occur. This presumption is codified in the Code of Canon Law, Article 2230, which exempts from certain penalties those who have indeed committed some crime, materially serious, but have not yet reached the age of fourteen, if boys, and twelve, if young girls, and Article 80.2, admitting Article 88.3, that already at least at the age of seven some degree of discretion or use of reason has been attained. However, *in foro conscientiae praesumptio cedit veritati*.[2] In the practical case of an individual child, how can it be truthfully ascertained that grave sin really occurred? Only by that person's sincere confession. Therefore, the obligation remains for the parents and parish priest to have the children also make their confession before their First Communion since Communion is a sacrament of the living, which requires the state of grace, either baptismal or recovered by the sacrament of Penance. Therefore, the pastor of the Three Holy Brothers..." But the taxi at that time stopped by the side entrance of the parish, and the rest had already been said.

After the boys made their confessions, the teacher had them do penance, and urged them to impose on themselves some other little penance of their own choosing, a small but nice sacrifice to Our Lady. Then she dismissed them. Things were now ending, with the last little girl just finishing her confession with Don Ciccio, when the door to the sacristy opened. The

---

2 "in the forum of the conscience, the presumption gives pride of place/cedes to reality/truth."

parish priest and a serious and dignified gentleman holding a large suitcase entered the main aisle and headed for the side exit. In spite of his extreme near-sightedness which was little improved by the thick lenses he wore, the parish priest noticed that the red light of his confessional was on. He walked up to it, threw open its curtain, and rudely asked:

"Who authorized you to come in here?" Don Ciccio did not answer. He finished confessing the little girl, blessed her, and then went out with the inner peace of someone preparing for a fight with the certainty of victory. It was a tranquility wrapped in an air of mocking irony, which only a Roman local knows how to put on in such circumstances. For a second, the parish priest experienced a moment of perplexity. Was it due to remorse? When he saw the ordinary Don Ciccio leave the confessional, all covered in dust, to regain his own demeanor in front of the austere gentleman with the large bulging suitcase, once again challenged the priest:

"Who authorized you...?"

"...to volunteer," Don Ciccio interrupted him, "In place of a deserter? I'll tell you right now: our Lord, and his vicar on earth!"

"Don't be an arrogant ass if you don't want me to kick you out, in the square, and send you to *Regina coeli* prison, and maybe even suspended *a divinis*. Right, Commissioner Market?"

"Certainly! I am a close friend of the Pope, benefactor to the Church, papal Commissioner..." But he stopped short, and looked quizzically at Camillo, Wong and, behind them, the Pope, who had approached the confessional that was at the center of the argument. The teacher, taking the hint, had started toward the exit, as if to escort the last little penitent out. "You, Mr. Osiris Market, are not yet a papal commendator," Wong told him. "You," Monsignor Wong then added, with a bow and a smile, "you lied!"

"And how much did he give you, Father, for that chalice

engraved with the Three Holy Brothers?" asked Camillo to the parish priest, "Ten thousand liras?"

The parish priest seemed to be dreaming, and as if in a dream, he mechanically replied:

"Ten thousand? What do you take me for? Two hundred thousand!"

"And do you know how much this benefactor of the Church has pocketed?" continued Camillo.

"Only five little million!" Mr. Market started to walk away with the bulging suitcase, which he had been holding onto tightly, but Camillo barred his way. "One moment, sir! You may go, but the suitcase stays!"

"But I've paid for it. I'm calling the police!"

"The police?" asked Camillo, "Do you really want to? I'm going, but I'll be back!"

He disappeared through the side door, but came back an instant later with Cincinnatus, to whom he had nonetheless made time to wink and whisper four little words into his ear. Cincinnatus, in a driver's uniform, looked like a policeman or security guard. Just then he had decided to go inside to warn the Pope of what was happening outside the church.

Outside, a little boy who had confessed to the Pope had raised the alarm. He had recognized the Pope! Many times, the boy had seen the short film, shot by a cousin of his in the Vatican gardens, because he never tired of seeing the doves. He had confessed to the very Pope of the doves! He had seen his beard so closely! He was not mistaken! He... His mother, who owned a flower store across the street, wanted to check with her own eyes. She had entered the church at the very moment when the pastor, appealing to all his remaining strength, solemnly exclaimed:

"I will go to the Vatican, to the Pope, and I will denounce you..." But the bearded old man took a step forward and interrupted him:

"There is no need for you to bother. You can make your denunciation right away, here, to me."

There was no doubt about it. It was the Pope, the one from his brother's son's short film. The flower lady hurried out of church and called to the teacher and the little boys she still had around her:

"Come, all of you, come here!" She led them in front of her store. She went in and came out quickly with a large bundle of flowers, and started handing them out to the little boys. "Take some, there are flowers for everyone. For the new Pope! You have confessed to the Pope! Now when he comes out, we can celebrate with him!"

The word spread quickly and in no time people flocked to the church. Many mothers took their youngest in their bosoms, and ran to the florist to ask for some flowers for their children as well.

"Ah, Filomena, I don't have any money. I'll pay you tomorrow!"

"Not tomorrow, not ever!" replied the florist, continuing to distribute flowers, "You take some too! All for the Pope, who has come to scold our parish priest. And may he leave his mark for a while!"

With no other choice, Mr. Osiris Market left without the suitcase. The parish priest opened his wallet, as if to return the money he had just now received for the sacred furnishings that filled the suitcase, but Camillo told him:

"Forget it! Can't you do the math? You are still on credit, right?"

Finally, the taxi driver got ready to pick them up out in front, as they had all been detected. It was useless to try to hide or escape by a side door. It was better to go out the front door with dignity:

"...and may God send us with good tidings, together with the Three Holy Brothers!"

So Cincinnatus and Camillo went forward in different directions. At the agreed nod and with perfect synchrony, they opened wide the two doors of the main entrance, like two ceremonial valets, and the Pope came out, and behind him Wong, Ciccio and the parish priest. As soon as the Pope appeared in the sacristy, an ovation rose from the small crowd that had gathered there. Mothers thrust out their little ones toward him as they requested,

"Holy Father, bless our little ones!"

The little penitents from a short time before crowded around the Pope, waving the flowers they held in their hands and kissing his hands. Meanwhile, the teacher had withdrawn into a chant, with tears running down her cheeks. When the parish priest saw her there, in that corner, he who had opposed her so many times, he could not resist any longer and threw himself on his knees before the Pope. Everyone fell silent, as if enchanted, and the Pope began:

"Praised be Jesus Christ!"

"May He always be praised!"

"My dear, dear children in the Lord, this is your pastor, your priest. He is here to assure me of his full cooperation for the good of your souls. He will resume the administration of the Sacraments, as is our desire, now that he has been able to have an authoritative clarification of the liturgical provisions in force. He will put back into working order this great consecrated altar, built by the faith, craft, and sacrifices of your elders. In the Holy Tabernacle, in the center of the high altar—which is its place—he will preserve day and night the Most Holy Eucharist, the perennial sacrament of the perennial sacrifice of Our Lord, Priest and Victim in perennial sacrificial act, with the lamp perpetually lit, with the *umbraculum*,[3] with flowers as fresh as the ones you are holding, dear children, and with the balustrade restored. He will put the altarpieces back in their places, he will put the statues of the saints back

---

3 "covering," i.e., with a veiled covering, either over the tabernacle, or sometimes as in a procession with the exposed sacrament.

in their niches, and before any other, and in the most solemn way possible, the statue of Our Lady of Sorrows at the altar of the Crucifix..."

At this point, the Pope was interrupted by the unanimous cry:

"Hurray for Our Lady!" At the same time, an applause erupted that was so spontaneous and cordial that it rewarded him for all the bitterness of the first thunderous but entirely conventional applause he received in the conclave when he accepted his election to the supreme pontificate. Then he blessed the crowd, and took his place in Cincinnatus' taxi, which had arrived at the edge of the parvis at that very moment. Camillo sat next to him. Wong and Ciccio went into the car of the florist's husband. Another small car, whose owner was unknown, went in front to act as a relay. The pontifical convoy then set off for the Vatican under a shower of flowers. It was preceded by the echo of what had just happened.

The Swiss guard had nurtured his good hopes until five minutes before 5 p.m. Then he resigned himself to putting on a happy face, and came up with a contingency plan. As he would still be on guard from 7 p.m. to 9 p.m., all he had to do was to warn the Pope to delay his return until 7 p.m., and the problem was totally solved. That said, having gotten off from guard duty, he would obtain a brief leave for a sudden and urgent matter. Then he would put on normal clothes, and take up guard duty in Piazza Leonina, at the entrance to the Via di Porta Angelica. But this was going on for a long time. He was too much in view just sitting there. He crossed the street, and took a seat at a small table outside the bar, immediately across the street. He ordered a beer, as the May day had been sunny and warm, and resumed watching the entrance to the streets leading into Leonina Square. Just as he was about to take the first sip of beer from an enormous mug that the busboy had laid before him, the latter said to him:

"Do you know the news? For you, a Swiss guard, it is certainly not news. If not, you would not have been there, across the street, half an hour waiting for him!"

"What news?"

"The Pope went incognito scold the pastor of the Three Holy Brothers. All the people there gave him a party. Looks like he started biting. It's about time!"

At that same instant, a procession of five cars emerged in Leonina Square. The first and fifth were police, and the third was Cincinnatus' taxi. Nothing else was needed from the Swiss. He put down the huge undrunk glass of beer and ran toward the St. Anne's Gate, hoping to have the gate thrown wide open at once. But it was already open, with the Swiss Guard lined up on either side, with some officers at the gate to keep the people gathering there to pay homage to the arriving Pope at a distance. And he, the trusted Swiss guard, had not noticed one thing! The Pope, when passing by and seeing him, smiled at him, as if to say:

"Patience! Everything went well!" and he waved "Hello!" at him.

At that moment, the Swiss guard thought of answering him with the military salute, but, out of uniform, he answered with the same confident gesture, "Hello!" which took aback those who noticed. After that, happy and satisfied, the guard went back to his beer.

15

Refined Surgery

"HERE IS THAT LETTER, YOUR Holiness!" Monsignor Taddei, head of the Correspondence Office, told the Pope, "It had been stopped by order of my direct superior. I took care to preserve it. I was not ordered to destroy it. After the visit of Your Holiness to our office, I tracked it down, but then thought twice because by then the date was so old! I could not ask Your Holiness's opinion without making you aware of this background information, and I did not have the heart for it. Now I am here at your disposal."

"Let's see what we can do," the Pope said. "It's dated May 2. It would be enough to add two, and could start with today's date, May 22."

"Your Holiness, if you will allow me to give a piece of advice. It is close to your heart that this reverend father be here as soon as possible. A telegram is quicker, and engages the recipient more than a letter does. It would be enough to let this reverend father know that Your Holiness expects him here as soon as possible, that he leave at once for Rome on the first plane, dropping whatever he is doing. He can later return to where he is now to get all his things together."

"Perfect! Send him this telegram: 'Come with the first plane. Pius XIV.' When will he receive it?"

"In half an hour. An hour at the latest."

"When can he be here?"

"Also in a couple of hours. Tomorrow at the latest."

"Thank you. Do it right away."

The monsignor was about to leave when a valet came in to announce:

"He arrived by plane..." and paused for a moment to read the name of the person about to enter on the note in his hand. This delay was enough for the Pope and Taddei to formulate an identical thought:

"Clearly, Father Aurelio has already carried out the order, even before receiving it!" But the valet read on his note the name of the newly arrived, giving the Pope no small disappointment:

"...Mr. Cardinal Friedrich Stolzkamm has arrived and wishes to be received at once."

"Do you see how effective your telegram was, Monsignor?" commented the Pope, "Someone on the plane has already arrived, but not exactly who I wanted right now! Patience! Let him in."

Left alone, the Pope knelt on the floor in front of the statuette of Our Lady of Good Counsel on his desk, bowed his forehead and, on his knees, waited for the hurricane heralded by the surname, Stolzkamm, that was about to break out. In fact, the cardinal held him for a good quarter of an hour under a barrage of names and titles, figures and statistics, organizations and associations, acronyms and documents, dates and deliberations, decrees and circulars. Suddenly it seemed to Pius XIV that even the cubic office was circular, with at least a dozen cardinals, oozing purple from every pore, swirling around him.

"The progressive and irreversible downsizing of all the load-bearing structures of our national Church, and at every level, which is demanded by the dynamics of the post-conciliar aggiornamento," Cardinal Stolzkamm said not without emphasis, "has been thwarted by these five bishops who are closed off to ecumenical outreach. They are made deaf to the needs of mature Christians and emancipated by a decadent, decayed, and inauspicious juridicism. They transform, degenerate, and prevent an authentic solution, and turn every pastoral problem into a doctrinal one. This is contrary to the principle that God is not conservative. In every discussion, they demand a prior *declaratio terminorum*,[1] which enables them to nail down, in the most rigid, fundamentalist fixism, every evolutionary impetus of thought, science, philosophy, dogma, morality, liturgy, sociality—in a word, the progress of peoples and the entire universe.

"These five are enough to hold back the work of all the others, and to disrupt our entire national Church! Eighty years *et ultra*[2] of tenacious work, in tune with the prophetic movements of other countries, with the *Sillon* of neighboring France, with the leading men of Catholic Action, with New Life and with the Worker Priests; eighty years *et ultra* of persevering underground work to repair the cruel divisions brought about by the *Pascendi* encyclical, by the document *Lamentabili*, by the anti-modernist oath; eighty years *et ultra* of tenacious and persevering work, often carried out at the fringe, and opposed by the very same official Church that should have favored it. We opened wide the arms of separated brethren, without torturing their consciences; we restored the authentic Gospel to the authentic People of God. Eighty years *et ultra* of a whole underground activity, and which only after Vatican II could finally come into the light. Yes, thanks to Vatican II understood, according to the spirit—*Littera occidit, spiritus vivificat!*[3]—according to its dialectic, its logic, its internal, intrinsic and essential dynamics.... And so, for five objectors, the marching wing of our national Church..."

---

1 "declaration of terms" (usually in battle as well as in debate)
2 "And beyond" or "and more".
3 "The letter kills, the Spirit gives life!" abbreviated version of 2 Cor. 3:2.

"... or eighty years *et ultra* restrained by papal provisions, like Prometheus tied to the column..." the Pope managed to say, taking advantage of the fact that the panting cardinal had to stop for a moment to catch his breath. The cardinal was in fact corpulent and somewhat asthmatic. The Pope added, "Once wings made them fly. Now, with irreversible progress, you make them march on foot. Mercury had wings on his feet; but a wing with feet is an absolute novelty. It would make a humorous cartoon! But let's not digress! Continue, Your Eminence, continue!"

Cardinal Stolzkamm rested a moment and looked at Pius XIV's face. But he saw such simplicity and sincerity that he immediately calmed down. Yes, this neo-Pope was naïve, docile, and harmless. However, taking up again the thread of the speech, he somewhat dampened energy and brought the first round to what he was persuaded was a happy end.

"Here are the names of the five *reverendi eligendi*[4] who are to succeed the five *deponendi*[5], who have gone so far as to allow secular and religious priests to wander about celebrating the pre-Reformation Mass at the request of the faithful, and this even outside their own diocese. Imagine, Your Holiness! In a semi-Protestant country such as ours, they are still celebrating the pre-Reformation Mass, which is hated by the Protestants, when precisely for the sake of our separated brethren the new Mass has been modeled. It no longer contains anything that could offend their convictions, in the cases where they differ from the Catholic ones.

"The deposition of these five transgressors is urgent. It is an imperative decision of the bishops' conference of our national Church. Nor would we have inconvenienced Your Holiness, in view also of his venerable age, if the last vestiges

---

4 "reverends who are to be chosen"
5 "the ones who are to be deposed/removed from office" — common terms in ordinations and official [re]placements in ecclesiastical offices.

of anachronistic legalism did not still reserve the designation of bishops to the Pope."

"Designation? I did not designate these five *eligendi*[6], you did. The Pope reserves the exclusive right, not so much to designate, but to confer, the jurisdiction for each and every bishop over a certain diocese, *et quidem tamquam conditio sine qua non*.[7] He can only receive this jurisdiction from the Pope, not from anyone else ever. Yes, this right and duty of bestowing and removing ordinary jurisdiction on bishops belongs exclusively to me. Is that clear? Do you then believe, Your Eminence, that those other five, the five *deponendi*, are all equally guilty? It usually happens that in a group, somewhat like in groups of any kind, there is always someone who is a little more of an expert in humanity than the others, who pulls the others' strings and gets them to act, supposedly of their own accord, but actually as he wishes. Don't you think so, Your Eminence?"

"Correct, Your Holiness! The one responsible, who first raised the banner of rebellion, is Monsignor Gordin. He ended up getting a hold on the four weak and easily persuaded bishops of the dioceses bordering his own."

"And so, before we proceed, *audiamus et alteram partem*![8] We will also hear from this Monsignor Gordin."

"Your Holiness, but then you doubt the seriousness of my grievances, and make no allowance whatsoever for the irreversibility of our collegial decisions! These are obstinate rebels! Every day that they remain in their positions is a greater danger to the dignity of all other bishops. The faithful lose esteem and trust in us, and they turn away from us more and more."

"Has this unfortunate situation lasted for a long time?"

"For some years. We have been patient, we have hoped for

---

6 "To be chosen."
7 *conditio sine qua non* means "an essential condition."
8 "Let us hear from the other side!"

their repentance, we have put forth everything in our power to bring them to their senses, but without success. Our patience was mistaken for weakness, for the fear of action that is peculiar to those who feel on the wrong side, and it made them obstinate, not to say aggressive. And so we were forced to resort to extreme remedies, postponing them until today, because we did not want to pour one last drop of bitterness into the heart of the late Pontiff, of holy memory."

"If you have been patient for several years, surely you will be able to be patient for a few more days. I will have Monsignor Gordin telegraphed at once, so that he leaves behind whatever business he has in his hands and comes immediately *ad audiendum verbum* [9]."

"Ah, no, Your Holiness! This is not possible! It will be a slap in the face to my brothers in the episcopate, whom I represent here, and who are only waiting for the formalities of the deposition to be completed. I have not come to provoke a trial and even much less a confrontation. There is no place for rebels among the bishops of our..."

"...National Church!" the Pope interjected, and in such a tone, that he took away the cardinal's boldness to interrupt in turn. They were both silent for a few moments. Finally the Pope resumed speaking:

"Your Eminence, I must tell you with all candor that I do not recognize any national church. I believe *unam, sanctam, catholicam et apostolicam Ecclesiam*, which by the will of its divine founder means only the Roman one. Do you not believe this? I think you agree with me on this. Otherwise they would be outside the Church, and there would be no need to depose them, to take any jurisdiction away from them, because they would have none at all. Just as I agree with you that there is no place for rebels in the holy Church of Our Lord Jesus Christ,

---

9 "to hear the word"—from Sirach 5:13, often applies to the wisdom of listening to whoever is present.

much less in the chair of the successors of His first apostles. Yes, in this I fully agree with Your Eminence."

The Pope fell silent, closed his eyes, prayed in his heart again to Our Lady of Good Counsel, and then resumed calmly but confidently:

"A rebel is someone who rises up against the provisions of legitimate authority, who challenges its strict orders, who misrepresents and mocks it. And who mocked and misrepresented and scorned and rebelled against, and induced as many as he could to rebel against, the encyclical *Humanæ vitæ* from his own diocese? Who said it reflected the private and therefore fallible opinion of the Pope of that time? It is known that the Pope of that time, as a private doctor, held an opinion contrary to the one he had to express in that encyclical as Pope, in spite of himself, in promulgating once again a traditional and unchangeable dogma of Catholic morality of all time. And who took a stand against ecclesiastical celibacy, amid congratulations from those who oppose God's laws, despite the most authoritative statements of the supreme pontiffs? Who rebelled against the Roman Pontiff's legal primacy by appealing to the collegiality of the episcopate, skillfully taking authority away from the Roman Pontiff? And who lets the theologians of his diocese, professors of self-styled Catholic universities, deny the divine motherhood of Our Lady, the perpetual virginity of the Immaculata, the very dogma of the exemption of Mary Most Holy from original sin, since they deny not only original sin, but sin itself in the true and proper sense, that is, theological? And who rejoiced with those who deny that the Mass as a sacrifice, with those who deny the real presence of the Incarnate Word in the Eucharist, with those who deny the ministerial priesthood, insofar as it differs from the simple common priesthood of the faithful, and approved that they concelebrate, those who denied, in their own way, together with Catholic priests? Who should instead believe all that?

And who went against—this has been confirmed to me now, here, Your Eminence—and who went against the provisions of the encyclical *Pascendi*, of the decree *Lamentabili*, of the anti-modernist oath, which was supposed to curb the spread of Modernism itself, the syllabus of all heresies? Would not this man be a rebel to be deposed? Your Eminence will remain in Rome until the arrival of Monsignor Gordin. I will receive you together, and..."

"Impossible!" exclaimed Cardinal Stolzkamm in a dramatic tone: "Impossible!" he replied as if his judgment were irrevocable. Pius XIV bowed his forehead, squinted his eyes, smoothed his beard, stayed silent for a few more moments, and finally pronounced the following:

"Then Your Eminence will remain in Rome, available, and the See of Your Eminence from this moment is vacant."

Cardinal Stolzkamm opened his eyes wide—they were incredulous, horrified, and almost threatening, but the Pope replied:

"That's right, Your Eminence! It is exclusively up to the Pope, who is me, to give and take away episcopal jurisdiction. Now I have taken away the one you had until a moment ago. You are no longer bishop of your diocese. Any attempt on your part to the contrary would be intrinsically illicit and invalid. Is that clear? Your arrival was unexpected for me. I did not yet feel prepared to face you, but it was Our Lady who allowed and guided this first surgery in the body of the episcopate. Now Your Eminence cannot understand it, but one day, I hope you will."

Cardinal Stolzkamm stood up, cast a defiant glance at the old man with the goatee who had spoken to him in such a manner, and walked out with a hurried step. At the sound of his footsteps, the vast Olympus of the whole Vatican seemed to tremble.

16

François René Visconte de Chateaubriand

During the walk in the Vatican gardens that afternoon, a surprise awaited the Pope. A gentleman came out of the grotto of Our Lady of Lourdes. He respectfully approached the Pope, knelt before him, and said:

"Your Holiness, I requested an audience with the Prefettura della Casa Pontificia, but they didn't grant it to me. I asked for an audience in writing to Your Holiness, but I did not receive any response. Then I saw a photograph of Your Holiness in the gardens, here by this grotto in a magazine. I had no choice but to wait for you here. I've gone through a whole adventure! I've had sorrow in my heart. My martyrdom grew worse when a certain prelate began to make public acts of repentance in the name of the Church. He asked for forgiveness for certain crimes he attributed to the Church itself. These were crimes committed by the bride of the Lord who is preserved in eternity, immune from all stains, like the Immaculate One whom we honor in that grotto..."

"Stand up, Mr...."

"François René de Chateaubriand."

"Viscount de Chateaubriand," said the Pope, who also added to the gentleman's name the title of nobility which out of modesty the latter had omitted. Then the Pope asked him with a smile, "The great author of the *Génie du Christianisme*?"

"I'm just a distant relative, an unimportant lecturer in the history of French literature at the University of Rome," replied the professor with a smile.

"I wouldn't say unimportant, Monsieur Vicomte de Chateaubriand."

Although still on his knees, his head was level to the Pope's shoulders. He was thin, bony, and all nerves. His attractive forehead was high, spacious, and smooth, and below that were two large, intelligent, deep-set eyes.

"Stand up, professor! And now just tell me, on the way, what you want to tell me. If that briefcase is a burden to you, go ahead and give it to Commendator Camillo."

"Thank you. I'm okay for now."

"You were telling me about your sorrow for certain acts of repentance, right?"

"Exactly! The Church should ask forgiveness from pretty much everyone, for what it has done and what it has not done: from Michelangelo and Raphael for having gotten them to paint the Sistine and the Logge; from the Muslims for having defeated them at Lepanto; from the persecutors for having survived their most thoughtful treatment. Ignorance? Bad faith? Inconceivable confidence in such historical falsifications to win the sympathy of the enemies of the Christian name and the current persecutors of the Church? You will understand, Your Holiness, I am a historian of French literature, but not only of French literature!" exclaimed the Viscount de Chateaubriand rather excitedly.

"How did you get here?" the Pope asked him, skillfully diverting the direction of the conversation for a moment to give him a chance to quell his emotions.

"With a group of German tourists. When it was time for them to leave, I hid and placed myself under the protection of Notre Dame de Lourdes."

"And Notre Dame de Lourdes bestowed her grace. Let's sit here, under this little kiosk, in the shade of these beautiful roses!"

"They are roses in bouquets, which we call polyanthus. They climb, and bloom so generously every year. Smell them!" said the gardener to the Pope. This was the same one from the first walk, who since that day at around that time always wandered over to that part of the garden, where he always found some work to do.

"Dutch, like those tulips?" asked the Pope. But the gardener, already out of range, gave no answer. "Commendatore, let's have a few things brought in. What would you like, Viscount?"

"What's good enough for a pope is good enough for a viscount," the professor replied. Camillo conveyed an order to the gardener, and returned at once to the side of the Pope, who was listening with interest to the professor. The latter's speech was dignified, dense, and passionate. He spoke with a slight French accent, but his phrasing was of Florentine-born propriety.

"Into the lake of my heart, as Dante put it, deep and filled with so much bitterness, poured a torrent of indignation, which stirred an uncontrollable storm there, the day I learned that the flag conquered at Lepanto had been returned to the Turkish republic. Returned? And why not to the Muslim League? History skips over the fact that at Lepanto the fleet of a then non-existent Turkish republic was deployed against the Christians, and that at least the Turkish republic, agonizing over having that flag, had asked and begged for it. Not even in a dream. The papal offer astonished them, made them smile, and was received with skeptical smugness, just like that, out of good manners. And the Lepanto flag ended up at the lost and found office, waiting for its rightful owner to go and collect it. Returned? To obtain the Sultan's forgiveness for the sin committed by the Church. It was committed when the Christians at Lepanto did not allow themselves to be thrown down, when they did not flee, but dared to fight. And they fought heroically and won, and saved us all from barbarism and the denial of the Faith. Because, if at Lepanto, we had been defeated, we would all be Muslims today!"

"In Palestine," said the Pope, "the foot of the Mount of the Franks, which lies just south of Bethlehem, is now permanently settled by a tribe of Bedouins who are descendants of the Franks, the most spirited of all the Crusaders. They are herd-breeders, called Ta'ámeri. They are all Muslims. Yet if on July 4, 1187, at Qurn Hattín, above Tiberias, the Franks had not been defeated by Saladin, the whole Middle East even today would be Catholic. The Lord uses men how and when He wills. And men who do not go along with God's designs betray themselves to their own harm."

"This was well understood then by the Pope and commanders, combatants and faithful," the Viscount de Chateaubriand resumed. "What indeed was flying on the Duke of Savoy's galley in the waters of Lepanto? The banner with the image of the Holy Shroud. What was flying on the red silk banner offered by St. Pius V to Marcantonio Colonna, admiral of the twelve papal galleys? The Crucifix and the motto *In hoc signo vinces*. What did the combatants do before the battle? They went to confession and received communion. What did the mothers, sisters, brides, and girlfriends of those who fell in the waters of Lepanto do when the news of the victory reached Venice along with the list of those who had perished in combat? They got dressed up!" Here the professor had to stop because he was so moved, as equally were the Pope and Camillo. Fortunately, at this moment the gardener arrived with four bottles of beer and four glasses: one for the Pope, one for the guest, one for Camillo and one for himself.

"Of course!" resumed the historian, "Twenty-four-year-old Miguel de Cervantes Saavedra, although with a fever, did not want to miss the great venture. He fought as a foot soldier under the orders of Marcantonio Colonna. He was wounded three times in the battle. He called those three wounds the 'three stars, which guide other men to the sky of honor.' He lost his left hand there, but with his right hand he wrote, 'If by a miracle I could be given a choice, I would always prefer to be present at that legendary battle than to be saved from my wounds by not participating in it.' So wrote the genius of Christianity, the author of *Don Qujxote!*

"Would the restitutors of that flag be happy if a new Selim II, on the advice of a new José Miquez, the Jew who suggested to him all the plans of robbery and slaughter, came to lay siege to them, as he did to Nicosia and Famagusta in Cyprus? Would they be happy if a new Mustafa Làla Bàscia, after having obtained the surrender with the guarantee of safety for all, and with military honors, had them beheaded — all of them — by the tens of thousands, except the commander, for whom, as for the martyr Marcantonio Bragadin, would be reserved the cutting off of the ears and the nose, and then flaying alive to the sound of fifes and timpani?

"Well, the flag was returned with a certain emphasis on the one hand, and accepted not without some disappointment on the other. It ended up in a corner somewhere and fell into oblivion. And then I had the idea..."

"...to reconquer it," the Pope said, "To erase a historical shame. Since France was on friendly terms with the Ottomans, it was absent when that flag was conquered. And so, on behalf of France, to erase that shame, you wanted to reconquer it. And did you succeed?"

"Holiness, not for that reason! A whole series of adventures happened. I will only mention the ending. Many presidents of Turkish museums and institutes had received the flag in their custody, but they didn't want it. The big problem for them was indeed to display it to the public with a caption that was historically true, and psychologically pleasing, but that would be squaring the circle. So it ended up forgotten in a historical archive in Ankara, where I tracked it down. But the road to get there was neither short nor easy.

"As soon as I suspected that it was in that archive, I did

some hard work to be admitted there, on the pretext of certain historical research of mine for a publication that was necessary for my career as a university professor. This was a work on historical-literary criticism, for which I knew that certain data could only be found in that archive. Six months of study! The problem was not so much with the documents that were so kindly made available to me, and of which I sometimes had a few excerpts translated, or had photostatic copies made. The problem I had was with the Turkish language. I had to learn as much of it as I possibly could so I could read the entries in the files for myself. It was difficult, but with determination I was quite successful. And I could also express myself discreetly. This won me the confidence of the porter and usher, and an archivist clerk. They were the only three people I dealt with.

"Actually, it was while talking to that clerk one day that I threw the word Lepanto out there, as if at random. The clerk picked it up at once, and, certain that he was doing me a favor, he said, 'Do you know that it ended up here, in my hands, the flag that the Christians detached from the flagship of Àli Muezzín Séde, the great loser of Lepanto? If we could display it with the caption—Lost at Lepanto, regained in Rome—that would be another matter. Not that we feel that we are the legal heirs of the glories and wrongdoing of the Ottoman Empire. The young do not even know what it is anymore. But when it was in its last location, the flag was in its proper place, and it didn't bother anyone. It's strange to send it to the Türkiye Cümhuriyeti—as if to remind us of a military humiliation that was suffered by others, because the truth of the matter is that no Turkish republic has ever been defeated at Lepanto since the beginning of the world! It is in the room adjacent to this one, in a red box, in the glass closet. And there it will stay until the rats have finished gnawing it."

After this news, which I confirmed by carefully checking the filing cabinet, I wrote to my mother. I must say that my mother—I owe her all of the little bit of good that is in me—when she heard of my project, she discouraged me. She told me that I just wanted to ruin my career, which had just begun. I am thirty-three years old. She told me that it was not in my heart to leave her alone, in pain, and who knows until when. My mother was widowed after two years of marriage, when I had not yet turned one year old. But when she was certain that I had weighed the pros and cons, that I was determined, that I was not doing it out of vanity or a spirit of adventure, and that Our Lady would help me, she then confessed to me what I had known from the beginning. She had contradicted me only to test me, and to know my intentions to the end. But she said that she was happy. She did not even say anything when I told her that I needed to ask for a break from teaching. She just wanted us to exchange Rosary wreaths. At the airport, just before we parted, she said, "If you need an accomplice, you can rely on your mother."

"So a few days after my letter, I was able to introduce my mother to the porter, usher and archival clerk. I resumed my work with the help of my mother, who, after secretly photographing the alleged Lepanto flag, returned to Rome. Fifteen days later she rejoined me. My mother is fifty-six years old, but I called her my sister. She brought back a copy of the Lepanto flag, which was also made on the basis of the data that I had accurately checked and rechecked in the archivist's file cabinet. The fake flag was a perfect copy. It had been reduced to such a state—including being full of dust—that it could be a perfect substitute for the authentic flag.

"I am not going to talk about how the substitution took place. I am not going to tell of our strong emotions when, in my rented room, we were able to unfold the stolen flag, and assure ourselves without any doubt that it was indeed the one we wanted. So far no one seems to have noticed the substitution. Who cares about the rags that ended up in that closet? And here it is!" While speaking, the Vicomte de Chateaubriand opened the briefcase he had been holding by the handle, and showed the large clear plastic envelope containing the carefully-folded Lepanto flag.

Then he continued:

"To conquer this flag, the encircled Knights of St. John, who were on the three galleys of Malta, died fighting—all of them, to the last man. To defeat it, the Venetian super-commandant Benedetto Soranzo set fire to his own ship, the Santa Barbara, and blew it up along with the Muslim ships, which were overpowering it. All of them ended up in the sea. In order to defeat the enemy, Agostino Barbarigo directed the combat of his men to the extreme. Although he had an arrow stuck in his eye, he resisted, and allowed himself to die only when he had seen with his unharmed eye this flag of the Crescent lowered down through the rigging of the Muslim flagship, and the banner of the Cross hoisted on it."

"And what about Don Juan of Austria? Have you forgotten, professor?" the Pope asked him.

"Don Juan? The 24-year-old supreme commander of the Christian fleet? In Santa Chiara di Napoli, he received the blue silk banner of the League with the image of our divine Redeemer crucified. When he was given the signal for battle, which came after the general absolution imparted to the combatants, he danced the Pyrrhic dance with two of his soldiers under the eyes of the enemy, who was advancing menacingly and observing him with stupefaction. When the two flagships docked and the Muslims were overpowering the Christians, Don Juan freed his galley slaves and threw them into the fray. Àli Muezzín Séde also freed his own slaves, but they were predominantly Christians. They turned their arms against their oppressors and secured the conquest of this flag.

"Return the flag of Lepanto? Don Juan of Austria, Marcantonio Colonna, Marcantonio Bragadin, the Knights of Malta, all of you: rise up, beat your chests, ask forgiveness, return this flag! It is St. Pius V himself who returns it, with many apologies, to the Bàscia of Algiers, to Ùhuds Áli, the Calabrian renegade Occhiali, commander of the Muslim left flank at Lepanto!"

A long pause ensued. Finally, the Pope spoke:

"Professor, do you see in the victory of Lepanto a victory of Christian artillery, as various historians claim, since in that battle it was double, or more than double, that of the Muslims?"

"Your Holiness, those historians missed a very historical dimension of that event that made October 7, 1571 a fateful date. They missed the supernatural dimension. The Muslim fleet as a whole was clearly superior to the Christian fleet. It was homogeneous, highly trained, reputed to be invincible, and deservedly so. Its name was sufficient to instill in the Muslim fighters the spirit that wins every battle. The Christian fleet had more guns, it is true, but it consisted of considerably fewer ships, was not homogeneous, and was not as well trained as the enemy fleet. The victory at Lepanto has only one valid explanation, which is the one that the Venetian Senate wrote under the depiction of the battle itself: 'Neither power, nor arms, nor duci; but Our Lady of the Rosary gave us victory.'

"That's why in Constantinople, in the church of Hagia Sophia, which had been reduced to a mosque, three admonishing fiery crosses had appeared. That's why the sea at Lepanto, which had been stormy until Oct. 7, calmed down on that day, only to stir again after the battle. That is why the wind, which, though initially favoring the Muslim fleet and sparing its oarsmen, had driven it against the Christian fleet, and had grouped it around the Christians in the shape of a waning moon, at the first cannon shot reversed its direction. The wind swelled the Christian sails and blew the artillery smoke, and then the smoke of the fires, into the Muslims' faces. That's why St. Pius V, from his office in his palace back there," and the professor pointed to it with his hand, "where he was in conversation with

Monsignor Bartolo Bussati, his treasurer, and Cardinal Celsis and others, interrupted himself, went to the window, opened it, looked toward the east, and then, turning to the onlookers, exclaimed, "This is no time for any more business! Hurry and thank God, for our army has won."

"I fear this Pope's prayers more than all the Emperor's troops!" Suleyman, the father of Sultan Selim II, had exclaimed. He saw his fleet destroyed in the waters of Lepanto. St. Pius V had called for prayers and penances and had been the first to set the example. On that same Sunday afternoon of October 7, processions of the confraternities of the Rosary were winding through the streets of Rome, singing and praying. That's why in Venice, when the news of the victory came, on October 19, all the rose bushes, which had already withered, were again covered in roses. These were the roses of Our Lady of the Rosary, the victor at Lepanto!

"Return this flag? Ask for forgiveness, as a sinner? No, Our Lady did not sin when she won at Lepanto!"

"Neither did the Church," concluded the Pope. To allow the viscount to catch his breath, he immediately added: "Those who ask for forgiveness left and right, as you mentioned, professor, for this or that alleged sin of the Church, confuse two realities that should coincide totally with no leftover residue, but which in fact often do not coincide: The Church, which is sinless, and Christendom, which is the sum total of the baptized, who can sin. The Church is holy. To be Church, Christendom must be holy too. There will always be at least one part of Christendom which will be Church, inasmuch as it is holy and a sign of God's holiness. It is raised over all nations, the only 'Sign of the Times' in the Biblical sense, and a sign of all times. But along the passage of the centuries there were certain parts of Christendom, certain parts of the baptized, which sinned and, by sinning, ceased to be Church. Should the Church, impersonated by its hierarchy, ask forgiveness from those who were offended by the sins of a certain part of what was no longer the Church? Will it have to promise to amend itself, to make reparation for a sin it never committed, and could never commit? These considerations don't even insist on the fact that those so-called sins of a certain part of Christendom are often simply presumed by certain short-sighted or malevolent self-styled historians. Those so-called historical injustices were often only acts of legitimate and duty-bound defenses, such as at Lepanto! And in such cases, those parts of Christendom that carried those actions out were not in opposition to the Church—they were the Church. But it is time to go back."

They got up, and started to leave the gardens. It was then that Camillo dared to speak his mind. In doing so, he made both the Pope and the Vicomte de Chateaubriand smile:

"Before we return this flag to them, they should at least return Marcantonio Bragadin's skin!"

The professor began speaking again: "Your Holiness, I have in mind to write something about all of this—either a novel on the adventures that I experienced in the reconquest of this flag, adventures of which I have only given Your Holiness a cursory summary. Or a history book, on the true and heroic history of that battle. For this second book, I have the first draft ready."

The Pope responded, "Professor, I would write both of them. The first, the one of adventures, would have to be under a pseudonym. Although I am the receiver of the stolen goods, I have no reason to fear serious trouble from the papal police. But for you, responsible for the flag substitution, and for your mother, a willing accomplice, the situation is different. You never know with Interpol!"

They both smiled. Then the Pope continued, "The second, the one of history, under your full name, François Réne viscount de Chateaubriand, and the title *The Miracle of Lepanto*. Now, what to do with this flag? Well, in the meantime, come up to the office with me to see this flag unfurled!"

Interlude

PIUS XIV BEGAN TO MOVE ON THE waters of the vast sea, on which he had been suddenly transported, cautiously and without moving away from the shore. He began to navigate along the coast, waiting for the arrival of those who could help him to attempt the high seas. The vision of the sea was inspired by his Palestinian and evangelical memories of the Lake of Tiberias and Peter's boat. This vision was sometimes replaced in his mind by the Dantesque one of the wild, rugged, and strong wilderness in which he suddenly woke up in the middle of a moonless night. He then had to proceed in order to get out of it as soon as possible, walking with extreme care and arms outstretched, and feeling the ground with his foot, before putting it down. Fatigue and tension would soon exhaust him. These figures appeared before him especially during log half-sleeps. In wakefulness, reality, illuminated by Faith, replaced them. This put an end to his nervous tension and fatigue, though not to all the effort.

His small coastal navigation included a thorough review of all correspondence, assisted by all the employees of the Correspondence Office. For these employees, the service under the direct management of the Pope was pleasing and light. They felt a bit like pontiffs themselves. After dealing with the mail, he would go through the list of audience requests and make his selections. He would receive all of the bishops, religious superiors, and missionaries, but, with some exceptions, only after he had in hand in writing what they wanted to say to him verbally. He did this in order to prepare suitable answers or to delay the audience, and in any case, to make the audience as effective yet brief as possible.

The Pope referred the purely formal, courteous, and business-like audiences to the polyglot Monsignor Bruno de Gaudenzi. He was an excellent papal representative, very cordial, effusive, and outspoken in the Roman manner. But he also knew how to appear noble and dignified like an emperor. He knew how to sweeten the pill of disappointment for those who had failed to obtain their requested audience, and to dismiss them serene and satisfied, with a fine pontifical souvenir and the blessing of His Holiness, which he himself imparted to them with such a priestly and solemn gesture, that any Pope himself could have envied him. When the list of applicants was short, and he sensed that the applicants would like it, he allowed himself to lead such little groups to even visit the Pope's private apartment.

Assuming a certain totally confidential tone, he would tell them, "You might know that it is strictly forbidden to everyone, *clausura stricta*,[1] but for you the Pope will make an exception, certainly." At other times, however, he thought it more suited to the visitors' temperaments to tell them, "You know what? It is strictly forbidden for everyone, *clausura stricta*, but if we can find the way clear, I will personally assume all responsibility. Come, this way! No photographs, mind you!" Other times he would add, "No photographs, mind you! Well, for you, I'll close my eyes. I won't see anything, but for goodness sake, let them remain only among you!"

The Pope's private apartment? They would behold the poverty of the papal bedroom—because the Pope a few days after his election had wanted it to be as such, and as such he had succeeded in obtaining. Everyone was edified and moved by what was a friar's cell, with no other furniture than a rough bed

---

[1] "strict enclosure," as with Carmelites.

made of iron pipes, a small table by the bed that served as both a writing desk and bedside table, a stuffed chair, a sheet metal closet, and an old-fashioned basin with a pitcher and towels, and a large bookshelf filled with well-ordered and labeled books. A single lamp dangled from the center of the ceiling. White lime walls, a bare floor with no carpet or even a bedside rug, not even a bedspread over the brown-colored woolen blanket, and only one pillow. A painting of Our Lady of Good Counsel, a large Crucifix hanging on the walls, and a holy water stoup with holy water on the inside wall by the door, at the height of the door handle. Following the example of De Gaudenzi, everyone dipped their right hand into the holy water and devoutly crossed themselves. In imitation of others, even some Muslims or Buddhists would try to make the sign of the Cross with holy water.

The first non-ecclesiastical figures to whom Pius XIV had granted an audience was Professor Amador Moreno dos Angelos, founder of the Mesogaios Institute, a multinational charity of Mediterranean culture, as its name implied. It included numerous Mediterranean European, Asian and African states, though several other countries from around the world had joined soon after it had been launched.

The Pope asked Professor Moreno if the Mesogaios Institute would be interested in moving its central office and would like to take over the management of the Vatican museums. The professor immediately grasped the full scope of such a question. This turned into an official proposal. He hastened to convene the executive council of the Mesogaios Institute and obtained its plenipotentiary faculties and sweeping assurance of the necessary funding. He directed the most highly-rated specialists to draw up a technical and legal outline of the whole undertaking, and then moved quickly to request a second papal audience.

In turn, he proposed to the Pope the transfer to Castel Gandolfo of some Vatican buildings, which would be reconstructed there with all the original items of artistic and historical value.

The most advanced techniques would be employed for the guaranteed safe removal and transport of valuable frescoes, mosaics, stuccoes, statues, and any other work, large or small. The funds available for this gigantic undertaking would allow the enlistment of a team of technicians large enough to complete the work itself in a few years.

At a later stage, the construction of a monorail for rapid transport between Rome and Castel Gandolfo could facilitate the flow of visitors, students and scholars since the project also included the establishment of a higher institute of classical arts and Paleo-italic, Etruscan, Greek, Latin, and early Christian archaeology. Additional buildings would be added gradually, but according to a predetermined, organic, and harmonious plan. For this reason, the new buildings would all be developed lengthwise, in Romanesque or Renaissance styles depending on the neighboring buildings, and without functional or modern oddities and discordance.

A monthly amount, to be agreed upon, would be paid to the Holy See for one hundred years as compensation for the transfer of ownership of the entire complex of artwork. It would be declared non-transferable to private persons in whole or part, and non-transferable outside the province of Rome. In order to initiate the detailed study of such a vast project, which already entailed significant planning expenses, Professor Moreno needed to present to the executive council of his Institute a preliminary report which, though not yet a contract binding on the Holy See, would bear the signature of the Supreme Pontiff.

"That's right!" the Pope had agreed. "Leave all your files here with me. I will have them examined and I will also personally review them, but we will see each other again soon. This is close to my heart."

With these words the Pope dismissed Professor Amador Moreno and the architect François Longueville, with whom he had taken a rather slow and very careful tour through the various pontifical buildings, apartments, and museums. Three hours, continually standing, observing, listening, and answering in Italian, Castilian, and French. He could no longer think about his afternoon walk, as it was already six o'clock in the evening. He returned to his office, tired, and overthinking a little:

"What a project! Yet this would greatly reduce the Vatican staff, which would be assigned exclusively to more purely ecclesiastical works. Expenses would also be reduced, and revenues increase, for seminaries, missions.... To compensate for this, we can expand and make the library and archives more accessible. And then... also replace Cardinal Stolzkamm, and find a worthy solution for him. And then... make those three musketeers of mine cardinals. And then... deal with the heads of the ecclesiastical dicasteries, who until now have not felt the need to submit even the smallest piece of a document to me for my august signature. Thank goodness! I know them neither by sight nor by name. Well, for the names, I will also be quick, as I have the Pontifical Yearbook here. But what I need is to know their character, their tendencies! And then... I should urge the bishops' *ad limina* visitation because so far only a few brave or desperate ones have shown up. Besides... who knows how many other good things a pope must know how to do. While I stay here, I cannot tell my right from my left.

My trusted advisor? Camillo. And then Caesar, the good gardener of Dutch tulips and climbing roses, which they call polyanthus, and we call bunches. Out there the roses, and in here the thorns! If only blessed Father Aurelius would make up his mind to come! 'He can be here in two or three hours, tomorrow morning at the latest,' said the good Monsignor Taddei. Instead, we are already on the day after tomorrow. Eh, *Mater boni consilii*, do you really want me to trust only You?!" he exclaimed toward the statuette placed on the bureau. Then he bowed his head and remained there dozing until he heard himself called.

"Your Holiness!" It was Camillo, but without the usual syringe for the injection. He went to the window, and then said, "Your Holiness, come and see the magnificent sunset!" The Pope got up and joined him by the window. Then Camillo lowered his voice:

"Holiness, these walls have ears. I don't know yet whose ears they are, how far they reach, or what they have heard so far, but besides the now useless expedient of injections, they have discovered a few other things. I have a thought to share these with you. So that they do not stop me short, we had better continue the discussion elsewhere so as not to arouse suspicion. Come with me to the private chapel. I brought you fresh flowers for the altar vases. Everyone knows that this is a practice that Your Holiness has reserved for himself, and which he carries out with such good taste."

So they went to do that. When they were in the small sacristy of the private chapel, as he helped the Pope beautifully arrange the flowers in the crystal vases of the altar, Camillo continued:

"Father Aurelio is in the convent on Via Merulana. He did not come here, because he wants to meet with Your Holiness first totally confidentially. He has his good reasons. He told me that he is well known. He has published things under his own name. Basically, he says that he has compromised himself, that he represents a specific theological current. An audience with the Pontiff could make people believe that the Pontiff himself follows that same thinking or has made it his own. He did not know how to make this known to Your Holiness, and he was racking his brains to find a way. Two hours ago, after delivering that letter from Your Holiness to the superior of the Convent of the Passion, who of course always asks me about their former chaplain, I took the liberty of telling her that Your Holiness was waiting for Father Aurelio. 'Father Aurelio Meyerbeer?' the superior asked me; and then she added: 'But he has been in Rome for two days already, in the convent on Via Merulana!' How that good Mother knows such things is a mystery to me."

"Because you have never been chaplain to nuns!" replied the Pope, smiling, "But I assure you that it is not a matter of insulting curiosity. Everything for those nuns becomes an object of prayer, and often also the occasion of the strictest penances. As for the superior of the Passion, she lives the life of the Church, and regarding the news that comes to her, she knows how to transmit it to her sisters in such a way as to commit them to it—regarding a certain mission or a certain bishop... In the letter I sent to you to bring to her, I even recommend a cardinal to her, and what a cardinal! This is how the superior keeps her sisters fervent and exercising the most exquisite form of Christian charity."

"Well, Your Holiness, if I have made a mistake, I will cancel the invitation, but the thing seemed urgent to me. I went directly to Via Merulana, to Father Aurelio, and I committed Your Holiness for tomorrow, during the walk, at the Madonna della Guardia."

"May you be praised ten times over! I must find a way to make you a cardinal too!"

They laughed together before Camillo escorted the Pope back to his office, lit the desk lamp, turned off the large ceiling light, and went out.

17

Father Aurelio's Ten Points

CAMILLO HAD MADE AN APPOINTment for Father Aurelio for four o'clock in the church of St. Anne of the Palafrenieri. This was the parish church and cemetery of the citizens of Vatican City. Father Aurelio arrived half an hour early. In order to prepare himself for his conversation with the Pope, a meeting whose importance he understood, he knelt at the balustrade and began to pray. Nearby, he found Camillo, who had entered the church punctually, just as the pendulum of the sacristy was striking its somewhat muffled four chimes. They went out together, with Camillo accompanying Father Aurelio toward the chapel of Our Lady of the Guard with a diversionary route.

"You too with a briefcase?" Camillo asked him on the way to fill the silence. "Like the Vicomte de Chateaubriand. Give it to me if it is a bother to you."

"No, thank you! As for Chateaubriand, I don't think it's his briefcase that has made him famous," Father Aurelius responded.

"Actually, yes!" replied Camillo, "It may be that His Holiness will mention it."

In fact, as soon as His Holiness had greeted Father Aurelio, he asked him:

"Have you brought me a flag in that briefcase, like the Vicomte de Chateaubriand did?"

"I don't know what color this viscount's flag is. Mine is

purple. I only brought it to you to please you. But it is for me. It is the purple of our last and long-deceased cardinal. I managed to track it down in the wardrobe of our convent in Landbergen. It fits me like a glove. I don't intend to wear the habit routinely. But on certain occasions, to open a few doors, I think it may come in handy. You never know! I put it in this briefcase as soon as I found it, and waited every day for a telegram from you. You, on the other hand, must have sent me at least a dozen letters, which were regularly stopped in the mail."

"Don't exaggerate. It was just one letter!"

"Well, dearest Pius XIV, you are formidable when it comes to the philosophy of law. Your graduation was called a carpet bombing on the doctrine of De Castro, from the heights of the metaphysics of law, and you left no trace of it behind you."

"Things from half a century ago."

"But regarding positive law, canon law... forgive me for being blunt: these are not your forte, do you agree? While I am getting fat between legal codes and the Justinian Pandects!"

"I can see that" exclaimed the Pope, and they both laughed. Father Aurelius was as thin as a stick.

"Now I said to myself, he will need a trusted jurist. Do you agree? How to create a cardinal—to create means to bring into being something from nothing. I will teach you later. My heart does not aspire to the cardinalate. For me it has only a middling reason, even boring. Instead, I care about becoming like you."

"Antipope, then, since there can only be one legitimate pope at a time. Congratulations!" Pius XIV jokingly replied.

"But I must resign myself to the fact that now you are the pope," Father Aurelio replied equally jokingly. He promptly added in earnest, "I am keen to become what you have been for many years, that is, to become a bishop, to have the fullness of the priesthood, and the grace that corresponds to the fullness of the priesthood. Neither the cardinalate nor the papacy, as such, could give that to me."

"When you have taught me how to make a bishop," the Pope said, "you will be the first, if only out of respect for the alphabet: Aurelio begins with A."

"Thank you! Look at the color!" said Father Aurelio as he showed the Pope the contents of the briefcase. Then he shook his head, "Thanks to the new simplified rite, you were not told *Sic transit gloria mundi*, but I repeat the *Vanitas vanitam* of Ecclesiastes if the wearer of this cloth is not of the cloth of a St. John Fisher or a Carlo Borromeo or at least Federico Borromeo, so well presented by Manzoni in *The Betrothed*. But let us come to the point, in order and summary. You did well to talk to Fathers Norberto and Gregory. They told me so. We had a brief conversation over the phone.

"You were chosen as a transitional pope so that the great electors would have time to agree on your successor, who would open some other window. The electors were confident that during your admittedly brief interregnum, you would not dare to close and lock up those windows that are already open. Remember? How many times..."

"...to the silent dying of an inert day," the Pope continued, quoting Manzoni's *Cinque Maggio*. The arrival of Father Aurelio had greatly revived in him his usual good humor.

"Yes, bravo! You were tired and had lost your voice from teaching and hearing confessions, and you call it an inert day! I said therefore—how often then, between the serious and the facetious—I addressed to you the Gospel greeting, *Ecce vere israelita, in quo dolus non est!*[1] Well Nathanael-Bartholomew allowed himself to be flayed alive, but he did not fail in the task for which Jesus had elected him."

"Thank you for the warning or the augury, whatever it is, but poor me! I cannot even bear to look at the statue of the flayed Saint Bartholomew, the one in the cathedral of Milan.

---

[1] "Behold, an Israelite indeed, in whom there is no deceit." (John 1:47)

I felt my skin crawl when the Vicomte de Chateaubriand told me about Marcantonio Bragadin..."

"...whose martyrdom gave occasion to the victory of Lepanto.... Ah!" exclaimed Father Aurelio, as if he was illuminated by a flash of insight. He then continued, "Perhaps I have understood all of this. The flag that the Viscount brought you is the one from Lepanto. He may not have told you that he tracked it down in an ancient friary, as I tracked down this purple cloth!"

"You have guessed the truth," the Pope told him. "It is a long story. He will write it all down, and I will get you a complimentary copy, but for pity's sake! Stop mentioning flaying to me. I can't stand it. Every time it rains, I get pain in my left ankle. I broke it once, as you know. Now where were we? You were telling me you wanted to get to the point, in order and in summary..."

"Do you think I have digressed? In fact, I'm moving on to the third point. I have already gone over the first one. It concerns the three new cardinals—and we know which ones. The second too: already noted and scheduled, *Dieu premier servi*, even if they were to flay you alive. The third point regards a refined surgery in the body of the hierarchy concerning the deposition of the leader of anarchy in the house of others, and of tyranny in one's own. It also concerns the medical deposition for the stricken in order to make an example for everyone else. This is the deposition of Cardinal Stolzkamm."

"Already done! Go ahead and move on to the fourth point.... Actually I didn't plan it, at least in the way it happened. Done *de jure*. But I don't know how this can be made concrete, *de facto*, and you will have to point that out to me."

Father Aurelio looked at the Pope without trying to soften his surprise:

"Congratulations! And they haven't set fire to the five hundred thousand volumes of the Vatican library yet? That's great!

I had judged it worse than it is.... Fourth point: we need to place priests who love prayer, the Eucharist, and the *Mater Dei* on all vacant Sees. I don't know if I'm being clear. I have a list of them ready."

Having said that, Father Aurelio took out the list he was talking about from his folder, and handed it to the Pope before continuing, "I promise to pay them a visit personally, to make sure that they really have calluses on their knees. A visit *in nigris*, of course, without the purple. The less I stand out, the better for both me and you.

"Ordinarily bishops and parish priests remain in their posts *usque ad mortem*.[2] We have no record of any of the Apostles retiring before they died. Yet even in those days people grew old and still worked hard, though with fewer meetings and less paperwork, and times were hard. And then it is necessary to require that the bishops regularly perform the *visitatio ad Limina Apostolorum*, prepared by sending the files of all the matters that are to be debated with the Pope and the prefects of the Roman Congregations."

"I have begun to do so with the few who have shown up. You will have some fun right away because, as I am alone, I had to leave quite a few matters unresolved."

"Fifth point: make it clear that national bishops' conferences have no authority other than advisory. This means that each individual bishop remains free to follow or not follow the recommendations of these conferences. This will make the local bishop once again feel that he is the shepherd of his diocese, and not a simple automatic executor of an impersonal and sometimes, we must agree, off-track power.

"The sixth point is the doctrinal examination of candidates for the episcopate. This needs to be a rigorous examination of many important documents of the pontifical magisterium.

---

2 "Until death."

These documents are too often completely ignored or misunderstood. These include Pius IX's *Syllabus* to Pius XII's *Humani generis*, against Modernism. These are the documents that candidates for the episcopate must know by heart—I mean by heart! And then there is *Mediator Dei*, the first and still the only dogmatic encyclical on the liturgy. It has been completely forgotten, with the consequences that we all see. But here's the list. I don't want to delay things right now by reading it to you in full. Please read it at your leisure and modify it as you see fit. You are the Pope, and I am willing to share even your opinions like a private doctor, well intended only in those matters in which it is permissible to have some private opinion either to me or to the Pope himself.

"Point seven addresses the renewal of the seminaries. We'll have to start from scratch, and transplant the new saplings in soil that doesn't have any weeds, any evil seeds—a soil that has been sterilized with fire. Therefore, those who must go through agony and die must be left to their fates. The new ones must be of the ancient style, of the style of St. Charles Borromeo, of St. Pius X, under the banner of piety, mortification, study, obedience. But *piscis foetet a capite*![3] There is an urgent need to replace Cardinal Geyser, who is currently presiding over the dismantling of the seminaries. You know who you need to put in his place."

"Father Norbert," said the pope.

"That's right. Point eight and the third last. I'll let you guess."

"What can concern a jurist if not the Code?" said Pius XIV.

"Yes, the Code! This *vacatio legis*[4] or hubbub, as you Italians say, must cease as soon as possible. This hubbub allows the bullies to impose their own arbitrariness as the law of the Church, and to destroy the law of the Church at their own will.

---

3 "The fish starts to rot from the head."
4 Mediating period after promulgation but before the date on which the law takes effect: "exemption of the law."

I had to record the last abuse of power in this area the day before I left Germany. The diocesan bishop pretends he can prohibit our friars from celebrating individual Masses in our sanctuary and demands that everyone participate in the great daily concelebration. Our rector fully indulges him, exerting all the psychological pressure on our friars that he can devise. He is moved by the hope of being proposed by the diocesan bishop for episcopal election. Well, let's open a parenthesis on concelebration!

"Concelebration means the loss of as many Masses as there are concelebrants minus one. If there are seven concelebrants, it is not the celebration of seven simultaneous Masses, but the concelebration of one Mass, done by seven priests.

"The Mass, as you know, is a sacramental renewal of the sacrifice of the Cross. Like every sacrament, the act of multiplying itself requires a multiplicity of ministers, of form and matter. Now this third multiplicity in our case of concelebration is lacking because those seven concelebrants consecrate the same and undivided matter, and not each one a distinct portion of this matter, to the exclusion of the remaining part, which would be consecrated by another celebrant. Therefore, even those who attend a Mass that is concelebrated by twenty priests attend only one Mass, not twenty. And will it be licit to demand the offering agreed upon for the celebration of twenty Masses from the faithful with a single Mass that is concelebrated by twenty priests? When will concelebration ever be licit? Whenever the celebration of several individual *digne, attente ac devote*[5] Masses would otherwise not be possible—in other words, only for the honor of God, and not for the convenience of the concelebrants nor to cheer up the faithful with some sort of fancy spectacle. On this subject I have much more to say, but let's return to the Code!

---

5 "worthily, attentively and devoutly"—words traditionally used in the prayer before the recitation of the divine office.

"The law is the defense of the weak, when there is adequate executive and judicial power. A Code is indispensable to the life of the Church. This is a true Code of laws and punishments, *penae ferendae sententiae, sed etiam penae latae sententiae.*[6] And one that does not shy away from anathemas out of a misunderstood sense of mercy, as the Apostle of the Gentiles didn't shy away from them. Until proven otherwise, he seems to have been a good Christian: *Cor Pauli, cor Christi*, it was said, and rightly so, of him."

"And you will have the Code nice and ready," the Pope said, "I was waiting for you for that too."

"Here in Rome we have a whole host of thoroughbred jurists, men who have been put out of work and forced to write anything and do anything—except canon law. We will review my code together. It will not take long. It will trump the debates and overbearing powers of so many assemblies, conferences, councils, organs and little agencies: *Esto lex, pereat Babel*![7] It is necessary for the Catholic to be at home with the exact same laws, rites, and language from one end of the Earth to the other."

"But you know the refrain, 'Unity is not uniformity'?" the Pope asked him.

"One of the thousand sophisms of the progressives to break the backbone of Christendom. Certainly if all the limbs of the organism were aligned with the head, they would be uniform from head to foot, but if their legs were not aligned like that, they would be lame."

"As for the ninth and penultimate point, I think I already know it, but I do not know if I will have time enough to execute it," the Pope told him. "Of course I intend to prepare for it."

"Father Gregory's Lateran VI? We will prepare it, and someone will celebrate it. You or your successor."

---

6   In canon law, *latae sententiae* refers to the sentence that has already been passed. *Ferendae sententiae* is the sentence to be passed.
7   "Let this stand as the law, let Babel perish!"

"My successor... And the tenth and final point?" asked the Pope.

"If you cannot guess it, it means it is premature to talk to you about it," Father Aurelio answered.

"It is time for me to leave. I will see you again tomorrow. By the way, you have welcomed me here, because there are prying ears there, right? Why couldn't we meet tomorrow in the Laurini Fathers' convent? There you could also have an office, eat your meals, and stay in your monastic cell."

They got up, arranged the meeting the next day and said their goodbyes. But as they parted, the Pope, holding Father Aurelio's right hand in his, asked him:

"Do you remember Gabriel Wong?"

"That little angel of a Chinaman? Never forgotten! Seminarian, priest, bishop. And since the day of your election as vicar on earth of Our Lord Jesus Christ, he has been ever more vividly present. God knows how to cultivate His lilies to perfection!"

The Pope closed his eyes, paused a moment, and then asked: "The tenth point concerns my successor, I know. I had thought about it, you know? He is here in Rome. I was waiting for you for that."

18

"Auri sacra fames"[1]

ROMOLO HAD COURTED CLELIA, Camillo's niece. But one day he made it clear to her that he intended to marry her on the condition that he could eventually divorce her. This was because he was an honest and loyal man, and certainly not because he did not love her. It was out of ideological consistency, and in accordance with legislation common to all truly free and civilized nations.

"Marriage is final," Clelia had replied. "If not, it is prostitution by a clock. Marriage is only between two. If not, it is not final, either between you and me or between you and me and some other person. Thus, when it is final and exclusive to two, it is from God. Whoever wants a different arrangement goes against God, but whoever goes against God, becomes broken just like what happened to your windshield last night. Do you really believe that with divorce man can remake and improve God's law on marriage? I would rather not get married than live in a marriage that is only an act, but that before God is a crime!"

Romolo did not understand these words. Later Clelia had learned that, even in the Vatican, where he had been for a short time, Romolo had already made a bad name for himself.

"If you are not faithful to God, will you really be faithful to me?" Clelia asked him. "You will not divorce in eternity! You

---

[1] "Sacred hunger of gold"—although always taken as "cursed" hunger of wealth, as in Virgil's *Aeneid*, 3.57.

tell me, but meanwhile you want a marriage with an escape valve. In fact, it seems you are not so faithful even to other men."

"What do you mean?"

"That would be to say that you have been employed in the Vatican for only eight months, thanks to the good offices of my uncle, and you have already made a bad name for yourself there as well."

"Ah, the spy! He'll pay for that!" exclaimed Romolo.

There could be no other spy than Camillo. After the exchange, which had wrecked his vague marriage plan, and with the benefit of greater reflection on his next step, Romolo began to spy on Camillo, to catch him doing something. Doing what? He couldn't assume anything. Why? He dared not confess anything. So Romolo began tailing Camillo as the latter went with Pius XIV on the evening of the new pontiff's election to the private chapel. After spending the night at the Vatican for that reason alone, the next morning he returned to look around, and caught Camillo serving Mass to the Pope, the old Mass, with the Pope celebrating it.

"Ha, ha! That's what I needed! To discover something like this! But how can I use it?"

He had thereby become aware of Pius XIV's confidence in Camillo and of the vacuum that some prelates aimed to make around the Pontiff. One had to know how to profit from such a situation.

The bad reputation he acquired shortly after being hired into the service of the Vatican was justified. He had indeed stolen two small valuable miniatures from a small room of reliquaries, but absolutely no one could prove that he had done it. However, a few days after the theft, a bundle of cash was left, as if forgotten there by an absent-minded person, in the same small room at the foot of a large statue of Our Lady. It was bait, and Romolo fell for it. He then tried apologizing:

"I said to myself, 'Someone forgot this here, and is looking for it somewhere else. I'll take it to His Excellency right away!' and I hurried out..."

"...to look around and make sure no one would see you. Then you put it in your pocket and went in the opposite direction from my office," Monsignor Steiner himself told him. "I watched you behind that curtain. I can report you, and also for the two miniatures, but I don't want to ruin you. You are young! I can give you time to fix yourself. Forewarned is forearmed!"

The only problem was that Romolo did not earn enough money. He had nothing and no one to support except himself. He was alone in the world. But in addition to himself, he had to maintain his own vices. He was always in need of money. He dreamed of having a lot of money at his disposal, but did not even imagine what he would be willing to do to achieve his dream as soon as possible. Now he had to find a way to turn the new situation created in the Vatican at that time into cash. But how?

"Osiris Market!" In him, he had found the help he needed. Osiris Market paid him honestly for those two miniatures, and had also mapped out for him a concrete, meticulous, and prudent work plan. Romolo unfortunately had to give up on the plan, after the reliquary room incident. On the other hand, a fresh path, his Gran Via, was now outlined before him.

Market immediately grasped the importance of the matter and had a plan drawn of the Pope's office and adjacent rooms, which included the path of the power lines. Providentially, an out-of-use telephone line ran right through the nearby locker room, which Romolo could access. Market taught him how to get it to work with a few devices to record what was said in the Pope's office. He also gave him some hidden microphones, a tape recorder, and empty cassettes. The job was not difficult. Romolo sometimes helped to polish the floor of the Pontiff's office, and with a certain amount of practice in installing electronics, he had it.

It was just a matter of letting time work things out, of acting cautiously and one step at a time, of doing a small part of the planned installation each day. The day arrived when Romolo let Market hear the first recording:

"...too am François Réne, like my great forefather. He made himself famous—and deservedly so, as you know. Meanwhile, I may become famous as the author of an Interpol-style theft."

"Give it here! Let's see it! There's no doubt about it—that's the one! We need to think calmly about how to use it, and in the meantime, where to hide it?"

That was all. The tape had recorded nothing else. The second voice was Pius XIV's, the first was the thief's. Romolo had seen that thief directly when He was leaving the Pope's office as serene as if it was Easter Sunday. He was a rather young gentleman, very tall and thin, with a briefcase in his hand which was certainly empty. Osiris Market understood that Pius XIV was in a relationship with an Interpol thief, and he had the proof.

"Thank you, friend!" he said to Romolo, "Carry on, and in due time we will draw our conclusions."

"Only thank you?" asked Romolo, "I came here to sell you this tape, not to give it to you as a gift." While saying this, he held out his open hand to Market.

"But I don't know what to do with your recording! I don't want it as something to sell or as a gift. What does it contain concretely? Two vague sentences, which can be interpreted as two wisecracks. A gift, yes. I want to give you a gift, as a friend!" He put some cash in Romolo's hand. "Take back that tape of yours. See you next time with something better!"

As soon as Romolo was gone, Market listened again to the two lines. He had dubbed them through a second tape recorder, which he routinely kept paired with the visible one, the same one he had used a few minutes earlier in Romolo's presence. Having listened again and again to those short lines, Market persuaded himself that they would be enough to obtain from Pius XIV, kindly blackmailed, the papal tiara as well.

Now, however, he cared more about the Pope's conversion, or even his elimination, than about the papal tiara. He had been struck by this idea when he had to lay down his most precious suitcase on the floor of the Church of the Three Holy Brothers. At that time, he came to understand that the time of plenty was threatened with an abrupt end at the hands of that intruder. It would certainly end, should the transitional Pope take too long in his transition. To make him come to his senses or accomplish the transition, he now felt he could give him a little push. But from what angle?

He came to understand it the next day, after listening to a second recording. It had been made before the one Romolo had played him the previous day as a trial. It was the entire conversation between Pius XIV and Cardinal Stolzkamm.

"Is this known in the Vatican?" Market asked Romolo.

"I wouldn't think so. After this audience, the cardinal came out of the Pope's office and walked past me with big strides. Apart from that excited walk, nothing else in particular was noticeable about him. Only later, in my dressing room when I checked the recording, did I learn of what had occurred."

"Actually, the media don't know anything about it." Market paused to reflect, and after a good minute, concluded, "Well, I don't know what to make of these quarrels between bishops! Bring me something better!"

"But commendatore, what more do you want? That I bring you the Pope's head on a tray, like the daughter of Herodias? If the Camerlengo found out..." but he paused. Could he bring such news to the Camerlengo himself, without Market in the way? In the meantime, however, he could try to squeeze all he could out of the situation, so he said in a tone of protest,

"Commendatore, you make me walk a tightrope, and then you ask, 'Is that all?' If those are the terms, I'll bring back your recorder, and won't do this any more!"

"How much do you want?"

"An advance, to be honest. I am not a blackmailer. I expose myself to risk for the honor of the Church, but I also need to eat."

"Here then, a check for you!" He filled it out for Romolo. "This is an advance on something of real value that you will bring me later. For now, you can also take back this second tape, which is not worth much more than the previous one."

"Terrific!" Romolo exclaimed in his heart, and he began breathing. Things had worked out well for him. He could actually take back his tape. He was going to let the cardinal Camerlengo listen to it. He took it back and left.

As soon as he was left alone, Market checked the result of the dubbing of the second tape he had obtained. Then he made a second dubbing of both recordings, and put a copy in his handbag along with a small tape recorder. He then telephoned the cardinal Camerlengo and obtained an audience for exactly four p.m. Since it was after three and he was keen to be on time, he hurried off to the Vatican.

As soon as he had returned to the Vatican, Romolo also hastened to telephone the cardinal Camerlengo to request an audience on a matter that was very important for the good of the Holy Roman Church. The audience was set for four o'clock. Later, arriving at least twenty minutes in advance and not yet having entered the reception room of the cardinal Camerlengo, the door of the cardinal's office opened, and Commendatore Market himself came out. The two momentarily looked at each other in amazement before each put his own normal mask back on so quickly that neither one noticed the other's astonishment. They did not even greet each other. It was as if one had lived until that moment in New Zealand and the other in Greenland.

As Market left, Romolo entered the cardinal's presence, and began speaking to him with the intention of telling him everything he knew about the thief François Réne and the deposition of Cardinal Stolzkamm. The Camerlengo stood and listened to him for a few moments in boredom, but soon he ended the audience and admonished Romolo to avoid collecting and reporting certain rumors, especially concerning such a delicate matter. He also refused to listen to the two tapes that Romolo had shown him, and quickly dismissed him.

Romolo realized he had the wrong address. On his way out of the Camerlengo's office, he laid his eyes on two tapes on a small table near the desk, similar to the ones he was putting back in his pocket. What were they doing there? Who had put them there?

"The jackal, Market, has brought copies of my tapes here, and the cardinal has given him a lot of money. That's why he doesn't need mine!"

In fact, the Camerlengo had sharply rejected the gift of the tapes offered by Market "out of deference and for the good of the Church." The cardinal then gave the same speech immediately afterwards to Romolo.

On his way out, Market had artfully and deftly laid the tapes on the small table. His Roman address stood out on the tape case. Perhaps the cardinal would reconsider, and phone him. One never knew. As for Romolo, he returned to his dressing room bitter with disappointment. He was about to remove the tape recorder and throw it out, but then reconsidered:

"If not for the Camerlengo, the recordings may one day be valuable for someone else, like a journalist. But I could also make a book out of them.... For what they cost me! I'll leave everything there for a bit longer!"

So he continued to record everything he could, about ten tapes, until the Pope changed his office and apartment. But he needed to find someone interested in the merchandise. It was no longer fitting to offer the tapes to Market. But against all his expectations, they were requested by the very man himself. Romolo immediately brought them. Market listened to them attentively, but dismissed their contents and offered to buy only one as a reward to Romolo for the good will shown and to testify to his sincere friendship.

"Friendship?" blurted Romolo, "A friend does not put his friend on the gallows! You immediately ran to tell everything to the cardinal Camerlengo that I had given you."

"What an imagination, young man!" As soon as he had recovered from the surprise of the encounter in the Camerlengo's reception room, Market thought up a suitable answer to Romolo's predictable protests: "You saw me there because I was called there and asked for information since I closely follow the trade of art objects in half of Rome. I told the prelate that I knew nothing, but that I would keep my eyes open, and that when needed would inform him if I spotted anything."

"The miniatures?" asked Romolo.

"Wild guess!" confirmed Market. Romolo did not breathe a word and left with his tail between his legs. Market, left alone, verified as usual this third dubbing, and bit his fingers. The tape of the hidden tape recorder had recorded nothing. Something had not worked properly. Understanding how to play a trick, Romolo had dropped some of his tapes on the ground, and as Market also bent down to pick them up, had moved the small lever, which knocked out the second recorder.

Yet Market needed to have the record of all that news! How could he get those tapes back from Romolo after so disdainfully rejecting them? Romolo himself showed up of his own accord early the next morning, but with more than just tapes! He had hurried back to Market early in the morning to be sure to find him. In fact, at that hour Market should still have been in bed—and was. At the first ring of the doorbell he jumped out of bed, ran to the intercom, and asked who wanted him and why.

"Auri sacra fames"

The man lived alone in a small apartment in a modest suburban condominium. Often, however, he was nowhere to be found, and there was no way of knowing where he had gone, or when or even if he would return, since no one could give such information. No one knew whether he had friends or relatives. The apartment building had no front desk, and Market dined in at least twenty different Roman diners. Romolo knew at least this much, which is why he had rushed to see him so early in the morning.

Market let him in, then retreated for a moment to make himself presentable. Romolo took the opportunity to put back in his pocket the tape which he had sold him the day before, and which he had spotted near the usual tape recorder. Market soon returned, washed and dressed, and began:

"So, perhaps you know why..."

"Give me a million, commendatore," Romolo said, extending his right hand.

"You are joking, young man!"

"I assure you that I am giving you a friend's price, a gift!"

"What's it about?"

"The liturgy!"

"Ah!" Market quickly pulled himself together after the brief slip.

Market owed his rapid enrichment to the collecting and trading of missals, vestments, sacred ornaments, statues of saints, and even altarpieces. He devoted himself, body and soul, to this. He had two warehouses full of these things, one in Rome and the other in Geneva. He curbed his excitement and insisted:

"Can you be a little more specific?"

"Well, let's do this. Half a million now, for the clarification. The other half when I give you what I came to bring you."

Market took out his checkbook from his pocket without saying a word. Romolo stopped him:

"No checks! I had some difficulties in cashing in the others. People in banks are always suspicious. I need cash."

Market went to the next room and returned after a few minutes with five hundred thousand lira notes in his hand. He put them in Romolo's outstretched right hand.

"It is the original of a draft decree or something like that," Romolo said, giving to the words he was uttering the greatest possible importance: "Of a decree, which His Holiness our Pope Pius XIV is preparing, to put an end—I say end—to the trade in books and sacred furnishings, to put back into service the books and sacred furnishings now lying in the closets of the sacristies and elsewhere. This decree provides practical rules to be followed by parish priests and bishops when canceling any contracts that have already been made, and to recover whatever has already passed to third parties, I'll say it again, passed to third parties. The decree also calls on the civil authorities to cooperate. And there's more. I found the draft in the basket of papers which were to be burned. This is a basket that I sometimes manage to take things out of before the contents are incinerated.

"This time I was lucky, and so are you. You'll be able to save yourself in time because this very important draft also contains a date and is signed by the Pope like everything else. You can be very sure!"

Romolo was wrong. The signature was not that of the Pope, but of Father Aurelio. He had drafted it with the Pope in a small room made available to the Pope by the Laurini Fathers in their small Vatican convent. The Pope had made an accurate copy of it, which had already been corrected once but was to be revised again. Then he had put the first draft in his pocket, so as not to throw it in the wastepaper basket at the Laurini Fathers. Before returning to his customary office, he had thrown it in the basket of papers to be burned.

"A date?" asked Osiris Market. "What date?"

"The other half million, commendatore!" replied Romolo.

Market hurried back to the adjoining room. He returned with five more brand-new hundred thousand lira bills and feverishly laid them in Romolo's hand.

"Is there a state mint back there? joked Romolo, but Market cut him short:

"The paper, show me the paper!"

"With a little bit of calm, you will be able to decipher everything, even the date—the date on which the decree went into effect."

So saying, Romolo took out from a folder a slightly crumpled sheet of paper that had no letterhead and handed it to Market. Where the crumpled paper had been in the folder he put the ten hundred thousand lire notes, thanked Market, and said goodbye with a polite bow. He added,

"And always friends, eh!" before leaving.

Market's face peered closely over the paper. It was authentic—he could feel certain things by instinct. He looked for the date, that tremendous date, and found three: July 2, August 15, and September 29. He consulted an outdated Catholic calendar which he kept among his paperwork. Not Catholic, he knew very little about the Church's feasts. He saw that July 2 was the Feast of the Precious Blood, August 15 the Feast of the Assumption into Heaven of the Blessed Virgin Mary, and September 29 the Feast of St. Michael the Archangel.

At best, it seemed that he had but a few months at his disposal to sell off, to transform, all that patrimony, but in fact properly appraising it would take several years. It was therefore necessary to prevent the Pope from promulgating the provisions or, at least, to delay their promulgation for a few years. Could this be done by blackmail, thanks to the Interpol theft? But what if it was just sarcasm and joking between the Pope and François René? Market gradually became obsessed with the thought of preventing the Pope from promulgating the provisions. It stole his sleep and appetite and made life generally impossible. As a matter of fact, Market had no need to fear much for his business from that decree, but on this issue his mind no longer grasped objective reality.

"A completely tenacious, bold, intelligent, and calculated work of many years! An immeasurable wealth! So many studies, projects, trips, jobs, and disgraces! And one old intruder who wants to bring it all down with that piece of scrap paper! We'll see! We'll see which of us will go up in smoke first!"

He sometimes felt ready for anything, but the anxiety in his heart prevented him from implementing a feasible and safe project. But Romolo gave him inspiration for one.

At this point the Pope was giving audiences in a small office with a reception room. This had been placed at his disposal and renovated to fit this purpose by the Laurini Fathers in their little convent. In that same convent, the Pope celebrated Mass every morning, ate, and spent much of his day and all night. He rarely appeared in the primitive and larger office. Camillo had been instructed by the Pope to gradually bring over certain needed items from the large old office to the small new office.

While doing this, Camillo discovered the spy microphones and realized that they were plugged into the out-of-order telephone line. Following the line route, he discovered it going through Romolo's locker room. When Romolo was absent—he frequently declared himself unavailable or sick and at the doctor's—Camillo entered the locker room, opened Romolo's locker with one of his countless keys, and found Market's tape recorder inside.

"What to do?" First, he carefully separated the microphones, but made them look like they were still plugged into the telephone line. Then he told the Pope everything. He would do the rest later, when he was calm, in such a way as to fool Romolo into thinking that no one had yet noticed his shocking behavior. The Pope was glad to know that this little espionage was due to the initiative of a mere jackass, and that the prying ears had been cut off. In any case, Romolo had no further occasion to record anything, given the Pope's rare and discreet use of the office. Camillo also tried to save the man by telling him in person, "The Pope knows that someone is betraying him. You have already risked too much. Stop doing this stuff! You can still avoid ruining yourself!"

Romolo shrugged and as Camillo left, he called the latter a spy.

Shortly thereafter, it was decided that Romolo's job there was superfluous, and he was offered a change to the garages. That position was somewhat more demanding, but also better paid. He accepted and then went to visit Market, though with nothing on his mind. He was nevertheless sure that the visit, as a papal garage attendant, would not be wasted time.

Market asked him, "The Pope's car is in those garages, right?" Without waiting for an answer, he lowered his voice and added: "If you were to work it in such a way as to cause a small accident, nothing fatal, of course, you would no longer have the sword of Damocles hanging over your head of a complaint about the miniatures, the clandestine recorder, the..."

"...and you would no longer have the sword of Damocles of the decree on sacred vessels hanging over your head!" Romolo retorted.

Market paused at length, then said,

"Five million would be well earned."

Romolo shook his head and made his counterproposal:

"As an advance: the other fifty, when things are done, to be sent to me according to payment methods to be specified. These methods give you no way out from the commitment you made. They don't leave me in trouble alone. For example: two lines, with the mandate you give me, signed, and the same promise spoken by you into the microphone and properly recorded. Simple, no?"

"You're really tricky!"

19

Catholic News

THE POWERFUL MEDIA'S BLARING headlines had announced Puis XIV's unexpected election. But the press had specified that he was a transitional pontiff with a brief and uneventful pontificate. The media could later confirm the soundness of their predictions by informing readers about the almost clandestine life of the new Pope, who had not yet appeared in public. Reporters attributed this pontifical seclusion to the Pontiff's age, the illness that had brought him low immediately after the election, and, finally, to his lack of competence in ecclesiastical matters. After that, the powerful media forgot about the existence of a Catholic or, as many preferred to say, ecumenical-universal Church, headed by Pius XIV, the Supreme Pontiff. A reminder was provided by unoffical news from the Vatican agency *Ecumenical Press* on the deposition of Cardinal Stolzkamm and his replacement, His Excellency Monsignor Gordin.

The faint rustle of the thin paper, which passed from hand to hand under the astonished and incredulous eyes of the editors for religious affairs of the world's main organs of information, produced such a thunderous echo that the globe seemed to shake on its hinges. As for the periodicals connected with or dependent on or financed by the Human Universal Fraternity, they reacted as if hit by lightning, to the point that several of the same periodicals, already set for dispatch, were held back, and then hastily replaced from scratch. To the Pope's unexpected and startling attack, it was necessary to respond with a counteroffensive so massive and synchronous that it would crush any chance of a reply.

An entire issue of the ecumenical-universal weekly *The World in the Church*, under the title *Thunder without rain*, as prophetic a title as there ever was one, assured its readers that the bishop of Rome's gesture, which it characterized as simply unconscionable, would have no effect. It would be withdrawn and repaired by his misguided author himself as soon as possible. With almost the same words, but with a more bitter, scandalized, and threatening tone, *The Sunday Clergy*, a weekly addressed to guide the pastoral and social activity of priests serving short or very short hours, addressed the burning topical issue. The authoritative *Temoignage Humain* merely offered a faithful French translation of what *The Sunday Clergy* had put out. However, some who noted the coincidence put forward the hypothesis that the original text was in French, and that the translation was the Italian edition. This was more than likely the case.

Under the single headline, "Whosoever bumps against the stronghold of collegiality, shatters and perishes," an entire issue of the universal weekly, *The Collegial Stronghold*, expressed outrage over Pius XIV's act, and added that he was inconsistent. It was irritated because the act was carried out by a simple *motu proprio* of the bishop of Rome, whereas the new authentically collegial climate, *ad validitatem*[1] of every act of the bishop of Rome outside his diocese, demanded an expression of this collegiality of bishops, *sicut era in principio*, that is, before Justinian, Theodosius, and Constantine.

An entire issue of the weekly magazine *The Kingdom of the Earth*, which was echoed verbatim across the Alps by the authoritative *Humanisme Integral* under the title "The Last

---

[1] "for validity"

Illusion of a Neo-Despot," demonstrated, with indisputable arguments, the historical irreversibility of the sunset of that baneful liberty-killing legalism that had stifled the development of the mustard seed from the era, *iterum*, of Justinian, Theodosius and Constantine to the post-conciliar liberation, followed by the authentic interpretation of the decree *Dignitatis humanae*, etc. etc.

After a slight delay, which was understandable given the circumstances and which sharpened the anticipation in its subscribers, it finally reached all of them on the five continents. It paid an extraordinary and unexpected tribute to numerous personalities of high culture, as well as to the main exponents of all religions and to anti-religious associations throughout the world. A special issue of the monthly *Superconcilium Permanens* was received by all. Its blurb bore the large letters of the eloquent title *De Pontifice Deponendo*. The issue dissected the controversy completely and with great analytical depth. Its assumptions were supported with a startling array of arguments. There was something prodigious about the issue, even more so when it became apparent that the doctrine had been formulated to make it appear thrown together within a few days of intense work, instead of being good and ready for at least a couple of months. It exhaustively analyzed the matter from every possible angle, that is, according to the five dimensions of modern thought. These are the historical, meta-historical, evolutionary, ecumenical and psychoanalytic. The latter part of the treatment in particular was astonishing due to its exhaustive and persuasive nature.

The origin of the indignation to which all the instruments of this vast universal orchestra were tuned was given by the fragile smokescreen of the Vatican *Ecumenical Press*. It characterized Stolzkamm's removal and replacement as an entirely personal and private gesture of Pius XIV which would have tremendous consequences. The most fearful consequence was certainly the mistrust of bishops toward their colleague in Rome, and the isolation of the latter, assuming that his specific and honorific task was nothing more than acting as a *trait-d'union* among all the bishops and rubber-stamping their collegial deliberations. This same news brought up the Pope's health, which was far from flourishing and even in decline, as was clearly demonstrated by the continued suspension of public audiences. Everything that was expressed in this communiqué was done so with dignified respect for the person of His Holiness, and with the liveliest trepidation for the fate of the ecumenical-universal Church.

In his modest office at the Laurini Fathers, Pius XIV quickly went through the whole bundle of periodicals brought by Father Norbert. Not an iota of their significance was lost on him. Father Norbert had, on his own initiative, placed big red marks throughout, sometimes on a period, sometimes on an entire page. It was true to a certain extent that the Pope was isolated in the Vatican, as the periodicals and the Vatican agency itself claimed, but this was less and less so than before.

Many of those in high positions in the Vatican and the various Roman ecclesiastical dicasteries had begun to close ranks around the Pope and were willing to put up a fight. The hope that was flourishing on the faces of many of the faithful encouraged these good curial members. Gradually, long, black cassocks began to appear more frequently both in Vatican offices and the streets of Rome, and many old-fashioned priestly clothes, resembling those of a disheveled messenger, disappeared. An inscription had appeared on Pasquino's bust:

> If a certain cardinal,
> Whose wings you cut off,
> Stares at you so coldly;
> Fear not, our Pius!
> We, faithful people,
> we all love you!

Pasquino was speaking the truth. The Pope had proof of this now, and he thanked the Lord for it. He would leave a less onerous task to his successor, he mused, and soon. At the end of the day, the progressives had not been able to hide their surprise, bewilderment, irritation, and fear behind the avalanche of fake news.

The Pope ordered a detailed written report on the structure, operation, cost, and financing of the Vatican's *Ecumenical Press*. He then wanted to hear from the principal heads of the agency. After that, he dealt with the problem through his trusted advisors and cardinals, Fathers Aurelio, Norberto, and Gregory, who were still *in pectore*. In fact, Father Gregory had also been able to participate in this council of war. The new responsibility he had been offered had shortened his convalescence considerably. After that, Father Aurelio reduced what had to be done to the following few points:

"The Vatican agency *Ecumenical Press* ceases to exist. Those who will suffer economic loss due to this closure will be fairly compensated: All employees of the agency will be given due severance pay, plus 50 percent. The Catholic News office has been established with the task, first, of making available to those who request it all communiqués that have obtained the prior authorization of the Roman Pontiff. Its second task is the editing of a weekly periodical, also entitled "Catholic News." It will offer news that pertains exclusively to the religious life of the Catholic Church."

The many clerks and employees working under various titles at the *Ecumenical Press* were replaced by the few employees of the Catholic News office. These latter employees were all clergy or religious and all permanently residing in the Vatican.

At the same time, numerous bishops and religious superiors received the order to suspend the publication of periodicals under diocesan authorities or religious institutes. They were prohibited from resuming the publication of these periodicals under any title. This was in effect until the Roman Pontiff's approval for new editorial boards of those periodicals. Numerous people had collaborated in the compilation of this list, under the direction of Father Norbert. He was well versed in ecumenical-universal publications and had carried out his work in the well-stocked newspaper library of the ex-*Ecumenical Press*.

A few bishops took this Roman encroachment very badly and assured editors of the coming fire and brimstone. What actually happened was that some of the periodicals died instantly, never to rise again, under neither the old nor new situation. Others broke away from ecclesiastical authority, at least formally, and continued publishing. They continued entertaining their readers on anodyne and controversial topics. They lost many readers. Still other publications openly conducted an anti-papal campaign. In losing all restraint, they also lost all remaining credibility. Others, in the end, aligned themselves with what they now clearly saw to be the Pope's line. These journals gradually gathered wider and wider support, even from very surprising sources.

Cardinal Stolzkamm, who while visiting Rome was hospitalized for surgery in the Immaculatini Clinic, followed the development of the situation. He moved from outrage to wonder, and from wonder to outrage.

20

THE GREAT SORCERER

THE SUPERIOR GENERAL OF THE Laurini Fathers was overjoyed when he heard that the Pope was the guest of his brothers at the Vatican. He was eager to pay an extraordinary visit to these brothers of his. He hoped for the opportunity to ask and obtain an audience from the Pope. This audience was dear to his heart, though he had not as of yet dared to ask the Audience Office until then. It happened that Father Vinicio entered the convent of the Laurini Fathers in the Vatican a little before the Pope was to leave for his daily walk in the Vatican gardens. It seemed to him to be the most suitable hour to meet, and ask him for the very brief audience, to be determined for a later date.

"Let's certainly determine a day!" the Pope said, adding, "do you have a car now?"

"Yes, of course, Your Holiness!" replied Father Vinicius.

"Then I will give you an audience in it. I have hoped to see your new Roman residence. Your good brothers have told me about it. After that, I would appreciate it if you would take me..."

"...I am all at Your Holiness' disposal!"

"Wait a minute, let me take any notes I may need, while Camillo can notify the Swiss at the gate."

By now there was no need for the Swiss of Grindelwald. The same message was extended to all the Swiss, and they all knew how to execute it properly.

Pius XIV took out and opened a folder of his papers, found the page he was looking for, and jotted down the program for a meeting that would take place that same evening in the premises of the Academy of St. Thomas Aquinas. He took a seat in Father Vinicio's roomy and comfortable car and invited him to sit beside him. The Pope was partially hidden by the priest's imposing build. They left the Vatican for the new residence of the Laurini Fathers. As in previous expeditions, Camillo sat in the front beside the driver. The Swiss threw the gate open in time, and immediately closed it behind the car without the customary salute. A precise delivery:

"Eyes wide open on the Pope, and pretend you don't recognize him."

This was not a difficult operation for a Swiss guard. Along the way Father Vinicius expressed to the Pope his own apprehensions, mostly of an economic nature:

"There are many offerings, but much fewer than before. Costs are high, much higher. The construction of the new Roman residence hall has bled us dry. We would like permission to take out another loan, without having to mortgage the hall, as we had to do for our academic school." From the new residence the talk shifted to the school of the Laurini Fathers, which offered academic degrees in the sciences.

Then the conversation moved from the economic challenge to the ideological one. For the Pope, this confirmed the decline, from confusion and dissension, that prevailed even among the alumni of that study center. The Pope was driven along the wide avenues that connected the various buildings of the Laurinis' new residence. The buildings had been built on a large estate between the Tiber, the Aniene and Monte Sacro. After walking through the interior of some of the buildings, the Pope wanted to see those of the academy. They were located on Rome's outskirts, but on the opposite side from where they now were. The city's new ring road brought them there in a few minutes.

"I see so many beautiful plants and through them can see so many beautiful buildings, but the pupils—where are they?" asked the Pope.

"Your Holiness, this academic complex was designed for five hundred during the years when we were thriving. But now we don't even have fifty," Father Vinicius replied sadly before sighing from the depths of his heart.

"'Rari nantes in gurgite vasto!'"[1] And at this very moment they are all submerged in the ocean of who knows what science!" commented the Pope, who continued, "All right! Thank you, Father Vinicio! Now will you give me a ride to the Academy of St. Thomas? If you can, you can stay as long as I am there. Then you can take me home and we'll have dinner together."

"Please!" exclaimed Vinicio, just like the good tailor in Manzoni and for the exact same reason. They found a place to park the car in the courtyard of the palace, which was the headquarters of the Academy of St. Thomas. Then what passed for the impossible happened: the porter paid no attention to the two latecomers, nor to the dignified, elderly gentleman, Camillo, who accompanied them, and much less to the driver who joined them on the stairs while fussing over a Football Pool readout. The Pope was able to make his entrance into the lecture hall without being recognized. He took a temporary seat in the last row of seats. The chairman introduced the very young, long-haired lecturer who nervously tortured the bundle of papers he held in his hand while reading his lecture notes:

"Marie Joseph Pierre Teilhard de Chardin, the founder of a new era of paleoanthropology, the universal philosopher, profound theologian, mystic, and saint. The following points will be covered in a comprehensive manner by our lecturer with his usual passionate vivacity. The program was printed in Italian,

---

1   Virgil, *Aeneid*, I, 118. "Few are they who [appear still to] swim in the great gulf of water," as in the *Aeneid*, regarding the fewness of those who make it through such ordeals.

but we will be pleased and honored that the lecturer will again express himself in his own mother tongue, which is also that of our great Master."

Having said that, the chairman motioned the lecturer to take a seat behind a chair, on which was the usual water bottle and microphone.

It was then that the Pope, followed by Father Vinicio in all his bulk, Camillo, and the driver came forward. When Father Vinicio, Camillo, and the chauffeur reached the height of the first row of seats, they stopped and took their places there. The Pope continued, climbed up to the podium, and took a seat behind the lecturer's chair, well in front of the lecturer himself. Immediately recognized, he was greeted with warm applause, and was invited to take the lecturer's chair. The Pope, however, briefly waved his hand to the chairman and, without any more hesitation, began:

"Thank you, Mr. President, but please remain comfortable in your seat. As a former member of the Academy of St. Thomas and, since it is a pontifical academy, also as Pontiff, I wish to address a few words to all those gathered. My starting point comes from the subtitles of the scheduled lecture which has been entrusted to the young lecturer here present."

In saying the word "present" he was reminded that he did not have in his hands at that moment the folder which he had taken care to take from his writings, but had forgotten it in the car. He couldn't send someone to get it now. He blew his nose and then put his handkerchief back in its place and drew from his pocket a packet of cards. They were covered with tiny writing, all in abbreviations according to a shorthand he had invented for his personal use during the long years of his life as a teacher. He commended himself to the *Sedes Sapientiae*, and then spoke directly:

"Let me speak to you in my mother tongue, but also with fatherly affection and directness. First point: Teilhard, the initiator of a new era of paleoanthropology. Listen to what J. Rostand writes about him in *Figaro Littéraire*: 'It is truly a lyrical fresco of evolution that Teilhard proposes to us. In this he is much more a poet and novelist than a man of science. It is undeniable that Teilhard's transformism stands outside science, as it eludes any experimental investigation and appeals to mysterious energies that we cannot in any way ascertain. His transformism, which is very superficial and confused, does not descend into the analysis of germinal organizations and structures. His transformism leaves aside all the precise problems that present themselves to every biologist who is seeking to clarify them, with the means of our time, the mechanism of evolutionary phenomena.'

"Listen to what P. O'Connel writes about it in *Science of the Day and the Problem of Genesis*: 'Teilhard's claim to be an authority in the field of paleontology depends almost solely on the remarks he made about Piltdown Man and Peking Man. In these two cases, he demonstrated that he did not possess even the slightest trace of critical sense and dispassionate judgment. He was nothing but a boy who never reaches maturity. He had an encyclopedic knowledge of all the terms used by geologists and paleontologists, but nothing more. It therefore remains tragic that the opinions of such a man, which were totally empty of any value whatsoever, could have influenced the teachings of otherwise eminent Catholic professors.' As for the theory of evolution in general, listen to what Professor Rabaud writes about it, in *Transformisme et adaptation*: 'Nowadays the latest transformists are considered to be people spending a lot of time dissenting.'

Indeed, the tooth that Dawson helped Teilhard find in the Piltdown quarry, which Teilhard believed to be of *Eoanthropus*, of the half-million-year-old Man of the Dawn, turned out to be the tooth of a recently-deceased ape, and the fossils of *Sinanthropus pekinensis*, that is, the Chinese Peking Man, turned out to be not of humans, but of orangutans who had been killed and eaten by hunters, by real men, the modern type. Those hunters were also artisans. They baked lime in the same quarry where the bones of the so-called *Sinanthropus* were found—the bones of men, who were hunters and artisans—and their tools and piles of ashes. But Teilhard, with the complicity of some other local pseudo-scientist, muddied the waters. He didn't mention the hole drilled in the skulls of orangutans by hunters which they used to take out the brains of the animals to eat. He made only a passing mention of the remains of the hunters of the modern type of humans in a sketch of the quarry. Teilhard called the piles of ashes from the stratified lime kilns 'fire traces.' Later, he forgot about these altogether, and therefore never brought them up again. As for the human fossils, found in the same quarry, they all disappeared. Rumors were spread that they had been stolen by the Japanese or Americans. Certainly they were too contrary to the evolutionary expectations of Teilhard and collaborators. As for the casts of the remains, which have survived, they are obviously artfully altered, and therefore of no value. Bathybius Haeckelii and the forgeries perpetrated by Haeckel and revealed by Father Gemini, are an innocent child's game in the face of those with which Teilhard de Chardin began a new era for paleoanthropology, the era of lies! And we come to the second and third points: the universal philosopher and the profound theologian."

The attendees could not believe their ears. They had long since been dissuaded from straight yes-is-yes and no-is-no talk. Their surprise at this unexpected and unbelievable event kept them glued to their seats, completely unable to react, speak, or move. The Pope was fully aware of this, and wanted to conclude before this enchantment ended. He therefore went more quickly, though he lingered whenever it was fitting to emphasize a certain expression. The Pope had a knack for this, which had become sharper from long use.

"Listen to what Teilhard wrote to Marguerite Teilhard-Chambon: 'The person is not an absolute being. He is in fact nothing more than the outcome of a process of concentration, according to the equation: Evolution plus Spiritualization equals Personalization.' How does he demonstrate this pantheistic monism? He does not even think it needs to be demonstrated: *Ipse dixit*! Not only is his system a fiction for whatever indulgences please him, without his bothering to prove anything, but a deliberately ambiguous and overly-critical system. 'I am sorry,' he wrote to Leontina Zanta, 'I am sorry that an excess of clarity and loyalty has provided an opportunity for three books by Edouard Le Roy to be condemned. They were put on the Index in 1931. To me they are beyond criticism. It also provided the opportunity to raise suspicions of certain tendencies and to glimpse the spirit of the dawn of a new Christianity. I feel confused when I think of the transposition that I have to make the common notions of creation, inspiration, miracle, original sin, resurrection, etc., undergo in me in order for me to accept them again.'

"Let us move on to the fourth and final point, which is the mystic and the saint.

"Listen to what Teilhard himself wrote to some of the women with whom he had a relationship: 'In the first place, even for a man devoted to the service of a Cause or a God, no access to maturity and spiritual fullness is possible outside of a certain sentimental influence, which succeeds in sensitizing the intelligence in him and to excite, at least initially, the capacity to love. Just as man cannot do without light, oxygen or vitamins, so he cannot do without the Feminine. There is more resounding evidence for this every day. An essential element would be missing in this message if I did not declare that, starting from the critical moment when I rejected so many old familiar and religious molds and began to wake up and truly express myself, nothing developed in me except under a woman's gaze and influence. Women's warmth and charm passed, drop by drop, into the blood of my dearest ideas. In certain moments, one must be deaf and blind to everything that passes in our inner self and becomes lost in action, and follow the currents of life passionately and blindly. Is not the Feminine the sensitivity and flame of my being? A certain love of the Invisible has never ceased to function in me, more or less excited and fueled by the influence of the Feminine.'

"And listen to what he says elsewhere, 'The world, the value, the infallibility and goodness of the world: this is ultimately the first and only thing in which I have faith. This is the faith that makes me live. This is the faith—I feel it—which, resisting all doubt, to which I will surrender myself in the hour of death.'

"Listen to what he wrote in *Christologie et Evolution*: 'I declare with all sincerity, that it has always been impossible for me to feel sincere compassion for the crucified man, inasmuch as that suffering was presented to me as the expiation of a sin which, either because he had no need of man or because he could have done otherwise, God could have avoided. What did he come to do in this jail?'

"And listen to what he states further on: 'It can be said that the modernization of Christology consists simply in substituting, in theological and liturgical formulas, for the word sin, the word progress, that is, the word fire for the word smoke. Is it really so difficult?'

"And hear this prayer of our saint: 'Holy matter, charming and strong, matter that caresses and makes strong, I surrender myself to your mighty resources. The virtue of Christ is transferred to you. With your attractions, attract me. With your lifeblood, nourish me. With your strength, strengthen me. With your tears, set me free. With your whole being, finally, deify me.' This is, as you see, a parody of *Anima Christi, sanctifica me*, by St. Ignatius, founder of the Society of Jesus.

"To Leontina Zanta wrote that 'a Super-humanity as the measure of the Earth, a Super-Christ as the measure of Superhumanity, a Super-charity as the measure of that Super-humanity and as the measure of the Super-Christ?' Ah, yes! The Word of God must be the measure of man, and man must be the measure of the earth! And this—he terms this evolutionary progress!

"Now know, dear beloved, that whoever prefers his own Super-Christianity to the Christianity of Our Lord Jesus Christ and the incorruptible and everlasting heritage of the Catholic Church, is an apostate. Do you not remember what St. Paul writes to the Galatians: 'Whoever dares to present to you a Gospel other than the one we preached to you, excommunicate him, let him be anathema! Even if it is I myself, even if it were an angel!'

"This is the seat of the Pontifical Academy of St. Thomas Aquinas, Saint and Doctor of the Church. I will not allow it to continue to be a venue for the propaganda of the aberrations of an apostate sorcerer! This seat will remain closed until—and this will happen soon—until courses cover both the two *Summae* and the Minor Works and Biblical Commentaries of St. Thomas. What may be added to this, for whoever presently feels the need, a course in minor logic as well. This course will teach—and not only to the young—them, if not exactly how to refute lies, at least how they can prevent themselves from being drowned in a sea of sophisms, which at times are as coarse as they are pernicious.

"Let's recall the prophetic warning we read in St. Paul's second letter to Timothy: 'A time will come in which they will not tolerate the preaching of what could save them. Instead they will go in search of a pleiad of teachers, who will caress their lusts, who will flatter them with lying words. They will give credence to all fashionable fantasies, and they will perk up their ears lest they have to admit the truth.' And now you may return, all of you, to your respective homes. The session is over!"

No one spoke a word. Camillo solemnly and gravely stepped up to the podium, and helped the Pope put on his *pastrano*. Father Vinicius, even more solemn and grave, lined up, with all his imposing bulk, to the Pope's right. Though he said nothing, he seemed eloquent. To Father Vinicius' right stood the driver. Those in the very first rows tried to slip away first. Behind them, the whole lecture hall emptied out. It was not very big, with few in attendance. Finally, the Pope with his companions also left. The president and lecturer lingered a few more moments, just so as not to join the Pope's group, before leaving, silent and pensive.

The rather fat porter climbed the two flights of the grand staircase, puffing and panting in the warm afternoon. He turned off the lights, locked the door, and descended the stairs again. He finally tossed the keys into a small drawer of a cupboard on which he had put a marble bust of St. Thomas back in its place of honor. The marble had been evicted from the lecture hall. He locked the drawer, put the last key in his pocket, and finally let himself fall, sweaty and transfixed, into his big creaky chair. He smoothed out the betting slip, which he had not yet filled out. He gripped his pencil and, while sighing, spoke fervently:

"Our St. Thomas and our beautiful holy Academy, *orate pro nobis*!"

He then re-started all the work. The Pope was able to re-enter the Vatican incognito. The police had not been notified and the Teilhardians had other things on their minds!

That evening only three dined in the Laurini Fathers' refectory, the Pope and Fathers Vinicius and Anthony. The latter was the local superior and Father Vinicius' adviser on economic matters. As for the small community's other four friars, one was in the kitchen serving as cook and another in bed due to one of his usual attacks of gout in his big toe. Only an extra piece of meat was needed to feed him. The other two friars had dined a little earlier because of an engagement at St. Peter's Circle. This allowed the Pope to divert the conversation, though only for a few moments, to something close to his heart. He did so without, however, turning the conversation itself into an audience, but also in such a way as to make a new audience to Father Vinicius unnecessary.

"Unfortunately, Your Holiness, it is a disaster! Especially among the young, who are melting away like snow in the sun. That leaves us, the old. We will have to turn some of our student houses, now deserted, into retirement homes for elderly and infirm brethren, but we lack the nurses."

"So if the old residence was enough for you, when you were growing in numbers, why should it not be enough for you now, when you are decreasing in numbers? All those beautiful and very comfortable rooms in your new residence, with the wide, bright corridors, the beautiful surrounding greenery, and everything away from the noise, would be a magnificent clinic. Give the new residence of yours to a hospital!"

"I have thought of that too, Your Holiness," confirmed Father Vinicius.

"Oh, me too, me too," Father Antonio added. "Also because of money."

"Relocate—carefully!—relocate the students of your school into some of your student housing, which can handle the inconvenience, and keep on conferring academic degrees. I'll lend a hand, if need be. And cede the school's complex of buildings to the University of Rome, which so badly needs them! You will solve the ideological-disciplinary problem and also the economic one."

"I had thought about that too, Your Holiness," assured Father Vinicio.

"Oh, me too, me too," Father Antonio confirmed in turn.

"But I hope you understand, Your Holiness," Father Vinicius continued, "I did not dare to make such a proposal to my collaborators. Please understand. I sponsored the building of those two complexes myself at the time!"

At that moment the cook brought grapes to the table:

"Uva dei Castelli. The very first early fruit from our vineyard in Ariccia."

" Excellent!" exclaimed the Pope, after tasting a few.

"If such is the mother, imagine the son!" exclaimed Father Anthony.

"He means the wine, Castelli wine," said the Pope, who continued. "I had just come from Mass. I was going to school, hearing confessions, helping the few priests in charge of a parish entrusted to our Order, but I was very tired. There was a lot of noise in the house, which also came from the nightly parish cinema. I slept very little. There was a lot of work and no rest. It was hot—it was the summer. I happened to pass by the wide-open door of the office of an old assistant priest of the parish. He had very weak eyesight, but a big heart. He realized what I myself did not: that I was gasping for air. 'Come here for a little, Father Pio!' he said, and waved me into his office. Then he took a large flask out from a closet, and said, 'It's genuine, from Marino, from my brother's vineyard.' He poured me a glass of the honey-colored ambrosia, and also for himself. We made a toast, and I left refreshed. Several times he again offered me that medicine. It was the most effective thing against all ills, and also the cheapest. That old man is long dead, and God will have rewarded him even for that act of exquisite charity, He who does not leave even a simple glass of cool water without reward.'"

"But you only drink a little of it, Your Holiness!" exclaimed Father Vinicius, who, as was fitting, drank in proportion to his size, which was truly out of the ordinary.

21

The Catholic School

AFTER DINNER THEY WENT UP TO the roof-terrace for fresh air. While slowly strolling about, the conversation turned to a very important topic. The two confreres, who had returned from the St. Peter Circle, also participated.

"That's right, Your Holiness!" said Father Vinicius. "We have been trying very hard to conform to the state programs. We have to put on a fine face for the state inspectors and commissioners, all so that we can put into the hands of our pupils a diploma with a state stamp on it."

"And what an expense," observed Father Antonio, the economic advisor.

"Patience about the money," Father Vinicio repeated, "but in view of the state stamp, we are going to sacrifice everything in our schools that would characterize them as Catholic. In the young person we end up seeing a graduate, supposing the state allows it at all. Religious, charitable, artistic, and recreational activities all take second place to cultural activity."

"You see, Your Holiness, how generous is our superior?" interjected Father Sixtus, one of the two who had just joined. "Our superior calls the Babylon that is found in schools today cultural activity. Now, in order to be up to date with this Babylon, we even abandon our timetables, if they do not synchronize with the timetable of the state schools, either because of the repeated vacations during the school months, or because of summer vacation, or because of time off due to strikes, since we also have numerous paid teachers. What do we have in our schools that is still private? Legal impairments, compared to state schools, and the economic surcharge to the families who continue to trust us."

"And we teachers," Father Augustine, the second survivor, said in his warm voice. He was the youngest of the group, but quite sensible. He had been resting for a few months due to exhaustion and nervous breakdown: "And we teachers, too, end up feeling reduced to mere instructors, no longer Christian educators. We engage in the activity of brain stuffing, for which the priestly character is entirely superfluous. It is an activity that frustrates our aspirations and destroys all enthusiasm. It turns us from being Our Lord's ministers into civil servants in the service of the minister of public education and, even worse, without salary, without insurance and without a pension."

"Well stated, Father Augustine," the Pope approvingly responded before asking, "From your schools last year, how many young men passed into become your order's aspirants?" Father Vinicius hesitated a few moments, arched his eyebrows, and finally answered:

"No one, Your Holiness, no one!" and sighed. "It is sad! Much more so when you read in the histories of our Order, that in the old days, among the young people of the higher courses, young people who had been living with us for a few years, many beautiful vocations matured. Sometimes a whole class would apply to be aspirants. This happened in my fifth grade gymnasium, for example. Not everyone was accepted, not everyone resisted the temptations of the world. But even today, there are still twelve of us, alive—twelve priests, all alumni of that magnificent fifth gymnasium."

"You know certain things, dear friends," said the Pope. "You know them better than I do. The ancient teaching orders, and yours before any other, did not need to adapt their methods, programs, texts, and schedules to the state's methods, programs, texts and schedules. They did not need to present their teachers to the state to obtain by grace the chrism that would qualify them to teach. The ancient teaching orders, and yours first of all, independently trained their teachers, and their schools were large, when those of the state had not yet been born. Great schools, because in them everything was permeated with Christianity, even the teaching of so-called abstract subjects. There was no need to comb through the state curricula in search of a legal pretext that would allow a few extra lines of Latin to be taught in whatever class. Nor did they feel the need to reach out to the state, and so pitifully, to receive a few crumbs of bread that the state gave mostly to own its schools. They survived because they were supported by Christian families."

"And speaking of Christian families, some are still around," Father Augustine observed, "eager to entrust their children to us, that we may make them good. How many times have I heard mothers and fathers—the best of all parents—how many times have I heard them say to me, 'I don't care so much that he learns to read, write and do arithmetic. I care that he becomes good, obedient, and that he grows up as a good Christian.'"

"Of course, of course!" nodded Father Vinicius approvingly.

"These families offer young people who are better disposed for a stricter Christian education," said the Pope. "Keep your methods, put them back in their place of honor! Modern psychology has taken apart the young person as someone takes apart a small car. Its principles may be useful for manufacturing a robot, but they ignore the soul and supernatural grace. That is, they ignore the historical datum, abstract everything, destroy."

"Our young people have destroyed so many bulletin boards thanks to modern psychology!" commented Father Anthony: "And then...movies, not studies; the stadium, not studies; a sightseeing trip all the way to Norway to see the fjords in the wild, when they have atlases, which would have enchanted us, if we had had them when we were kids! Expenses, expenses, expenses, and parents complain. And what gratitude! Patience to us, but not even to their parents. By the fruit you know the tree!"

"Leave the State its crumbs, if it offers them unsolicited to you someday. But keep your methods, curricula, texts, all made by you, for the in-depth development of truly Christian young people. Keep your timetables and teachers, approved by you alone, and prepare your diplomas, your own, with the sign of the Cross on it in many places instead of the state's stamp. Believe it or not, a graduate of yours will not be left standing at the door when he applies to a real Catholic university. An accounting graduate of yours, even if he doesn't have the image of the state stamp on his diploma, will be happily received by any bank that needs him, and there is no bank that does not need competent and honest accountants. Just as a surveyor graduate, even without that state stamp, will be well received by any construction company because he is competent and honest."

"True, true!" approved Father Vinicius. "Our electricians are welcomed without a blink at Tecnomax, as one example, and it's the same with our tailors at Petronius Arbiter, though without the stamp."

"Even degrees today give no guarantee of competence, let alone honesty and virtue. The crown of laurel leaves could be replaced by a crown of donkey ears," Father Sixtus solemnly concluded.

Then the Pope resumed: "Having made the young person good, virtuous, and pure in a Christian way, on the basis of Catechism, the Last Things, Mass, Confession, and Communion, you will also have an able young scholar. And then the qualification as a private school graduate—because your schools, independent of the state, would be strictly private schools—well, such a qualification would become synonymous with the exceptional student."

"True, true," Father Antonio agreed.

"Allow me to make a clarification, which His Holiness certainly had in mind," said Father Augustine: "When the state diploma was indispensable for certain careers, it could easily be obtained by our young people when they were twenty-three, the age at which, according to the law, they are even admitted to the high school matriculation examination, without the need for previous qualifications. In that case, even a young man admitted as an auditor in any university could then be enrolled there regularly."

"In conclusion," said Father Vinicius, "We really need to go back to doing *ad litteram* what our holy founder did. We need to observe *ad litteram, sine glossa et adamussim*[1] what he prescribed. It is not outdated! And to innovate, but validly, we must redo exactly what our founder did and established and codified in various regulations. But this is a problem, a real problem!"

"Start with a few institutions," the Pope urged them. "Then you can make adjustments to the whole thing as you go along."

"Yes, a few schools, a few pilot colleges. We could even start them for the next school year, if we hurry to communicate with the families."

"Do it, do it!"

"We will, we will certainly do it, Your Holiness," Father Vinicius concluded.

"Our Lady and your holy founder will bless you."

A pause followed. The air had cooled somewhat. The Pope felt tired and looked at his watch before asking:

"Isn't it time to retire? They all went down to the chapel, recited the evening prayers, from *Vi adoro* to *Gesù, Giuseppe e Maria*. Then each silently retired to his own room. Leaving the

---

[1] "literally, without commentary or gloss, and accurately"

chapel, the Pope found the cook waiting for him with a cup of chamomile tea in his hand. He had been instructed by Father Anthony to have it ready for him by that hour.

"Here's your tea, Your Holiness, hot, aromatic, and with a slice of lemon. It will help you sleep. But...."

"But?" asked the Pope, interrupting to sip the chamomile tea, "But?"

"But," the cook spoke with an air of connoisseurship, "A glass of Castelli, instead of chamomile tea, Your Holiness! It is a true medicine against all ailments, the most effective and also the cheapest!"

"Well, if you say so, Brother Ambrose, I really have to believe it. Another time. Thank you, my dear, and holy night!"

"Holy night, Your Holiness!"

22

WITHOUT THE CHURCH THERE IS NO HOLY SCRIPTURE

"We ARE AIMING FOR PUBLIC OWNership of the means of production and compulsory education," Monsignor Consalve, from Central America, stated with a certain degree of prosopopeia.

"And do you know what the famous Aldous Huxley said about these two great reforms?" Wong asked him, with a big smile and short bow. "He said that compulsory education has proved to be the most effective tool for state-imposed regimentation and militarization, even of those citizens who had previously escaped the influence of organized lies and silly and degrading collectivist seductions, and that the state's takeover of the means of production replaced the tyranny of money with far more ruthless tyrannies of mindless and heartless police and bureaucratic political power."

"I don't believe that! Those reforms have been proposed by the youth, and we are with the youth!" asserted Consalve somewhat resentfully.

"You are with the young people? What are you saying, Your Excellency?" exclaimed Wong before he continued: "You are with the grandparents. Mao was a great-grandfather, and as for Marx, he is obsolete!"

They were walking in the Vatican gardens in the Pope's company. He had wanted them with him that afternoon to complement the morning audience. And in fact he was getting what he had promised himself he would get—Wong trying to set Consalve's ideas a bit straighter. Though well-intentioned, the latter was perhaps a little too zealous, and as eccentric as his attire. He dressed like a traveling salesman. The fact that he presented himself to the Pope so poorly-dressed revealed him immediately for what he was, despite the saying, "It's not the habit that makes the monk." In fact, he had appealed to this saying in the face of Wong's discreet remonstrances. Wong had responded to him with an episode:

"A priest of mine had started going around pretty much like you dress. An old Catholic lady then said to him, 'Father, is there really a need for the good of our souls for you to blend in like this? No one is persecuting you here.' That priest had responded just as Your Excellency did a moment ago:

"'It's not the habit that makes the monk.' To which the old woman replied, 'It's true, at least in part, that it is not the habit that makes the monk, but it is quite true that it reveals it and preserves it. Thanks to the habit, your black cassock, you preach eternal life even without opening your mouth. Without that habit, you give the testimony of the chameleon, who makes himself into the color of the environment, out of fear of being seen. And then—believe it, my father, for I am old and I know certain things—for our families, to our women and daughters, you priests also appear too much like ordinary men, without cassocks. And our men then prefer that you stay away from their women, both those present and more so their absent ones. A word for the wise!' That priest of mine allowed himself to be convinced. It was in fact himself who reported this episode to me."

"And another such incident happened to me, but a sweet one," the Pope added. "A few months ago, after preaching for four days to older ladies, the mothers of our order's missionaries, I took the train back to Rome, to the monastery of the Passion. I was, of course, wearing the black cassock of our order. I had just barely taken my seat in a compartment and was sitting there alone, when I was approached by a little girl who, I later learned, had recently turned six and was named Daniela. She stood watching me for a few moments, with the only eye she had. She had a black patch over her right eye, which was held in place by her glasses. That was the good eye, she explained. But she had to exercise her left eye, to strengthen it. So she stood looking at me for a few moments, then approached me and said in a soft, confiding voice:

"'You are a good priest, though, because you wear the long habit.' So she sat down in front of me, spoke in a familiar way, and confided that her teacher was very strict, but that 'this is better for us children, who learn more that way!' She spoke with joyful honesty about her First Communion. She wanted to know so many things about the Land of Jesus and Our Lady. She wanted to transcribe her own name in Hebrew characters, the ones Jesus had to learn in school, and under the individual letters she wrote their meaning:

"*Dan* means judge, *i* means mine, *El* means God, and *ahè* is used for the ending of girls' names.' And then she made me buy a letter-sealing stamp from an anti-tuberculosis campaign. When I had to get off the train, she went back to her mother's side, and from there she waved me a nice 'Bye!' It was a lovely meeting, which soothed my soul. I always pray for that little angel with the black patch over her right eye, and who with her left eye saw and judged a priest by his black robe."

"There are various places, Holiness, and various circumstances," Consalve observed. "And then Our Lord did not go around to divide, at least if we give credence to Scripture, the basis of the Faith and the Church."

"Are we conforming to Holy Scripture, the foundation of the Church?" Wong asked with a new smile, "Monsignor, the hemorrhagic woman healed by Jesus had touched one of the four bows that the faithful Israelite was supposed to wear at the four corners of the square cloak. This was the uniform of the true Israelite. So Jesus wore the cloak of the uniform prescribed for the faithful Israelite, which not everyone did."

"Whereas today," said the Pope, "certain illustrated catechisms depict a proletarian Jesus wearing a slave's smock and wooden clogs. Yet the painter cannot be unaware that Jesus wore those sandals, of which John said he was unworthy to untie. Moreover, at least during the institution of the Most Holy Eucharist and the Mass he also wore a special vestment, the seamless and precious priestly tunic, which the executioners did not dare to split into parts, so as not to destroy its value. And once resurrected, He still wore a uniform—the stigmata of the crucifixion in His glorious flesh. If you, Monsignor, wore these latter, certainly no other uniform could add anything.

St. Francis of Assisi got rid of his worldly, elegant clothes, and dressed in sackcloth. Of course, if that sack had thus been filled with potatoes, it would not have affected anyone's conversion, but even St. Francis, as long as he went dressed in the fashion of the world, converted no one.

"As for the assertion you made, Excellency, that Sacred Scripture is the foundation of the Church itself, I object to something in that, but that would be a long conversation, and so I'll postpone it to another occasion, also because my throat is a little sore today. But are you really so sure that Sacred Scripture is the foundation of the Church?"

"How not? Who can doubt it?" asked Consalve excitedly.

"I do, Your Excellency," Wong answered. "And if Your Holiness has no objection to it, I would like to remind Your Excellency of it as well. I would like to remind you of it because it is a doctrine that you, Your Excellency, has studied like me.

"Without the New Testament there is no Holy Scripture, in the same way that there is no human life without oxygen. Now the Church already existed before the New Testament. The oldest writing in the New Testament is in fact the first letter of St. Paul the Apostle to the Thessalonians, a letter dictated by Paul not earlier than the year 51 of the Christian era, when the Church had at least four intense decades, was in full missionary expansion, and had already been stained red with the blood of St. Stephen, the early martyr who was stoned to death, and with the blood of St. James the Greater, the brother of St. John the Evangelist, who was beheaded.

"It's not only that. You cannot also say that Sacred Scripture founded the Church even if you really mean to say that the Church acquires authority from Sacred Scripture. The opposite is true. It is the Church that guarantees that those particular writings are sacred, that they were inspired by God as their principal author. And it's not even all that. You cannot say that Sacred Scripture is the foundation of the Church even if you intend to say that the Church acquires all its doctrine from Sacred Scripture because Scripture is but a reminder to the Church, and a partial reminder, inasmuch as the Church's doctrine is broader than that which the apostolic Church itself fixed in writing in Sacred Scripture.

"So the great problem of the sources of Revelation, which was dealt with during the Second Vatican Council but left unresolved, as if it did not already have its own infallible and binding solution for all Catholics, already offers a good solution, which is this: God inspired the doctrine which is called Apostolic Tradition, in which all the truths of the Faith are gathered together. Part of this Tradition was also fixed in writing in Sacred Scripture, before the death of the last Apostle. After the death of the last Apostle, who was St. John the Evangelist, the charism of divine inspiration of the hagiographers ceased. But what remained was the charism of the infallibility of the ecclesiastical magisterium. This is held in a personal way in the pope when he teaches as pope. This charism is contained in the Apostolic Tradition and is therefore infallibly transmitted and, what is implicitly contained therein, is made explicit to a certain degree.

"In short, the ecclesiastical Tradition that is constituted by the Apostolic Tradition is identified with the authoritative and infallible papal magisterium, which makes explicit and transmits this Tradition. No other sources of Revelation can be distinguished which, possessing various aspects of Catholic doctrine, would result in a synthesis of the whole Catholic doctrine. No, there is but one source, ecclesiastical Tradition, which is identified with the teaching Church. In short, Jesus did not come to found a library of writings, however inspired by God, but to establish a society of living persons, which he assured would have perfection, even doctrinal perfection: the Catholic Church.

"Without it, Scripture has no authority, whereas the Church without Scripture would still subsist, though like someone who had lost part of his memory, who would always remain capable of reintegrating the lost part. Let it be said by others, Your Excellency, that the Bible is the foundation of the Church! Can't you see that without the Church the Bible has founded nothing but a group of quarrelsome sects?"

"But...but, we kept the faithful away from Sacred Scripture," Consalve said, just to say something. That was also something unexceptional and commonly admitted.

"Your Excellency, how many people are illiterate in your country?" Wong asked him in a friendly tone. Wong was an accomplished chess player who knew how to take every possible advantage of any unconscious move of the opponent.

"How many people are illiterate? Who has counted them? The so-called official statistics go so far as to say that 72 percent of the total population is illiterate, but in the countryside and mountains it is as high as 90 percent and more. The population in the city centers, which is considerably more educated, brings this number down."

"And you, Your Excellency, are you sure that if you put the Bible in the hands of that illiterate 72% of the population of your country, that population would benefit greatly? And in Northern Europe and North America, what has been achieved through the direct reading of the Bible after it was put into the hands of everyone who can read due to the Protestant dogma of private inspiration? More holiness of life? More purity of customs? More unity in the Faith? Think of Sweden! Think of Denmark!"

The Pope cleared his throat, put a lozenge in his mouth—he had received a nice bag of them, sent by his sister, the one with the T-shirts and socks—and then decided to speak, at the cost of exacerbating his sore throat a bit.

"A mother does not offer bread to a nursing infant, not because the bread is bad, but because it would hurt the child. No one with common sense but lacking experience in mountain climbing, and who wants to return home safely, dares to start climbing a daunting peak without a proven guide or at least very good preparation to guarantee him success in his undertaking. Simply reading the *Divine Comedy* is of no use to a child, who will be bored with it very soon. Even the high-schooler finds it difficult and feels the need for a teacher. That teenager will not grasp the vast scope of the poem, however, until a more mature age when life experience has taught him something about the mysteries of the human heart.

"Holy Scripture is a far more difficult book than the *Comedy* that later generations called *divine*. It is not divine by forceful attribution based on the readers' admiration, but because the main author of it is truly God Himself, and God remains mysterious even in the way He reveals His mysteries to us, which seems like a paradox. Who can gaze into the sun without being dazzled by it? After an instant of great light, you'll see nothing more than a black background, nothing more. Is this perhaps from a defect in the sun's light? No, but from a defect in sight. Something similar also takes place with regard to Sacred Scripture, the Word of God. All the human sciences must cooperate and bow with reverence before the Word of God, in order to interpret it. This is also done under the guidance of the authoritative magisterium of the Catholic Church, by which Sacred Scripture itself was inspired."

"But how?" objected Consalve, who was now sure that he had found an irrefutable argument. "God is not capable of making himself understood, and man is? God is obscure, man is clear! Does God need a human interpreter?"

"Exactly!" replied Wong, intervening to give the Pope's throat a break. "Exactly, because God willed it that way. He could have done otherwise, and He still could, but in regard to Sacred Scripture He willed it that way. He inspired it for His Church, and reserved exclusively to the Church the faculty of authoritative and infallible interpretation of it. He wanted all secular human science to bend reverently, as the humble handmaiden of the Church, in the work of interpreting Sacred Scripture, in the work of deepening the inexhaustible treasures of truth contained therein. Besides, Your Excellency, do you not remember the episode of the disciples of Emmaus?"

"What a question!" replied Consalve with a shrug. He was beginning to show some irritation.

"And then can you tell me what the Lord explains to those two, to Cleophas and his traveling companion?" insisted Wong.

"But Your Excellency, don't you know that I know the whole New Testament by heart? I know the Vulgate version, in Latin, but I think I can translate for you that passage from Luke's gospel into my poor Italian: 'And referring to Moses and the prophets, he went about explaining to them everything in the Scriptures alluded to Him.' There, are you happy?"

"So," Wong resumed, "Jesus, on his way to Emmaus, explained to those two the true meaning of a few pages of the Old Testament, which means that they had not been able to understand those pages rightly, though they were the Word of God, either individually or aided by the explanations of the rabbis. And in the Upper Room, didn't the risen Jesus, after dining with the Apostles, repeat something similar?"

Flattered to be able to confidently flaunt his biblical culture, Consalve replied: "Of course, in the episode immediately following that of the disciples of Emmaus, Luke himself tells us a few verses later: 'Then Jesus illuminated their minds, so that they might understand the meaning of the Scriptures.' That is, Jesus also explains on the evening of Easter Sunday to the Apostles and disciples, who had gathered in the Upper Room, as He had to the two disciples of Emmaus, the meaning of the prophecies that were contained in the Pentateuch, the books of the prophets and the Psalms."

"Don't you see, Your Excellency, how well you know these things? Your nonstop activities have overwhelmed you, making you forget them a little. Now you must admit that Jesus' explanations wouldn't have been necessary if the Holy Spirit had inspired each of the readers of these writings just as He had inspired each of the human authors of Holy Scripture. Thanks to such a private inspiration, not only the Pharisees, priests, Sanhedrists, and other notables of Jerusalem, but also the humblest and least educated among the children of Israel, would have seen in Jesus the foretold and invoked Redeemer. Likewise, even the New Testament, thanks to such a private and individual charism, couldn't be misunderstood by anyone, contrary to what St. Peter declares in reference to the letters of St. Paul: 'There are some expressions that are difficult to understand, misrepresented to their own detriment by those who do not have due preparation and by those who do not have firm foundations, which, moreover, they do with all the other parts of Scripture as well.' You see then, Your Excellency, how Scripture itself warns against placing Scripture in the hands of anyone who is not illiterate!'"

"In short, you want to skin me alive," Consalve exclaimed, bursting with resentment. The conversation went silent. Having lost from every angle and feeling the silence weighing on him like a condemnation, Consalve searched frantically for any topic to restart the conversation. He finally managed to throw in a sentence with a certain ring to it:

"All right, from the doctrinal point of view you may be right, but from the pastoral point of view things are quite different. I alluded to Scripture, meaning by Scripture the quintessence of the Gospel, that is, the basic foundations of liberation theology and liberating revolution. Excuse me very much, but I don't mince my words. I live in a poor country. I have to bring the people to the gospel of total liberation. Freedom, that's what the people want. I say it and let me repeat it to Your Holiness," he added solemnly as he put his hand on his tunic instead of his heart in a dignified manner: "And I don't say this in a personal manner, but on behalf of the seven million—seven million!—of my countrymen: we want the Gospel that gives us freedom!"

"Freedom?" Wong asked with a smile that this time really seemed to mean, "Now I'll set you right!" So he repeated, "Freedom? I, too, say it, and if it is ever necessary I will repeat it to Your Holiness—but in a personal capacity only, because I have no way of questioning the seven hundred million of my countrymen, not counting those in the Diaspora—that I think freedom is like the word 'thing.' It can mean anything. Now what do you, Your Excellency, mean by that word, freedom?"

"By freedom, I mean liberation first of all from the yoke of capitalism. You who come from the Far East, you cannot dispute that Mao, that this freedom..."

But Wong raised his hand toward Consalve, as if to ask his permission to interrupt and question him, so the latter said to him, "Go ahead. Say it," and was glad to be interrupted because he sensed that he had walked into a minefield.

23

INTROIBO AD ALTARE DEI

"YOUR EXCELLENCY," WONG ASKED him, "Have you never been in prison?"

"No, I've never had the opportunity."

"I did. I was there as a visitor, chaplain, and also inmate. I was an inmate for two years, in a closet that was three feet wide and four feet long. I could never lie down, in that closet, for two long years. I could only curl up on the floor. I could stretch my legs, however, and soon I devoted several hours a day to this exercise, to push-ups and jumping jacks. The dirt floor properly muffled any noise. When they brought me food, they would spit in it, right in front of me, but I always ate it. I had no intention of starving and dying there.

"Well, that freedom had its own gospel: Mao's little red book. And Mao offered it to me, by force. Why was that? Because in matters of religion I thought differently from him. Just because of that. Would you have adapted to thinking like Mao even in matters of religion?"

Consalve did not answer, and Wong continued:

"I did not die in that prison, because I escaped. Do you want to know how? It was a great adventure! If I had time, I would write a movie script or a novel entitled *Introibo ad altare Dei*.

"Strange!" Consalve declared.

"Do you think so? But you will quickly understand why. My presence in that prison was useless, both to me and to my Christian brothers. There was nothing left for me to do but try to escape. During the short hours of marching and standing at the barbed-wire fence, I saw in the garbage heap two plastic bags, a ripped shirt, and many orange and lemon peels. In one of those bags I put those peels and the shirt, and in the other, I would fill in due time with cooked rice, which I would subtract from my one meager daily meal. I studied the habits of the sentinels for a long time, usually observing them from a crack in my cell's doorway. And then I made up my mind.

"One evening, around sunset, when the sun was low on the horizon and with the help of a bamboo pole, I jumped over the fence. I was always very agile in jumping, given my height and thinness, and although very weak, I made it. When the alarm was sounded, I was already a hundred or more meters away. I ran toward the sun, so that the sun rays would burn the pupils of those who would shoot at me from behind. In fact, a shot reverberated, and a bullet whistled past my right ear. I let out a cry of pain, and let myself fall as one who is shot to death falls, but just where I wanted to: into the bottom of a ditch. Crawling on all fours through the water, slime and vegetation, I reached the nearby reedbed, and hid there.

"The sentries did not hurry much, as they were all certain of the fact that they were all sharpshooters, and until that day they had not missed a single shot. Taking advantage of those few moments of their lingering, I stripped off my rags, and put on the shirt, full of the smell of oranges and lemons that were basically spoiled. That way the dogs would not track me down so soon. Each time the reeds swayed in the evening breeze, I moved too, to get as far away from the camp as possible before darkness fell over everything.

"The next morning, before sunrise, I arrived where I promised myself I would: on the outskirts of some kind of agricultural cooperative. There, no one owned anything and everything belonged to everyone, at least in theory. I immediately tried to put that theory into practice. There was a clothes rack with clothes in all shapes and colors hanging on it. I took what I needed and that fit me and that was in good condition. In fact, several of the garments were well washed, but they also had an indescribable number of patches on them. On the windowsill of a ground-floor window, I saw a water bottle complete with a consortium stamp: it had certainly been placed there in the cool of the night so that the contents would not spoil. Milk? Rice brandy? That was not the time to solve the riddle. For good measure, I took it and then set off at a brisk pace across the fields so that, as soon as possible, I could reach the paved road that should in the long run bring me closer to Hong Kong.

"I won't tell you about all the hitchhiking I did in the early days of escape. I will only tell you about my last day of escape from Mao's subject territory. It was dawn, and I was walking, very tired, along the paved road, when I heard a military truck coming up behind me. I later learned that the driver was the attendant of an officer, and that he was going to pick up the officer who was returning from near Hong Kong. When the truck came close, I put a handful of rice in my mouth, began waving with a clenched fist, and asked for a ride. They picked me up. I sat down beside the good soldier and handed him the canteen, which did indeed contain rice brandy, but he shook his head, and started the vehicle again. I asked him for a cigarette, I who have never smoked in my life, but he shook his head again, and with a gesture that meant: 'If you annoy me any more, I'll throw you out!' So I opened my plastic bag again, and tried to give the impression that I was eating with two palms; but in fact I aimed to consume very little of the rice because I wanted to have enough more to fill my mouth with whenever I had to speak.

"The attendant was going all the way to Shenzhen, near the border between Red China and Hong Kong, but I could not risk going all the way there. I decided to ask to get off as soon as we reached the first houses of a village, still some 20 kilometers

Introibo ad altare Dei

away from the border. After a quarter of an hour's journey, the good little soldier also took aboard a little old lady, who had a nice basket of fresh eggs to take to the same village. I then moved to the back seat of the truck, next to the old lady, and gestured for an egg, without saying a word. She looked me in the face, and then gave me three, choosing the largest ones. I sipped all three one after another, but I held the empty shell of the last one in my hands because I had seen a police truck coming toward us. I barely had time to fill my mouth with a handful of rice, when the truck barred our way and forced us to stop. One of the two policemen got out, pulled up directly beside me, and asked me:

"Are you another one running away to Hong Kong?" I gave him a nod that meant:

"Are you crazy?" and with my right hand I pointed out to him the town to which we were headed, but without uttering a word because my mouth was full. Then I brought the empty shell to my lips, which I held in my left hand, as if I wanted to drink some more. Then with a calm and amused gesture I threw it across the road; and then finally I handed that policeman my bottle. The policeman saw the stamp of it and his face broke into a grimace, which meant:

"I wonder where this agricultural cooperative is?" and motioned me to put it back on my shoulder as well. Meanwhile, the old woman had spoken for me as well:

"Both of us are going to the village with all these eggs here. We'll be back for the collective exercise in the morning."

The policeman said goodbye to her, went back to his vehicle, and we each carried on in our own directions. I got out on the outskirts of the town, as did the little old lady. We walked a little way together, me carrying her basket of eggs. At one point she stopped and said to me:

"Give me the eggs. Now go down that path until you get to that reedbed over there, and wait there for the night. Here are some more eggs also," and she gave me three more. "Courage, father!" she said before resuming her way. She was certainly a Christian, and had recognized me as a priest. I reached the reedbed, hid myself there on the ground to rest a little, and fell asleep. It didn't seem real to me, after two years, that I could lie down so comfortably! After a few hours I woke up, recited the Mass of my Saint from memory as a prayer, ate all the rice I had left, with those three eggs, drank a few sips of that rice brandy behind it, and waited for the night to return.

"So I reached the paved road again. At every sound of a car, I lay down flat at the edge of the road, and did not move until the car had disappeared into the darkness. Shortly before dawn I left the asphalt road, and continued towards Hong Kong through the fields, until I reached the barbed wire fences. Here I began to do things that I won't describe to you because it would make you sick, as it made me quite sick as well. I came out all bloody. It was all the worse in the last stretch of the crossing because, looking around at a moment's pause, in the dawn light, I had caught sight of a patrol of sentries a few hundred yards from me. Thank Heaven they were marching in the opposite direction, but there was no way that I could linger. I made a last effort, leaving on barbed wires the last scraps of cloth and skin, and arrived on the other side of the barrier. I fell on the grass and fainted.

"I came to when I felt something pressing on my chest. It was the barrel of a sentry's rifle. It was a British sentry. I breathed, somewhat relieved, but was unable to utter a word. The soldier asked me in Chinese: 'Who are you?' I answered in English: 'I am a Catholic priest. Take me to the bishop!' 'You're a Catholic priest? How do you start the Mass?' It had been two years since I had celebrated it except mentally. I answered promptly, *'Introibo ad altare Dei!'"*

"'*Ad Deum qui laetificat iuventutem meam!*' he answered me, and then he knelt beside me, gave me a sip of whiskey, and helped me up and to his truck. And then to a barracks, and then to the bishop. I saw him again some time later. I went to find him to thank him. His name was Patrick O'Brien. He told me that the usual formula he used as a watchword, when some fugitive declared himself a Catholic, was the first of those two Latin phrases: that of the priest, *Introibo ad altare Dei*, to which the faithful must know how to respond. Whoever responded to it promptly, and there had already been many, were welcomed and rescued. Whoever, on the other hand, who had not known how to respond, were communist spies, and were sent back to the sender."

"Who will still be able to assert that liturgical Latin is of no use at all?" asked Pius XIV.

24

Every Promise is a Debt

As every Friday afternoon, the Pope performed the pious exercise of the Stations of the Cross in the Laurini Fathers' small chapel in preparation for his weekly Confession. He finished at around three o'clock, when his confessor, Father Gregory, still only a cardinal *in pectore*, punctually arrived.

After Confession, Father Gregory told him, "Even a pope is not exempt from fulfilling his promises."

"Are you so keen on becoming a cardinal?" the Pope asked him.

"There is no hurry for that. A young man like me should not be afraid to die before he gets there. I'm talking about the promise you made in my presence to Sister Rosa, the director of the Santi Cosma e Damiano clinic. Have you forgotten that?"

"Not at all! Now get something hot or cold, and then I'll tell you something about that nun."

Shortly afterwards the Pope spoke with Camillo, who laid out the simplest and most practical plan to fulfill the promise.

"Notifying the sacristan of the chapel of the Blessed Sacrament too early is not convenient. It would shake up half the Vatican, we would have inconvenient protests, and people would be upset. Yes, the sacristan will be notified, but at the appropriate time. He won't know until a few minutes before the event. We have to do it like this. You will put on the sacred vestments for the Holy Mass in the private chapel of your former apartment, which is always at your disposal. I will personally have them ready for you, as we have done since the first Mass of yours after your election. Then I will get the ushers and valets ready. Only at that point will I announce that the Pope is about to enter the Chapel of the Most Holy in St. Peter's Basilica. They will be speechless, especially at seeing you with the sacred vestments on. But who will dare say anything negative? Certainly not the sacristan. Oh, he will have the most wonderful surprise of his whole life with this all! I can just see it, the look on his face! And then he will run around lighting the chandeliers, and then the candles, and then he'll take away the forty-pound Bible and put the most beautiful missal on the lectern and fill the largest pyx. In fact, I think Your Holiness will want to put the Blessed Sacrament back in His dwelling, in that beautiful Bernini Tabernacle, which has been empty and deserted for so long! You enter that beautiful chapel, as big as a church, all lit-up and gold. You notice that the Tabernacle of God is empty. You feel that there is no one there waiting for you. You feel alone. And you come out feeling so sad."

"The large pyx?" asked the Pope, "I think one that is so large will suffice. It will also be more manageable. Besides the clinic director and the donor of the chalice, I don't think many other people will come."

"Your Holiness," Camillo said in turn, "Better that consecrated particles should be left over than that they should be lacking unless Your Holiness feels like multiplying them as needed and at the appropriate time. There are already four of us coming: me, the sacristan, the clinic nun, and the benefactress. And don't you think, Your Holiness, that each of us will invite a few close friends to your Mass? I suppose you won't mind!"

The Pope returned to Father Gregory, and told him what to report to the clinic director:

"Tomorrow morning, a little early, at seven in the Chapel of the Blessed Sacrament, in St. Peter's Basilica."

The next morning, the Pope arrived already vested for Mass in the sacristy of the Chapel of the Blessed Sacrament and waited until Camillo and the sacristan had put on the cassock and surplice. He then had to wait for the ringing at seven o'clock. As soon as the sacristy pendulum had struck the seventh chime, the sacristan solemnly commanded:

"*Reverentia cruci! Procedamus!*" He opened the door to the chapel, and the Pope entered it, his eyes downcast, collected, and seeing nothing. But he had the definite impression that the chapel was full—of angels—perhaps. The day was Saturday, the date July 2, the feast of the Visitation of the Blessed Virgin Mary to St. Elizabeth, according to the traditional calendar of the Catholic Church. The missal was open, printed in such large type that even from the balustrade one could easily read the *Introit: Salve, sancta Parens,* by Celius Sedulius, a fifth century Latin poet, an *Introit* that was later adorned with the well-known Gregorian melody. Pius XIV began:

"*In nomine Patris... Introibo ad altare Dei...*"

He was so surprised at what happened next that for a few moments he could not continue. His subdued *Introibo ad altare Dei* had been answered by a concordant, devout, and sonorous chorus of a thousand voices. The chapel was packed to overflowing with the faithful and even beyond the gates, in the nave of the basilica. So many of the faithful had thronged to hear the Pope's Mass, the Mass of which they had been abruptly deprived without their knowledge, against all their expectations, and without faculty of appeal; the Mass that since a sad Sunday of Advent they had come to love even more, the Mass of the Apostles, the Mass of all time. The sacristan had noticed the crowd, but had not wanted to notify the Pope, for fear that he would change the program. And now, all happy, he returned to the sacristy to fill more pyxes.

Starting from the day on which the celebration of what many had called the true Mass had ceased, a sincere religious sister from the Santi Cosma e Damiano clinic began telephoning the donor of the chalice, and a few other people whom she knew with mournful hearts. She telephoned only a few because she was aware of the delicate nature of the matter. She knew that great caution was needed. But among those few were other religious sisters who in turn issued confidential invitations here and there. Meanwhile, the lady of the chalice communicated the news to some supportive people who since the time of the Second Vatican Council were associated with the defense of the traditional liturgy. Among those was a printer who wanted to know which Mass the Pope would celebrate.

"The Feast of the Visitation of the Blessed Virgin Mary. That one!" the chalice lady assured him over the phone.

"But are you certain?"

"Totally certain!"

"But it no longer appears in the reformed calendar!"

But in that of Pius XIV it is still there!"

In fact, she only imagined it as such. She was of such temperament, however, that she would not hesitate to approach the Pope, even at the foot of the altar, to beg him to celebrate that very Mass there.

"And how many will there be?" asked that printer again.

"One thousand!" the lady answered in a tone that dispelled all doubt.

The printer and some of his family members worked the whole night. The next morning, at half past six he and his people were already by the gate with two thousand copies still smelling of ink, with the Mass of the Visitation, in Latin and the vernacular, in two columns side by side and error-free. He distributed them all. He wanted nothing. He was happy!

After finishing the Confession at the foot of the altar, the Pope went up to the altar, kissed its table, stood *in cornu epistulae*, and was about to pronounce the first three words of the *Introit*, when he felt as if swept away by a wave, a mighty, sonorous wave, which descended majestically from the choir loft, invaded, and immediately submerged the entire enormous chapel, and then, more moderately, the naves of St. Peter's Basilica.

Salve, sancta Parens, enixa puerpem regem sang thirty voices in beautiful Gregorian. They were lively yet devout. *Qui caelum terramque regit in saecula saeculorum.* Who were they? Who had opened the door of the chancel and organ to them?

The lady of the chalice had also given notice of the Pope's Mass to a baritone from the Sistine Chapel. The latter had made it his duty to immediately transmit the happy announcement to two of his friends, two brothers, a tenor and a bass of the Lateran Chapel. Each had relayed the news, the former to a tenor of the Giulia Chapel, and the latter to the archivist of the Association of St. Cecilia, who was an ultra-deep bass. Calling each other back that same evening, they made their schedule:

"There are five of us, and so we will be able to perform at least two polyphonic motets properly, one at the *Introit* and the other at the *Communio*. As for the chancel key, I know how to do it!" concluded the archivist, who would bring the scores and act as both organist and baton master. But then by the morning of the Mass the voices had grown to about thirty. All of the singers knew each other very well. There weren't enough copies of the hymns to go around. Singing without music was neither prudent nor dignified. As the prudent and responsible chapel master that he felt he was at that unforeseen juncture, the archivist started distributing the copies of the *Liber usualis*. He had located them nearby in a closet under a nice layer of dust. As a lover of classical polyphony, he revered Gregorian music as its legitimate mother, and therefore did not mind in the least having to change his schedule that morning.

"Hurry, hurry. The Mass has already begun." He ordered the singers, "Page one thousand nine hundred and ninety-one. Let's all start together: *la-do-re-mi-re*." He hummed to give the intonation. "Ready?" and gave the sign to begin. From the choir arose in unison the majestic *Salve, sancta Parens*. Celio Sedulio, the fifth-century composer, who had heard it sung and re-sung an innumerable number of times, was prompted to look down from heaven. The singing made the sacristan's head rise up towards the choir: He had let five, five in number, pass by, so where had this army of singers originated?

After the Gospel of the Magnificat, the Pope stood for a moment, hesitating about whether or not to give a short homily. It had not occurred to him before. He could have told them a little about what he had considered during that morning's meditation. He could have told them of his visits to En-Karem, to the house of Zechariah, in a hilly area because it was in Judea. The house was at the bottom of a little valley that descends westward from Jerusalem. That was the exact place where Our Lady let burst forth from her whole being the canticle which from the day of the Annunciation resounded in her heart:

"*Tegaddél nafshi et Yahwéh! Magnificat anima mea Dominum!*"

Along the road from Nazareth to En-Karem, whenever that exclamation escaped her lips, St. Joseph would turn toward her. But he would immediately and demurely lower his gaze from beholding all that light. Once in Jerusalem, he did not want to linger. St. Joseph had never seen her hurried before. They hurried together on their donkeys down the charming little valley for almost an hour and then crossed it. They passed by the spring that gives its name to the village, the Generous Spring. They went up the southern side of the valley for a few minutes, and entered one of Zechariah's houses. And Mary turned to Elizabeth and greeted her. At Mary's greeting, Elizabeth felt the child she was nourishing in her womb jump with joy. Invested by the Holy Spirit, she exclaimed with a sonorous voice:

"Blessed are you, among all women, and blessed is the fruit of your womb! How is it that I have this fortune? That the mother of my Lord should come to me! I have understood it very well, because at your greeting, my child's joy flows forth from my womb. Yes, truly blessed, for you did not hesitate to believe that everything that God told you would be fulfilled!"

Mary then let her canticle flow from her own heart:

"Tegaddél nafshi et Yahwéh!"

And Mary said: "My soul doth magnify the Lord. And my spirit hath rejoiced in God my Saviour. Because he hath regarded the humility of his handmaid; for behold from henceforth all generations shall call me blessed."[1]

The Pope saw himself again on his way from Bethlehem to En-Karem by the Virgin's Way. It was stony, dusty, winding, and all ups and downs. He was on pilgrimage, on foot, with his Rosary in hand. He saw himself descending from the ridge of the hill, by the rough and uneven path, which forced him to make big steps and even jumps. He was among patches of flowering broom, making his way toward the Church of the Magnificat, which overlooks the nearby Church of the Benedictus just beyond the spring. He arrived again to celebrate Mass, the same Mass as that day, the Mass of the Visitation, in the church. The Franciscans had rebuilt it with care and love. They were the faithful custodians of the Holy Land. The church was built on a Crusader church, and they had built theirs on a Byzantine one. The Byzantines in turn had built theirs on the house of Zechariah.

In the church, which was filled with frescoes and color, but almost always deserted with the sharply falling number of pilgrims, he saw again two priests, one old, one young, who had come from afar, from northern Europe, to fulfill their vow, which was to sing the *Magnificat* right there, where it had been sung the first time by Our Lady herself. Father Pius had joined in their singing, a little out of tune—for they were not singers—but all done with faith and joy!

---

1   Lk. 1:46-48.

Of course! Something to say to all the faithful, who at that moment crowded the Blessed Sacrament chapel. They had been attracted there, unbeknownst to each other, as if by an irresistible call, to that papal Mass. But of course! He would find something to say to them that was in his heart and mind. He no longer had any doubt. He decided for the affirmative. He turned to them, and looked at them, and they all looked back at him. He opened his mouth to speak, but a sob came out. It was a contagious sob. The whole chapel was filled with quiet and poorly-restrained sobs. They continued, in a moderate and demure but irrepressible crescendo, until some good angel inspired St. Cecilia's organist to start working the organ keyboard. The first notes of the Gregorian Creed III spread throughout the chapel, and the alternate singing of the Creed gave way to the expression of feelings that cooled the tears.

Among those gathered were many religious sisters who knew the responses and how to sing. But there were also many mothers, with their little children who had been woken up early that morning. The children did not know how to answer or sing. They had never seen or heard anything like that, but it seemed to them as if they were in Heaven for the first time.

Many priests, young and old, were also there. Just before Communion, some of them donned their surplices and stoles and organized themselves for the distribution of Communion. The sacristan had arranged about ten pyxes on the altar before the Offertory. These were all that he could find. Almost all attendees took Communion. In a few minutes all the communicants were able to approach and kneel at the balustrade to receive the Most Holy Eucharist there. Everything happened in an orderly manner. The singing of the *Adoro Te, devote* died out just as the Pope finished with the last communicants.

He recognized the last communicant. It was the little sister. She had stayed last on purpose, because she felt it to be a very special act of faith and piety to receive the Eucharistic

Jesus from the hands of His vicar; and then it also seemed to her that she had deserved that privilege, if not actually being entitled to it by virtue of the Pope's promise.

Yes, the Pope recognized her, although she was not dressed in white, but all in black. Since there were no more than three particles in the pyx, he laid all three on that sister's lips. True, it was not a strictly liturgical gesture, but it seemed to him that this time the Lord had arranged things this way in order to testify His approval to the director of the Santi Cosma e Damiano clinic, who, with her humble request, had given occasion to that unexpected, spontaneous manifestation of such intense and devout faith. To the faithful who still lingered in the chapel a voice announced:

"For the seven o'clock Mass, to be celebrated in this chapel by the Holy Father, it will be useful for the faithful to bring the bilingual Missal, which is the traditional Missal."

Thus many Missals that had long remained venerated but unused, that had been placed in the most sacred part of the homes of so many families, by the statue of Our Lady, or at the foot of the Crucifix, were once again to be devoutly leafed through by so many faithful, and then by their heirs.

25

"Principiis Obsta!"

THE REVERBERATION OF THE CELebration, though the celebration had been so discreet, spread rapidly, and with an impressive crescendo. From the Vatican, it reached the various ecclesiastical dicasteries of Rome. From Rome, it reached the four cardinal points of the *orbe terracqueo*, including all of the most renowned prelates. In the face of such fundamentalist and retrograde audacity, their faces turned pale with holy disdain.

The transitional Pope had dared to celebrate, and in public no less, the pre-Reformation Mass, the Mass of earlier times, the Mass as it had been celebrated by St. Clement in Rome and then in exile in the Chersonese; as it had been celebrated by St. Irenaeus in Smyrna, and then spread by him on mission among the Celts of Gaul; the Mass as it had been celebrated by the holy doctors Augustine and Jerome in Asia and Africa; the Mass that St. Leo the Great celebrated three times at Christmas; the Mass that St. Gregory the Great adorned with new hymns, just as St. Ambrose had already done; the Mass as it had been spread among the pagan converts of Ireland, England, and Germany by the apostles Augustine and Patrick, and then by the holy martyr Boniface; that Mass as it had been loved, desired and devoutly celebrated by Saints Bernard and Bonaventure, and enriched with immortal canticles by St. Thomas Aquinas; that Mass which had inspired a hundred polyphonies, among them Pier Luigi da Palestrina's

Missa brevis, and Ludwig Beethoven's *Missa solemnis*; that Mass that Christopher Columbus had spread to the far West, and St. Francis Xavier to the farthest East; the Mass for which John Fisher, bishop of Rochester, whose own blood had turned the cardinal's purple purple, and for which the English Martyrs had died by tens, hundreds, even thousands; the Mass of the ecstasies of St. Catherine of Siena and St. Teresa of Avila; the Mass of St. John of the Cross and St. Margaret Mary Alacoque; in short, the Mass of all the Saints, Martyrs, Confessors, and holy Virgins hitherto canonized.

How horrible! How scandalous! That little Pope had dared so much!

Action had to be taken. Immediately. *Principiis obsta!*[1] Any delay could allow the defeated traditionalists to feel a little life, to breathe again, to raise their heads. Any delay could jeopardize the process and progress that the perennial dogmatic renewal of the last non-dogmatic Council considered to be irresistible and irreversible.

Thus, from the four cardinal points of the globe, by the fastest way—for there was no need to spare any expenses!—following a whole series of dramatic intercontinental phone calls, the most zealous and decisive prelates gathered in Rome, determined to save humanity. None were missing. The big three were there, inevitably first and foremost Cardinal Stolzkamm, who was unanimously recognized as the indispensable leader. Other prelates who were present included those who had been proposed for the cardinalate by the cardinal Camerlengo to the last Pope and left *in pectore*. Then there were the very many who, though somewhat less determined, would certainly become more determined by the decisiveness of the others.

---

[1] Proverb about the crucial resistance or cooperation at the initial moment: "resist/stand firm at the beginnings!" It is usually followed by "look to the end"/ "medicine is offered too late."

They were there to work out a contingency plan. Its implementation would be simple and quick and put things back on track, or would get the stubborn sclerotic pope out of the way. The three arrived punctually and simultaneously to the meeting to elaborate their strategy, at the headquarters of the Academy of St. Thomas. The *primus inter pares* of the triad urgently notified the doorman and janitor:

"Open the small room for us immediately!" And then, turning to the other two, he explained, "It is more suitable for the work we have ahead of us."

"You cannot have either the small or big one!" they heard the fat man reply. "Orders are orders."

"Whose orders?" Quira, the *primus inter pares* of the trio, asked, astonished.

"Orders from those who can give them to me and also to their Excellencies," the fat man replied. Quira thought he understood. He was sure he had the key to all the doors of the *Urbe* in his pocket as he had been to Rome many times. He immediately made use of it. He drew from his pocket a pad of travelers' checks and wrote on one of those cards:

"Mr. Giorgio Cicibello, twenty-five dollars." He signed and laid it on the table in front of the doorman under the eyes of Mr. Giorgio Cicibello. Indeed, Quira thought that he and his people would need that little room again and again, and so he arranged to give the keeper a good tip in advance, once and for all. Faced with such an *argumentum ad crumenam*,[2] the good janitor would certainly have had nothing more to object to nor any contrary orders to execute. Instead, Mr. Giorgio Cicibello looked at the check with supreme contempt, and then with no less contempt spat on it. Then to their Excellencies he ordered:

"Eccellentissimi, turn around!"

"But...But...But..." stammered the three.

---

2 "argument aimed at money/purse, i.e., bribes or other such pecuniary expediency.

But Giorgio Cicibello repeated, "But nothing!" in such a tone and gesture that their Excellencies could do nothing but change the program. Quira, very sensitive to the voice of duty, felt it was now his duty to raise the morale of his collaborators. He tried to fulfill this duty as soon as possible and in the best possible way.

"Let's meet in a small lounge in my hotel," he told the other two. "It will be a bit expensive, but no expense should be spared. It's better that way! Follow me!" he enjoined, in the electrifying tone of the great mercenary leaders of the good old days. Their three taxis followed one after the other, through Rome's streets, to Quira's hotel.

As the first thing, Quira telephoned everyone, all the minor conspirators, whom he had already invited to cancel the invitations with vague and pedestrian excuses. He advised them of his availability there, at his hotel, at any hour, day or night. They were not to hesitate to wake him up even in the middle of the night. The urgency of the matter could not tolerate any hesitation, delay, or further consideration. He got down to work, like a military strategist before the most decisive battle. He adopted an attitude of extreme confidence although in his heart he felt something was wrong. Wasn't the 'about-face!' and the contemptible spit on the check an unimaginable, inconceivable, and unbelievable sign of the times? A sign that the wind was changing direction?

How was it that the fat man, who on other occasions had always found an inventive way to display the tremendous work that certain gatherings caused him, who had been able to think up ever new and fresh ways of soliciting adequate financial reward, how was it that he had refused, and in that way! A windfall of twenty-five dollars?

Mr. Giorgio Cicibello had been one of the faithful who had attended the Mass of the Scandal, on the day of the Pope's Visitation. It had been so many years since he had gone to Mass, since he had set foot in Church! He had solemnly sworn to himself, one when, in the middle of the church, in the middle of the celebration, when he had already been completely stunned by the loudspeakers, incessant chatter, sharp din of the guitars and drums of the new circus liturgy, he could no longer resist, and had shouted, "Clowns, clowns, clowns!" before running out.

But on that July 2 morning, just before seven o'clock, he had the good mechanic from across the street drive him to St. Peter's. He spotted a white-haired priest in a black robe on his knees at the balustrade waiting for Mass and begged the priest to hear his confession. This gave him comfort. He felt a knot in his throat throughout the entire Mass. This, however, did not prevent him from devoutly receiving Holy Communion. He had made the resolution to fight by the Pope's side, the battle that Pius XIV had begun at the Academy and had carried on with that Mass. He always learned certain things, he knew them all better than Quira and his shoe-shiners did. And he had walked home, as if flying, on the wings of hope and grace. He felt light, so light, he who, even then, though still fasting since midnight nevertheless weighed about one hundred kilograms.

In that quiet little salon, the three main conspirators discussed things for half an hour or more. The more they talked, the more problems they found needed to be addressed, not least because the definition of their scheme's purpose was itself a scheme, one that was far from easy to prepare. It seemed to them that they were heading into thicker and thicker darkness when the arrival of Consalve was announced to them. They hailed this arrival as they would the arrival of the sun. Consalve would bring them light and health. Yes, it was divine Providence that had provided the maternal gestures of giving Consalve such a fateful surname and preventing the same from returning to the diocese immediately after the papal audiences. He was thus able to brief his colleagues on many things of vital importance. The first thing was that he had found Pius

XIV set in his ways and closed off as only an incurable arteriosclerotic can be.

"What did I say?" Quira exclaimed triumphantly. "These are all the symptoms of a chronic, progressive, and irreversible atherosclerosis that results in insufficient blood supply to the meninges due to the obliteration of the lumen of the capillaries that need to detoxify them with a constant and well-dosed blood flow and reflux. The result, in the affected subject, is a pathological mental imbalance, close to senile dementia."

The others, faced with enough science as to outcompete Hippocrates and Galen, could only nod their heads energetically, and soon the nodding became words:

"He has demonstrated it spectacularly! Only those who have lost much of their intellect can act as this Pope has." So deemed Monsignor Arras, while Monsignor Speakering maintained his golden and eloquent silence even then.

"Pope?" Consalve asked before answering his own question. "Pope, yes and no, my dear Excellencies! After the second and last papal audience, I went immediately to the cardinal Camerlengo, who is a great man, a man of extraordinary stature. He tried to protect himself, out of diplomatic habit, of course! But he had to agree with me that he had proposed to the late Pontiff, of holy memory, a number of prelates for the cardinalate. There is no doubt that we are all on that list, all four of us, and with a few others of ours. Well, the cardinal Camerlengo confided to me that he had been to Pius XIV to let him know that in the conclave he had been elected under certain conditions, and that not fulfilling these..."

"...He *ipso facto* ceases to be the legitimate Pope, the See remains vacant, the Camerlengo gets together the conclave, and the new Pope is elected, and then acts first to complete the College of Cardinals," Quira continued.

"Well, actually, the Camerlengo, by diplomacy, you mean! He was not so explicit about it. According to the Camerlengo, based on canon law, Pius XIV would be pope. He had been to him with the purpose of telling him that he was willing to resign if..."

"...the Pope himself did not resign!"

"What if he doesn't resign?"

"The answer to this question is certainly to be found, based on canon law..."

"Right, right!" shouted Quira in annoyance, "But by now it would be time to have messed up all this post-Constantinian legalism, which has nipped in the bud the development predicted to the mustard seed!"

"Law, law, Your Excellency! There was a certain development of the mustard seed even after Constantine, so that the Church, from Palestine, also reached your country, across the oceans. And then without a core, I say a well-enucleated core, of canon law, what right could you claim over your diocese and in the universal Church? That of speaking over others, of insisting more strongly than others, of maneuvering more skillfully than others—but you see the consequences. Your Excellency?"

"Unfortunately!" Quira sighed, calming down somewhat. "A nucleus, a well-enucleated core, of canon law..."

"Well, the solution is there!" Consalve continued. "It may be old, because it goes back to the scholastic theologians of centuries gone by, but it is still valid. We must not, by virtue of the canon of cosmic progress, make *tabula rasa* even of the part of the past that can be useful to us in the present for future progress. Precisely because it is connected with future progress necessarily, it still remains necessarily valid. Discretion, Your Excellencies! Well, there it is, the solution: *Papa haereticus deponendus est*![3] Some people will be sorry to hear the word 'heresy', and even I, in the past, had the idea of replacing that adjective, *haereticus*, with a more modern adjective now that today certain heresies of times gone by have become truths

---

3   "a heretic pope is to be deposed!"

of faith or almost. But any other adjective that I could trace back does not adapt to the existential situation determined with the election of Pius XIV, and therefore we must leave that aphorism as it is: *Papa haereticus deponendus est!*"

"It is now a matter of finding the charges, of making a separate one," Quira observed. But Consalve smiled, as about something that was not only already thought of, but already well and truly carried out.

"Excellency, I know what to do, but I don't want to anticipate anything. Everything in its own time. Now you, too, get moving, find all the charges you know and others you can find out about, and then we will meet at the Camerlengo's, in full force and... and one thing will lead to another."

"One thing will lead to another!" repeated the other three in dismay. All of them were full of new hope and a little bit of the beer they had drunk during the fiery session, and each went their separate ways.

26

Father Medina and his Page

Cardinal Stolzkamm did not attend the meeting, apologizing in rather dry terms. Father Medina had also not gone because at the exact same time he had an audience with the Pope himself. He had asked for it, indeed demanded it. The Pope had no objection to granting it. He would thus have had the pleasure of meeting for the first time this father who had a truly exceptional curriculum vitae.

While he had been entrusted with liturgical reform, various prelates had succeeded one another at the high commands of the dicastery of the sacred liturgy itself. Several of his collaborators, even prominent ones, had been removed. But he had always stood his ground. He had not prevented the Pope from endorsing an extremely important document that contained Luther's definition of the Mass, which the Council of Trent had declared heretical. This declaration had been an obvious error. Only a fuller understanding of the cause would allow apologists to show that he had not actually pledged the Pope's authority. He had assured everyone that, thanks to the grand reform, which was a true creation of a whole new liturgy out of nothing, the Church would welcome back the dissenters and convert the pagans. Yet he had disappointed the expectations of bishops, irritated pastors, and embittered the faithful. He had allowed every sacred thing to be profaned and the churches to decline tremendously. Despite all that, he remained there in his place longer than any other. After his ouster, he had regained it in one bold move. Now, if he descended from that throne, it was only to go to the audience of Pius XIV, which was solicited, indeed demanded.

He had warned that he would come to this audience accompanied by one of his associates, and the Pope made no complaint whatsoever. In turn, Pius XIV welcomed him in the presence of Wong. He was keen that Wong be present at the audience, which would certainly be demanding and important. The Monsignor had not yet been able to return to his own diocese. The Pope had begged him to stay in Rome a little longer. He had good reasons. Both to lighten his expenses and make it easier for him to enter the Vatican, the Pope had gotten Father Laurini to make available to the Monsignor a small room in their order's house within the Vatican itself.

And Father Medina began. He was not the sort to lose himself in compliments. Even if required to do so, he would not have been constitutionally capable of making any. In addition to everything else, he was a graduate in psychology. He was very certain that he was one of the rare experts in humanity. He—yes, he!—had made people dance! People were the keyboard and he a skilled organist. He always knew how to bring out the chords, but also the dissonances that he wanted. He had only seen Pius XIV in photographs. But to him, a born physiognomist, the photos said it all.

He was authorized immediately to the Pope's presence. This meant authorization into the magnificent hall and ancient office without waiting in the reception room, because the magnificent hall was where the Pope had wanted to receive him. As soon as he was admitted into the presence of the thin, little old man with such an insignificant presence, with his little goat's stubble and half-closed, seemingly half-asleep eyes, with his hands joined like a novice's as he sat on the edge of an enormous chair as if afraid of spoiling what was not his and as if he was ready to spring to attention at the first command of

Father Medina and his Page

the last to arrive—well, as soon as he arrived in the presence of Pius XIV—Father Medina knew that he was going to win him over. His analysis of the photos had been perfect, which reassured him. On the trip over, in fact, his hesitation had led to his ceaseless overthinking and gnawing anxiety. Father Medina began, mixing a dignified calm with the confidence of an experienced cat playing with a mouse.

"The charge entrusted to me by the People of God," he said, "imposes on me the duty to remind Your Holiness that every gesture, every word of Your Holiness, no matter how secret, is proclaimed on the rooftops: *Quod in aurem locuti estis in cubiculis, praedicabitur in tectis*,[1] to quote Luke. I do not mean to say that the pre-Reformation Mass is *radicitus invalida*,[2] but it is certainly *graviter illicita*[3] whenever it hinders the progress of the reform."

From the way he pronounced the word *reform*, it could be safely inferred that he always wrote the word with a capital letter. He continued, "All the bishops have stopped it, that Mass, which is anachronistic and annoying in so many ways. One can count on the fingers of one hand the bishops who have not rejected it. All the elderly faithful have thereby been freed from it, and can breathe new air. All the young faithful, the future of humanity,—he spoke the word *humanity* with the same emphasis with which he spoke the word *reform*—have never known it. They would laugh at it or be so shocked by it as to be traumatized in their faith. The unity of the faithful demands the unity of the Mass. Respect for this unity is most binding on those who are in the highest positions. It therefore binds the Pope most of all. He is consequently obliged to defend it *et quidem sub*

---

[1] "That which you have spoken in the ear in the chambers, shall be preached on the housetops." (Lk. 12:3)
[2] "Invalid at its roots."
[3] "completely (at the roots) invalid," "gravely illicit"—moral theology terms for sacramental validity.

gravi."[4] He pronounced this *sub gravi* with the same gravity with which a judge pronounces a verdict of a final and unappealable death sentence.

"*Et quidem sub gravi!*"[5] repeated as a faithful echo Father Viso, Father Medina's companion, though in a soft and squeaky voice. The Pope closed his eyes and smoothed his goatee. He then reopened them and turned them to Wong with a questioning look. Father Medina, being a skilled psychologist, clearly saw in this the last half-hearted look of someone who, hit by a blow to the head, is about to collapse to the ground. Wong gave a nice bow to Fathers Medina and Viso, smiled broadly, and then said:

"A few years ago, in a very authoritative ecclesiastical periodical appeared an article entitled 'Unity does not mean uniformity.' This article advocated a certain form of liturgical pluralism as the fatal and irreversible goal of the ongoing liturgical reform. The author of that article was a certain Ramiro Medina. Was that another Ramiro Medina or was it you?"

Father Medina felt a jolt of surprise, but quickly recovered. "Those were different times. Pluralism was necessary back then to make way for the redoing of the liturgy. One could not, from the beginning, totally substitute the new for the old. We had to proceed in stages: first move a comma, then change an adjective, then replace a formula, then modify a rite. All this gradualness and prudence was necessary to destroy *sensim sine sensu*[6] the taboo of the intangibility of the ancient liturgy so that we could bring about the state of psychological fusion which would enable the remake of the entire liturgy. So yes, the concept of the liturgy of the Second Vatican Council is radically different from that of earlier times. Therefore, an *ex nihilo* creation of a whole new liturgy was urgently needed.

---

4 "And indeed under heavy weight."
5 "and certainly under [pain of] grave [sin]"
6 Commonly used phrase for "imperceptibility" or "little by little," without noticing or sensing it.

Father Medina and his Page

This was a huge undertaking, one that would make anyone who did not have our determination tremble all over. Between the point of departure, uniformity in the old, and the point of arrival, uniformity in the new, a period of pluralistic transition had to be tolerated, in which the old and the new would coexist *ad tempus*.[7]"

"You've answered with such extreme clarity," Wong said approvingly.

Hearing the unexpected praise, Father Medina could not suppress his pleasure. He thought to himself, "I am getting back on track. Just a little bit more, and then, at the first wrong move, I'll throw a left to knock him out of the ring." Boxing was his favorite recreation.

"Yes, you answered very clearly," Wong repeated, "condensing into a few sentences what others would not have been able to express even in long speeches. Would you allow me to give a brief recapitulation?" Increasingly pleased, Father Medina nodded his agreement.

"First: unity in the faith, that is, in the *lex credendi*, requires unity in the liturgy, that is, in the *lex orandi*."

Father Medina nodded again.

"Second, unity in the *lex orandi* demands uniformity in the *lex orandi* itself. There is therefore one Mass, which is identical for all and which means that any other Mass is illicit, *et quidem per se sub gravi*, except for special extenuating circumstances."

For the third time, Father Medina nodded. He couldn't believe his ears. He had won! What an easy victory!

Wong continued: "Third, this uniformity was always your goal, from the beginning, even when you had to tolerate non-uniformity—pluralism." Father Medina was about to nod yes for the fourth time, but Wong raised his hand as if to say, "Let me finish!" before continuing: "You aimed at uniformity, even when you had to tolerate, introduce, and advocate

---

7 "For a while."

pluralism, and you had to demonstrate that this pluralism was a necessary and irreversible goal of liturgical reform."

Father Medina began to wonder what the hell was on the mind of the very kind Chinese man standing in front of him and who, between a smile and a nice bow, continued:

"You, Reverend Father, thought that uniformity was necessary, and you aimed for this goal. And to achieve it, you wrote that it was not necessary, but that non-uniformity was necessary. You were demonstrating to everyone the opposite of what you really thought, and you were aiming at the opposite of what you were writing. Or am I wrong?"

To this question, which remained unanswered, the Pope looked at Father Medina, who finally understood why the Pope had allowed him to come to the audience accompanied by someone—to also be in the company of the damned Chinaman! He wanted to slam his fist on the desk that was just before him, jump to his feet, get close in on him and say, "I will see you again in Philippi, my handsome Chinaman," and leave, slamming the door. But he preferred to imitate Farinata degli Uberti in the city of Dis in Dante's *Inferno*. He did not move his neck, nor bend his ribs, as he held the Chinese cockerel in great displeasure.

He had convinced himself that he could no longer gain anything useful from the audience. But it had not been entirely useless, as he now had confirmation that the Pope was nothing other than the puppet that some prelates of the conclave had sought among a thousand. He also knew that the main papal puppet master was this Wong, who had rushed to Rome immediately after the conclave and was still there, in the way. And Wong appeared to him to be the most traditionalist of traditionalists, who was in addition benefiting from the great distance that separated him from the Roman dicastery of the sacred liturgy. A way had to be found to get him back to his home, and as soon as possible! Subverted by the hypnotic suggestions exerted on him by Wong's black, penetrating eyes, the Pope would be knocked out of the game at least in the second round, since this first one had gone badly. It was an audience of doom! What need was there now for more audiences? He would act from his office, from his plenipotentiary throne, making use of.... At this point Father Medina's lightning-fast reflections became somewhat confused, because at other times he had indeed had at his disposal the Vatican agency *Ecumenical Press* and the periodicals of the Universal Human Society. But now the former was dead. Would the latter publication, without the support of *Ecumenical Press*, have the means and persuasive effectiveness of past years?

"Enough, enough!" he ordered himself. "Now I must record exactly everything this fellow is blurting out. As happens to talkative and conceited people who think themselves clever, he will miss those two words, which will enable me to nail him down!" Having established this, he nodded to his companion, to say, "If you really want, then speak. I'm not saying another word."

Meanwhile, Wong continued his talk:

"Fourth, the Vatican II concept of liturgy is radically different from the concept the Church had before the Council. You affirmed this a moment ago, Reverend Father, when you repeated in other terms what you wrote in other times. It must then be agreed that the concept of the *lex credendi* of Vatican II is also radically different from the concept the Church had before this Council, given the relationship of necessary correspondence that exists between the *lex orandi*, the liturgy, and the *lex credendi*, the dogma. But won't your paternalism be mistaken in interpreting the liturgical Constitution of the Second Vatican Council in this way? In any case this interpretation coincides with your personal conviction. Now you know that anyone who admits that dogma can change radically is a heretic. Not only that, but this pastoral Vatican Council II wanted precisely to call itself pastoral because it did not intend to shift a single iota or a single peak of traditional dogmatic doctrine. So that assertion of yours, already written down, and now repeated here orally a moment ago, which is formally heretical, is totally unrelated to the conciliar declarations. Oh, there is no need to worry about that, dear Father! There is the objective formality of heresy. But subjective heresy depends on personal warning. I certainly do not intend to set myself up as a judge."

Medina reacted like a cat held down by a mountain lion. For his part, Father Viso wanted to intervene on Medina's behalf. Although nothing came to his mind, he expressed his desire to speak. But Wong, smiling kindly, spared him such a risky intervention that would have prompted only nonsense.

"Fifth, what was the liturgical reform?" Wong asked, before adding, "according to you, Father Reverend, the liturgical reform was nothing but restoration work. You also wrote this not too long ago."

Father Viso breathed. He had thought of something to add: "Sure, restoration, removal of duplication, and the return to the basics," he said all in one breath, as if he was reciting a lesson learned by heart without understanding even the punctuation.

"Well, dear Father!" Wong replied approvingly, "removal of duplication like the Offertory of the traditional Mass..."

"Exactly!" Father Viso interjected triumphantly again. "A crude anti-liturgical duplication because it offered the exact reality that would be offered again after the Consecration. It was, moreover, a rhetorical duplication. It was imploring the acceptance of an offer that is known to be necessarily accepted."

The Pope looked, almost amused, at Father Viso, as if to say to him, "What a good memory! You've learned the lesson so well!"

Interpreting the look as approval, Father Viso smugly turned to the Pope and said:

"Thank you, Your Holiness!" He actually did have a photographic memory of all the bulletins he had typed and retyped.

Wong, however, continued: "Dear Father, in the Offertory of the traditional Mass the intentions of the sacrifice are formulated, which could not be tolerated by the unbelievers, in homage to whom it was abolished, under the pretext that it was a duplication. Can you dispute this historical fact? Yes, several times the prayer is repeated so that the sacrifice is received graciously. Even Jesus in the Garden of Gethsemane repeated his offering for three hours, and always with the same formulas. The Offertory thus comes to have the character of a pre-consecration because no bread and wine is offered in it because it is the fruit of the earth, the vine, and human labor, but with the bread and wine already pre-consecrated symbols of the divine victim. Precisely because with this character of pre-consecration, the Offertory is an integral part of the sacrifice of the Mass. It is characterized as a sacrifice in a clear and unequivocal way. A Mass amputated of this can no longer be said to be intact. And, moreover, it is easily transformed into a symbolic supper.

"Duplications! In order to simplify the Mass, you have amputated an integral part of it, and then infused it with refrains, sometimes puerile, sometimes simply strange, and which you make everyone repeat *ad libitum*[8] to the point of boredom. And you call this the elimination of duplications? The return to the origins! Only if you, Reverend Father, heir to a cyclical apocatastasis[9] of the universe, can think that it is progress to return to the origins since with the passing of the last hour of the universal year, everything will start all over again."

Father Viso opened his eyes wide, and then energetically protested: "But no, Excellency! It is not the apocatastasis of Egypt!"

---

8 at one's "good pleasure," as it pleases for what is at the discretion of the one to whom it is directed.
9 Ἀποκατάστασις. It means "return" or "restoration." Origen (185–253) is the most famous exponent of this doctrine. He argued that all beings would ultimately be saved.

"And so how can you reconcile your proclaimed irreversible progress and rejuvenation with the return to the origins? These origins are certainly a little outdated? It's just that when it pleased you to impose something brand new and unprecedented to destroy the old, you spoke of rejuvenation; and when it pleased you to destroy some other part of that sacred liturgy, which organically grew and matured down the centuries through the work of so many doctors, pontiffs and saints... because the liturgy must be had in here, first of all. If it is not in here, you do not make it, but you undo it!" Wong said as he pointed to his heart.

"So when you preferred to hide both the adoration due to the most holy Eucharist and the Mass as a sacrifice behind a curtain of fog to give it the appearance of a symbolic dinner, and when you decided to drown the Holy Mass in an ocean of words, as Luther had planned, then you appealed to the simplicity of the origins.

"Even then, however, when you dug up ancient texts, you purged them of all dogmatic content that clashed with your modernism. A return to the origins as they historically were would contradict the dogmatic-liturgical development of so many centuries of the Church's life. This development was vivified by the Holy Spirit. Would an oak tree progress by returning to its beginning as an acorn? It wouldn't be able to do so.

"Yes, yours was a return to the origins, but not of the true Church of Our Lord Jesus Christ. It was a return to the origins of Luther's heresy. Didn't Luther say, 'It is necessary for the word to take over, and thereby destroy the Mass as a sacrifice'? For a religion of defrocked priests, such as early Protestantism was, there can be no sacrifice. A meal is enough. There can be no priesthood. A presider is enough."

Father Viso took a deep breath. He glanced timidly and questioningly at Father Medina. But he may as well have looked at an empty chair for Father Medina had melted into his.

Wong continued, serene and relentless and without a tone of reproach:

"Let us return to the fifth point. Father Medina wrote that the liturgical reform was a work of restoration, of peeling away. It had begun without anyone knowing precisely what would be found underneath once the crusts were removed. Instead, he knew at the outset that it was a revolution, thanks to which old rite would be replaced entirely by new rite, old formula entirely by new formula, old content entirely by new content, old liturgy entirely by new liturgies..."

At this point, the Pope turned to Wong and said:

"Your Excellency, let's stop here. Five points are enough for now."

Then he turned with a kind expression toward Father Medina and said:

"Think about these things, dear Father! Then, in a few days, if you can give me a hand, we will make a decree on the liturgy. For the title, I will make your term my own: *Restauratio*. Let me offer you the chance to repair so many faults, which you have partly been responsible for. I offer you the possibility to repair this as much as you can. You are obliged *et quidem sub gravi*. Don't you think so?"

The Pope pronounced this last expression with a smile, as if to soften it. However, to Medina, both the smile and the conciliatory words seemed mechanical and impersonal, as if imposed on a robot by its maker. The audience ended like that. In accompanying them toward the exit, Wong said to Medina:

"Reverend Father, if you want a record of this audience, we will get it for you later today. We recorded it. Our tape recorder, which is in that desk, is a bit bulky. But on the other hand, it is much more accurate than all the portable recorders, which are so small that they could be concealed very well even in a pocket of Father Viso's cassock. Anyway, this is good to know!"

The two liturgists walked in silence toward the cardinal Camerlengo's office. Father Medina grumbled something to himself. He needed to vent to someone, and that someone could only be Father Viso, whom he walked a step behind, and who occasionally looked timidly toward his director. The micro-recorder weighed so heavily on his heart in his left shirt pocket, although he was sure he had put it much lower down, in the large trouser pocket on the right.

"You can't do anything right! The only thing you can do is spoil everything! You always have your hand in your pocket playing with the tape recorder! If only I had never given it to you! Yes, it really took you to silence that bewitched Chinaman!"

"However," Father Viso dared respond, "however, I think he could easily be made to return to his country."

Father Medina looked at him with astonishment. What a wonderful idea he just thought up! "Of course!" added Father Viso. "A telegram telling him that his mother is sick would be enough."

Father Medina shook his head:

"She's sick in the other world! Who knows how many years she has been dead! Don't you know that those Asians look young, even when they are old geezers?" They entered the Camerlengo's office, followed by a very mean look from Father Viso, who, left there alone in the reception room, repeated:

"However, if I succeeded, he could no longer say to me, 'You aren't good for anything,'" and began pondering this.

27

Not Westernizing the Church?

THE MOST FORTUNATE ROMANS had already left the city for their holiday resorts. Many of the less fortunate spent their afternoons at the nearby beaches, Anzio, Nettuno, and the Maccarese Reclamation. Everyone else had to be content with the cool breeze blowing from the Tyrrhenian Sea, the Ponentino, and put up with the heat whenever the breeze didn't come. Someone even proposed to Pius XIV to move to Castel Gandolfo.

"With the signing of the Lateran Pacts, the popes resumed the ancient custom of spending the hotter months in the papal residence of Castel Gandolfo. When does Your Holiness plan to go there?"

"For now, I prefer to stay in Rome. The heat is good for us old people," the Pope replied. "Yes, later, we'll take a detour to Castel Gandolfo. I'll put it on the agenda."

However, he did accept the suggestion of a little more time on the daily walk in the Vatican gardens. On the same afternoon that someone suggested Castel Gandolfo, and while on his walk, he offered Wong a fresh opportunity to reveal his fine gifts of mind and heart, and to save himself the trouble of a conversation, perhaps even an argument, with Father Lesage.

Father Lesage was the *matamoros* of Latin. He sincerely and zealously fought the use of Latin, though certainly not because of the monotonous four Latin classes in his distant high school days, but only because he wanted to prevent non-Western

Catholics from westernization due to the use of Latin. The issue of Latin being taken away from Western Catholics had not ever crossed his mind.

Events in his life had made him a journalist, though he had never thought about why this had happened. He was neither cultured nor intelligent. He was, however, a fast writer with a witty though somewhat stumbling style. This style often bristled the reader with its shocking neologisms like the adjective, *matamoros*, which Father Lesage used with particular frequency. He strutted about with it, modestly considering it the happiest of his linguistic innovations. His lack of a metaphysical foundation or in-depth historical knowledge left him without a critical sense. Therefore, to the readers of the various periodicals, who paid handsomely for his articles, he could offer, with the warmth that only the certainty of fighting for the good cause can nourish in a sincere heart, the summary of only a limited aspect of a complex problem while ignoring all other parts. He therefore inevitably arrived at a solution that was very often completely wrong.

Although he was neither a bishop nor a religious superior, he had immediately obtained a papal audience. He gave the Pope a detailed description of his journalistic activities and ideological campaign. Modestly though correctly, he considered himself an important, not to say main, leader of this campaign.

He was still relatively young and attractive in appearance with a straightforward and stately manner. His brief and rare nervous outbursts took nothing away from this. These outbursts were totally understandable if one kept in mind that for a long time he had gone from tranquilizers to sleeping pills, and from sleeping pills to hypnotics, in order to get some sleep. All that remained was to go from hypnotics to narcotics, a step which, he sometimes said to himself, and with all sincerity, he would by no means take. He was a man to keep even the promises he made to himself.

For a long time, the journalist had had no break from his fevered activity, with the attendant shifts of place, travels and interviews, not even a single day's respite. For a long time, the urgency to write and write and write would have caused him to lose the ability to read, if it had not been maintained by so many newspapers and periodicals, all coming from the pens of writers far inferior to him. Even this judgment, which he could not help but make — because facts are facts — infused a heartfelt sense of superiority and confidence which spurred him on in his very demanding and exhausting career.

Father Lesage considered himself most fortunate to have obtained such a fresh and ornate audience. He considered himself even more fortunate when he saw that he had been admitted into the audience in the company, perhaps serendipitous, he thought, of Wong. Wong, as a genuine Asian in the flesh, was a sure ally and patron of his thesis. Indeed, he had promised himself that he would succeed in inducing the Pope to utter a few words in favor of his thesis. He would need no more than that to obtain a whole series of informative and exciting articles from the Holy Father. And by now he was sure of his facts. Contradictory rumors that were whispered in certain journalistic circles were certainly without any serious foundation, as so often happened. In any case, with those two words, the Holy Father would entirely rehabilitate himself, if there was any need, in the eyes of Father Lesage and many lesser journalists.

Father Lesage also had a beautiful, thundering voice with clear, accurate pronunciation and a harsh, but compelling directness. In short, he spoke as he wrote. This made him enchanting to listen to. He himself often could not escape this enchantment, and as he spoke, one could say that he was smugly listening to himself. At that precise moment, and in the shade of the flowery and fragrant little kiosk in the Vatican gardens, Father Lesage was making his beautiful voice resonate. He asked Wong a rhetorical question, as the answer was completely obvious:

"Would it please Your Excellency if Western missionaries westernized the sacred buildings of your country, if they built churches in the Far East in the style of, for example, Holy Trinity of the Mountains?"

"Would Your Paternity be pleased," Wong asked him in turn, "if, in order not to orientalize the citizens of Rome or let's say even of Paris, Buddhist missionaries were to build in Rome or Paris their pagodas in the style of St. Trinità dei Monti or in the style of your Eglise de la Madeleine? Would this not be a kind of deceptive mimicry? Who told you that our Asian peoples are happy to enter churches identical to the pagodas of their ancient and repudiated superstitions? Or to worship statues of the Immaculata, bearing the effigy of some great goddess, and adorned with the symbols of her vices? We want Our Lady depicted as she was and is historically. We want to be Western in everything Western that Jesus wanted His Church to be."

Wong smiled and bowed to Lesage, almost as if to apologize for giving an answer that differed from the expected and desired one, before continuing:

"That's right, dear Father Ive Lesage! Asians by natural birth, we are spiritually born again and want to be Westerners. Jesus wanted His Church to absorb and transfix the Western Greco-Roman civilization of His time. We, Asians by birth, want to be spiritually Roman, and spiritually we feel ourselves to be Romans of the Romanitas for which Our Lord is Roman. This then in a very special way in the matter of liturgy. Those who do not feel Roman will never be able to enter the inner sanctum of the sacredness of the liturgy. At the bottom of so many aberrations, not only in matters of liturgy, but also in matters of dogma and morals, lies too often the lack of Romanitas, and Romanitas is essentially Western."

"But tastes in the East are often different from ours, and people there have their own specific requirements," Father Lesage struggled to say as he tried to avoid looking like an ancient grammar school student. "Just think of the popular swallow's nests. Such exquisite delicacies!"

"I could tell you that Westerners who come to the East also like them very much, but I prefer to tell you what you say in the West: *De gouts et des couleurs il ne faut pas discuter*.[1] Now we do not speak of preferences, but of dispositions of the soul that are far deeper, and even inherent in human nature itself, and as such these are universal and perennial. Do you want an example of this? Do you know what is studied in music conservatories in the Far East? Carissimi, Scarlatti, Frescobaldi, Bach, Handel, Haydn, Mozart, Wagner, Beethoven, Chopin, Liszt, Gounod, Debussy. They try to westernize themselves a little, and at great cost! And do you know, Reverend Father, what music was awarded the first prize overall last year in Japan, that is, in the most eastern of Far Eastern countries? The most Western and Roman of music, Gregorian chant.

"I think that you, Reverend Father, the day on which you could start to find some time to study the subject well, you could then write a whole series of articles on Gregorian chant, as music par excellence, as universal and perennial music. Perennial because every time music wanted to return to interpretation without any pretenses, in the sincerest and most perfect way possible, with the noblest human feelings, it summarized the modes and rhythm that belongs to Gregorian chant. It did this spontaneously, almost reinventing itself behind the suggestions of nature.

"But also universal. I do not intend to give an exhaustive list of examples. This is certainly not the time or place. I will simply report to you what the tribal chiefs said about Monsignor

---

[1] "There is no arguing about matters of taste."

Jekune Amlak—it was he himself who confided it to me—when, in order not to Westernize them, he had given them permission, granted by Rome, to substitute local languages for Latin in church, and the local vocal and instrumental music for Gregorian and polyphonic chants for a Latin text. It was said that as soon as he dared to sound the language of their ancient blasphemies, and the drums of their ancient orgies, none of them came to church anymore. It was heard, from the mouth of the word-bearer of all the tribal chiefs of that region that there was only one language of their prayers, of their Mass, which was that of their baptism, Latin, and that there was only one music of their songs, Gregorian and the associated polyphonies. This comes from the tribal leaders in the heart of Black Africa! You have certainly read *Treasure Island*, by Robert Louis Stevenson."

Father Ive Lesage smiled, nodding.

Wong continued: "I do not know if you have also read by the same author *The Ancient Capital of the Pacific*. In this book, Stevenson describes a pilgrimage to California. His story is just right for us. He writes something like this: 'The Indians gathered in groups. Their multicolored clothes contrasted with their dark, melancholy faces. There, in the midst of a crowd of very non-religious tourists, you could see God served with moving attention, perhaps more so than in any temple existing under heaven. There was an Indian, about eighty years old, completely blind, who led the singing, while the other Indians made up the choir. Yet he knew the Gregorian chants so perfectly, and pronounced the Latin so correctly, that I could follow everything. I had never seen more vividly radiant faces than those of these Indian singers. This constituted for them not only an act of worship paid to God, not only an act that reminded them of better days, but also an act of culture in which all their learning in arts and letters was condensed and expressed.'

"I think I translated this page quite faithfully, because I know it by heart in English. I had to learn it when I was a young man here in Rome and was a student of His Holiness; and you know, Reverend Father, what you learn at that age, you never forget."

"But what could those poor people understand?" blurted Father Lesage. He was unable to understand the full meaning of the page recited by Wong. The latter immediately came to his aid:

"To understand, they went to catechism. They did not go to Mass to understand anything, but to pray, having understood and learned what they themselves should say and sing at Mass. Was it not so since apostolic times? Without sufficient prior catechesis followed by an adequate mystagogical catechesis, which is to say, the initiation into the arcane mysteries—ultimately into the Holy Sacrifice of the Mass—no one was admitted to Baptism, and thus to participation in the Mass itself. Remember the '*Ite, missa est catechumenorum; maneant solum fideles!*'[2] You taught me, dear Father, that this was addressed to the catechumens who were not yet sufficiently catechized, and not yet able to duly participate in the Holy Mass. That Mass was celebrated quietly by the bishop or a priest, almost completely obscured by the curtains of the iconostasis. They saw almost nothing, heard almost nothing, in those vast basilicas that obviously had no voice amplification systems. But they had been well prepared by catechesis, and therefore they participated in the Holy Sacrifice, praying and adoring."

"However, the first catechesis, it has been said and repeated by renowned liturgists, is and remains liturgical catechesis," Lesage asserted, without sounding the least argumentative. He was serene and not at all discouraged by Wong's words, even though they were so contrary to his expectation.

---

[2] "go, this [was] the Mass of the Catechumens; let only the faithful remain"—filling in one of the common interpretations of what the *Ite Missa est* stands for or what it stood for.

"It is true," Wong nodded before continuing. "What you just said has already been said and repeated by many others. But it is not accurate. Liturgy can be neither the main form of catechesis nor even less the only form of catechesis, as unfortunately is happening. Do you want proof of this?

"A few days ago I was celebrating in a chapel at St. Andrew of the Valley. At the time of Communion, a lady beckoned to me that she wanted to take Communion, but I had already consumed the Consecrated Species, so I could not help her. After Mass, the same lady wanted to thank me from the bottom of her heart for the beautiful Communion I had given her that morning. What had happened? The altar boy, a little guy, had gone to the sacristy, taken a particle out of the sleeve, and brought it to the lady, who thus took Communion. The lady attended Mass daily, and had therefore received from the liturgy a catechesis like few other faithful."

"Will Your Excellency permit me to bring the discourse back to the matter that is close to my heart?" Father Lesage asked very politely. Without waiting for any response other than the Pope's gesture of encouragement, he added: "The sub-Saharan Africans want Latin and the Native Americans of California sing in Latin. Yet the Church always translated the liturgy into the language of the various peoples, to whom it addressed the work of evangelization. So the Mass was born in Aramaic, the language spoken by the Apostles. It was translated into Greek, the language spoken by the Corinthians, Thessalonians, Philippians, and so on. It was then translated into Latin in Rome. It was translated into the language of Malabar in India, which then founded the Malabar rite. It was translated into the language of Ge'ez in Ethiopia. Among the Slavs, Cyril and Methodius translated it into their language.

"Thus thanks to the Mass celebrated in the living language of the various peoples, they were converted to the Faith."

Father Lesage paused in satisfaction at this proof of uncommon erudition given in the presence of the Pope himself. It was not difficult for Father Lesage to see in the Pope's gaze all the complacency and approval of the Holy Father himself.

"It is true," the Pope then told him. "What you have said has already been said and repeated many times in defense of the vulgarization of the liturgy. But it does not correspond to the truth. The explanation, the proof, would be long, and I really do not have the breath to do it. It may be that dear Monsignor Wong will feel like briefly taking my place in this thanks to his skills at synthesis. You will certainly be pleased, Reverend Father, because we can say that you have the exact motto that Manzoni had Carlo Imbonati recommend to him: *Il santo vero mai non tradir!*[3] This, dear Father, is certainly your most beautiful talent."

It was true. Lesage was not offended by Wong's candor. He was not highly educated nor very intelligent. But he was very devoted to the truth, even if he rarely had the chance to come to know it. But once he had glimpsed it, he longed for it, even if it required him to overthrow his own habitual positions, as was happening right there in the course of that magnificent audience.

"Yes, dear son," Pius XIV added in an even more confidential tone and look of kindness. "We can see it in your eyes. You are constitutionally incapable of betraying the known truth, and this fine gift makes you especially dear to us!"

The Pope's last words moved Lesage deeply. He could not stop himself from wiping away a tear. This disposed him even better not to miss a syllable of what Wong would say.

"In ninth century Moravia, Saints Cyril and Methodius could not translate the liturgy into the Slavonic language for the simple reason that a Slavonic language did not yet exist.

---

3 "Never betray the truth!"

The various Slavonic dialects that existed were unsuitable for liturgical use. The two saints, indeed certainly Saint Cyril, did not adopt these vernaculars, but constructed from pre-existing disorganized elements a language for liturgical use, a language that was later adopted for literary use. The Slavonic of the Slavic liturgy was never a vernacular. It was born as a sacred language, that is, removed from vernacular use, and reserved for addressing God. But even later, it never became vernacular. None of the various Slavic languages, which developed at a later time, can be identified with the Slavonic of St. Cyril's liturgy. This is the historical truth, apart from a judgment on the merits of St. Cyril's work, namely whether his having isolated the Slavs was really a good thing and whether his evangelization would not have been more Catholic if he had brought the Slavs closer to the Greek-speaking Catholic Church and to Greco-Roman civilization through a common liturgy and alphabet. The Slavic torpor in certain fields certainly was caused by this cutting-off of the Slavic peoples from the Greco-Roman body, which was carried out by St. Cyril. He was not content that those peoples understood catechesis, biblical readings, and homilies, but was also eager for them to understand directly even when there is nothing more to understand, but only prayer and worship remain. However, the islands of German people, scattered among the Slavic peoples, asked that the readings also be done in Latin, not because they understood Latin better than the new sacred language, constructed by St. Cyril, but because Latin was the language of their conversion to the Faith, and they loved it as they loved their Faith itself.

"And in the seventh and eighth centuries in the England of St. Augustine of Canterbury and the Germany of St. Boniface the Martyr, among people who spoke anything but Latin, the Faith was extended through the use of Latin in the Roman rite. And in Ethiopia, from the seventh century on, the liturgical language of Christians was Ge'ez, an erudite language which became a sacred language precisely because it was different from the spoken and vernacular languages. And the five hundred thousand monks of Egypt in the fourth and fifth centuries spoke Coptic as their first language to the extent that they needed interpreters when welcoming Greek-speaking visitors. Yet they still participated actively and piously in the liturgy that their bishops and abbots celebrated in Greek.

"And in Rome in the fourth and fifth centuries, Greek and Latin coexisted in the liturgy. Both were quite different from the Roman vernacular. We are talking here about a Greek and Latin remade expressly for liturgical use, with expressions and meanings that were totally unknown to classical Latin and Greek. They had already become languages that were reserved for liturgical use. They were not based on the language of the general public, who knew very little about them. Yes, I repeat, this is a Greek and Latin that were remade expressly for liturgical use. These are therefore sacred languages *a nativitate*,[4] and are far from common usage!

"And in the ancient Phoenician colonies of North Africa, the vernacular language was Punic or Berber. Yet St. Augustine, in the fourth and fifth centuries, celebrated in Latin, the common liturgical language in those regions. And in the second and third centuries, St. Irenaeus catechized the Celts of Gallia-Lugdunensis, but celebrated in Greek for those who neither speak nor understood Greek. Yet the Faith in France was born and spread in this way, as indeed everywhere else, where it has come down to the present day.

"Today the use of the vernacular in the liturgy has not taken the Church forward in any way—perhaps many steps backward. A Lutheran pastor said, 'We have been using the German language for sacred services for four centuries now and what is the outcome? We have divided ourselves into as many sects as

---

[4] "From birth."

there are believers, believers each in his own way. In addition, our churches are deserted, even on the holiest and most solemn days.' In the United States, between 1945 and 1965, there were about a million conversions to Catholicism a year, despite the Latin liturgy. Today, although the liturgy is in the vernacular, conversions can be counted on your fingers while millions fall away, and this does not only concern the ordinary faithful, but also priests, religious and cloistered nuns themselves.

"What about during the apostolic era? St. Paul in Corinth preached in Greek, the Corinthians' vernacular language. But he wanted everyone in the liturgy to pray in tongues: '*Volo autem omnes vos loqui linguis. Et loqui linguis nolite prohibere.*'[5] So writes St. Paul in two places in his first letter to the Corinthians."

"But Chapter XIV of that letter is the warhorse used against Latin. I confess that I too have appealed to it over and over again." Father Lesage candidly confessed and continued: "For in it St. Paul says that he prefers to utter five words that are understood, rather than thousands *in linguis*!"

"Dear Father, you can also feel completely authorized to use it. Did it not appear in the documents of high prelates? They, however, despite the vaunted biblical revival by them, certainly never fully read that chapter and the following one, or did not understand them. Because St. Paul in those chapters makes a clear distinction between the language of preaching, which is to be directly understood by the faithful, and the language of prayer, the liturgical language, which by necessity is esoteric, that is, its meaning is known only to the initiated. Now among the esoteric languages in those chapters defended by St. Paul, is Hebrew, we may assume, since St. Paul claims to be able to speak *in linguis* better than a thousand others. But certainly there was no vernacular language.

---

[5] "For if I pray in a tongue, my spirit prayeth, but my understanding is without fruit." (1 Cor. 14:14)

"And Jesus himself, in instituting the Holy Mass, did not use vernacular Aramaic but liturgical Hebrew for the blessings and prayers prescribed for the Passover rite, the Exodus readings, and the singing of the Great Hallel. But the liturgical Hebrew language, in even more ancient times, that is, before the exile in Babylon, was similar to the language of the various other peoples of the ancient Near East in that it was poetic, priestly, and just different from profane and vulgar Hebrew. And after the Babylonian exile, it was different from Aramaic, which became the vernacular language of the repatriated Jews, although it had changed somewhat from what it had been centuries before.

"Among all peoples, the liturgical language differs from the spoken language. It is a special language, to be used exclusively for addressing God. This is a law of nature. I could speak to you, Reverend Father, about the sacred languages of the Far East, and I think I know a few things about them, but that would take a really long time. As well, who does not know that Muslims everywhere, even in India, also learn ancient Koranic Arabic for prayer? And that Jews, living everywhere, learn Biblical Hebrew for prayer. It is quite different from Hivrit, which is modern Hebrew?"

"However, in India there is the Malabar rite. This shows that the liturgy that St. Thomas brought there, certainly in a different language, was translated there into Malabar," observed Father Lesage, who was now, despite this point, no longer so sure of his own science.

"This rite is more accurately called Aramaic-Malabar, because it preserves the ancient Aramaic language. So even in this case no translation of any kind took place, much less in Malabar, a language that never existed even in Malabar. The Bible was translated into different languages, but only in our time has the liturgy been translated from scratch, and in such an urgent and peculiar way!"

"'However, if you want the people to pray or sing, in other words, to actively participate in the Holy Mass, they need a liturgical language they are familiar with," Father Lesage observed again. With these words he did not intend to defend either himself or a cause he considered already defeated. He simply wanted to have a solution to the difficulties he himself had so many times accursed Latin of bringing.

"Actively participate? The supreme liturgical activity is the worship of each of the faithful, who *per Ipsum, cum Ipso et in Ipso* comes to be united with everyone else worshiping. They are equally united to the same center. Otherwise a blind or deaf person would surely be cut off. As for certain chants in the vernacular, I have been here in Rome for some time, and I have heard several of them, sung, let us say sung, by the microphonist, amidst the patient silence of the faithful. The microphonists! The great directors of the new liturgy. And the more the speakers boom, the less the faithful dare to sound their faint voices. With the microphones removed, what would be left of the new liturgy? On the other hand, you, Reverend Father, remember how until a few years ago the faithful sang the *Ave, maris stella*, the *Tantum ergo*, the *Te Deum*, the *Magnificat*, the *Benedictus*, the *Miserere*, the *De profundis*, the hymn *O salutaris Hostia* and many others. I remember the attention of my Chinese listeners when I would explain these beautiful chants to them, and with what joy they would then recite them, discovering more in them than I had indicated."

The energetic gust of the Ponentino, swept away the petals of a withered rose, stirred up the foliage of the colorful kiosk, and reminded everyone who had been conversing under it that it was time to go home. On the way, the Pope wanted to bring together the best parts of the audience. Turning to Father Lesage, he said:

"I want to speak in confidence to you, dear Father. I do allow you to spread the news, just as I would be pleased if you would include what was said in this hour we spent together as the subject of some of your articles. Well, the confidential part is this. In a few days, we will decree the restoration of Latin to its rightful place in the sacred liturgy. Not so much because it is a sacred language that is removed from the corruptions of spoken languages, and is reserved for when one addresses God, as because the abandonment of the Latin formulas has compromised the dogmatic content contained in them. Have I made my point?"

"Do you really believe, Your Holiness," Father Lesage asked, fully won over by the Pope's benevolence, "that the crumbling of the Faith and therefore of customs, which we have been witnessing, and which has authoritatively been called the self-destruction of the Church, has been caused by the abandonment of Latin?"

"The abandonment of Latin is certainly not the only cause, nor perhaps the main one—certainly it is not the most profound one. Are you surprised, Reverend Father, if a Pope tells you that the ultimate cause of this self-destruction of the Church—I repeat the famous phrase, however questionable it is—well, that the cause of all this is not theological, but first of all philosophical, metaphysical in nature? It comes from the misrecognized objectivity of being. But the abandonment of Latin is also responsible for it to an important extent, as a very efficient negative cause, that is, as being very destructive. Chronologically speaking, the destruction of the stronghold of the Faith began with the elimination of Latin, which constituted its outer wall of defense. The death of Latin brought the death of a whole civilization!"

"Dear me!" Lesage exclaimed. His spontaneous gesture and facial expression drew a good laugh from both the Pope and Wong. They were immediately joined by a far more sonorous one from Lesage himself. "Your Holiness," he then added, "I am on your side, body and soul. I could use some of Monsignor's culture, though."

"Gabriel Wong," Wong said, introducing himself.

"Write to him, dear Father," the Pope concluded. "Write to him, and every letter of reply from Monsignor will offer you subject matter for some article."

"Only if you are pleased with that as well," Wong said in turn to Lesage.

The latter replied with sincere enthusiasm: "Pleased?" Say delighted, Your Excellency!" And thus the beautiful and erudite floral walk ended in glory.

28

Romolo Gives Himself Away

ROMOLO HAD NEVER DECIDED TO commit papacide. He had only decided to make money—lots of it and fast. The self-styled commendatore Osiris Market now possessed an immense emporium of sacred ornaments. The material, artwork, antiquity, rarity, and uniqueness made them extremely valuable. He had inestimable treasure. Romolo knew all this. This made Osiris his gold mine. The problem was to become a co-owner of the mine, or at least an associate of the company, which at that moment was owned only by the commendatore. Romolo believed that he had found the solution to this problem. In theory, reaching the solution did not seem difficult to him.

Market had committed the money he had managed to pull together from the liquidation of all his assets to the purchase of the sacred ornaments. He risked everything in the bold venture. The sale of the items at prices that were a hundred or even a thousand times the purchase price, though occurring at a snail's pace and with infinite precautions, had already greatly compensated the commendatore for the expenses. However, mentally and physically worn down, he was becoming a shadow of himself. He did not realize this, and had no one in the world to tell him so, for he had no one in the world who loved him. He had no children, and had also lost his bride some time ago. The emptiness had brought him to the brink of suicide, but a barrier of sacred ornaments had risen up before him to bar the way, to prevent him from carrying out such a useless, foolish action. However, some sort of madness or disposition to madness stayed with him. This was the obsession of losing at one stroke what until now remained for him his only reason for being, which was turning the treasures of sacred art into money.

Romolo understood this well. Almost without needing to think about it, in other words spontaneously, a perfectly logical and multi-stage plan formed in his head:

"First, agitate the commendatore with the bogeyman of the papal decree on the sacred ornaments. Second, make the commendatore fearful of losing them all at once. Third, plant in him the conviction that replacing the Pope is the only solution. Fourth, weaken his risk-aversion by convincing him that it is an indirect risk that needs to be carried out in order to free, if not the Church itself, at least humanity, from a senile despot. Fifth, induce him to put in writing a contract that goes something like this:

"X amount of euros goes to Mr. So-and-so—which would be me—for the incident in which the unfortunate Pope...etc., etc. Signed, stamped, and dated."

"I have no intention of getting my hands dirty, but that contract in my pocket automatically makes me the co-owner of that thief's treasures, just as he becomes my partner in a crime, which he may care about, but which I let some other person deal with. That piece of paper is enough for me, so that I can milk the commendatore as long as he lives, and then become his sole heir."

Market, however, hadn't been born yesterday, and he was a businessman. He knew all-too-well what a word, date, and signature on a piece of paper meant. He was overwhelmed by his obsession, especially when he dreamed, as he now often did, of a fire, robbery, flood, or earthquake that destroyed all of his treasures. He had been on the verge of yielding to Romolo's

Romolo Gives Himself Away

suggestions many times, but as soon as he imagined himself ready to sign the piece of paper, pen in hand, he stopped, as if overcome by an instinctual repugnance, and resolutely declared:

"I am a man of my word. In all my purchases over the years, I have never needed to sign anything. My word has been enough for everyone. You have my word! If you want it, I can give you an advance, up to half of the agreed sum. I'll do it to prevent you from risking your honor by having your name written on that piece of paper. I'll do it for you.

"I know how to cope. I keep almost everything in Switzerland. That includes a spare personality with documentation. You don't have any of that!"

"Well then, give me a date for the advance," Romolo replied.

"It depends on you. Today you give me the details of the plan. If I feel like it, tomorrow I will get you the advance in the currency of your choice."

Romolo, however, was not up to specifying the plan. It would need to be easily-executable so as to meet the commendatore's desires. He had drawn up more than one plan, but only after getting high. While high, each plan seemed more perfect and executable than the previous one and equally payable on sight. But after, if he could remember any of them, they were merely fragments that appeared bleakly improbable.

Could he turn to an expert? He had some acquaintances among the Bresciorsini group, but this matter was so delicate that he could not trust anyone from there. Besides, an expert had to be paid, but he, Romolo, had already used up all the funds from Market and was himself in urgent need of money. His vices and drugs bled him dry.

While waiting for the execution of the plan and finally get his hands on the twenty-five million advance, before disappearing, why couldn't he exploit the recordings of Pius XIV's first papal audiences, first confidences, first fatally unwise decisions, which were certainly the most compromising ones? The cardinal

Camerlengo had only the first two tapes, sold to him—Romolo thought—by Market. He would certainly be interested in coming into possession of the remaining ones as well. But he didn't feel like going back to the cardinal to offer them to him. And so he confided the matter to Consalve.

Romolo understood that Consalve was tackling something extremely serious in regard to Pius XIV. It was not for nothing that Consalve had been received by the cardinal Camerlengo for the first time dressed as a layman and the second in ecclesiastical garb. Then he returned a third time in the company of another prelate. All the comings and goings of vehicles certainly indicated a coming great offensive, a kind of pre-conciliar council, in which those leaders would make some historic decision.

"I am distressed by what I have to see and hear from this observation post of mine," Romolo confided one day to Consalve after refusing the tip the latter offered him while retaking his seat at the wheel of his car. Consalve did not in fact have at his disposal a car and driver from the Vatican. He drove a rental with rare skill even in the midst of the chaotic traffic of certain Roman streets. Pleased so much with this skill, he sometimes confided it to himself:

"I should've been a driver! That was my vocation! I wouldn't have all the headaches I do now! But Providence has its ways!" Romolo said, "I am very distressed with all the oddities that are being committed in high places here..." before abruptly stopping.

"Here? In the high place? From whom? Don't be afraid to confide in me. Besides, this is well-known. If I were Italian, I would say with you that it is an open secret. Who does not dislike certain stances of Pius XIV? Right?"

And through such conversations, Consalve found out that Romolo had recorded many of Pius XIV's odd moments.

"I was perfectly aware of this," Romolo confided to him. "It was a risk I was taking, a heroic risk, for the holy Church. But

Romolo Gives Himself Away

I am not boasting about it. Any other true Christian in my place would have felt the duty to do what I did, to go to the same expense because, unfortunately, there aren't too many in Rome nowadays who work for an idea. I had to resort to working with mercenaries. I got into debt up to my nose. Some saint will provide. I am a man of faith. The maturity of certain promissory notes is near, but there will be a prelate to give me credit. An interest-free loan will also be there for me." Consalve put his heart in his throat, totally moved. He got out his wallet.

"Is two hundred dollars enough for you? You can pay me back when you can. There's no hurry."

"Oh thank you, what a Providence! You're too good, Your Eminence!" Romolo knew very well that Consalve was only an Excellency. But an Eminence thrown in at such a moment could yield something more. "Then I can begin to silence my worst creditor, the one I owe the least yet who demands the highest interest."

"Well, let's make it $1,000," Consalve concluded. I can't afford any more now. Someone else will understand your situation, and come to you. I will speak about it myself, if need be, to those who are in the right position. So then, you are one of us! Have your equipment ready. I will specify the place, day, and hour in due course. We'll probably get together here, at the Cardinal Camerlengo, any day now."

"You can count on me, Your Eminence."

His Excellency sighed at the Eminence, who had been addressed so sincerely for the second time. Then he jumped behind the wheel and set off in a hurry. He had to tighten the ranks of what, at first jokingly, he had called the Catiline Conspiracy. In fact, it had seemed quite easy, that everything would come together naturally. All that was needed was for someone to take the initiative. Then the light handful of snow, blown by the wind from the ridge of the mountain, would begin rolling down the slope and gradually grow into an avalanche.

Not that Consalve had pictured the thing in his mind in terms of a snowball and avalanche, things never seen in his country. But he was convinced that the whole Catholic world was disappointed, indignant, and alarmed about Pius XIV, and that everyone would rise up as one to demand his deposition as soon as the reality was aired by someone. And at that moment, that someone was Consalve himself.

In practical terms, however, the parable of the wedding guests had been repeated. As a result, for now, he and the others, determined as he was, had had to fall back on a project with a more limited scope. This would be a limited meeting, of an exploratory nature, at the Cardinal Camerlengo's. Being there meant that even though it was limited, it nevertheless remained high-level.

Now Monsignor Quira and his two colleagues, Monsignor Arras and Monsignor Speakering, Father Medina with his faithful collaborator, Father Viso, and the activator of it all, Consalve gathered around the Camerlengo in the latter's office. Cardinal Stolzkamm had excused himself from the meeting, saying he was very busy with an extremely important matter.

"More important than this!" Consalve had shouted to him over the phone. "What else in the world could be more important than this for a cardinal?"

But the cardinal responded by laying down the receiver with dignity, leaving Consalve with nothing left to do but imitate him at the other end of the telephone wire. However, the cardinal Camerlengo himself did not appear very enthusiastic about the gathering. Perhaps it was his diplomacy. Perhaps it was his great concern over the importance of diplomacy, thought Consalve, who occasionally shot the same cardinal a questioning glance. For both he and Quira had not hesitated in underscoring the very bold theme of their gathering.

"First, based on a recent issue of the journal *Superconcilium permanens*, totally dedicated to the problem *De Pontifice deponendo*,[1] we can draw up a detailed and precise list of the main charges, in order of importance and gravity, that would force Pius XIV to acknowledge himself to be in error and therefore required to resign, or that would prove Pius XIV no longer *compos sui*,[2] and therefore without any doubt *dimittendus*.[3] Second, the way to proceed in either hypothesis *ad validatem atque ad liceitatem dimissionis Pontificis*.[4] Third, and optional, time permitting, perspectives on the upcoming conclave."

On hearing this plan of action, the Cardinal Camerlengo brought his right hand to his mouth to hide a yawn. Given the extreme importance of the plan, Consalve attributed the yawn to nervous tension.

The opening solemn declarations were made by Consalve himself. These were followed closely by no less solemn and serious ones by Arras. With great passion, the latter touched on the central problem. He examined every element at every level, from the progress of peoples to literacy and the fight against malaria, from democratic freedoms to a more fat-rich diet, from anti-cholera sanitation to the oil crisis. Medina, who acted as secretary, put everything on record for history. He begged those present to use concrete, short, and precise sentences for the charges against Pius XIV, according to the first item of the agenda photocopied and sent around by Viso beforehand, as a reminder to each of those present.

The men gave the impression of being in the Sanhedrin, bringing forth the corrupt witnesses and their contradictory accusations against the Lord.

In order to bring an end to such a situation which could have jeopardized the outcome of so much effort, travel and expense, had it gone on a bit longer, Consalve saw that the time had come

---

1 "on or regarding the pontiff who is to be deposed"
2 "of sane mind"/of his wits/in control of himself
3 "to be replaced"
4 "for the validity as well as liceity of the deposing of a pontiff."

to bring in Romolo and his recordings. This was the Monsignor's trump card. And so Romolo entered, carrying with him Market's tape recorder and a few cassettes. The cardinal Camerlengo already knew a few things about the cassettes, including something he wanted to object to. But he thought better of it and let it go. Trying to portray a demeanor befitting the solemn moment, Romolo plugged in the machine and remarked,

""Let me plug it in. It works better than with batteries." He then checked the number marked on the little box he held in his hand, carefully slipped it into the recorder, and waited for the command to press the sound button. The command came. *Conticuere omnes intentique ora tenebant.*[5] Then the recorder began to buzz for a good minute amidst the total silence of everyone present. The calm was interrupted as the moving notes of the chorus of Nabucco burst throughout the hall:

> Va, pensiero, sull'ali dorate; va, ti posa sui clivi e sui colli...[6]

Performed by the La Scala chorus, it was a perfect performance, the most faithful recording!

"What on earth is this?" Consalve burst out. He was not in the least moved by the rather moving music. Good musical taste was not among the many talents bestowed by Mother Nature on him. His Excellency, on the other hand, greatly enjoyed jukebox records. Romolo immediately pressed the stop button. He apologized, carefully read the wording he had inscribed on the case of a second tape, placed it in the recorder and, at Consalve's renewed command, pressed the accursed button a second time. New buzzing and anxious waiting, and the final eruption into the austere hall of the somewhat less austere notes of

---

[5] Virgil, *Aeneid*, 2.1. "All became silent and beheld intently," when all listened to "Father Aeneas."
[6] "Go, thought, on golden wings / Go, lay thee on the cliffs and hills ..."

Romolo Gives Himself Away

> La donna è mobile, qual piuma al vento,
> muta d'accento e di pensier...[7]

which flowed from Beniamino Gigli in all his vigor.

"Go to hell!" shouted Quira as he slammed a fist on the table on which the recorder was laid. It was such a gigantic fist that, as if struck by an apoplectic stroke, the recorder fell silent while Viso broke out in uncontrollable laughter. Romolo hastily gathered up his things, but was not fast enough to prevent the cardinal Camerlengo from throwing the two tapes at him which Market had left him.

"Take these, too, young man!" he told him. "Maybe there are some excerpts from *La Gazza ladra*[8] in them!"

What had happened was this: After reporting the discovery of the tape recorder to the Pope, Camillo had gone back to Romolo's dressing room and replaced the tapes with the first ones he found. He put them in the cases of the tapes on which Romolo had written titles.

The gathering at the Camerlengo's ended without Romolo. While dismissing everyone, the host said to them with some sympathy:

"Il n' y a pas des roses sans épines![9] If they are roses, they will bloom! Let's give time to time!" Stepping out, Father Viso hummed, almost without thinking:

"La donna è mobile," and burst into a second howl of laughter.

---

[7] "The woman moves, like a feather in the wind, / silent in accent and thought..."
[8] Rossini's 1817 opera *La Gazza ladra* (*The Thieving Magpie*).
[9] "Every rose has thorns."

29

"Tischreden"[1]

IN FAITHFUL DEFERENCE TO AN ancient discipline of the Laurini Fathers, in the two main refectories, even the Pope's diners would eat in silence as they listened to something from a book or periodical. On that day, Father Sixtus was reading an article from a monthly magazine in French. He gave the noble language a Roman's forthright pronunciation. He was reading about the events of the Combes Law, by virtue of which in March 1904 religious congregations were denied the right to teach, although the right remained for individual members. The speaker, Buisson, was addressed with an objection:

"Leaving some congregations with the right to teach will be enough for them. They will change their attire in order to continue their harmful activity with the same corrosive spirit. It's not the habit that makes the monk!"

To which Buisson replied:

"'It's not the clothes that make the man!' goes the proverb. Well, I'm here to tell you that it is indeed the habit that makes the monk. In fact, for the one who wears it, for those who see him in the habit, the habit is the permanent sign and symbol of his being set apart, the sign and symbol that the religious is no longer a man among men. The habit is for him a force. It is a force that keeps him apart, and it shows the hand of a master

---

[1] "Table Talks." This was the title of a book of Martin Luther's musings around his dinner table.

who in this way no longer lets his slave escape. We are in a world of dreams when we delude ourselves that we can snatch such prey from the master until the prey is in the right habit.

"Everything will change as soon as the religious has taken off the uniform of the militia in which he enlisted. He'll inevitably find the freedom to belong only to himself. There will no longer be a Rule that locks in his whole life moment by moment. There will no longer exist a Superior, whom he must obey at every moment for his own existence. He will no longer be the man of the Congregation. He will inevitably return, sooner or later, to be a family man, a man of the world, a man of humanity!

"It will also be necessary for the religious to begin to earn a living like everyone else. We won't ask him for anything more. And here he is free! For a time he will still cling to his religious ideas, but let's not work miracles. Let him secularize himself, with the help of life. We can rely on nature, which will gradually and irresistibly push him to take back all his rights as a man like everyone else. Don't forget that in order to remain a religious, it's necessary to do incessant violence to nature, while all he needs to become a layman again is to reopen both the eyes and the heart."

At this point Father Antonio gave a signal with the bell. The reading ceased and the conversation started.

"Earn a living like the worker-priests and priests on reduced service," Father Sisto commented, putting away the periodical he had been reading up to that moment. "Reopen your eyes and your heart like Adam and Eve, say a bachelor's farewell and get married!" He then turned to Father Antonio: "Dear Father, you got me to read this article because it was for me!"

"What on earth does it say?"

Father Antonio answered: "I only knew its content in a rather vague way. How could you think that?"

"'I thought that because whoever is at fault is suspect,' replied Father Sisto. "Let me explain. Several times before going out into the via di Porta Angelica on the way to the Circolo San Pietro, I put the Roman collar in my pocket. With my bright and fashionable attire, no one could take me for a priest or friar. But from now, on I will always go out with a friar's cassock. I love celibacy. I hope that's clear."

The Pope responded, "Dear Father Sisto, years ago I agreed to take part in a very demanding mountaineering excursion that banned the wearing of a cassock. The decent young men who had wanted me in their company found a rock climber's outfit for me. Arriving at a refuge, in perfect mountaineering camouflage, a man came out of the little building and, seeing me, opened the door in front of me and said, 'Praised be Jesus Christ! Come in, reverend,' and he let me in."

"That's right!" Father Antonio commented. "The priestly character is invisible, but it sends a light..."

"...until, with our long years of indifference to meditation, the Eucharist, and chastity, we extinguish every glimmer of these virtues," the Pope said before adding, "Once, one of our fathers was preaching at a retreat for us in preparation for priestly ordination. One morning he came to us a little late, and excused himself by saying, 'I heard a knock and when I opened the door, I saw a man begging outside, with a slipcover shoulder cushion in the style of a saddlebag. I told him I was in a hurry, that he had to be patient. He stretched out his hand and said, *Bis dat, qui cito dat!*[2] I immediately put something into his consecrated hand. I too am a priest!' But my priestly character no longer gave light..."

A pause followed, which Monsignor Wong ended by saying:

"If the diamond of celibacy is removed from the priesthood, what kind of a young man will feel attracted to it? Someone may be attracted by a salary. In this case he is a mercenary. He will no longer be a good shepherd, to whom the sheep belong, and he knows them, and for whom he is ready to give his life."

---

[2] "He gives twice who gives promptly!"

Father Sisto added, "Of course, if Father Maximilian Kolbe had been a father of a family, how could he have given his life to save that of... a father of a family? He would have said, like Manzoni's innkeeper, 'I have nothing to do with it. I'm the innkeeper!' But he would not even have become the patron saint of innkeepers... he would have said, *Uxorem duxi, et ideo non possumvenire*."[3]

"*Sed omnis qui reliquerit etiam uxorem propter nomen meum, centuplum, accipiet, et vitam aeternam possidebit*,"[4] Monsignor Wong added. He then threw out the question, "Why did Jesus entrust his own mother to St. John the Evangelist?"

"The other apostles were married," Father Agostino replied.

"Nothing requires us to believe it, to assume it certain," Wong said.

"But at least it is certain that St. Peter was married," Agostino insisted. "Because he had a mother-in-law, and therefore he certainly also had a wife."

Wong retorted, "But he left her. St. Peter was able to say to Jesus, *Ecce nos reliquimus omnia*.[5] Jesus, enumerating the components of that *omnia*, also lets the bride enter. At least it seems to me that is how that pericope of St. Matthew in chapter 19 should be understood. As for St. Paul, there is no doubt that he was celibate. He exhorts the simple Christians of Corinth to celibacy, while recognizing their right to marry: *Volo enim omnes vos esse sicut meipsum*.[6] He declares that the young woman who abstains from marriage for the love of God is more blessed than others."

The Pope said, "The hundreds of thousands of monks of the first centuries are the most eloquent response to the advice of

---

3 As in the Gospel account: "I have taken a wife and thus I cannot come." (Lk. 14:20)
4 As in Scripture, just slightly adapted, "but everyone who leaves even a wife for my name's sake will receive a hundred-fold and will possess eternal life." (Mt. 19:29)
5 "Behold we have left all things, and have followed thee." (Mt. 19:27)
6 "For I would that all men were even as myself." (1 Cor. 7:7)

St. Paul and the Lord himself. It's advice for the faithful and obligation, now tested by the centuries, for the clergy."

Antonio replied, "Strange that the proponents of progress who have no historical memory are so keen to return to the era in which ecclesiastical celibacy was in decline. Progress, progress! But as for celibacy, they want to go back to the good old days of the serf clergy, but with a prosperous wife and dependent children..."

"...following the example of Luther," Father Sisto added. "Then these convivial conversations of ours would automatically acquire such an evangelical stature and scope that they would be collected, codified, and published in a critical edition. They would be translated into every language and widely disseminated throughout the centuries to come for the edification of true believers, as was done for the seven thousand Convivial Sayings, the Tischreden, of Martin Luther, formerly Father Martin. It would be enough to stuff them with lowbrow stories and vulgar and atrocious buffoonery against the Pope and friars."

The Pope noted, "In the Middle East, where the lower Greek Orthodox clergy are not held to celibacy, they understand more clearly the importance, the indispensability, of celibacy for the priest who wants to be what he should be, totally for God and totally for souls."

"Here are some very attractive young men and hopeful ladies, so joyful, all seated, bundled up in tandem, like sandwiches, if you prefer, on the carousel. He, she, he, she, and so on. And that they pass that beautiful sugar-coated lie from mouth to mouth." And in so saying, Father Agostino circulated a photograph among the diners: "They are seminarians in a Catholic oratory of an Order of modernized educators."

A pause followed, while a shadow of sadness descended on everyone's faces. The Pope tried to dispel it, speaking again:

"Years ago, when I was leaving the Middle East, I wanted to say goodbye to an important, non-Catholic personality who, after having mentioned the chronic state of war in those regions, suddenly changed the topic and said, 'You Catholics are educators. You possess the secret of the art of education. You men educate the boys and let the sisters take care of the education of the girls. One of the secrets of the educational effectiveness of your Catholic institutions is right here, whatever modern psychology says about it. On the contrary, thanks to modern psychology, we practice mixed education from kindergarten to university. This interchange leads to the early corruption of customs under the mask of innocent, irresponsible spontaneity. I have two daughters, one in high school and the other in college, and I am anxious about their virtue.'"

Monsignor Wong added, "And going from the Middle to the Far East, I will say that we only admit such interactions in the family, that is, between brothers and sisters, because they are all under the eyes of the parents. No alternative opportunities exist until young people are of marriageable age, have begun to work at a profession to support themselves with their own family, have good health and, for us Catholics, also have a solid foundation in faith. Because only then, under the constant prudent guidance of their parents, will they be able to prepare seriously for marriage. Any other form of interaction between the sexes *in malo est*![7] As for such interactions in religious institutes, it is expressly prohibited by the Code of Canon Law."

Agostino exclaimed with measured irony, "The Code, the Rules? I am anything but the letter! The letter kills. It is the spirit that gives life!"

Wong observed, "In fact, by the letter St. Paul means the Old Testament, and by the spirit the New, so that pericope is almost always invoked inappropriately."

"The spirit and the letter.... What has the spirit to do with shoes?"

---

[7] "It is evil!"

Everyone looked with amazement at the Pope, who had thrown out the question. He himself replied: "When St. Teresa of Avila wanted to reform the spirit of the Carmelites, she made them take off their shoes."

Father Sisto exclaimed, "Monsieur Buisson's dress is back! A parish priest of Lyon traveling to Venice said to me triumphantly, 'Nous avons laissé tomber la soutane!'[8] At the time, it seemed logical to me. Today, however, I would answer him, 'Pour commencer!'"[9]

> Martin Luther
> threw away his tunic.
> Throw away your constraints
> human thought,
> And shine and thunder
> surrounded by flames.
> Matter, arise.
> Satan has won...

The Pope confirmed, "The spirit has its own components. Once those are removed, the spirit... expires!"

Everyone smiled, but soon turned, their eyes filled with curiosity, towards Monsignor Wong, with the interest of grandchildren looking at their grandfather, because the latter had begun to say:

"Once upon a time, a Chinese mandarin returned from a long journey to India with a very precious Indian dagger that had a blade of a very rare steel, all damask. The dagger was more expensive than gold. It had a handle of gold, ivory, and mother-of-pearl, and was encrusted with gems and diamonds. Falling into poverty, the man was forced to sell the blade of his Indian dagger. He replaced it with a tin blade, but he always spoke of his Indian dagger. Later, once again to get some money, he was forced to sell the handle of the dagger. He replaced it

---

8 "We have stopped wearing the cassock!"
9 "To start!"

with a bamboo handle. But he continued to speak of his Indian dagger, although of his Indian dagger, only the..."

"...spirit!"

Father Antonio said, "At the Pontifical Gregorian University, perhaps the nicest of all the teachers I had the grace to have in my life, during a course on the history of religious Orders, said to us: 'By dint of improving the Rules, which they always justified as necessary to keep the spirit intact, all the religious Orders that have died down the centuries up to the present day have done this. The ones that preserved or restored, *ad litteram et sine glossa*[10], the observance of the primitive Rules were saved from ruin.'"

"*Sine glossa*!" nodded the Pope before adding, "When Napoleon was told, as if it were good news, that an edition of his code had been published along with the necessary glosses, he exclaimed: 'Mon code est perdu!'[11] But I can tell you that there are some religious houses that ask and are granted a return to the ancient observance, and also that on the initiative of holy priests, seminaries are being opened according to the ancient discipline, inspired by St. Charles Borromeo and St. Pius X. They quickly fill up with young people."

"If they knew they could live there as they pleased, that they could find the comforts of their own home, they would have no reason to leave their homes. They also quickly adapt to strict wallet control," Wong observed.

"You understand, dear Father Sisto," Father Antonio said. "You who do nothing but ask me for money?"

"You know very well that it's not for me!"

"For you or for others, it's all the same. I have to fork it out!"

"Certainly," Father Agostino began to say. In terms of poverty, he could've been considered a second St. Francis. "Certainly,

---

10 "literally and without a gloss/commentary"
11 "My code is lost!"—i.e., it didn't turn out how Napoleon wished... because the Code was meant to be confusing so it was now lost or hopeless.

some practice poverty in the household and perhaps in what they wear, but if they do that with a fat wallet and offer nothing to others, but keep it all for themselves and their own discretion, well, that's called hypocrisy. And it's only worse when one speaks at every turn of the Church of the poor."

"The Church of the poor?" the Pope asked, and added: "The newborn Jesus in Bethlehem, while welcoming the relatively poor shepherds, sends a star that guides the rich Magi to Him from the Far East with their rich gifts. At Cana in Galilee, to please Mary Most Holy, Jesus miraculously gives a few hundred liters of excellent wine to the young spouses, who had invited him as their guest. It is a gift from a rich man, and given not to hungry poor people, but to banqueters, already full and somewhat tipsy. Jesus has nowhere to lay his head, but he appreciatively accepts for himself and his apostles the hospitality of the house of Lazarus, Martha and Mary. They are rich to the point of being able to house so many people without special discomfort. Jesus appreciates the prodigality of Mary of Bethany, who pours a pound of pure and precious nard on his head and feet. He condemns Judas, and those who echo him, who are concerned about the poor. Jesus praises the widow who deprives herself of bread to offer two pennies to the Temple, which was overflowing with gold.

"The Church of the poor! Jesus counts the rich Joseph of Arimathea and the wealthy Nicodemus among His disciples. One of these embalms the body of the Lord and spends his inheritance on the purchase of a hundred pounds of myrrh and aloe. The other, Joseph of Arimathea, in addition to purchasing a valuable shroud in which to wrap the body of the Lord, places the body in the princely sepulcher that he had dug for himself in the living, peaceful rock of his garden.

"And weren't Constantine and St. Helena and St. Louis IX rich? Very rich? And yet they belonged to the ranks of the Poor of the Lord, the poor in spirit of the Beatitudes. Conversely, there are many who are poor in wealth but rich in spirit, that is, full of greed and envy, ready to seize wealth, even by violence. They esteem wealth as the supreme good. Even the rich can belong to the ranks of the poor in spirit beatified by the Lord on the Mount of Beatitudes. However, those belonging to the ecclesiastical hierarchy and religious, ordinarily, will also have to be poor in wealth, if they want to be more similar to the divine Master."

It was the moment for them to leave the table, as some time had already passed. Father Antonio gave the usual ring of the bell and everyone stood up to recite the prayer of thanksgiving *Post prandium*,[12] the *Confiteantur*,[13] just as they had recited the traditional *Benedicite* before eating.

---

[12] "after lunch"
[13] The *Confiteantur* is Psalm 144:10 prayed in the "after lunch" prayer at monasteries and seminaries.

30

Stravinsky's "Fireworks"

ROMOLO WON A PRETTY UNBELIEVable victory. He was about to rid himself of the thousand dollars that Monsignor Consalve had just given him, to make up for the setback suffered by the Camerlengo on account of the messed up tapes, but stopped himself in time.

"Now I've got nothing, and have to find the twenty-five million advance. I need to come up with something that will please the commendatore. If I give him something to remember, he won't be able to deny me the money. Then I can cut my losses and make a clean break. I don't want the commendatore to make my life impossible. I have to find a specialist, someone who comes early for things and doesn't talk much. Vassily never talks, and is a great expert in ballistics. I can give him up to five hundred dollars. I don't think he's ever seen that much in his life. For now, I have to stop spending money." He sighed. "I have to sacrifice so much just to make a couple of bucks! But I don't want to take any chances."

The next afternoon he was at the Pincio. It was a Thursday. The Rome Underground Band, a well-known group, was playing. It wouldn't seem out of place for two young men to start hanging out by chance at the kiosk of the musicians, both listening to great music on a great day.

"Why don't we sit on the bench over there, by the well of Moses who was saved from the waters?"

"What about over there by the water clock? It's so sunny by the bench, but there's more shade down there."

"Fewer eyes and the band will bother us less."

"What is it?" Vassily finally asked while offering a cigarette to Romolo and adding: "You'll like it. There's a pinch of weed, a small, decent dose. It's my invention."

"You can make explosive things, can't you?" asked Romolo.

"They say."

"Are you any good with fireworks?"

"A little bit. During the holidays, at the fair, you know? In my country, we have fireworks. We compete with each other. I like to enter contests. There are also some prizes." Vassily looked him over closely, planting his magnetic pupils in his face, in his eyes. He turned to the flower bed and tore off a dry leaf. Grinding it with his teeth, he began to speak through nearly closed lips, but in correct and succinct Italian:

"You work in the Vatican. So, it can only be a Church-related device. A sort of clockwork breviary. It'll cost a thousand, half as soon as possible and the other half on delivery, next Thursday, here."

Romolo squinted his eyes. The thought flashed through his mind, "This is a policeman and wants to deceive me. A setup! No. Impossible. He doesn't even have Italian nationality. Anyways, be careful!" He said loudly, "A breviary of Egypt! I need only some information on the most common pyrotechnic material and how to get the most spectacular effects without putting anyone in danger, of course!"

Vassily smiled skeptically and offered another cigarette.

"This should enlighten your mind and help you choose the quickest option, which is what I propose and offer to you."

Romolo didn't believe him. Vassily said, "All right, do what you want! So, five lessons at a hundred each, that's five hundred. And for the materials for practical experiments, that's another five hundred. It's the same total: One thousand dollars.

So again, I advise you to get a breviary, a beautiful breviary. One that is guaranteed to help you pull it off. All you would have to do is get yourself a breviary case suitable for where you want to put it."

Romolo insisted on lessons, perhaps because that option would take the longest time, and he had not yet made a final decision. The lessons would give him time to think again on what to do. Or perhaps it was because he would need two breviaries and two thousand dollars, but didn't have the money or the breviaries. But even if he had all that, he would not throw it so naively at Vassily.

"So you're afraid of the air too," Vassily said, a little upset. "Do you really think the longest way is the least dangerous?"

In response, Romolo handed him five hundred-dollar bills.

"You're paying! You're in charge!" Then he asked, "When do we meet for the lesson?"

"Next Thursday, I still have the whole afternoon off."

"Yes, Thursday at three o'clock on Tiburtina Street, at the intersection of Torre Cervara."

"Why all the way over there?"

"You'll understand when you get there."

After saying this, Vassily stood up and said: "Come on, they're playing the *Feu d'artifice* of our divine Stravinsky. Listen to this!"

They both approached the musicians' kiosk. When the performance ended, they applauded loudly. The master turned to thank the crowd repeatedly. Then Vassily disappeared under the trees of Viale dell'Obelisco. Romolo turned and walked towards the balustrade of the great terrace overlooking the Viale Gabriele d'Annunzio. He looked down towards the Piazza del popolo and then towards St. Peter's Basilica Dome, which appeared misshapen. He decided to return home. He wanted to go through something else in his mind while walking the vast horizon, so dense with history, from the Monte Mario to the Janiculum, from the Janiculum to the statue of St. Paul and the Column of Marcus Aurelius, to the white mass of the Vittoriano, to Trajan's Column and the statue of St. Peter.

The following Thursday, arriving a little early in his economy car for the appointment, Romolo said to himself, "Patience! I'll wait for him." He found a parking space, turned off the engine, got out, and looked straight at Vassily. How had he gotten there? He was wearing a fishing suit: a thick shirt, cap, and rubber boots up to the knees. He was holding fishing baskets and a strap and line in his hands.

"What's with the disguise?" Romolo asked.

"My lessons are practical. Without the relevant educational material, they'd be of no use to you. If I'm caught fishing along the Aniene with a little explosive, I get only a few days in jail. That's it. Understand?"

They reached the shore of the Aniene and started to walk along it, going with the current, to a grove of bushes and reeds that were lapped by the water. Vassily seemed to know the area well. He threw the fishing line into the water, lodged the fishing rod into the ground, and sat down nearby, Romolo by his side. He then took explosives out of the basket, electrical wires to connect the charged batteries in different ways depending on the desired effect, and a small clock-like device for timed ignition.

Under Romolo's wide open eyes, he dexterously and confidently assembled and disassembled the material several times in different ways. It looked like he was handling bars of chocolate, not explosives. Then he cautiously passed each of the pieces to Romolo, and guided his hands to help him work out the various problems that he presented to him one at a time. Once the five fundamental problems were worked out, everything was resolved.

"And now what you need is this," Vassily quickly said at the end of the exercises. So quickly, in fact, that Romolo was unable to follow all his moves as he would have liked. He put together a device with the shape and dimensions of a medium-sized breviary. "Here it is! Just enclose it in its case, and you're all set. When it comes to placing it, for example, in a car, behind a cushion, you just need to move this lever to the minutes you need, up to a maximum of sixty minutes."

He broke into a satisfied smile. A second later, he had taken the whole thing apart again and made its elements disappear into the fisherman's basket.

"When are the next lessons?" Romolo asked, relieved by the thought that this was only the first one, that he would be tutored again, and that he would have plenty of time to reflect properly and make his decision before the end of it all.

"They're all done already. Five problems, five lessons. Everyone has his own method. I always do that. What more do you want? Your Orsini and Bresci[1] knew much less than you, I assure you!"

After a long pause, Romolo replied, "I'd like to practice a little myself. Give me some of the material."

"You know the price," Vassily told him as he extended his open hand towards Romolo, who gave him the last five one hundred bills.

"I'm giving you everything we've handled so far. You cannot say that Vassily is not generous. I'll take it to your car. However, first let's take a stroll along the Aniene."

Having said that, he withdrew the fishing line, slung the basket over his shoulder and, followed by Romolo, began to climb the bank against the current. Romolo grew increasingly upset and felt like saying something rude when Vassily turned to him and, offering a cigarette, said, "Here, take this. It works against distrust!" The bomb expert then resumed walking without

---

[1] The revolutionary Felice Orsini (1819–1858) attempted to kill the French emperor Napoleon III in 1858. On the contrary, the anarchist Gaetano Bresci (1869–1901) succeeded in assassinating the Italian king Umberto I in 1900.

saying a word. When he reached a patch of reeds dominated by an isolated poplar, he slipped into the patch while moving the reeds to the sides to make his way. Romolo followed. After a few more steps, Vassily finally said, "Here we are. This is the place! It's the most suitable place for a hands-on demonstration. I think you will trust me a little more now that you have proof of how much I trusted you. I only reveal my Pentagon to the most intimate and secure of people. I won't tell you how long it took me to find this place, and the gradual tests and counter-tests that I had to do before being sure that it was what I needed. To get here without getting lost, keep an eye on that isolated poplar. You can see it from far away. So, when you have your breviary, you secure it to a string. Tie the string to the top of a reed like that one there."

He pointed out one of the tallest canes of the reed bed to Romolo. The cane spanned the entire bend of the Aniene on both banks, and hid the two men from the eyes of anyone who was not on the other bank directly opposite. "It's long and strong. Then adjust the time. I recommend five to six minutes for the experiment here. A beginner can't do it in less time, but more is too much for anyone, and might give someone time to get close. Then sink the breviary here, in the water, near the shore, right here. Remember it well! As soon as you feel it touch the bottom—and you'll realize it immediately, because you'll no longer feel the weight of the line—take cover in the trench there, the embankment of volcanic rock. I think it was made on purpose to allow such experiments in complete safety. Please, don't hurry! Otherwise you may also end up in the water. I'm not telling you to count the seconds, because you do it instinctively. You will be able to see the quality of the material of these fireworks. It's all high precision. The detonation should be dull, and won't go far. I've done it many times, so I know. In any case, it can easily be mistaken for a military jet in the distance breaking the sound barrier. If, hypothetically, it doesn't happen—but it will certainly happen because I saw that you understood everything instantly—but if it doesn't happen, just take care to hide the tool holder rod among the weeds on the bank, and then leave everything there, and call me immediately at the number you know, even from the nearest bar, saying any sentence in which the word Aniene appears. And then just go about your business. I'll take care of the rest. All free, that is, everything's already paid for. And now let's go back to the Via Tiburtina."

Along the way Vassily gave Romolo another piece of friendly advice:

"If by chance a fisherman surprises you, don't say a single word, and immediately pay him off. It will cost you less than the fine, at least if he finds you in a fisherman's outfit."

Once they reached Romolo's parked car, Vassily took out of his basket the green plastic bag that lined it and contained the material given to Romolo. He let it fall on the floor of the car and said:

"All goods guaranteed for the bomb test...Oh, some people are coming! They better not see us going the same way. Good luck!"

He went back down towards the Aniene and disappeared.

31

Broadcasting

"DO YOU THINK THIS IS A SUITable song for the Pope's radio?" the cook asked the Pope. Father Antonio had allowed Brother Ambrogio a small radio but not without carefully defining how and when he could use it, including the condition that it not disturb anyone's quiet life. But in practice, since Ambrogio was basically deaf, sometimes the little radio placed above the refrigerator in the kitchen disturbed everyone around him, including the Pope when he was there.

The Pope needed to rest a little after lunch, but his very sensitive nervous system prevented him from tuning out the music. Unable to doze off for the twenty minutes reserved for his nap in his daily timetable, he walked towards the source of the music, intending to politely tell Ambrogio to turn down the volume and keep the kitchen door closed. However, the cook had anticipated him with a question:

"Do you think this is a suitable song for the Pope's radio? Silly thought, to say the least. Hoarse drunken voices. The music of sickos. I set the dial to Vatican Radio. How do you want to change this situation? What should listeners expect from the person who is responsible for the religious radio station? Sacred praise, prayers of good Christians, the lives of the saints, and the catechism with the commandments of God."

"Are you going to burn anything?" the Pope asked him.

"No, I don't have anything on the fire right now," the cook replied.

"Then let's both sit here for a moment, like good friends... That's it! So, dear Brother Ambrogio, when you will be pope..."

"Holiness, I am a poor cook, and an old one at that."

"Anyone of the people can become Pope: *Quisque de populo*,[1] and even when one least expects it. You also have the advantage of being twenty years younger than me. What, did I expect it, to become pope? And St. Ambrose, your protector, when he wasn't even baptized yet, did he expect to be elected bishop of Milan?"

"And what a bishop! Well, at least I've been baptized, and confirmed."

"So when you will be pope, you will realize that between saying and doing..."

"...there is a sea. I didn't have to become Pope to find this out. How many times have I heard myself say—you know the saying!—that to make zabaglione, the real zabaglione, you have to do this, like this and then like this. But then when I tell them, 'Ok, do it!' either they don't, and I have to do it, or if they try, they let everything get burned. It's always like that!"

They both laughed. Then the Pope said to him, "Meanwhile that little radio now does nothing but disturb our conversation, just as before it didn't allow me to doze off as I had planned..."

"Oh, Holiness, I'm so sorry!" Ambrogio hurried into the kitchen to turn off the blaring device. Then coming back, he repeated: "I'm so sorry, Holiness, I'm so sorry! Tonight I'll give it back to Father Antonio, and we won't talk about it anymore. I'm so sorry!"

---

[1] "anyone from among the people," i.e., the laity.

"Keep it, and use it, at a moderate volume and with the kitchen door closed, as Father Antonio told you, since I really hope that even the Pope's station will improve its programs. I am very grateful to you for the suggestions you have given me."

"Suggestions? Your Holiness, I didn't mean to suggest anything to you. I spoke like this, from my heart, because you are a trustworthy person. I spoke as I would have spoken to my father, good soul!"

"And yet in a few words..."

The doorbell rang.

"It is Master Camillo, with the usual bunch of letters. I'll get the door for him, and then bring him the usual coffee. He likes my blend so much, and with a lot of sugar. He doesn't have diabetes, if you can believe it! And if he continues like this, he will live for a thousand years!"

While Camillo sipped the coffee brought by Ambrogio, the Pope happily chatted with both of them on the same subject.

Camillo interjected at a certain point, "Your Holiness could speak with Mantellini, who's an engineer. He's the technical director, really valuable and deservedly respected by everyone. If he can assure Your Holiness that it's possible with the current system to transmit on many wavelengths 24 hours a day, no one will be able to hide behind reasons of technical limitations to sabotage a given programme."

"Sabotage?" the Pope asked.

"Ok, an improper word, I agree, but the day when a program is too religious, too bigoted—too much *whatever* according to some of them—they'll twist their noses. They'll say, these self-proclaimed anti-bigots, they'll say that first you need to do a work of persuasion, which dissolves distrust, which arouses sympathy. They say that preliminary work must be done for religious work, and the religious work, in which Our Lord Jesus Christ is clearly spoken of, is put off forever. And never carried out. Am I right?"

"I would say so."

"Many times I have personally asked a Christian—or you could even ask a pagan who knows that the Pope is the authority of the Catholic Church—what do you expect to hear from the Pope's radio station? The truths of the Catholic religion. The events of the Catholic Church, perhaps beginning with Adam and ending with persecutions of believers under the communist yoke. The defense of the Catholic religion from errors and slander. The responses to objections. The celebration of Catholic solemnities.... How many times, not being able to do the Spiritual Exercises like when I was in boarding school, would I have been happy to be able to listen to meditations and instructions from the Pope's radio station. And I wondered, and I still do, why there isn't such a broadcasting program for the community of the faithful since religious and priests can no longer easily find what is right for them in other places. And not only in Italian, of course, but in all the languages of the world, at least in the main languages, but also for languages that have a small Catholic population, so that also those people know our Lord and Savior, Jesus Christ, at least this way."

"I imagine it will take an army of translators," the Pope objected, but only to provoke Camillo to continue.

"There already exists, if not an army, certainly a large group of translators and interpreters which, there, in the midst of all those priests and religious, I don't like at all."

"Would you get rid of them?" the Pope asked.

"The non-essential, of course! With a settlement to prevent any claims and protests. As for the indispensable, I would reserve them for translations that can also be done at home. Translators and interpreters are different. Interpreters have to be present at the recordings, but not translators."

"Thanks, Camillo, and thanks to you too, Brother Ambrogio. I'm sure that Monsignor Wong is waiting for me. Let's get back to our desk!"

"You at the desk, and I at the sink. I peel potatoes, and you fry your fish,"[2] said Brother Ambrogio in a solemn way of concluding. Then he renewed his assurances to the Pope, who was leaving: "And please be certain about the radio and please excuse me again."

Arriving in front of his office, the Pope found Monsignor Wong there. The latter said to him:

"It's three o'clock, Your Holiness. I thought I'd find you in the office."

"I went to see Brother Ambrogio because of his little radio."

"Your Holiness has also been disturbed by it? I prepared what you told me. Here's the memorandum. In any case, the conclusion is always the same: lifting the excommunication placed on Marxists and Freemasons is equivalent to turning a red light that needs to stay green. What I mean is, it's equivalent to sending them down the road to perdition, since until the one group of them renounce materialism and atheism and the other group rationalism, evolutionary pantheism, and religious indifferentism, they are and remain outside God's grace, and therefore outside his Church. An ecclesiastical authority that declared them readmitted into the bosom of the Church, just because times have changed, would betray its mandate and deceive those unfortunate people. It's obvious that lifting the excommunication would be completely ineffective *in foro interno*[3]: it would remain completely outside of Church law."

"Agreed! But I need a fresh mind to conclude this matter, and I need Father Aurelio's steady hand. Let's put it off for another day. I'd like to take up the discussion begun with Brother Ambrogio and continued with Camillo."

He entered his office, followed by Wong. They recited the

---

2 "Gatte da pelare," literally "peel your cats," or "skin a cat" means "have other fish to fry."
3 Ecclesiastical law, meaning "in the internal forum." This can refer to a person's conscience or when discussing matters privately in the confessional or other religious setting.

Actiones nostras[4] together, sat down, and talked for a long time. They finally concluded the conversation with a first draft of the seven points of a general programme, to be re-examined and further specified, for Vatican broadcasting. After that, Wong read them again:

I. Practices of piety of the good Christian: the traditional *Angelus* three times daily, with three *Aves* and three *Glorias*. The *Vi adoro* with the usual morning and evening prayers, including the *Acts of Faith, Hope, and Love*, etc., God's Commandments, etc. The Holy Rosary, which on the feasts of the Madonna is to be solemnized by the song of the mysteries. The *Via Crucis* every Friday. Mass and Vespers on days of obligation. Generally, all the other more important liturgical and devotional functions.

II. Daily popular lessons in Catechism, Sacred Scripture, Church history, hagiography, apologetics, and Christian art and archeology.

III. Daily lessons in liturgical Latin and Gregorian chant, particularly to teach the singers and the faithful in general the variable parts of the Mass and Vespers on the days of obligation.

IV. Fifty-two annual series, of seven days each, of Spiritual Exercises for the community of the faithful. The Exercises will consist of two meditations, two instructions, and one outline for the examination of conscience for each day.

V. Catholic news, with particular chronicling of news concerning life in distant missions, will aim to instill priestly and religious vocations in both the active and contemplative lives.

---

4   From the Breviary and after Mass prayers:

Actiones nostras, quaesumus Domine, aspirando praeveni et adiuvando prosequere: ut cuncta nostra oratio et operatio a te semper incipiat, et per te coepta finiatur. Per Christum Dominum nostrum. Amen.

Direct, we beg you, O Lord, our actions by your holy inspirations, and carry them on by your gracious assistance, that every prayer and work of ours may begin always with you, and through you be happily ended. Through Christ our Lord. Amen.

VI. All broadcasts are to be made in Latin and the most widely spoken modern languages, both for Catholic nations and for nations with a relatively small Catholic population, including Russian, Romanian, Chinese, Lithuanian, Arabic, and modern Greek.

VII. Each daily program must last as long as possible, even 24 hours a day, bearing in mind different time zones, and therefore duplicating the broadcasts in the following languages: French, English, Portuguese, Spanish, and Latin.

After reading this first provisional programme, they went out for the afternoon walk, which naturally had as its destination the Vatican Radio building at the end of the gardens. On the way back, the Pope was also escorted by the director general of the radio, the engineer Mantellini. The technical problems could be solved, with financial support and a proportional expansion of equipment. The more serious problem remained that of finding the trustees for each individual topic of the program.

"Among our current collaborators," observed the director general, "we have a good number of elected minds and hearts of apostles, Your Holiness. But for such an original programme, I think it will be necessary to find others as well."

It was understood that the director general himself would give the Pope a list of names, mainly clergymen and religious, as was natural, and that he would evaluate the issue of the layoffs of some staff members. The Pope and Mantellini would be in touch with each other as soon as possible.

"Well, thank you from the bottom of my heart. See you soon," the Pope said as he dismissed them, before immediately adding, "But couldn't certain songs be replaced with music worthy of the name, making it a little more like a radio station of the Pope?"

"Certainly, Your Holiness," the director general replied, not at all surprised by the question. "We had planned it for some time, but without direction from above I didn't dare."

Back in the Laurini monastery, the Pope and Monsignor Wong stopped in the sitting room for the usual cup of tea, which they hadn't had before going out. While he was serving them, Brother Ambrogio asked the Pope, "How did it go, Your Holiness?"

"It's gone," the Pope answered. "You won't hear any more of those songs, not even if the volume is turned up to the max!"

"Wow, what a Pope!" Ambrogio exclaimed, making both Wong and the Pope laugh, with the latter nearly spilling his cup of boiling tea on his immaculate pontifical cassock.

32

"Ludwig and Friedrich"

THE TWINS LUDWIG AND FRIEDrich were quite close. They were alike to the point that when one of the two complained of a stomach ache from overeating, their mother hastily administered an equal dose of castor oil to the other as well, sure that it wouldn't go to waste. Inseparable at school, they would divide the exam material. Sharing the same gift for literary subjects, they quickly agreed to do half the work in the other subjects, especially those they disliked and therefore found more difficult, the hard sciences and philosophy. Thus on several occasions, each took the same exam twice, the first time under the name of Ludwig and the second time under that of Friedrich. This ensured success with less effort.

They even attempted the same fraternal and selfless collaboration at the end of the first year of the seminary. However, after the seminary authorities learned of their boasting at the dinner table of their success with this scheme at other schools, they were separated despite the lack of evidence that they had done such a thing at the seminary. Friedrich continued in the same institution while Ludwig was sent to one in a different diocese.

The separation, though temporary, was the first of their lives. It turned out to be very painful. Never before had they understood how close they were, and how one was the perfect copy of the other, even emotionally. Nevertheless, they came to sacred priestly ordination with somewhat differing aspirations. Ludwig fostered in his heart the ideal of unspoken sacrifice for the salvation of souls, and Friedrich the ideal of the Christian social apostolate. This difference of orientation in no way damaged their friendship. It had simply led Friedrich to the episcopal chair and the purple, and left Ludwig in hiding in rural chaplaincy. Then the second, with some regret, reoriented his life in becoming a canon of a cathedral in order to please his cardinal brother.

From this vantage point, he began to look with fear on the first irregularities of his cardinal brother, but didn't dare condemn anything. He preferred to think he was wrong in judging him. In any case, he offered for his brother all the humiliations that he had to suffer from the prisoners, for whom he was chaplain, and prolonged his endless hours of adoration in the episcopal chapel. He increased his abstinence and fasting in imitation of Jesus in the desert, always for his brother. Nevertheless, his brother continued to gain weight, and had already become massively built, with a thick neck and head sunk between powerful shoulders. His great and feverish activity required a generous diet so he would not be weakened with abstinence beyond what circumstances inevitably imposed. Nonetheless, apart from the difference in color between the purple and the purplish mozzetta, at first glance they could still be mistaken for each other.

Ludwig had kept the serene though jocular demeanor of his childhood, while Friedrich's gaze had become scrutinizing, at times cryptic. This was understandable. Contact with so many people, many of whom were subtle and deceitful, added to multiplying worries and difficulties, had left a few wrinkles on his broad forehead. None were yet noticeable on Ludwig's completely flat and bright forehead.

Always very close, they enjoyed a relationship of respectful affection, which in Friedrich bordered on veneration of Ludwig, and in Ludwig, a motherly trepidation towards an endangered son. This feeling had grown in Ludwig from right after the death of their mother. When dying, she had said to him, "Help your brother!" and to Friedrich, "Be humble! Give the lie to that ugly surname of yours!" Since Stolzkamm meant "proud crest."

The trepidation had suddenly sharpened in Ludwig's heart when, shortly after the election of Pius XIV, he had seen his frowning brother leave as quick as lightning for Rome, like someone leaving for war. Then, long after that, the news of his brother's deposition had reached him, brought by Monsignor Gordin himself, who did his best to sweeten the bitter news. Ludwig had awaited a direct report from his brother, but only a few letters came, filled with vague and conversational content. Finally, he plucked up his courage and went to Rome.

He tracked down Cardinal Stolzkamm in the latter's normal college residence in Rome. They tearfully embraced each other, but Ludwig had no words to mitigate the fury that his brother nurtured against Pius XIV. Friedrich was still too emotional. Finally, when parting at the Termini station on a hot evening, after a few moments of hesitation, Ludwig whispered, almost imploring:

"Friedrich, what would mom tell you? Bow your head!"

Friedrich reacted in a completely new way to this unexpected recommendation. He looked at his brother in astonishment before his eyes sharpened, like that of a treacherously wounded person who would defend himself to the last drop of blood. His look differed completely from Caesar's lament-filled gaze after the emperor was stabbed. Saying nothing, Friedrich turned his back on his brother, quickly got into his car, and disappeared into the night.

With an anguished heart and sweat beading his forehead, Ludwig went to the train station, boarded the train, and huddled in a corner of his otherwise empty compartment. He took the rosary between his fingers and began to cry uncontrollably.

The first to set foot inside, the inspector, was the one who found him still crouched in his corner, rosary between his fingers, no longer weeping, but unmoving. He had died of a heart attack.

At the news of his brother's death, Cardinal Stolzkamm seemed to go crazy with pain, worsened from the remorse for having killed him. What did he care now about the chair and the cardinalate purple!

"Ludwig, Ludwig!" he called out, on his knees as he shut himself up in his room. "Forgive me, Ludwig! We have always been so close! You forgive me, don't you, Ludwig?"

Those who saw him feared that he was about to have a heart attack too. After a few days, he retired to a monastery of Passionist fathers, where Pius XIV's condolences reached him. The cardinal couldn't question the sincerity. The Pope apologized for not having come in person. He feared that his visit might displease His Eminence.

After a month of spiritual exercises, prayer, penance, and tears, he conveyed his thanks to the Pope for the condolences and let known his continued availability to him. The Pope, seizing the opportunity, immediately went to see him by the simplest means, the new taxi which Cincinnato had previously supplied for similar outings. The second taxi, used at other times, was now known and monitored.

As initial evidence of his submission, the Pope asked him to act as celebrant of the rite for the episcopal consecration of Fathers Aurelius, Gregory, and Norberto in St. Peter's Basilica, in the Pope's place. Such a ceremony would certainly tire His Holiness too much. The acceptance of that first obedience would also be very welcome in Paradise for his brother.

Cardinal Stolzkamm couldn't believe his eyes when he arrived at St. Peter's for the ceremony. A sea of heads filled the entire church—the central nave, the transepts, and the apse. Someone from the crowd of faithful, seeing him enter with the other two consecrators and the three candidates, began to wave his handkerchief. Almost immediately, at an agreed signal, the expanse of heads disappeared under a white tide of silently waving handkerchiefs. Soon the forty thousand waving handkerchiefs were joined by forty thousand voices, varied and uncertain at first, but soon forming a single voice. It began to articulate in unison, and at length:

"Long live Pope Pius! Long live Pope Pius! Long live Pope Pius!" with such a crescendo that, at its climax, it seemed as though it would lift Michelangelo's dome. Then, as if by magic, it stopped and gave way to prayer and singing. The long ceremony seemed to last only a few minutes, and everyone went back home, as joyful as at Easter.

33

The Prodigal Son

YES, EVERYONE RETURNED HOME as happy as if it were Easter Sunday—all but one, the Cardinal Camerlengo. Not that Cardinal Stolzkamm's reconciliation with the Pope displeased him. But since he understood that there was nothing left for him but his own reconciliation with the Pope, he now had to find a way to do just that, and as soon as possible, without turning into something like a second Henry IV in Canossa.

The opportunity was presented to him by a very polite bore who dedicated himself to disseminating artwork, especially modern art. He confessed his ups and downs, his financial wins and losses. Yet he ceaselessly declared his determination to carry on his trade for humanity's artistic elevation. This apostolate had also enabled him to build more than one villa for himself and his heirs, both on the French Riviera and the shores of Lake Saint Moritz in picturesque Switzerland.

He asked the Camerlengo for authorization to dedicate a current editing project to the Pope, a series of biblical pages illustrated by this famous Michael Raphael Leonardel. The first time he met Leonardel, the Camerlengo thought of sending the good gentleman back out the bronze door with a flood of courteous words. While discerning the best such words among the many that appeared in his mind, he had a very bright idea that got him to immediately correct his aim.

"Do you have any specimens of the work with you?" he asked his visitor.

"Here with me, no. At the hotel, yes. I can get you a few copies in about half an hour."

So within an hour or so, after the Pope's return from his afternoon walk, the cardinal Camerlengo presented him with a beautiful and shiny briefcase under his arm.

"I hope that in your goodness, Your Holiness will excuse me. After the first audience that Your Holiness kindly granted me, I didn't ask for a second one. I was already so ill that day, and, what's more, I was obsessed by so many fears over all the news, which since the closing of the conclave had given me no break, day or night. That pressure might have given my words a different coloring from what they should have had, and which they certainly would have today."

"Are you feeling better today?" the Pope asked him, smiling.

"I would say so. For this I took the liberty of requesting an audience with Your Holiness so that, as Camerlengo..." and he lingered over this word, to see what impression he would make on the Pope, but the Pope did not hesitate at all, and replied:

"One moment! Does your Eminence remember that he immediately withdrew his resignation, given in that first hearing?"

The Camerlengo gasped at the question. He was ready to throw himself on his knees in front of the Pope, but the latter prevented it by declaring,

"So from that moment on you were no longer Camerlengo of Pius XIV, present here. Do you agree?"

The cardinal ex-camerlengo bowed his forehead, and the Pope continued: "But Pope Pius XIV, present here, needs a Camerlengo, practical and decisive. Do you know of anyone suitable for this highly trusted position? Who would your Eminence suggest to me?"

"Actually I...on the spot...I don't know..."

"... if you have nothing against it, I would offer this position of extreme confidence to you, and I would be happy if you accepted it. Think about it, and when you're finished thinking about it, tell me what you think."

"But I, Your Holiness, can only say to Your Holiness: I obey!"

"Like Garibaldi!" the Pope added, smiling again and making the Camerlengo smile too, who also heaved a deep sigh of relief. Then the Pope continued: "With the difference that Garibaldi only had a cheap red vestment, while Your Eminence has that wonderful cape, a river of purple. Other than this little white garment! But does Your Eminence know that it suits him? And I would like to say something to those who go around saying that the habit does not make the monk! Even the magistrates, in the exercise of their functions, care about their attire, and they are successful. If the signs of thought were removed, how would we communicate with each other? By the *scientia media* [1]? In any case, Eminence, to what do I owe the pleasure of this visit of yours?"

"A trifle, but one that would offer me the opportunity to reconnect with Your Holiness. As my goal has been accomplished, this trifle is no longer worth considering. I think I was blunt."

"Let's hear it anyway, Your Eminence, this trifle! Especially since I see that you've come with a rather large folder, and all in that beautiful shimmering satin. It must be a rather aristocratic and voluminous trifle."

"A publisher wishes to dedicate to Your Holiness the artistic edition of a certain number of biblical pages selected and illustrated by the painter Michael Raphael Leonardel, who is stranger than his stage name, and better known for his quirks than his art. Not that he doesn't know how to paint. He definitely knows all the secrets of the trade, but seems hardly ever to commit

---

1 The *scientia media*, "middle knowledge," endeavors to reconcile God's knowledge of future events with human free will.

himself seriously. Even more rarely does he deal with religious subjects, which, as another point to remember, he doesn't seem able to deal with religiously. I think I speak with a certain competence about the case, if only because during my studies I had the opportunity to specialize in the field of sacred art, and even afterwards I have always tried to pursue this subject."

"I have read with interest all your publications in this field, Your Eminence, and let me now offer you my congratulations."

"Thank you, Your Holiness! This folder contains samples of the work. Because I'm busy with something else, I haven't yet had the opportunity or desire to examine them. Here you are."

As he was talking, the newly appointed Camerlengo took out of the folder the reproductions of large-format color illustrations and passed them to the Pope one at a time.

"What does this represent?" the Pope asked. "I would say that it can only represent the *tohú wa bohú*[2]—deserted and empty—of the first day, before the Lord had separated the light from the darkness, don't you think, Your Eminence?"

"Let's check it out! 'The universal deluge' is written in English on the back."

"Oh yes, it's true. A deluge of ink! Less spontaneous, however, than what I painted in second grade, when I overturned the inkwell on the calligraphy notebook. A slap from the teacher extinguished the artistic power in me in the bud, when I was not yet able to exclaim, as Suetonius makes Nero exclaim in the act of killing himself: *Qualis artifex pereo!*[3] And this second table...What is it? A second deluge, I would say!"

"Actually, it says in Spanish behind here: El paraiso terrestri.[4]"

"I would rather say El paraiso tierra-tierra, and before the creation of the sun, moon, and stars. Unless modern biblical scholars have been able to prove that the great river of Eden

---

2   Hebrew. Gen. 1:2: "void and empty."
3   "What an artist the world has lost in me!"
4   "The earthly paradise."

was made of Chinese ink, with a natural wave here partially in the foreground. But perhaps everything here has a purely symbolic meaning, symbolizing the stain of origin... And what is this? The same garden after a fire?"

"So, behind it is written in French, 'Le prophète Ézéchiel.'"

"Ezekiel or the smoky bottom of the frying pan that the prophet erected as an insurmountable barrier between himself and Jerusalem? And then from which side should we look at it?"

"No caption. However, given the pan's circularity, I think you can look at it from any side. If not Ezekiel, at least the frying pan shouldn't have serious reasons to take offense."

"And what does this represent?"

"Something written on the back again, though in German: 'Der prophet Hesekiel.' However, I think that some trade has taken place in the application of the captions on the reverse, if only because these patches of color, which are dull and flat, do not seem to me to fully bring out the features either of Ezekiel or of his frying pan, which we find expressive in the previous illustration."

"Unless the overleaf captions were chosen by lot. And what does this other illustration represent? Oh, but this, because it is not really understood, can be easily mistaken for pornography! Put it away, put it all away! Send everything back to the publisher, and tell him that if he mentions the Pope's name, he will be excommunicated. If he wants some good advice, he should return all the originals of those masterpieces to their author himself."

"Impossible, Your Holiness. the author has already got rid of them, and the publisher has already paid for them."

"Expensive?"

"Only ten thousand French francs each. There are forty, but the painter will send him another forty pictures in about ten days, because they are now urgently needed for the edition that has already begun. On the other hand, they will be more spontaneous and without any second thoughts."

"Leonardo took years to make the Mona Lisa, while this Leonardel knows how to make four masterpieces a day, and earns something like four million lira a day..."

"...profaning values he can't understand. Yet some people will buy such marvels!"

"Because there are those who know how to market their products and enchant the wealthy customer. They play on their vanity to overcome the more elementary and natural good taste and common sense."

34

A Lesson in Aesthetics

"DURING MY STAY IN PARIS WHILE studying, one Sunday afternoon I went to the Louvre, and ended up in the Mesopotamian archeology department. The marvels of Mari, the capital of Zimli-Lim, destroyed by Khammurapi, King of Babel, had just been set up. These marvels had remained for about four millennia under the sands along the Middle Euphrates, with some dating back to the fifth millennium before the Christian era. They had been brought to light mainly thanks to André Parrot. I was able to talk to various scholars, in search of possible connections between these archaeological finds and Sacred Scripture.

"One Sunday, feeling particularly tired, I thought of briefly returning to the Louvre and immersing myself in the river of colors that flows along La Grande Galerie and ends in the lake of La salle des États. It is overflowing with the brightest colors of the masterpieces of Italian painting, especially of the Venetian school. It is right in the middle of La Grande Galerie, with a background a large red velvet drape that dominates the portrait of the Mona Lisa. I was there with my secretary. He was a fine young man from Brittany. We were quietly exchanging thoughts when we were surprised to see a group of visitors pass in front of the painting, glance at it in passing, and hastily pull away as if looking for something better. They were soon joined by a guide, who made them retrace their steps. The guide began to hypnotize them with his uncommon eloquence in extolling the virtues of the Mona Lisa. After that even those visitors turned their gaze from the eye-catching red velvet drape to the frame of the picture of the Mona Lisa, expressing many prolonged Ahs! Ohs! Heys! of the most artificial admiration. Leonardo's art was too high for them. But the art of the guide had reached them with a rhetorical art, a far cry from the pictorial kind. A kind of pseudo art, like that which we just held in our hands. It circulates in the world only because of a skilfully concerted rhetoric. The art that has to reveal itself, that needs rhetoricians, is nothing but a lie. I'm speaking of rhetoricians, not teachers or educators. True art needs neither guides nor captions. At the feet of the Pietà, Michelangelo did not feel the need to put an inscription that specified what he intended to express with the statue."

"He limited himself to sculpting his own name along the strap of the Madonna, they say, to assure even the unbelievers that he had sculpted it himself. In fact, he was only twenty-five years old!"

"Or rather as an act of devotion to the Madonna? Of course, in his death, Our Lady would have immediately welcomed him with open arms and would have said to him: 'You have made such a great sculpture of me, my Michaelangelo!'"

"And yet anti-Catholic fanaticism has wreaked havoc on that face," the Camerlengo sadly commented. "And even among Catholics, there are those who demand a disembodied art, to prevent the faithful from stopping at external forms, to induce them to reach the supersensible depths."

"In fact, Our Lady in Lourdes appeared disembodied, in the form of a skeleton! But she appeared beautiful to you, as she is!"

"It's true. They want disembodied sacred art, and then they embody it in the most simian and filthy way. They amputate the wings of the angels to combat anthropomorphisms, and grant them a satanically provocative body. They repudiate the formal exemplars of the great masters, and copy the fetishes of Easter Island or the two-coloured graffiti of the Paleolithic troglodytes..."

"...to return to the pure intuition of primitives in the spirit of irreversible progress! A child who speaks like a child is adorable. If he spoke like an adult, even with the voice of a Tamagno[1], he would be scary. The opposite is also true. An adult who speaks like a child can only be a mentally challenged person or a ventrilogist or a small-brained jester."

"And the fight against formalism? Against techniques?"

"They mask incompetence and the disengagement that is the least result from their inner filth. That is the minimum. Sometimes they are treacherous masks of the stubborn will to profane and desecrate everything that concerns the worship due to God and required by God. This is the only way to explain the multiplication of many immodest disfigurements of what God willed to be beautiful and holy. These are blasphemies that are put on canvas, in marble, in bronze. Never before has matter itself been so contaminated! Do you fight against technique? High imagination would have lacked all power if Dante had not perfectly known the technique of the gentle idiom. Even the most sublime aesthete is mute without technique. Conversely, every technician has nothing of his own to say without aesthetic inspiration. In his condition he is either a copyist or an empty talker. The artist is a poet when he has full mastery of the technique that he requires to tame the material that is offered to him as a possible vehicle of his spiritual feeling. This is to say, he is an artist in the complete sense. His expressive activity is the communication of a gift, of a particular ray of God's light which shines in creation. By giving that gift to others, he embellishes it and enjoys it in communion with others. On the contrary, only by giving it and multiplying it, does he realize that he fully possesses it, and in that way obtains the maximum possible possession of

---

[1] Francesco Tamagno (1850–1905), a famous Italian tenor.

it. Despite its impact on the senses, art remains in its depths an eminently immaterial and ultimately theological fact."

"But then all art is sacred, and we cannot distinguish a piece of art that is specifically sacred from art in general!" the Camerlengo exclaimed.

"All art is sacred, but not all art is religious, and much less ecclesiastical or liturgical in the Catholic sense. I limit myself to this specification both because it is more pertinent to what is close to my heart now, and for the sake of brevity... Don't you think, Your Eminence, that I have detained you quite long and on such a subject? But I didn't do it on purpose. Not that I wasn't expecting you—in fact I would have ended up sending for you—but I couldn't imagine that just today I would have the pleasure of your visit. Permit me—" and as the Pope was talking he offered the Camerlengo a lozenge for his throat, and then took one for himself too. Then he continued: "So all art is sacred in a generic way, but not all art is liturgical or ecclesiastical in a specifically Catholic sense. Let me explain. Precisely because it is the revelation of God through an imitation of nature, in which God has left His own imprint, art is necessarily always sacred. But to be ecclesiastical or liturgical in the Catholic sense, it must also be an immediate revelation of God. This is to say that it must have as its object a datum of the supernatural revelation of the mysteries of God, of the direct interventions of God in human affairs. In other words, it must have as its object something that can only be grasped when illuminated by the light of faith. The natural light of reason is not enough for that."

"But then a believing artist is required for the art of our churches!" the Camerlengo exclaimed.

"Believer and practitioner! It is not enough that he be a believer and express a truth of the faith or a fact connected with the faith. But he must be a believer of faith alive with hope and alive with theological charity. I say theological. Fraternal horizontalism is not enough. In conclusion, a disgusting art, an art of confusion, an art that does not make one pray, if anything, is still art, but it is absolutely not ecclesiastical art and if it enters any church, it must be evicted.

"This is why the ideal church artist is a Fra Angelico, who paints on his knees. Without this, his inner emotion will be insincere sentimentality, not authentic religious sentiment. In this latter case, the artist's technique will only give physical form and therefore appearance to a lie. Such a piece of art will be able to amaze onlookers. It will be able to attract others by its spectacular characteristics. But it will not help souls. Therefore, if we have to choose between an artist in possession of a highly-developed but less mystical technique and one less rich in technique but more mystical, our only choice is the latter. The latter will make the faithful pray more than the former, superficial but highly-developed one. Certainly it is less difficult to find an Alessandro Filipepi than a Giovanni da Fiesole!

"This is why not only theatrical music, but the instruments commonly used in the theater cannot enter our churches. This includes jazz, although in some of its forms it is sometimes not without a certain suggestiveness that may seem religious."

"How many works of art would come out of our churches, if we were to adhere to such a criterion, which I dare not call rigorous, because I have to admit that it is true!" exclaimed the Camerlengo before adding, "Even from the basilica of Saint Peter!"

"It is a fact that certain works of art, even in some churches in Rome, disappoint the most understandable and pious expectations of many pilgrims. Nothing other than pious and rigorously modest art should enter churches. This is another reason why we welcomed the proposals of Professor Amador Moreno of the Mesogaios institute to place many masterpieces of the same Vatican museums elsewhere. The Pope's house must be like a church!"

"What a pity!" the Camerlengo exclaimed, almost talking to himself.

"You are upset?" the Pope asked.

"Very much, for not having brought a tape recorder, which would have allowed me to listen to and transcribe what Your Holiness has been saying so far. Thank goodness I have a good memory."

"In any case, here is the memorandum," the Pope said while handing him some protocol-sized sheets. "You will find in this synthesis more than what I have just said talking with you here. It is the first schematic draft of a *Decretum* or *Motu proprio* on sacred furnishings. You know how many end up at antique dealers, though totally altered and used for profane uses. And now *finis*! It's late in the day. It's time for spiritual reading. I have to get to the chapel. I don't want to keep the Laurini fathers waiting. Nobody says anything to me when I'm late, no one, that is, except Brother Ambrogio, who very diplomatically finds a way to speak his mind when he brings me tea in the afternoon."

They stood up and recited the *Agimus tibi gratias*. Then the Camerlengo said:

"Holiness, could I ask you a favor, which is an advance on the overtime salary for the double work entrusted to me? It is no longer practiced, but I ask anyway. Will you allow me to kiss your hand?"

"Only this?" the Pope asked, and the Camerlengo embraced and kissed him effusively. As he left, still moved, the Camerlengo repeated to himself with the utmost conviction: "But what a beast I have been! To tell such a man that he was *Papa sub conditione*! What a beast, what a beast, what a behemót—to put it in Hebrew—what a hippopotamus!"

But he was also much more peaceful than he had been before the audience. He felt lighter, like everything had been renewed with a healthy bath.

35

Legitimate Defense

COMMENDATORE OSIRIS MARKET returned from Geneva to Rome exhausted and worried. Nothing had been removed from the Geneva safe, but someone had forced the lock. A mistake by the painter who lived downstairs who tried to enter an apartment that wasn't his? Artists always have their heads in the clouds! But if that had been the case, the artist wouldn't have fumbled so much, he would have noticed immediately that the key didn't turn in the lock, and he wouldn't have kept forcing the lock. Instead...

The storage space was in a third-floor apartment of a modest, old house on Geneva's outskirts. The uninhabitable ground floor was unused. The first floor stored pharmaceutical products. The painter's starving family lived on the second floor. They had recently settled there and kept the stairs clean. They didn't bother anyone and were always the first to extend a greeting. Their presence was a guarantee, both for the storage below and for the one above, the latter close to the commendatore's heart. The attic above the third floor was uninhabited except for the rare mournful owl whose brief nocturnal visit brought bad luck.

Seeing that the lock had been gently forced, the commendatore cautiously opened the door and saw the strip-seal that he usually glued to the base of the second door of the entryway. It was intact. He breathed in relief. He then carefully reviewed all the objects that he had accumulated in the three rooms before unpacking the ones that he brought from Rome in his suitcase. He used to keep the suitcase in full view and half open on the train. It was well known by now to the inspectors of the railways on this side of the border. They were careful not to open it completely when examining the confusion of shirts and socks, which were pressed by a pack of handwritten school assignments that stuck out.

Once, at the beginning of these trips, a zealous official, spotting the suitcase when it was closed and half hidden by an overcoat, wanted to verify its contents. This elicited complaints from the commendatore. Making things worse, he couldn't find the key, which prompted the intervention of a police officer, who opened it up in front of everyone just when the commendatore finally found the key. The noisy though polite discussion continued, and attracted the attention of other officials so that Market, at the right moment, suddenly and in front of everyone dumped all the contents of his suitcase onto the seats.

"There is it, gentlemen, that's all! How much are the customs fees for these things? These nice pajamas, green like my pockets? Or for these slippers? Or for my pupils' homework, the despair of the *damnatus ad pueros*?"

With the skill of Virgil's character, the Greek Sinon, he knew how to turn drama into comedy. Everyone laughed heartily, and then parted ways with apologies and goodwill. After that, luck always assisted him: all the customs officers knew him, and greeted him first in various languages, depending on the mood of the day

"Good morning Professor! Bonjour, monsieur le professor! Guten Tag, herr Professor!" they said, knowing that he was a professor of modern languages. He was forced by his occupation by the generator of appetites to live like a pendulum, going back and forth on both sides of the frontier. When they found him with the packet of scholastic exercises that needed to be corrected, some spread out on the small table by the window, others sticking out from the half-open suitcase, so as not to distract him, they limited themselves to brief nods. He replied with his own slight nod, so as not to lose the thread of reading, along with a benevolent wave of the hand which was invariably armed with red and blue pens.

Thanks to this strategy, he had managed to supply the warehouse in Geneva with less bulky but no less valuable items. The transport of the more voluminous ones required various couriers and packaging systems, all personally handled by him. He arrived in Geneva ahead of the packages, had them carried up to the third floor and set down outside the apartment on the landing, and then took it from there.

The packages included the usual old books from which he hoped over time to make back the little money he had spent on them. It was a mania of his! But who didn't have a fixation? At least his didn't hurt anyone.

He packed the books with such care and skill that he rarely had to complain to himself about minor damage caused by the shocks of the journey. For each object, he drew up a regular and detailed file in duplicate, confident that one piece of the information would be the hook to procure him the highest profit possible.

In short, he was a man of order. He loved the old adage: *Serva ordinem, et ordo servabit te.*[1] But now the old storage area no longer seemed so secure. He had to move everything to an apartment guarded by a good and honest caretaker—honest above all.

"A good and honest caretaker—especially honest! The move is urgent, but what is more urgent is the caretaker. Can I find someone here too? With a decent salary, I think the painter below would agree. It's worth a try!"

The painter wholeheartedly accepted! He and other members

---

[1] "Keep the order, and the order will keep you." Often attributed to St. Augustine. Many Jesuit schools have used it as a motto.

of his family would track every step of anyone who walked up the stairs, especially to the third floor. The third floor, thin and creaking with every step, was directly above their heads. They heard every step of the commendatore when he was there, even though he apparently had a light step! He could leave in peace, and almost forget about moving.

"Let me tell you how happy we are with the salary, even though it's not much! Just to let you know, we'd hate to lose it!" He ran to tell his wife. He was sincere because they were starving to death and the few coins they received from the commendatore were a real boon. Despite all that, Commendatore Market left for Rome with the intention of returning to Geneva as soon as possible to put it all in a safer place. He didn't feel at all obliged in conscience to support the painter and his family with his sweat. Hell, he could either learn to paint better or change his profession!

Returning tired and worried to his Roman home, he immediately threw himself into bed, although it was still far from midnight, the hour at which he used to interrupt all work, however urgent, to go to sleep. He needed to sleep twelve hours straight. The fatigue he felt at that moment would make him sleep even more than that and without the usual sleeping pills. He still took the normal dose. But a few minutes later he jumped out of bed to turn the sink faucet tighter because of the unbearable drip.

A little later he jumped out of bed to wrap the alarm clock up in a towel and to put it and its loud tick-tocking—the loudest he'd ever heard—in a closet. He didn't care if he couldn't hear it the next morning. It didn't matter. Some time after that he jumped up to close the shutters tightly because they'd started to creak with every movement of the wind. This was followed by infernal orchestral outbursts that had suddenly begun from the Tre di Coppe bar. Was it really a good time to make all that noise? And was there really a need for all those tam-tams to beat so perfectly? What was the Minister of the Interior doing, if he didn't know how to protect the silence of the night, with so many edgy nerves among the population for lack of sleep? And the Minister of Public Health? The damned bar continued to produce sound waves, waves of intermittent noise that could drive someone crazy waiting for one wave after another.

Oh, I have tallow balls!"

He jumped out of bed, opened several drawers, and finally reached for a small box containing twelve balls of a paste similar to tallow and chewing gum. He pressed one to the opening of his right ear, and placed another in the other.

"True, I can still hear everything, but less. Now I'll finally be able to fall asleep!"

He got back to bed. The ear plugs bothered him a bit, but he hardly heard the crashing orchestra, with his head wrapped up in the blanket.

"Finally some silence! But the pillow is so hard and the blanket so suffocating! I can't breathe."

Frustrated, he leapt out again to throw the blanket away and arrange the top cushion properly.

"Oh, now I just have to fall asleep!"

He managed to doze off. While doing so, he began to hear the arterial beats right at the level of his ears and felt them in sync with his heartbeat. Then he realized that both made the bed itself vibrate.

"Amazing how the heart of flesh can keep an iron bed in vibration! Meanwhile, even though I'm so tired, I still can't sleep! And with all the work that awaits me tomorrow! And the urgent need to return to Geneva for the move! I really have to get rid of all the goods quickly, even at the cost of losing money. If not, I'm going to end up going crazy. All I have to do is reserve the best and least bulky things to sort out: precious stones, jewels... A couple of suitcases of stuff or at the most a dozen suitcases, if they're almost the size of hail; rather big, much, much bigger…" and he fell asleep, and dreamed a whole series of strange dreams, until he saw a moving van appearing from the end of the street which stopped on the landing on the third floor. The painter opened the gate for him, and the van entered the apartment, in the midst of all the suitcases. All of the painter's people, and the two sales assistants of pharmaceutical products, hurriedly threw the suitcases, sacred furnishings, and sacred vestments, into the van in one big heap, spoiling everything.

He said:

"Slowly. Respect these things! Let's get the suitcases in the van so we can get going!"

But they threw it all in, hurriedly. Then, as the van moved, it slid down the slippery, stony slope. It was very steep and narrow! They weren't even going the right way! He stood in front of the van, signaling them to stop and go back, but they stared at him with glassy, immobile, traitor eyes as the van came upon him. He then began to run to avoid being crushed, but the van went faster and faster, still behind him. So he ran even faster, to outpace it, but the van, seeming to have wide open jaws, was still behind him. He could feel its suffocating breath. He reacted by darting to one side, but there wasn't any space. The side was closer than the van itself. It was as if he was enclosed in a steel suitcase and they were about to flatten him while staring at him with glassy, motionless, traitor's eyes. By this time he was running with all his strength but was so tired, he could no longer move his legs. He had nothing left to do but make a leap, to launch himself onto the open nose of the van, and thus escape from the steel suitcase, which gripped him like an iron vice.

He bent down on his steel legs, but they didn't want to bend. He made a superhuman effort, and took the leap. He fell on the rug, began dragging the sheets with him, and woke up.

He was panting, sweaty, bruised, but it had only been a dream! His deposits were safe. He was in Rome, and the painter was watching over his things in Geneva.

"That traitor! But no, I was dreaming. He's a very good person, even if as a painter he's not worth anything at all."

He took off his earplugs and heard the loud rumble of a van passing in the street. He ran impulsively to the window and flung it open just in time to see a military truck disappear around the bend. He breathed and closed the shutters. Daylight filtered into his room, but he was too tired to get up. He threw himself back on the bed and resumed daydreaming, until the phone rang.

It was Romolo. He told Market everything was ready, that he could have a practical demonstration at any time, and that was ready to be paid. At first Market was surprised and hesitant. Then he thought:

"It's just a test! As for the money, I'll only give it on my timeline, if there really is a need for it."

But on the other end of the telephone line, Romolo demanded that he set a date for the experiment and payment delivery. Cornered, Market had to accept the date suggested by Romolo himself:

"Thursday at half past seven, on the via Tiburtina, at the crossroads for Torre Cervara."

But having given his word for the experiment, he also had to keep his word for the money. Finding twenty-five packets of one hundred bills of ten thousand lire each wasn't difficult for him, but he had no intention of depriving himself of this for the sake of Romolo's innocent act. But he began to get the money together.

He knew the feelings towards Pius XIV of the Roman delegate of the Human Universal Fraternity for the integration of Humanism. Having spoken to him, he had gotten what he had wanted. It was nicely packaged, like a nice dictionary.

He put it in a small bag and later locked it in the safe in his apartment.

Wednesday evening arrived without Market fully realizing it. He'd been so absorbed in his work in the goods depot that he had on the mezzanine floor of the apartment building. To safeguard the deposit, he had also had to rent the rear garden that was filled with brushwood, filled with four leafless and semi-dry shrubs, called thujas, that stretched upwards. They looked like four gigantic headless human skeletons, arms outstretched as if imploring the infinite.

Before leaving for Geneva, he felt the need to make a file as precise as possible of the material in the Roman depository. Then he would move to a new warehouse in the city before beginning to sell all its goods. In order to make a decent sale, such as to someone in the United States of America, he needed a catalog with photos, as complete as possible. He fretted about such a catalog since he was not much of a photographer and didn't think of hiring a professional photographer.

On the other hand, there was a certain urgency because he didn't have any receipts for the goods, and therefore could, strictly speaking, be accused of possessing stolen goods or, at least, of evading taxes. This had become a possibility from the moment when parish priests, chaplains, abbots, mother superiors, and others received the pontifical decree regarding sacred furnishings. Maybe he hadn't fully paid them all at the agreed price, in cash. But he was an honest person. In business, nothing is achieved without honesty. Dishonesty ruins everything. This he knew and practiced.

He was a very honest person. In fact, he had overpaid everyone, and all the stuff was his. It was his rightful property. No one had the right to touch it, not even the Pope. That old fraud had made him put his suitcase down on the floor of the parish church of the Three Holy Brothers! By what right? With the right of arrogance! Because it had been four against one. But now that man would no longer hook away the tiniest of those treasures from him! He had tightly closed all the windows and then walled them up, locked all the doors tightly, and walled up the doors too, all twenty-five or maybe even twenty-seven doors. They were all walled up with stacks of banknotes and massive railings. Then there was the painter with all his family members, who kept watch, day and night, armed to the teeth, and with a string of bombs on their shoulders. Then all around there was that barbed wire. Nobody could cross it.

However, a van, full of suitcases, was passing over it.

He ran after it, to get his suitcases out, all the suitcases. His suitcases. The vehicle accelerated, but he grabbed it, and held back all his suitcases. But then came a procession of popes, who passed by, and snatched his suitcases. They snatched away his silver candelabra, which was so big! And the monstrances. So big! The glasses. So big! The little doors of the Tabernacle. So huge! The Crucifix of the main altar! But he held it tight.

The little fraud pope snatched it from him. That screeching barn owl grew stronger and larger! More and more overbearing, more and more threatening and smirking. But he held back one Crucifix, like a mad man, with all his strength. It began to slip through his hands, but he held on tight with invincible strength. The tractor of a barn owl was huge, and he pulled the Crucifix behind him, on the fence. The smug barn owl's tractor hauled him along too, but he didn't move. His neck was caught. He felt a tug in his neck by the rope that held him and pulled by the tractor of the laughing fellow. He didn't let go. He squeezed harder and harder. He was invincible, but the silver Crucifix slipped inexorably from his grasp, slowly, now gone but still within the reach of his fingers.

"No, no, no!" he cried out, making a titanic effort before waking up. But even when awake, he cried out again, "No, no, no! All that stuff's mine, it's the fruit of my work, it's the bone of my bones, it's the flesh of my flesh! There is not a pope in the world that I can let touch it! Whoever laughs last laughs longest!"

He threw the blanket that he had kept wrapped up tightly around his chest across the room. Then he unwound from his neck the lamp switch cord that was at the head of the bed. He pressed the button on the switch and the lamp came on. It was all askew, nearly ripped from the wall. He would have a mark or bruise around his neck. He looked at his watch:

"Seven o'clock!" He looked at the wall calendar. "Thursday! What did I have planned for this Thursday? Ah, you grinning, decrepit fraud of a pope, I'll show you who my stuff belongs to! I'll show you what Osiris Market can do! Keep your commendation as well!"

He hurried to put himself in order. In order? To shave he soaped himself up with toothpaste. By the time he noticed it, he was already bleeding in different spots.

"Blood? Legitimate defense against an unjust aggressor! Doesn't the law protect me? I can defend myself! Any risk? Today I risk fifty, one hundred million, but tomorrow I'll lie down on a bed of billions."

About to take the little bag with millions in it out of the safe, he hesitated. "Don't risk the certain for the uncertain! But now, what's left for me with any certainty since that decree...that sword of Damocles hanging over my head? And I've not yet said I'll give them to him! I'll start showing them around."

He arrived almost punctually where the Via Tiburtina is crossed by the road that goes to Torre Cervara. He saw a small car parked at the edge of the road and pulled his own car up to it, stopped, and got out. Romolo saw him step out of the car, like a ghost coming out of a tomb, and became afraid. But soon the tragic was replaced by the grotesque, and he had to make an effort not to laugh in his face, seeing the half-shaved face full of cuts. Market too gave a start when he saw Romolo in a fisherman's outfit. In fact, he was wearing Vassily's getup which he had borrowed the night before. There was no point in wasting time.

"Let's go, Commendatore. Come with me!" Romolo said to him. "A walk along the Aniene will do you good."

After walking for a short stretch of road, they descended to the riverbank, and then began to go against its current as far as the reed bed which was dominated by the solitary poplar. They moved forward among the reeds and reached the place of the experiment. Market had followed Romolo like an automaton, nervously and without asking where they were going. He had already understood enough, just as Romolo had understood that the bag Market was holding had the agreed-upon loot. There was no need to ask questions.

"You can see those people, but they can't see you. Here, this is a breviary. We attach it to the top of this barrel. There's a timer in here, and we set it to five and a half minutes, right. Now I immerse the whole thing right to the bottom of the river, near the shore. And now we take cover behind here, and wait."

They crouched behind the pozzolana[2] embankment, and fixed their eyes on their watches. Exactly between the fifth and sixth minutes, a dull but powerful explosion was heard. The ground shook and a shower of water flew over them. The stems of the plants in the bushes where they were hiding bent as if under a gust of wind, but straightened up immediately. Everything became calm once again. The Aniene flowed peacefully, and anyone who had not been looking directly at that spot a moment earlier wouldn't have noticed a thing. But Vassily had noticed it from his excellent observation point. He had followed the two early-morning hikers with binoculars and had noticed the bag carried by the stranger following Romolo. He perceived the detonation that had caused the momentary geyser.

---

2   Pozzolana is a fine volcanic ash. It is mainly used in construction.

"Well! He's brave!" Vassily exclaimed. "Even the charges are really noiseless. The test is also done. Kharashò!"

"Well then?" Romulus asked Market. The latter gathered his thoughts together one last time about the next step, but his mind was blank. As soon as he closed his eyes, he saw the tractor again, the suitcases, the van, the grinning wannabe pope. He instinctively clutched his bag to his chest. This gesture shook him out of his anguished visions. He reopened his eyes, threw his bag at Romolo's feet, and said:

"The sooner the better. Afterwards, the other twenty-five, actually twenty-seven million, are waiting for you, but it's a hundred thousand lira less for every day that passes, from today. Agreed?"

Romolo bent down to pick up the bag which he then opened. He took out and unwrapped the package and peeked at the contents. He put it back into the fisherman's basket, gave the empty bag back to the commendatore, and repeated:

"Agreed!" Market looked at him sideways and asked him: "How?"

"A breviary behind a car cushion."

Market locked up the bag, gave a shrug, and walked quickly away. Romolo waited until he had gone a little distance, and then returned through the reeds and went slowly along the Aniene with the current. Mission accomplished.

"And now I just have to change my demeanor. I'll claim I'm sick and get a medical statement right away. Then I'll quit and go to Naples."

As soon as Vassily had seen them both moving, he had left his observatory and preceded them to their respective cars. He was well hidden in a grove a little further on. When Market hurriedly passed by his side, without spotting him, Vassily carefully scrutinized the purse that the man gripped nervously with his left hand, and said to himself:

"It's empty. Romolo has collected the advance." And then he went down towards the Aniene to meet up with him.

"What are you doing around here at this hour?" Romolo asked when he saw him.

"I thought you might need me. I wanted to tell you last night when you asked me for my fisherman's outfit. You yourself told me that you needed it for this morning, very early, and I hurried to get it to you. But it looks good on you. Well, how did it go?"

He offered one of his cigarettes to Romolo. Smoking in silence, they reached the street. Vassily asked again:

"Well, how did it go?"

"What do you care?"

"I was hoping that a pinch of grass would help loosen your tongue and take some of the nervousness off. You're used to it. It shows. For me a pinch is enough. It makes me generous right away. So then I have to be alert because I end up saying everything... and let me tell you, I'm interested in knowing how it went because we're dealing with newly acquired material."

"And I was your guinea pig."

"I would've given you a hand too. I would've checked everything first. That's why I came so early, but you still got here before me. Would you at least give me a ride? I had to hitchhike to get here. Take me wherever you're going, but at least up to Piazzale del Verano. From there I can take the tram. If you no longer need the getup, I'd like to get it back as soon as possible, except the trousers, of course, which belong to you."

"Take it!" Romolo snapped. Now a step away from his car, he started to untie the basket, but suddenly remembered the loot inside, and stopped himself. He said, "I'll get it back to you within a day."

He got in behind the wheel. Vassily got in next to him and began to smoke. Romolo started the engine, but before engaging the gear, he stretched out a hand towards Vassily, gesturing to the cigarette. Vassily handed him the entire package. Romolo took one. Vassily lit it for him, and that was it.

When Romolo came to his senses, it was ten o'clock. He had a severe headache. He realized that he was in his car, parked by the cypresses, in front of the entrance to Campo Verano. He was still dressed as a fisherman. He slowly began to remember. He remembered the dope. He looked for the basket. It was on the seat next to him. He had used it as a pillow. He opened it. The money was still there. With difficulty he started the car again, and set off on his way back. But what exactly had happened? Vassily had fed him a fast-working narcotic! Why? He took one more look at the basket, and began to wonder about something. He pulled to one side and stopped the car. He grabbed the basket, opened it, and took out the package. Under it were many packets of cigarettes. He feverishly unwrapped the parcel.

"Asshole!"

The parcel was filled with explosive material and related accessories. Among the explosive tablets was also a carefully folded note, which he read while trembling: "Dear Friend, These will easily give you something more than what I have taken from you. You just have to get yourself a breviary case. As you can see, I've taken care of everything else. In these types of situations, it's customary to go halfway, like good friends. I've given you all my brain, and will settle for the lesser part. The fisherman outfit fits you perfectly. It's yours. To prove my honesty, here are all these cigarettes. I made them myself. Also, to make up for the headache that the drugged cig certainly left you with. These take away all headaches. Try one now! Don't look for me! In a few hours I'll have given myself who-knows-what name and who-knows-what nationality, and will also have changed my physical features. So what good would it do you to look for me? So always good friends! Yours, Vassily. Good luck."

"Go to hell!" Romolo shouted.

"And the sooner the better! Twenty-seven million. One hundred thousand lira less with each passing day!"

Romolo turned to see who had whispered the words in his ear. No one. Crazy! All he had to do was stick to the cigarettes, of which there were many. They would last for a few weeks, depending on their strength. With their blue, rosy, golden fumes, the cigarettes gradually hid the horrors of the crime from his sight and made many beautiful shells glitter before his eyes, overflowing with many precious stones. Ever larger shells, ever more precious stones. Sparkling. All colors. Radiating around him like a magical, immense iris.

36

Lateran VI

"HERE! BREAD FOR THE PONTIFIcal doves," Brother Ambrogio said while placing the usual transparent bag in His Holiness's hands that contained a few scraps of dry bread. The Pope passed the bag to Camillo, and they went out with Monsignor Wong towards the gardens.

"What a beautiful day! What beautiful flowers! Everything's so lush and green! What a pleasant Ponentino!" But soon their conversation turned more serious. Camillo remembered that he had to say something to the regular gardener, and discreetly moved away from the group.

"Do you remember, dear Gabriele, the euphoria felt right around here of those past days? Like a distribution of prizes or honorary degrees to Congar, de Lubac, Maritain..."

"...who had not yet published *Le paysan de la Garonne*, to repair, though unsuccessfully, the damage caused by his *Humanisme intégral*," added Wong.

"Some even awarded the degree to the memory of Teilhard himself. They considered him to be the inspiration of the Second Vatican Council, which was then closing amid such triumphal language!"

"And the springtime of the new Pentecost was announced as imminent. Indeed it had already begun!"

"There was no shortage among the clergy, of those who understood only one thing, that the era of freedom had begun.

Each one gave himself to following his own ideas, more often those deftly spread by modernist propaganda, which had captured the monopoly of the means of social communication."

"And winter began!"

"Was there any resistance to such a colossus? It was enough to utter the magic formula, *Vatican II*! And then there were some of the most energetic bishops, some of the most authoritarian religious superiors, who supported this all, without examining the situation or demanding credentials or having any discussion on it. To avoid appearing old and outdated, they competed to outrun the craziest innovators.

"In making concession after concession, one arbitrary decision after another, they absorbed themselves in the new pastoral dynamics, in solidarity with and therefore accomplices of the modernists. They were forced to act against their deepest pre-conciliar convictions."

"Having taken the first bad step on the slippery path, they kept slipping till they reached the bottom, and declared that it was a responsible and irreversible choice to drown in mud and treason."

"Sown skilfully, the weeds grew rapidly and thickly. How much wheat withered or died or is now dying!"

"Soon certain conciliar texts, however open, were said to be outdated. The Council became the spirit of the Council, the dynamics of the Council, the logic of the Council, the mentality of the Council. These all demanded the radical conversion of every pre-conciliar mindset, even if this implied, in practical matters, going against the clear and explicit texts of the Council itself."

"What Mass did the Council Fathers celebrate? The traditional, apostolic-Roman one. What did they establish with the fourth article of the conciliar liturgical constitution? To keep that Mass. What is now being declared in the name of the Council? That it is prohibited. What did these Fathers establish with the thirty-sixth article of that constitution? To retain the use of Latin. What is now declared in the name of the Council? That the use of Latin is a sign of rebellion against the Church and a cause of schism."

"And the Council became synonymous with revolution. Then the deceitful people who had fanned the fire were heard barking in dismay, 'Too hot!' The naive had not considered their belief that the old was to be abandoned in the light of faith not because it is old, but because it is false and evil and the new was to be welcomed, not because it is new, but because it is true and good."

"In such an atmosphere, they changed the Mass as one changes attire. The most dismayed faithful were comforted by being told, "Here is finally a clean shirt, lighter, if you like, but functional."

"The Lutheran reform brought about a clear schism: either with or against Rome. The reforms that followed Vatican II brought about a series of schisms within the very heart of the Catholic Church, within every Catholic community, in the heart of every Catholic family. There were very painful tensions in the very heart of the conscience of many Catholics."

"It's now a question of carrying out a work of counter-reformation, which is certainly more complex than an anti-Protestant one, because it must be radically anti-modernist, and modernism is yet another arm of the octopus of early Lutheran Protestantism. We need to start a work of restoration of the Catholic tradition, of reconciliation of the faithful in a single and incontrovertible *lex credendi*, expressed faithfully, unequivocally, and explicitly by a single and common *lex orandi* that is specifically Catholic."

"Where to begin?" asked Wong.

"I was chosen against all human expectations as vicar of the Lord. I felt as if I had been transported up high, almost lost. This first impression was succeeded by the one St. Peter had after he climbed over the edge of his boat and had enough trust to take his first steps on the waves of the stormy lake. But I didn't doubt. I immediately began to commit myself to being better, to praying better or at least a little more. I limited myself to undoing from time to time the knots that from time to time came to roost, or to cut them, as I did with the Teilhardian society. At the beginning, I did this when I was given occasion, but I didn't have any organic plan. But I was soon convinced that the consequences deriving from a Council which was intended to be pastoral couldn't be fully remedied except with a Dogmatic Council. And this is exactly what I wanted to talk to you about before you go back to the Far East."

Their walk brought them to the pool of water lilies where they lingered to admire the few pinkish-white flowers that had blossomed among all the floating green discs which covered a large part of the surface of the water. Under all of that, goldfish could be seen darting here and there in groups. Camillo and the gardener approached the Pope and respectfully asked for an audience.

"Holiness, look at this stone!" the gardener told him. "It was found in Castel Gandolfo by a colleague of mine while he was digging a hole for a transplant. It looks like it came out of a volcano."

The Pope examined it with curiosity and then passed it on to Wong, saying:

"It looks like a meteorite."

"In fact, it is," confirmed Wong, who, turning to the gardener, continued, "This stone is not of terrestrial origin. In fact it fell from the sky. It is a piece of star, which became a shooting star. Falling towards the Earth and having reached the atmosphere, due to the friction of the air, it became incandescent and traced a luminous trail, consuming itself in part. It nevertheless managed to reach the surface of the Earth before it was completely consumed. It is certainly iron, perhaps with nickel and carbon. Nickel steel. This piece of star, which shone up there, hasn't been on the Earth for long. Otherwise it would be corroded by rust."

The Pope added, "The chisels that the ancient Egyptians used to carve granite, and also other stones that were harder than granite itself, were certainly made of stellar steel! However, some archaeologists, since they did not find such chisels in the layers of the soil they explored, say that Tubalcain[1] couldn't have been the father of the copper and iron smiths, because the use of copper would have begun only six thousand years ago, and iron only four thousand years ago or a little more."

The gardener, believing himself authorized to confirm the Pope's words with his own experience, said:

"Don't archaeologists know that the iron in the ground decomposes? I lost a grafting knife and found it a few years later, hoeing around a rosebush. I recognized it from the handle, which was bone, and it was still there, but the metal was almost all gone."

"But do you see?" the Pope added, "According to certain scholars, the only things that existed back then are the things that they find in excavations, and that anything that they do not find there, couldn't have existed and didn't exist. Since the caves still exist, while the huts and houses were destroyed, they assert that ancient man lived only in caves."

"And since they didn't find any feathers in the caves," Camillo observed in turn, "will they perhaps say that the primitives weren't hunters of birds? And if they find nothing in a cave, they'll say it was uninhabited, when maybe it had simply been carefully cleaned at the time."

"Nevertheless archeology, treated seriously by real archaeologists, is also very useful for biblical studies. For example, if we go back to Tubalcain, his name means 'smith-smith': *Tibira*

---

[1] "Sella also brought forth Tubalcain, who was a hammerer and artificer in every work of brass and iron." (Gen. 4:22)

in Sumerian, *Qàyin* in Hebrew. He lived in what is called the Paleolithic era, the era of the ancient stone, as the stone tools used by man of that time are the crudest known. However, the Book of Genesis makes Tubalcain the progenitor of the iron and copper smiths, and perhaps himself a metalsmith. 'From what metals, in an age of stone tools?' some archaeologists ask skeptically. My answer: meteoric iron.

"Well, iron was called the Metal of Heaven by the ancient Egyptians, and the cuneiform ideogram of iron has the same meaning. Even philology confirms this conclusion: in Greek it's called iron, *sideros*, what in Latin is called star, *sidus sideris*. Even today the natives of Greenland have tools made with star pieces."

The gardener said, "But I, I couldn't get anything out of this piece of star."

"Give it to me," Wong said. "I'll place it in the museum at my seminar, with a nice tag, the name of the kind offerer, and the place of discovery. And many thanks!"

The walk resumed in groups of two.

The Pope went on: "And if, continuing with what we said at the beginning, if this Lateran VI has to be dogmatic, here we are again with the same question: where to begin?"

"I asked that question a moment ago, and now I would like to try to answer it. We must begin by putting the Church in first place, putting the Gospel in second place. First, living people, then things, their instruments. Let me explain. The modernists present themselves as champions of the Gospel, of the Gospel that the Church supposedly hid, disfigured, and denied. They shout: 'Gospel yes, Church no!' For some, it's an illusion mostly from crass ignorance, in other words, the deception of finding the Gospel outside the Church or even against the Church. For others, however, it's a formal and diabolical lie. They mask this true aim by claiming to reform the Catholic Church on grounds which they say are evangelical, but they want to destroy it."

"The Luther illusion."

"Much worse, Your Holiness! Luther was incapable of reforming his own habits. He couldn't bring them back into harmony with the Commandments of God. He became a helpless slave of his own flesh. Then he found an alibi for his inner anguish. This alibi was the exterior struggle. So he set out, spear in hand, against the Church based on his alleged fidelity to the Gospel. But the wound inflicted by Luther on the body of Christianity gradually became more and more purulent, gangrenous. It began as Protestantism and degenerated into modernism.

"St. Pius X did not hesitate to act, like a determined surgeon. But it was a malignant cancer. Enucleated from where it appeared most developed, it metastasized throughout the organism, subtly during the pontificate of Pius XII, but then boldly extending all its tentacles with Vatican II. Didn't modernism aim to shame the agony of Pius XII? He had kept it in check. And no one expected to reform the Church structures themselves in the spirit of Vatican II—according to them! They never specified what they meant by structures because the aim was only deformation and destruction? What healthy aspect was left? In the name of the Bible and out of fidelity to Christ—listen to them!

"The new Pentecost actually aimed to start things from scratch, which meant first of all reducing to nothing everything that had been built up since the first and only true biblical Pentecost. They found nothing good or evangelical in the Church, the same Church that had been completely filled with the Holy Spirit at the true and unique Pentecost. In the two thousand years of life of the Church, they saw only two thousand years of errors and infidelity to Our Lord and to the Gospel. Two thousand years of faults that required repentance and requests for forgiveness, if not from God, at least from men.

"And then we have the critics with their semantics and the experts with their demythologization in search of some primordial and literal sense of the sacred texts, as if they had never been correctly understood before. They sought the distillation of the authentic spirit of the early Church, as if they had then been an active part of it of the first importance, at least on a par with the apostles. They found that everything had been the opposite of what the uninterrupted two-thousand-year-old tradition of the Church had transmitted until then. Instead of the infallible Magisterium, we had the infallible Hans Küng and his by-products!"

The Pope added, "Boileau-Despréaux.[2] He said that every Protestant, with the Bible in hand, is Pope."

Wong added, "But to the modernist, for him to feel himself as both Pope and Church and Church founder, he doesn't even need the Bible. His own impudence is enough for him! To launch his message, for him it's enough to scrutinize the Signs of the Times on the pages of his favorite newspaper that are dedicated to the news of the previous day.

"I've tried to identify the intrinsic causes of this cancer of modernism, and would reduce these to the Enlightenment, the belief in democracy, and universalist humanism. When the Enlightenment denies divine revelation as infallibly delivered to the teaching Church, it deludes itself into believing that it's finally discovering the genuine truth for the first time and under its own power. It declares that this genuine truth involves a continuous dialectic between contradictory phases. Democracy rejects the Church as how its divine Founder wanted it to be, namely monarchical and aristocratic. Democracy replaces this with a pseudo-church that's structured like democratic parliamentarians and soviets. This new church is consequently at the mercy of demagogues. Finally, regarding universalist Humanism, it denies the worship that is due God. It devotes

---

[2] Nicolas Boileau-Despréaux (1636–1711), member of the Academie francaise, poet, and classicist, wrote the influential *L'art poètique*. He satirized public figures.

itself to the worship of man and forgets eternal life. It worries about this life, which is as fleeting as a shadow. It is only concerned with the earthly progress of peoples towards a future of eternal damnation."

At this point the white doves descended in flight around the Pope in order to assert their rights. Then Camillo approached the Pope and handed him the bag of dry bread.

As the Pope broke off little pieces of bread and threw them to the doves, he began to recount, "During the war, we wouldn't have thrown even these scraps of bread to the doves. Bread! One Sunday, I had gone to celebrate Mass for displaced citizens in a small country church. It was winter. Very cold. The silver of the goblet was icy, and during the ablutions, the water in the cruet had already turned to ice. The chaplain then gave me an exceptional reward: a nice loaf of white bread, over half a kilo, still warm.

"With that loaf of bread under my arm, and my hands tucked into my sleeves—because, to tell you in confidence, I had given my beautiful woolen gloves to a Thai brother of mine who suffered from the cold much more than me—therefore, with my loaf of bread, I set out to return. But when I turned a corner, I saw a little girl in front of me, with worn out boots on her feet, and a boy's shorts and jacket. Near her chest, by means of a cord that descended from her shoulders, and with her red and swollen hands, she was holding a box that had many compartments. It was filled with strings, ribbons, spools of thread, and other trifles. As soon as she saw me, and that I was a priest, she didn't dare offer me her wares, and from those hungry eyes, large and pensive, came a look of profound disappointment. But she recovered and said to me: 'Can you at least give me charity?' I had no money. However, I had the precious bread, with which I had promised myself I would cheer up some of my brothers who were in bad health. But I didn't hesitate. I unwrapped it from the sheet of newspaper with which it had been wrapped up, and I deposited it on the box of the small itinerant haberdashery. She widened her eyes and exclaimed:

"Bread! It's mine?"

I nodded yes, greeted her, traced a small sign of the cross on her forehead, and went on my way. After a while I looked back. The little girl, now far away, had turned around at the same time and so greeted me by waving the loaf of bread.

"Now this, on the other hand, wastes so much bread! And all the while there are entire populations that need it more than these doves. But this dry bread will end up in the trash anyway. So I might as well give it to the doves!"

At the chapel of the Madonna della Guardia, the Pope and Wong sat down and resumed talking about the future Council.

"First of all, the sixth Lateran Council must declare unambiguously that it intends to be an act of the solemn, dogmatic, and infallible magisterium, in continuity with the ecclesiastical magisterium, and therefore in continuity with sacred Tradition. And for this reason, it's still rooted in that part of sacred Tradition which has been enclosed in Sacred Scripture. In this way, the possibility of appealing to Scripture as a way to go against the infallible magisterium is nipped in the bud.

"Furthermore, Lateran VI must declare that the only certain and authoritative interpretation of Scripture is found in Tradition, and that the only certain and authoritative interpreter of Tradition is the infallible ecclesiastical magisterium with its fulcrum in the very person of the Pope as Pope.

"It must be established, then, that the Church is not the so-called People of God which expresses by itself all doctrinal and disciplinary authority, but that it is the mystical Body of the Incarnate Word. It is governed by the Pope, who has supreme power of direct jurisdiction both over the other bishops and over each individual believer. It is governed by bishops who are united with the Pope. They have the power of personal and direct jurisdiction over all the faithful of the diocese entrusted to them by the Pope. In the exercise of their apostolic activity, they are not bound to conform to the deliberations or recommendations expressed either by the majority or by all the bishops of other dioceses, however those are grouped together.

"Lataran VI must restore what has not already been restored from what was destroyed in the appeal to *Sacrosanctum Concilium*, on the liturgy, and sometimes in contradiction with it. This must be done so that the *lex orandi* returns to conformity with the Catholic *lex credendi*, and not to the cloudy ideals of the modernists.

"It must then repair the damage caused by the Lutheranism that is latent in certain declarations. These have led to disqualifying the priesthood, making the priest the presider of an assembly of his equals, or a transmitter of the Bible to men. But in fact he is in the first place a priest for the sacrificial cult that is due God. It is necessary that the due punishments will be determined for anyone who dares to undermine celibacy priestly.

"Lateran VI must divert apostolic and missionary activity from social concerns, that is, from the construction of the Tower of Babel of the world, and from the obsessive-exaltation of the world itself with all its worldly values, its fairy tales and fleeting shadows. Above all, it must bring this activity back to the search for eternal life and personal sanctification through theological charity. Only this can lead to true fraternal charity. It is quite different from any sentimental and moralizing humanitarianism.

"Therefore it must declare that *Ad gentes divinitus* missionaries are sent not to bring to the peoples the expected democratic liberator and promoter of earthly progress, but to convert and welcome the mysteries of the faith, to get them to renounce Satan and his idols along with the concupiscence of the eyes and of the flesh, and the pride of life, to offer them baptism and purification from Adam's sin, and from their personal sins, and to make themselves worthy of Heaven. This is the only service that the Church can and must render to the world. This is the purpose that Our Lord founded her for. The rest is none of her business. This must be defined in classic terms, very clearly, without drowning it in a sea of digressions and eloquent but meaningless formulas. In other words, the missionaries who prefer the digging of wells to the catechesis of eternal life can go home.

"The Church must no longer be considered and defined by those who imagine it in their own way. This is the greatest revolutionary force of our time, stronger than Communism itself, which could do nothing against the West without the complicity of progressive Christians. This madness that makes the revolution divine and supernatural and declares it to be the Gospels must cease. It naturalizes the Gospel and reduces it to a cookbook for a higher standard of living. *Regnum meum non est de hoc mundo*.[3] This should be meditated on by these unfortunate guerrilla priests who, out of the entire Gospels, only remember Jesus casting out the profaners from the temple."

"They should also meditate on the words spoken by Jesus to Peter: 'Put your sword back in its place, for those who live by the sword will die by it. Do you not know that I can ask my Father, and he will immediately give me more than twelve legions of angels?' I'm for universal peace. I'm for conscientious objection. I'm against the death penalty... and they kill the soldiers and policemen of the countries they enter to bring freedom!"

The Pope and Wong had resumed their walk before stopping to observe the rainbow which formed intermittently in a large fan of water droplets that a sprinkler forcefully threw and the sun vaporized. The Pope turned back to Camillo and the gardener and said:

---

[3] "My reign is not of this world."

"Today this system of spraying is widespread in Palestine, above all on the initiative of the Jews."

"Oh, the Jews! They say they work miracles there," the gardener declared.

"They would certainly do much more," said the Pope, "if there weren't political and military tensions. I happened to walk for half an hour on the shores of Lake Tiberias, on the most fertile land in the world—blackish loam of loose basalt, deep, and with abundant water just a stone's throw away. I walked for half an hour in an abandoned banana grove. The head of the nearby kibbutz told me that there was no manpower to work it. The young men do not have the makings of pioneers, and moreover they have to spend a long time in the army. That was a kibbutz without the bet tefiláh, the house of prayer."

"How come?"

"Because out of five hundred people who belonged to it, there weren't ten men who could assure everyone that they would visit it regularly. Other kibbutzímins have their own beautiful synagogues; and in them truly *fervet opus*, despite the fact that everyone has to live there with weapons close at hand, as in the times of Nehemiah..."

"...and in a land which, if we keep to the Scriptures, would belong to them by divine right," observed Camillo.

The Pope also explained, "Truly, Scripture also demonstrates that the heir to the divine promises implied by the Old Covenant, now, according to the New Covenant, is the Catholic Church, of which the people of Israel were but a mere forerunner. We, however, are satisfied that pilgrims can visit the Holy Places freely and without danger."

"However," Camillo observed again, "without Palestine, the Jews would go back to being wandering Jews."

The Pope explained, "I will say that only a minority of Jews are Zionists. And at least 80% of Jews don't want to live in Palestine. They're comfortable where they are. Despite the pressure exerted on them in years past, they didn't want to move there. Sure, if they could freely and fearlessly enter the whole boundless empty space of the Middle East, without setting up a political and military state there, they would quickly establish a vast economic and cultural empire with undeniable advantages also for the populations who have lived there since time immemorial. Jews generally retain those talents, bestowed upon them by the Lord, that allowed them to succeed as missionaries of monotheism and be the prophets of Catholicism. They keep those talents even now when they no longer have that divine mandate, and they know how to trade them like that shrewd servant of the ten minas[4], and even better. Then they would not need to contend with the desert for a few palms of sand to be reclaimed and irrigated to make it fertile, much more so because water in Palestine is scarce and expensive."

"But what about the Sea of Tiberias or the Jordan River?"

"They don't provide enough. Also water is taken from the lake near the few ruins of the very ancient Sea of Galilee and sent to the Négev—the southern or arid region, as its name suggests—so that water doesn't feed the Jordan, which flows out of the Sea of Galilee."

"But if it is true that Palestine is slightly larger than Lazio,[5] I believe that water for irrigation should not be lacking, as it is crossed throughout its length by a river like the Jordan."

"Oh, the Jordan," the Pope replied. "It's a River Po only in name.[6] In reality it ordinarily has a flow rate lower than the average of the Tiber."

"It's a River Po its name? What does it mean?" Camillo asked.

"The Latin name of the Po is Eridanus and its Greek name is Eridanàs. Now, if we pronounce the name Eridano poetically, we really have the name Giordano, which means outflow or

---

[4] Lk. 19:11–27.
[5] A region of Italy, where Rome is located.
[6] The River Po, Italy's longest river, flows through the north of Italy.

river. The names Rodano, Arnon, Reno, Nera and so on, and even Euphrates, can also be traced back to the same root. Several local places have a peculiar coincidence with Semitic words. The Semitic for plain is paddán, and we have the Po Valley. Álpu stands for ox and pasture, and we have the Alps. Abode is bet, and we have the baite, or huts, of the Alps. Haddéh means fast, which is perhaps the river Adda. Lily is shusluán, and we have the Susa Valley, and so on. Now it may be that we are dealing with pre-Semitic words that the Semites borrowed. But if the words were originally Semitic, we have to agree that tribes of Semitic nomadic shepherds had been sent to the Po Valley even before Abraham."

Back in the house, after having had the usual cup of tea in the living room, the Pope and Wong ended their conversation.

"Finally, the VI Lateran, possibly in a second session, will have to deal with the relations between the Church and non-Churches and reconfirm the dogma *extra Ecclesiam nulla salus*[7] unambiguously and in the correct sense. It must therefore rectify *Dignitatis humanae* on religious freedom, because that document contradicts the immutable doctrine of the Church that declares *ore rotundo*[8] the absolute and universal supremacy of the one true God, Who is called Jesus Christ. The duty of all non-Catholics is to convert to Catholicism. They don't have the right to refuse to enter even if the executioner's ax is hanging around their necks. Let them know that eternal damnation hangs over them. And let Catholics also know that it's not enough to believe in God to be Catholic, but that they must believe that Jesus Christ is God and that there's no other God than Jesus Christ.

Lateran VI must specify that *Unitatis redintegratio* does not open a broad path to some sort of confusing ecumenism in which everyone pretends, during common pseudo-liturgical

---

7 "There is no salvation outside of the Church."
8 "With open mouth." In other words, loudly and clearly.

ceremonies, that they get along with everyone else, while in fact believing quite the opposite, that the other is very wrong. *Unitatis redintegratio* consists exclusively in the return of the dissidents to the one fold under the one supreme doctrinal and juridical pastor. Therefore, the prohibition of *communicatio in sacris*[9] which takes place in those hybrid celebrations must be renewed, since, prior to the law canon, they are condemned by the natural law itself as grave immoralities by virtue of their very nature.

"Finally it must clarify the *Perfectae caritatis*[10] by defining the characteristics of Christian perfection, according to the evangelical counsels. This must all take place under the auspices of Mary Most Holy, proclaimed Mater Dei et Virgo perpetual."

As they walked slowly up the two flights of stairs together to go each to their own room, the Pope asked Wong:

"If you were in my place, what would you do with the Vatican?"

Without hesitating for a moment, Wong replied: "The citadel of prayer, with permanent Eucharistic adoration, also in the chapel of the Blessed Sacrament of St. Peter's basilica. Isn't it right that God should be adored like this at least in the capital of his Church?"

"And where would you like to take the Catholic Church?"

"To the hour of annual worldwide Eucharistic adoration for the feast of Corpus Domini, with all the faithful having the use of reason. I think that having obtained so much, even the conversion of the unbelievers would be more easy, if not completely accomplished."

The Pope then threw out a third question, one that was very close to his heart: "If you could no longer govern your diocese, who could replace you?"

---

[9] "Communion in sacred things."
[10] Pope Paul VI, *Decree on the Adaptation and Renewal of Religious Life* (1965).

"Monsignor Filippo Yu-min-ten, my current vicar. He has all the gifts that I would like to have, and he did a seven year apprenticeship in communist prisons."

While the two were talking, Camillo told Ambrogio the little story of the itinerant merchant, and of the loaf of white bread. Ambrogio then confided to him:

"Do you see? So that I always have scraps of dry bread ready, I take a nice fresh and beautiful-smelling loaf, cut it into pieces, and put the pieces out on the windowsill, in the sun until the next day. There they are, on the windowsill, ready for tomorrow. Now, however, we really need to save the bread, so that one day it won't run out, and that we won't have to regret it. I need to find some dry bread that is more... natural!"

37

"Traditionis restauratio"

OF ALL THE PIOUS PRACTICES OF pilgrims, by now the most important was the Mass of the Pope, in the chapel of the Blessed Sacrament of St. Peter's Basilica. The news of this celebration was spread by pilgrims throughout the Catholic world. As a result, requests for details and for permissions flooded onto Father Medina's desk. In some dioceses, several bishops favored the restoration of the unreformed Mass.

Father Medina was not up to facing the Pope a second time, either alone or supported by Father Viso's assistance. He therefore went to a colleague of his, Monsignor Corsuccini, under the pretext of asking advice on what to do about expected resistance to editing issues in an appendix in one of the many soon-to-be-released liturgical books, but he skilfully brought the conversation around to the true purpose of his visit. This was the scandal of the Tridentine Mass celebrated by the Pope himself. This posed a mortal danger to the entire Vatican II reform and consequent nullification of so much work and expense. He convinced Corsuccini so kindly that the latter declared his determination to go to the Pope himself. He would make his most heartfelt protests, convey the cries of pain which the faithful emitted in chorus from many parts of the Church against the liturgical innovation constituted by the Tridentine Mass, and induce the Holy Father to put an end to his daily celebration. This celebration was upsetting to the People of God, scandalous to fearful souls, and discouraging to true liturgists. Naturally, Father Medina was careful not to inform him of the outcome of the visit that he himself had made to the Pope for the same purpose in the company of Father Viso.

"*Gutta cavat lapidem!*"[1] he had said to Father Viso, commenting on the impending assistance after the slick talk with Corsuccini. "Our words were the first drops and those of Monsignor Corsuccini will constitute the second. Then, if that's not enough, we will organize a third, a fourth series of drops: *Gutta cavat lapidem!*"

"That's enough! Enough!" Father Viso exclaimed. "Your words are more corrosive than sulphuric acid. Just give them time to act. They will also hollow out the stone."

After addressing these expressions of comfort to his superior, he passed him a letter which had arrived shortly before. The letter immediately put an end to Father Medina's euphoria that had been sparked by the conversation with Corsuccini. Father Medina had been summoned along with various other liturgists to a restricted meeting or audience by Pius XIV himself.

"So he escapes the dripping. Meanwhile I might get another cold shower. Let's hope that damn Chinese fellow isn't there too! In any case, I won't be alone. There will be many of us, and we'll form a group around the reform! It's a question of getting in touch with them before the hearing. And I'll require that they too can participate in it. When will all these dealings end for this reform. They almost make me dislike it too!"

And he grabbed the phone.

Corsuccini arrived well in advance for what he was to turn into a collective embassy of protest by real liturgists against Pius XIV. Given the number of churchmen who had been summoned, the hearing wouldn't take place in the Laurini monastery, but in the large old office. In the office's waiting room, Corsuccini spotted Father Norberto. Although the latter was

---

1 "a drop [of water] hollows stone," i.e., not by force but by repetition.

now a bishop, he still wore his black friar's cassock. He was leafing through one of the new, very short Italian breviaries. Corsuccini guessed that the friar, despite his age, was one of the reform group.

"The breviary, the Hours, in a living language!" he said to strike up a conversation, and continued: "It's about time! The People of God in our assemblies no longer understood a thing, and they demanded it."

Norberto looked at Corsuccini, greeted him, and then said:

"The Hours or the Minutes? I wasn't aware that your People of God are so enthusiastic about it. On the other hand, the Breviary was not conceived as a prayer of the faithful, but as a prayer of the clergy for the faithful. But listen to this story! There was an excellent organ in a cathedral, one of those old-fashioned organs, of very high workmanship and a great deal of religious sense, built by one of the best organ specialists of those times. But the cathedral had a terrible organist, one of those modern electric guitar racket-makers, who elbowed his way to power and, with his up-to-date views, kicked his predecessor out and took over. But when he played the keyboard, everyone left the church. Having heard about this from the presbyteral council, what did the bishop do to repair such a misfortune? He changed the organ!"

"You mean that..."

"...I mean?" Norberto interrupted him. "No! I mean that a more effective participation of the faithful in the Holy Mass, and the liturgy in general, requires a more accurate catechesis, without any need to redo the Missal. Haven't you read anything, dear Monsignor, by Prosper Guéranger, by Ambrogio Amelli, by Pius Parsch? Don't you remember Pius XII's encyclical *Mediator Dei et hominum*?"

"And yet, despite the fetishists of that Tridentine organ, the People of God deserted the churches," insisted Corsuccini, who, though he could not be blamed, was not so flexible.

"And now in terms of frequency, how are we doing?" Norberto asked him. "What do your statistics tell you?"

"Statistics must be interpreted. Otherwise, they can be misleading. Concerning numbers, quality must be considered above all. Now attendance has qualitatively improved," concluded Corsuccini.

"That is, now there are fewer faithful in church than before, but on the other hand..."

"...in compensation," Corsuccini said, interrupting Norberto, "in compensation they participate *cum participatione magis actuosa*[2] in the liturgy."

"And they continue it outside church too," said Father Gregorio, who in the meantime had arrived, also *in nigris*,[3] and sat down next to Norberto.

"That's right!" Corsuccini exclaimed. "Repeat it, respectful of this Father, that thanks to the reform, active participation goes beyond the simple church hall. It ceases to be a place of privileged and exclusive sacredness, inasmuch as all the places where the People of God gather and live become equally sacred,"

Corsuccini concluded triumphantly, with an emphatic Petrarchan overflow. Indeed, he quoted a sentence from a recent article of his on which he had had to work harder than Hercules had during the most strenuous of his famous twelve labors.

"That's right!" Gregorio in turn exclaimed, adding, "And they continue their *actuosa partecipatio* even outside the sacred place, which by now is no longer exclusively sacred. I'm thinking of those little boys who made a nice collection in their home, as one does with butterflies, sticking pins in many consecrated hosts, received during Mass by hand, and devoutly placed in the pocket—at least—those that they had not dropped under

---

2 "with more 'actual' participation"—obvious reference *Sacrosanctum concilium* quote about "active" / "actual" participation, made popular by St. Pius X.

3 "In black [vestments]".

the pews. And like those workers who stuck some to their own machines and others on the glossy walls of washroom stalls, by virtue of the principle just stated by Your Excellency, that all the places blah blah blah. The girls of a female religious institute made balls with the sacred particles received in the hand to play with."

"There were always profanations: *Necesse est ut veniant scandala!*[4]"

Corsuccini's liturgical competence was recently acquired. He hadn't done much research on the subject and wouldn't have profited much from it even if he had because he had never exercised a pastoral ministry. However, he had turned to journalism, producing at least five articles of at least almost two entire columns length about liturgy for an unimportant publication in which he reported on the course of the ongoing reform. He had been paid a rather modest writer's fee, but received much glory. That's where his true reward was.

He had also received an illegibly-signed letter so filled with praise that it seemed to promise advancement if he continued to support the reform. It didn't take anything more to confirm him as irreversibly among the champions of the reform itself, which he then saw in all its splendor. When defending it, he felt as if he was defending part of himself. For this reason, he couldn't be discouraged, and he wasn't, in the face of the short-sighted opposition of the two fathers, all the more since by now he wouldn't be alone against them. In fact, precisely at that moment in that room, he perceived the footprints of Father Medina himself and the shadow of his faithful page, Father Viso.

"You have a good saying!" Corsuccini said, reassured: "But only now, finally! In liturgical assemblies everyone understands."

"Excellency," Father Norberto asked him: "Have you been a Christian for a long time?"

---

[4] "For it must needs be that scandals come." (Mt. 18:7)

"What? Have I been a Christian for a long time? I was baptized right after birth! My ancestors *ab immemorabili* were all men of faith, and what a faith they had!"

"From the altar, as they say" Father Gregorio suggested.

"You can really say that," confirmed Corsuccini: "From the altar, and more than certain bigoted saints, whom we've finally set aside."

"Like St. Gabriel of Our Lady of Sorrows," said Don Gabriele De Giorgis, who had arrived in time to understand the subject of the discussion. He was part of the large group of marginalized liturgists, as they were politely called, marginalized by the reform's torrent. The torrent hadn't lasted long enough to overwhelm them or carry them away on its own waves.

Norberto asked Corsuccini: "And those old people of yours, those practicing Catholics, and altar saints too, did they understand absolutely nothing in church? So why did they go there? And why did God himself, having inspired the Psalms, inspire them in a sacred language that differed from the faithful's vernacular one?"

Corsuccini stood there with his mouth open before shrugging his shoulders, and attacked De Giorgis' joke:

"As for St. Gabriel of Our Lady of Sorrows, reverend, ask Father Medina for an account, along with all the events on the calendar. Right, Father?"

Having sensed the treacherous air, Father Medina had taken refuge in a corner, protected on one side by Father Viso. The thought he sent from his deepest gut to Corsuccini was so powerful that if it had been a physical expression, he would have stunned the addressee. In fact, he confined himself to tracing a vague gesture in the air, which said everything and nothing. He continued to look between the lines of a very important letter, which he held in his hands, without realizing that he was holding it upside down. De Giorgis moved in for the direct attack, approaching and asking:

"Reverend Father, does St. Gabriel seem to you to be one of those hypocrites, to which Monsignor Corsuccini alluded a moment ago. Was his name entered by mistake in the register of saints?"

"It's not a question of a mistake, reverend," Medina answered. "It's that the *Feriae quadragesimales*[5] must not be overshadowed by the feasts of the saints. Thus St. Thomas Aquinas passed from March 7 to January 28..."

"And St. Gabriel, from February 27 or 28. Can you tell me where on earth you would transfer him? The Greek Kalends, my fair lord!? Why never? You were annoyed by his office. Too bigoted, too derogatory of the world, too filled with devotion to Our Lady of Sorrows, too hypocritical. Do you really believe that knowing that a certain day is the *Feria secunda*[6] of *Dominica tertia*[7] is more edifying for the faithful than knowing that that day is the feast of St. Gabriel of Our Lady of Sorrows? Did it take so long to combine *sicut erat*[8] the commemoration of the *Feria* with the feast of the Saint of the day or vice versa? But under the pretext of giving due historical importance to the *Feriae quadragesimales*, you have purged the calendar of various embarrassing saints."

"How dare you say that?" Medina defying said in turn before adding, "We have carried out a work of enrichment..."

Showing a large folder, De Giorgis retorted, "I dare to say it, because in this folder... because in this folder there is a synoptic representation of the old missal alongside the new one, which one of your collaborators themselves defined as a hasty abortion. Enrichment? Would he like to tell me which dogmatic principles have inspired him, liturgical plenipotentiaries, for this sort of enrichment? Or does he not feel like confessing them openly out of his natural modesty?

---

5 Lent.
6 "Second weekday," which is Monday.
7 The third Sunday.
8 "As it was."

"Enrichment? You are joking, reverend Father! In the traditional missal there are five hundred Masses, with a characteristic unitary and harmonious architecture around a central theme. In your missal there are only two hundred and fifty, and almost all came to be architecturally ruined by the *lectio continua* of Biblical readings that are all autonomous from one another."

"The traditional Mass lasts half an hour. Yours lasts less than a quarter of an hour, less than it takes to shave one's beard and shine one's shoes. Before there was a sacrificial Offertory. Now there are two good formulas for the Confederation of Direct Growers. What did you not make disappear from the *Oremus* that out of scientific scrupulosity you wanted to call *Collectae*? Miracles, fasting, long prayers, contempt for the goods of this world, eternal life, religious families and families of holy virgins, unity in the true faith, the fight against heresies, former believers recalled to the true faith, the keys of the kingdom of heaven entrusted to St. Peter, the merits of the saints, the intercession of the saints, souls to be saved, the weight of sins, the defense of sacred images, the call to death... and, elsewhere, the everlasting regard for the holy virginity of the Madonna.

"But you were afraid of the yes-is-yes and no-is-no. and you have wrapped yourself in the smokescreen of turmoil over the liturgical calendar. Messing up the calendar enabled you to weaken the cult of saints, or even throw it out altogether, starting with certain saints and certain hypocrites, to quote Monsignor Corsuccini here. Hello! Purifiers of the Roman Martyrology, enlightened critics, that if someone doesn't show you his birth certificate, you feel obliged to show him that he was not born and that he has no right to exist."

With that, De Giorgis closed his folder noisily, but didn't shut his mouth. Everyone was listening to him:

"As for the tampering you have perpetrated against the traditional missal to resize it for the use and consumption of Protestants, well, this tampering constitutes a whole series of points, which, joined together by a dash of line, as in certain appendix tricks, in the end provides the outline of a clear figure. This figure is the swaggering, flaccid face of Martin Luther. True, today there are also some cardinals of the Holy Church who participate in symposia in honor of Martin Luther, and offer dithyrambs to his sanctity. True, now the mystical, mixed, and diverse center of the Catholic Church is the Calvinist nest of Taizé. Nevertheless, there is still too much Catholicism in the reformed neo-liturgy! They are waiting for much more of the new Prefaces, the gentlemen who make it their own!

And how many miracles have you reduced to mush!

And now you are crying out from your liturgical dicastery. These are cries of lamentation and warning because there are those who dare to touch the work of your hands! Who dared to raise their hands to tamper with what you say is more sacred and intangible than what is in heaven and on earth? Towards Mass! Who dared to raise his hand to tamper with what is most sacrosanct and intangible in the Mass? Towards the Canon! Who dared to raise his hand to tamper with what is the most sacrosanct and intangible in the Canon? The Consecration! What intangible thing can you now present to the clergy and the faithful, after that with very different intentions of Uzza, you raised your hand, not to support, but to tamper with the most sacred and intangible Ark of the New Testament? Tell us, Father Medina, tell us, if you know! Is your liturgy Protestantized?

"To enforce it, you first sought to destroy the taboo of untouchability, and because the insertion of the name of St. Joseph in the Roman Canon also contributed to this, this introduction made you rejoice. You rejoiced for this reason alone, Most Eminent. After the first adjustments, you made the situation fluid and confused, with orders and counter-orders, deeds and misdeeds. Then you preached irreversibility, while performing the heart transplant by surprise. Then you proclaimed that the heart operation had succeeded perfectly, with no symptoms of rejection. But the patient wasn't breathing, and you didn't realize that it was dead, frozen to death!

"Your collaborators in good faith—I don't exclude the fact that there was good faith—were unaware that the reform aimed at distorting the Catholic liturgy to Protestantize it. They deluded themselves that they could renew the ancient liturgical structure in perfect continuity with tradition. They operate analogously to what Herod the Great had done, he of the massacre of the Innocents, with the temple of Jerusalem, in which the sacred functions continued without the slightest interruption in the decade of the tremendous work of dismantlement and replacement piece by piece, and the seventy years of the finishing work. The liturgy, in fact, is rather like a clock. You cannot change the dimensions of a wheel, without stopping it, without needing to change all the other parts. It follows that your liturgical reform necessarily had to lead to a revolution. If any liturgy needs reform, it is your reformed neo-liturgy!"

At that moment the Pope entered, followed by Monsignor Wong and Father Aurelio, now Cardinal Aurelio Meyerbeer, clad in the old purple unearthed in the monastery of Landbergen. Pius XIV apologized for the delay, entered the great office, followed by all those who had been waiting for him in the antechamber. He recited the *Veni, sancte Spiritus* and an *Ave Maria*. He had everyone sit down and began speaking about the decree on the sacred liturgy that he had in mind to promulgate.

"Dear children," the Pope began to say, speaking in Latin. He extended his little speech by a good quarter of an hour in order to ask all those summoned for their expected diligent collaboration *"ad operam restaurationis sacrae atque traditionalis liturgiae, centrum habentis suum in Missa quae quodammodo impropere tridentina seu sancti Pii V comuniter dicitur, cum sit ipsa Missa ecclesiae nascentis."*[9]

---

9 "for the work of the restoration of the sacred and traditional liturgy, which [liturgy] has its center in the Mass that is commonly—albeit in

He also asked that all those present reflect on the advisability of introducing the so-called Perpetual Calendar if they had not already done so. This would make each year perfectly superimposable on any other from a liturgical point of view. This would result in considerable advantages also from an economic point of view for the populations that would adopt it. And he then dealt with various other subjects.

The Pope's speech was followed by serene conversation, which included talk of the elimination of the altars placed nearer the people for the new Mass and of the obligation to celebrate Holy Mass with all due genuflections and *versus Tabernaculum et Crucem* instead of towards sometimes-empty, sometimes-occupied pews. They also discussed the obligation of the maniple at least for prelates, which would be optional for all others ordained from the subdiaconate upwards. The subdiaconate would be restored. Everyone present consented as soon as the Pope made it known that he was granting a prelatical title to those who still didn't have one. Father Viso, unfortunately, remained without this honor, because, after having waited for a certain time for the Pope's arrival, and being aware that he would arrive again in Wong's company, had gone off to attend to other, more urgent matters.

---

some manner improperly—called Tridentine or that of St. Pius V, since it is the very Mass of the nascent Church."

38

"Felix culpa"

FATHER VISO WAS NOT AT ALL THE stupid one as commonly assumed at first sight. He was not lacking in imagination and tenacity. When he set a goal, he didn't let go, like the bite of a donkey, which hangs on until it fractures a bone. It wasn't a question of transcendental goals. He didn't aim very high. His present goal was to demonstrate to the bear of a man, Father Medina, that he was by no means a wimp. That was now the ultimate goal, to achieve what he had to achieve, as a proximate or intermediate goal: The removal of Monsignor Wong from Rome. Father Viso had once studied moral philosophy, and therefore knew how to clearly distinguish among the ultimate, proximate, and intermediate ends.

To have Wong removed from Rome, a telegram would be enough as long as it were something like the following: "Mother unwell. Return home. Stop." But he had to be certain that the Monsignor's mother was still alive. Father Medina gave her up for dead, but what did he know? On what did he base this categorical statement of his? On the void! Instead he, Viso, would verify the matter. He was a prudent man. It was enough to have it clarified by Wong's secretary. An official request would have to be sent. It would have to have a long form with many questions to camouflage the purpose. It had to be a great form, with at least a thousand copies printed. It was an expense, true, but of very little value, in comparison with the expenses imposed by the Dicastery for Divine Worship on the priests of the renewed Church of the poor for the purchase of ever-new liturgical books which were to be surpassed in the short space of a few weeks, to be replaced by newer, momentarily more definitive ones. And now that Wong was endangering the liturgical reform, the little money for the thousand forms, of which only one would be used, would be worth it.

When Wong's secretary in Asia received the sole form that was sent out, he promptly filled it out as meticulously as possible. True, it seemed to him to have little relevance for the liturgy. but coming from the Dicastery for Divine Worship, he was unsurprised. At this point, if the dicastery ordered him to blow up their beautiful cathedral with TNT, he would not have found it so strange.

The minor task didn't require the secretary, a few years older than his bishop, to gather information because he had known Wong since the latter was a boy in a Shanghai hospice at a time of grave mourning. The hospice in Macau was directed by Father Ardens, whose great intelligence, energy, and heart gave consistency to his projects.

He always challenged his listeners in a way that allowed for no indifference, as he would observe, "You are all baptized. You love the Lord and Our Lady, live in God's grace, and walk towards Paradise. Now I come from Shanghai. There, few of your peers are as lucky as you are, and Shanghai is a very big city. Think then, in all of this immense region of East Asia, how many souls are still waiting for someone to preach to them about the Lord. There are those who promise them a Paradise on earth: wealth, knowledge, power, glory, and with very little effort. Such speakers delude these people with high hopes yet disappoint and leave them sad and desperate in the end.

"Jesus commanded His apostles to go and preach what He had taught them. What did Jesus teach the apostles? Why did the Word of God want to assume human nature from the ever Virgin Mary, through the work of the Holy Spirit? You know why. So that we eat a little better and become a little fatter? So that we dress more hygienically and have more comfortable homes? So that we escape all diseases, and know how to ward off all typhoons and earthquakes? So that everyone can read, write, and do arithmetic, and enjoy the freedoms invented by the French and October Revolutions? In short, so that we stay well on this earth for seventy years and even a little more, given that the afterlife is remote and uncertain? And shouldn't we think about things like that? Just the opposite! Jesus commanded us to seek the Kingdom of God and His righteousness, that is, holiness. This consists first of all in the love of God, since everything else, concerning this short life, will then be given to us in addition.

"How will they receive this doctrine of God, those to whom it was never preached? To preach it, here in the East, one must know the languages of the East. Poor me! As soon as I open my mouth, you immediately realize where I come from. That wouldn't be a terribly bad thing. But I feel unable to duly present the Lord's doctrine to you because of my tongue. I feel half deaf and half dumb, and this is certainly a great evil. If among you there were someone to whom the Lord turns his gaze of predilection, like that young man in the Gospel, and says to him, 'Come, follow me! I want you to be my apostle!' But you can't imitate the young man in the Gospel who says no! Instead, imitate St. John the Evangelist, imitate his brother St. James the Greater. They both left the nets and their father with the mercenaries, in the boat, and followed Jesus.

"A few months later, four young men from the hospice, the first four vocations, set sail from Macau to Shanghai, where Ardens was waiting for them. In Shanghai, they would begin their studies with a view to the priesthood. After nearly two days of sailing, and the delights of seasickness, they finally came within sight of the desired port. Ardens would be waiting for them on the dock, so they had to be ready, with their suitcases in hand. Renouncing the interesting and cheerful sight that the port and city of Shanghai offer to the sailor from the sea, the four of them went down into their cabin to get their suitcases in order and bring them up to the deck.

The pagan and therefore superstitious Chinese captain of their little ship slowed his engines when he sighted a fine large English ship just about to leave port. He waited for her at the gate, ready to force the engines again at the opportune moment, to cut off the way of the beautiful ship, and steal her fortune. But the steward of the English vessel was also Chinese and pagan, and consequently at least as superstitious as his colleague on the approaching ship. As a consequence, unimpressed by the audacity of his rival, he maneuvered so as not to let his fortune be robbed. This resulted in a fatal collision. The incoming small vessel was split in two. The passengers, almost all on the decks, ended up in the sea. They were rescued by the numerous boats that rushed to their rescue. But our four aspiring missionaries, surprised with their suitcases, still in the cabin or climbing up the ladders, were overwhelmed by the whirlpools and dragged to the bottom of the sea with the remains of the ship.

From the depths of the sea, all four immediately went up with euphoria to Paradise, and after the customary pleasantries, all four asked the Madonna to comfort their family members, especially their mothers and fathers. They also asked that she also comfort Ardens, by sending him some good young men in their place, even better than they.

"Father Ardens, after the evening prayers, had to give the sad news to the young men of his hospice in Shanghai. He joined the words with his tears in a heartrending way, and was unable to finish his brief words with the exhortation that he had intended to address to them. Those words remained in his heart. But how many times was his heart more eloquent than his lips! The following morning, during the brief recess which he kept after breakfast, a young craftsman, a mechanic, the eldest son of a nice set of brothers and sisters from a long-standing Christian family, approached Father Ardens, and asked him:

"What will you do now, Father?"

"I'll look for some other good boy, and those four, from heaven, will help me find him."

"Do you still plan to go to Macau to look for some, Father?"

"If I could find any near here, I wouldn't need to go there."

The young craftsman sighed, and his clear and sparkling eyes were brimming with a light veil of tears. He saluted and started to go away, but Ardens held him back.

"Gabriele, what are you thinking about?"

"I think I would be happy if those four thought of me too some day."

The difficulties inherent in birthright were not minor, but were overcome one after another. Gabriele Wong was able to pass from the lathe to Cornelius Nepos, Julius Caesar, Marcus Tullius Cicero, and also to Tertullian, Lactantius, Augustine, and so on. Then he sailed for Italy before returning to the East, where his mother saw him go up to the altar and celebrate like an angel. He treated the consecrated Host as Our Lady had treated the body of the Lord taken down from the cross. Then she saw him celebrate all the other Masses like this, like his first Mass, after which she saw him as a missionary, then parish priest, and finally bishop. At present, his mother spent almost all of her time in the episcopal chapel, the Rosary in her hand, before the Blessed Sacrament, to implore only one thing from God, holiness for her Gabriel. As for herself, she would be happy if the Lord threw her wherever He would like for all eternity, because, from there, she would continue to thank Him forever.

"She's a holy mother!" exclaimed Wong's secretary, who had known her for a long time. He also called her, according to the ancient custom, Leon-ciao, that is, woman dearest to me or woman closest to me. These expressions of respect substituted for the name of mother. But having reached this point in his digressions, he realized that he hadn't yet answered even the first of the questions on the form, and decided to finish without further digressions or wasting time.

"Paternity: Francesco. Maternity: Lily Tsang Kien-zie. Living brothers and sisters..." As soon as Father Viso glanced at the form, he let out the cry of Xenophon's men, followed by that of Archimedes:

"Thalassa! Eureka! Goal!"

Then he continued: "The father passed away, but not the mother. She is twenty years older than Monsignor, which makes her eighty. Nothing more natural than a good heart attack. And now to work on the telegram!"

It was the kind of work of which he considered himself a champion. His presumption was not gratuitous. During the war, in fact, he had had the opportunity to specialize in the manufacture of various documents of all colors. These were necessary to escape from all sorts of serious problems. For various reasons, people compromised in their dealings with different and opposing authorities. Ochre sheets were for telegrams. He had quite a lot of these. Stamping the necessary sentences was a game. The text was already decided: "Mom serious. You come. Stop." At this point the language problem arose.

"Hm, what language do we put it in? The secretary added two lines of Italian to the Latin form. But it is unlikely that he would send a telegram in Latin or Italian to his Chinese bishop. He would certainly send it in Chinese."

And then he took the telephone receiver, dialed a number, and began:

"Reverend Mother, I'm sorry if I'm bothering you again after the translations of the liturgical texts. This time I only need you to kindly help me send the following sentences in Chinese from the *Song of Songs*: 'Flowers sprout on our land. The rains have ceased. The vines spread their scent. Mom is serious. Come from Lebanon.' Enough for now. Please, have the Chinese translation marked well and clearly under each single sentence...Call the Chinese nun? She's fine. I'm waiting on the phone...Ready! In Mandarin Chinese? Whatever works for you works for me...Of course! All transliterated as usual in Latin letters...During the day? May God repay you!"

He put the receiver down, rubbed his hands together, and exclaimed:

"Blessed be the Song of Songs together with King Solomon, if it was he who wrote it!" A few hours later he had the desired translation in hand. He stamped the fourth of the sentences and the beginning of the fifth on the telegram strip. He added the surname of the secretary, Chang Viu-lam. He glued the strips in place, pasted the address, perfected the other details, paused to contemplate the work of his own hands, and modestly applied to himself, albeit somewhat modified, the phrase from Genesis: "And Elohím turned to contemplate the work of his own hands, and he had to admit that everything had been done well, indeed very well." And he rubbed his hands a second time.

As to how to get the telegram into the recipient's hands, there would be no particular difficulties. He would have the bell of the Laurini fathers' monastery rung at the time when the cook would most probably open the door because the others, he knew, would be busy with other matters. In fact, the cook himself did come to the door.

"I'm in a hurry this time. My tyrant boss is waiting for me. Since I was already on the way, the folks in the Correspondence Office, damn slow, gave me this telegram..."

"But at least a cup of coffee!"

"Put me down for next time. I'm really in a hurry. Arrivederci!" He went straight off, without looking back. The cook immediately took the telegram to Monsignor Wong. Wong knew the classical tastes of his secretary, but applying it precisely in a telegram of that sort was strange! And he had never before signed with his last name! Then the telegrapher had made two mistakes in the transliteration of the same surname. It was something to wonder about. First of all, he immediately had an urgent telegram sent to his secretary, asking him to reply immediately and with a few more words. There was no need to skimp on the expense. At the table, however, the Pope reflected, briefly prayed, smoothed his stubble, and said to him with half-closed eyes:

"You are right. The thing is not at all clear. You were right to ask your secretary for clarification. It could be an error. It could be a joke of questionable taste. It could be a deception... But your mother is really waiting for you. You risk nothing by leaving. I was the one holding you. Now I tell you: do not wait for the answer to your telegram, and leave immediately!"

The Superior of the monastery, Father Antonio, booked the plane for him, paid all the expenses, put another wad of cash in Wong's hand, and accompanied him to Fiumicino airport, where he arrived just in time for takeoff. After that the central office of the airport received a phone call:

"Secretariat of His Holiness, Pius XIV. Notify Monsignor Gabriele Wong that the famous letter has been found... I'm waiting on the phone... Hello! Has he already left? No, there's no need. We'll cable directly. Thank you!"

Father Viso put down the receiver, rubbed his hands for the third time, and exclaimed: "I want to see if the bear will still have the courage to call me a good for nothing!"

As soon as he arrived in his diocese, Wong went to the secretary, who, when he saw him, exclaimed:

"Are you here already? I received your telegram in which you ask for clarifications regarding a previous telegram of mine. But I didn't send the earlier telegram. Following your telegram,

I have sent you this, which will have reached Rome after your departure."

He handed Wong the draft of the telegram which he had sent him the day before, and which said exactly the same as that made by Viso, albeit in non-classical Chinese.

After a pause, he said, "A heart attack. But she's very calm. Wait for the warning."

A few minutes later Wong was at the bedside of his mother Leon-ciao. He knelt next to her, without saying a word. She looked at him, and then slowly spelled out:

"You were right to come right away. I was waiting for you, to die more happily. I asked Our Lady for it!"

39

A Mountain of People Twice Murdered

It was a particularly crowded morning. At least a thousand faithful had flocked to the chapel of the Blessed Sacrament for the Pope's Mass. This had been occurring almost daily. The Pope addressed them in the manner of *homilia infra Missam*. This allowed him to give an audience to pilgrims, addressing them with the words of eternal life.

With nonchalant elegance, Monsignor Bruno De Gaudenzi took care of the audience of the most distinguished personalities and onlookers almost daily. His unique style made people appreciate the privilege and left them satisfied. He continued to bring them to the papal apartment although the Pope had not set foot there for some time. This left the Pope with strictly ecclesiastical audiences that concerned his specific mandate. But even these were often numerous and demanding. At times they left him tired, voiceless, and with a sore throat. Then at table he apologized to the Laurini fathers for not being able to participate a little more animatedly in their conversation, as he would have wished:

"You can understand. I no longer have the lungs that I had as a student of philosophy and then theology, when I was also a cantor—not that I had a great voice, but I was sufficiently in tune. At the time, I never missed any of the Gregorian chant

A Mountain of People Twice Murdered

and polyphony lessons that Monsignor Casimiri and Abbot Ferretti imparted as equals to the Roman seminarians, in a very large classroom of the Pontifical High School of Sacred Music. Every Thursday morning we hurried to the Piazza Sant'Agostino, to the school. We owe that school so much for the revival of sacred music, which today has suffered a setback."

"That setback has lasted for years, Your Holiness!" exclaimed Father Antonio.

It was true, and had caused much suffering. Sacred singing was dead or dying in many churches of Rome, while jazz had triumphantly entered the high school and pontifical school of sacred music.

That same morning while in audience, the Pope received first of all Monsignor Dimitri Novascky, who had spoken to him about the mountain of corpses which the Soviets had amassed in the Ukraine, and which the manipulators of world public opinion had agreed to bury under thickest silence.

"Nobody talks about it anymore. Nobody defends its memory anymore, not even the ecclesiastical authorities! The First World War and subsequent civil war forced collectivization, famine, and permanent and uninterrupted persecution. Millions of Catholic Ukrainians died as a result. But the storm continued, right until today. Our entire episcopate has been suppressed by the Soviet regime. Thousands of Ukrainian Catholics are locked up in prisons or in deportation camps. However, today Vatican diplomacy considers these Ukrainians, martyrs for their fidelity to Rome, as...—sorry for the word, Your Holiness. I learned it in Rome—jerks! True, the Vatican has tried to favor the Latin Catholics who are under the Soviets, but no one has spoken in defense of the six million persecuted Ukrainian Catholics. When the Patriarch of Moscow declared the union of the Uniates with Rome void at the Synod that had elected him, none of the Vatican delegates, who were present to add prestige to the ceremony, raised a cry of protest.

"Despite the persecutions, the Catholic faith still survives in the depths of the log huts and the secrecy of consciences. But to celebrate Mass and administer the sacraments, we must go down into the catacombs because every outward manifestation of worship and religious instruction is immediately and ruthlessly repressed. Do you want examples? There are countless! Here are some of them!"

Monsignor Dimitri Novascky placed a large folder on the Pope's desk: "All documentation with names, localities, dates, crimes, and years of harsh prison, or rigorous concentration camps and forced labor, or deportation even beyond the Arctic Circle, or buried alive in some madhouse, a penalty compared to which death is light. Here is what is systematically kept hidden from those who should know!

"Your heads burst when you hear of the persecutions that take place in certain western countries, but who talks about the persecutions which believers in Soviet countries are subjected to? The Church of Silence is silent because no one lends their voice! And while clandestine seminarians in the fields of Siberia suffered for the faith, several Vatican prelates listened without batting an eye to the new Patriarch of Moscow, in the Synod of Leningrad, declare that such an abomination, which cries out for vengeance in the presence of God and his angels, would be continued, because he considered it suited to the established order.

"The Catholic media, on whose behalf the Vatican solicits the charity of Catholics, regularly throws away our letters, while at the same time saying 'Bless you!' whenever a Soviet despot sneezes. And why on earth does it exalt as heroes—heroes of the new faith?—priests who plot against their respective governments, against radically Catholic governments, or against governments that at least let the Church operate freely, while this same media wants Catholic priests in Hungary, Czechoslovakia, and so on, to collaborate with their respective governments, which radically and brutally deny God and execute His prophets? Since when did communism, which is inherently immoral and perverse, show its radical transformation and convert itself from materialism into spiritualism, from atheism to belief in God? Has it demonstrated this by granting religious freedom to the peoples it keeps under its thumb? Read, Your Holiness, the samizdat, the Russian clandestine publishing, and you will get an idea!"

"I know the samizdat publications, I know them, Monsignor! However, please briefly prepare for me all the points which you believe should appear in an encyclical against atheistic materialism, against the deniers of religious freedom, and against their accomplices. Then come again."

As soon as Vladimir Rostropovich entered the Pope's study for an audience, he saw the Pope leafing through the thick folder left on the desk by Monsignor Dimitri Novascky. He was delighted, and helped the Pope to read some Ukrainian proper names correctly. He was not, however, Ukrainian, nor even Catholic. He was Orthodox. He'd been in Paris for many years, where he pastored a group of Orthodox Russians who reject the envoys of the Moscow Patriarchate, that is to say, of the Kremlin. He had always felt nostalgia for union with the Holy Mother, with Rome. He professed himself a disciple of Solovyov, and had read and reread the Russian writer's seven volumes of *La Russie and the* Église *universelle*, the most beautiful apology of Catholicism and the Primacy of the Pope of Rome. But now he felt great apprehension in his heart, in the face of so many changes that were convulsively underway in the Catholic Church that he, from Paris, couldn't fail to notice. In the common view of many reflective Orthodox, these changes were, unfortunately, deepening the gulf between the Catholic and Orthodox Churches.

"I must honestly tell you, Your Holiness, that we Orthodox are scandalized by what is happening in the Catholic camp.

Since the Second Vatican Council, the rift between us Orthodox and you Catholics has been getting bigger and bigger. You are getting rid of a whole patrimony of traditional values so carelessly. To us, this patrimony is of incalculable importance. It seems that you are ashamed to proclaim the most holy Virgin Theotòkos, Mater Dei, almost as if this privilege, which is fundamental to the nature of the most holy Virgin, constitutes an obstacle to our journey towards the divine Saviour, her Son and Son of God. You are destroying the sense of the sacred which is everything in our churches. It would seem that you do not have the slightest idea of the place that holy icons occupy in our piety and liturgy, and you destroy them like the iconoclasts do, or sell them to junk dealers, which is much worse! You are forgetting the absolute priority of individual prayer and individual penance in the Christian life. And you fill your mouth at every opportunity with the word ecumenism, so that this word has lost any serious and acceptable meaning, if it ever had any. I don't know if by now you have already reached or even surpassed this general betrayal on the whole front of the faith at the same level as the most rationalizing Protestants, but what I can tell you is that you now discourage Orthodox Christians. But is it possible that you don't realize this? Most of my relatives are still in Russia."

"Now I am sorry to have to tell you such bitter things, but I must also tell you, because I came to Rome for this very reason. Instead of helping us, or supporting us in our fight for the faith, you join our persecutors in their efforts to destroy the holy Church of God in the midst of the Russian people.

"And do you want to speak of ecumenism? Our posterity will talk about it again—not so much about ecumenism, but about reunion with the Church of Rome. They will talk about it again with the remnant of Israel, that is to say with the remnant of the Church of Rome, the survivors of the storm that's tossing you so terribly. But let it already be clear from now on that true ecumenism is union with Rome, under the primacy of the pope of Rome, in the faith and liturgy, and in discipline. This is a completely different thing from your romantic and voluntaristic *embrassions nous!* while you close your eyes and keep certain dogmatic points of the Catholic Church under the table. These points cause difficulties for some Orthodox. They must first of all be discussed and resolved! There can be no union in the chalice if union in dogma and total faith has not first been established. Diverging from that chalice, each one drinks what he believes, some this and others that. Some drink the blood of the Lord and others simply the wine. This wouldn't be a union in the chalice of the Lord, but in the chalice of Satan, the father of lies!"

At this point the Pope was able to insert a joke of his own:

"The oceans said to the continents, 'Don't you see how many shores we have in common? Why don't we unite ecumenically?' And everything returned to the way it was before God separated the earth from the waters!"

This unexpected allegory changed Vladimir Rostropovich's indignation to hearty laughter.

The Pope continued: "This is where the great road of ecumenical confusion would lead to, dear reverend, while, as you said very well, the Lord indicates the narrow path of conversion to those who want to belong to his Church."

The Pope willingly resorted to such figurative speaking, which he had learned from the Arabs in the Middle East, because it allowed him to say a lot in a little, effectively. It also allowed him to avoid arguments and a sore throat, the latter being no small thing.

"Allow me, Your Holiness, before leaving you, to read you a few lines from a letter, which arrived a few days ago from a friend of mine from behind the Iron Curtain, a Catholic and a priest! He will show you how the state of mind of true Catholics is no different from that of true Orthodox, today, in the face of what is happening in the Catholic camp. Here then: 'They put me in prison for twelve years because I remained faithful to Rome. They subjected me to torture, because I didn't want to deny the Pope, and indeed I didn't deny him. I lost everything for the faith. But this faith instilled in my heart a peace, a security, which transformed those years of detention into the most intense and precious years of my life. Then I visited the West, the post-conciliar West.

"'Now you Westerners ignore us, because remembering us would make you burn with shame. You no longer find peace in God! You undermine the foundations of true faith, and cling to the mess of your topsy-turvy theologies. Your acclaimed total liberation of man is nothing but unbridled libertinism, beyond any dogmatic, moral, liturgical tradition, particularly the most sacrosanct! You have extended your desecrating hand to everything, to redo almost everything from scratch, with your own lights, the first ones that have finally been lit under the vault of the firmament! You no longer believe in *Lumen Christi*! You have soiled everything, even the Holy Mass of all time! You have disappointed me bitterly. Rather than live among you, I prefer another twelve years in a communist prison.

"'Forgive me, dear Vladimir, if I have made personal reproaches to you that are for others. I did it so that these words of mine can be useful to you as they are, for whoever is interested, without obliging you to touch them up.' That's it, Your Holiness, and that's enough!"

"Yes, reverend, that's enough!" confirmed the Pope before he added: "And to conclude, I will repeat to you what you yourself have said so well. The movement into the Catholic Church will happen for Christians, regardless of their denomination, who today are anxious about so many errors, that is, for those who shun compromises and pseudo-ecumenical confusion, and await the counter-reform from Rome. This union does not require anyone to dust off the historical facts that separated us. That comes with the danger of making some wounds worse. But it requires the resolution of the dogmatic problems that divide believers. Trying to ignore them *non prodest, sed obest*[1]!"

---

[1] "it does not benefit but prevents" or "it does not stand to help but it stands in the way."

40

English Attitude

It was then the turn of the Anglican pastor Reverend John Power. Forty-something, his mother repeatedly urged him to get married, but he harbored in his heart the secret desire, if not intention, to become a Catholic priest one day. For this, he had seen in celibacy not only a *sine qua non* to that goal, but also a way of ascetic perfection to prepare him for it. Paradoxically, it was precisely his mother who oriented him towards Catholicism, in the evening of a distant November. Having returned from the Anglican cemetery, adjacent to the Catholic one, she burst into tears.

"What's the matter, mother?"

"You see? Those good little Catholic women this morning were at Mass for their deceased, and this afternoon they were at the cemetery to pray. They recited the Rosary to obtain the end of purgatory for their dead, willing to pay themselves in person instead of their beloved deceased, if the good Lord permits it. They still feel united, in communion, with their family members, even when they are in the afterlife, and they consider themselves capable of still contributing to their supreme good, eternal life. They told me this with simplicity and conviction.

"I was so tempted to join them in those suffrage prayers! Then I was so sad when I returned to the section of our tombs, to your father's. I rearranged a few things of those closest to us, and thought of the uselessness of all those tombs if there is no purgatory, if our communion with our loved ones is broken with death. The saved don't need us, and the damned can't receive our help, so we can't love them anymore! This impossibility of loving them again cannot come from God until his mysteries have been revealed to us too in the light of God."

"Look at the crucifix, mother!" John Power had replied, pointing to the antique crucifix, in ivory on ebony, which he had bought in Rome and had wanted to hang on the wall of his studio. He continued, "Won't you give credit to a God who dies on the cross for us? What other proof do you want, and from God Himself, to trust God, and leave Him with the task of providing for our eternal fate? Faith in man is a risk, but faith in God destroys all risk and flourishes in hope. Now hope is the most granite of all certainties!"

"I know that Christian hope, when it is true theological virtue and it comes from God, is certainty. But purgatory seems to me not to conflict with Christian hope. It can be reconciled with the sacrifice of the Cross," concluded his mother.

But now Power hesitated at the threshold of his conversion to Catholicism. Like him, thousands and thousands of Anglicans, already out of their shells, already on their way to Rome, had gone back into their shells. Earlier, they had begun to move towards the Catholic Church in their attraction to its specific treasures. But the Catholic hierarchy itself, or rather the most powerful and busiest part of it, had thrown those treasures up into the attic.

As for him, he had acquired a much-publicized Catholic catechism, a so-called Catholic catechism, which the Holy See itself had authorized to be translated from the original language. He had opened and skimmed through it with keen interest, only to be more and more disappointed. Before reaching the last page, he opened the door of the coal stove and threw it in to burn forever in hell, the only place it deserved. All the truths of the Christian faith, the most fundamental and indubitable ones, were presented in an emotional way, increasingly ambiguous, clouded with a questioning attitude, or reduced to questionable and optional opinions.

And what about the liturgical books? Like Power, other Anglican pastors had also repeatedly gone to Rome to purchase Roman vestments, furnishings, and liturgical books. They had often achieved something very close to the Catholic liturgy, but that liturgy frequently lacked any certainty of having a soul, invisible but guaranteed by faith, because he didn't often have the certainty that the celebrating Anglican minister was a real priest. In any case, there was no communion with Catholics, who adored the same Eucharist. Hence the shift towards Rome, stimulated in a particular way by the resurgent devotion to Our Lady, after the impulse given to this devotion by Faber and Newman.

The Pope interrupted the reverend Power at this point, to remind him that he too, at Oxford, had prayed at the foot of the beautiful statue of the Madonna, in the University Church of St. Mary the Virgin on High Street. This was the church where John Newman, still a Protestant pastor, had been a zealous chaplain.

Then Power resumed his business:

"But now Rome has set out on the same path that led the English to schism and then heresy. You remember the stages. 1534: denial of papal jurisdiction. 1539: stripping of the Churches and fighting against the cult of the saints and of Our Lady in particular. 1547: suppression of the laws against heresies, communion under both species, and the struggle against priestly celibacy. 1548: communion according to the Lutheran formulas and the increasingly widespread replacement of generic and collective confession in place of particular, spoken, and individual confession. 1549: transformation of the sacrifice of the Mass into a commemoration of the Last Supper and the Lord's death, concomitant and consequent recasting of the missal, the breviary, and the *Rituale romanum*. 1550: destruction of the ancient liturgical books, replacement of the altars with tables for supper, a new and completely Protestantized catechism. 1558: Biblical readings and prayers of Mass in English, then all Mass and other rites done in English. 1559–1560: the whole liturgy, with the Act of uniformity, is brought into line with the Protestant heresy: denial of the priesthood, denial of the Sacrifice, denial of the permanent real Presence. After all of this, the persecutions raged, alternating with periodic and deceitful professions of fidelity to the true faith as a way to overwhelm the last resistances of the simple.

"Now I have carefully examined the Acts of the Second Vatican Council, especially those that deal with the priesthood, as well as the declarations of the highest Catholic authorities on the same subject. For me, these things are particularly close to the heart, as they concern the very heart of the Catholic Church and had made me love her. Am I wrong, if I seem to find both in the Acts of the Council and in those declarations a conception of the priesthood different from that of the Council of Trent? This new representation replaces the altar that is there for the sacrificial adoration due to God with the word that is preached to men. It makes the priest the man of the word, and leaves out the fact that, before everything else, the whole man of sacrificial adoration makes the priest a servant of man. It forgets that he instead is first of all a priest for the worship that is due to God.

"Few Catholics seem to realize exactly what is happening to their faith. Yet the track record of the evolution in liturgy doesn't leave any room for doubt—the shipwreck of faith in the priesthood, the Real Presence, and the sacrifice at the altar.

"How did all this happen? By the work of everything that the Catholic Church had already condemned under the name of modernism. Modernism had its adventurers. They undermined the foundations of the citadel of the Catholic faith from within. The frightening crisis of the faith afflicts Catholics and frightens all Christians of every denomination. It frightens every believer in God, even the non-Catholic. But first of all, it frightens us Anglicans, who feel, rightly so, the closest to the Church of Rome. We are therefore also the most seriously injured, the most in danger of being overwhelmed by those same whirlpools.

"Now we are organizing our defense, but we feel weak, and the attitude of the highest levels of the Catholic hierarchy discourages us. For this reason, I dared to ask for an audience with Your Holiness. It's time that true Catholics, comforted by true bishops, and by the bishop of bishops, let their anger explode against the lying slogans of so many despotic tyrants. They demolish the spiritual life in favor of philanthropic action. They are sacrilegious towards God in favor of the promotion of man and destroyers of the sacraments. Their prophecies destroy everything."

Power had taken up the charge, hurling lightning from his light blue eyes, his thick golden hair jumping with every gesture.

"I wish he could see and hear you right now," the Pope said to him. "I mean, the fellow who spread the rumor of the proverbial English attitude, calm and impassiveness!"

"Please excuse me!"

"I do not excuse you at all. I congratulate you, dear reverend. I heartily congratulate you! And do you remember any of those sayings that you, in the American style, called slogans, and that we, in the Greek style, call aphorisms?"

Power smiled, and then, after a few moments, he was back at it:

"Are they talking about crises that come from growth? Of course. The growth of evil! They say times have changed... Sure. For the worse! They call this a transitional age? Sure. From an avalanche that overwhelms everything! They try to cause inaction, saying, 'Everything will pass!' but they don't say that it took the Assyrians six hundred years to pass! Are they talking about scaling? Sure, at present they are like little mice deciding to downsize the cat but at other times by starting a fire that reduces everything, absolutely everything, to ashes! Do they fight without even saying who they are really fighting, the bourgeois? They ignore that we owe what was great and lasting over the centuries to the bourgeoisie. So often, they, the bourgeois I mean, worked anonymously, courageously, industriously, and responsibly for the communes and republics, lordships and monarchies, in the streets and cities, from cathedrals to universities, hospitals to theaters. Those gentlemen are against bourgeois life, and they get up at noon!

"They say, 'I am against individualism, and for the *tous ensemble*. Only as a team can something good be built!' Really? Think of the team that wrote Shakespeare's tragedies, that sculpted Michelangelo's Moses, that composed the ninth symphony of Beethoven, who was already deaf. With the team, they aim to escape all responsibility, and drown in the mass that can come up with something! They push the team to destruction and then wash their hands of it. They are innocent. The fault lies with the team, with the voting assembly. An intelligent sociologist, Célestin Bouglé, went so far as to state that the intelligence of an assembly is proportional to the intellectual quotient of the biggest ass of the congregants, divided by their number.

"Do they want to adapt everything to today's man? In doing so they destroy everything that is required of eternal man! Do they want to adapt to the preferences of the people? In doing so they spread their depraved tastes to the people, without saying that Seneca considers the taste of the crowds an indication of the worst and without saying that according to Nietzsche the wise man does not join the crowd. Do they always declare themselves tightrope walkers in the golden mean? As if between two mistakes, there couldn't be a third and worse mistake right in the middle. They speak of an update? They don't realize that society is dying and the darkness of barbarism is descending!

A whole civilization is shipwrecked! Do they self-elect charismatics and prophets? In doing so they don't think of the warning, *Attendite a falsis prophetis*[1], endowed with charisma in every way, but from Satan!"

At this point the Pope interrupted him to allow him to catch his breath:

"You mentioned those in the highest levels of the hierarchy, who would have betrayed their mandate. How long have you been waiting, reverend, to become a Catholic? You cannot say that the Pope doesn't have an urgent need for bishops of faith and courage!"

At this statement by the Pope, Power blushed like a girl. No! He hadn't yet thought of becoming a bishop. But he recovered quickly and replied:

"Why not? *Si quis episcopatum desiderat, bonum opus desiderat.*"[2]

"And you know how that *bonum opus* is translated into English, don't you?" the Pope asked him before immediately providing the answer: "It must be translated as a very heavy burden!"

Power confirmed, "I don't doubt it! Just think of the revolutionary climate we live in. We are actually in the middle of it. I don't know, Your Holiness, if you perceive all the dangers of this climate, which is encouraged by people I benevolently called—out of Christian charity—'adventurers.' All revolutions happen in a romantic climate. Romanticism is anti-logic. Anti-logic is anti-metaphysics, and anti-metaphysics is Gnosticism, it is anti-truth, it is a lie. All revolutions conjure up or promise the imminent arrival of a new millenarianism. They all resort to what you, Your Holiness, have classically called aphorisms.

---

[1] "Beware of false prophets." (Mt. 7:15)
[2] "If a man desireth the office of a bishop, he desireth a good work." (1 Tim. 3:1)

"They must be formed, these aphorisms, with ambiguous, shifty voices. They must be repeated, hammered, reaffirmed, and even imposed so that they become phantom, unnoticeable routines in the brains of the brainless, the brains of the impressionable. The masses are the most impressionable. Individuals in every assembly, even an assembly of council fathers—pardon my impertinence, Your Holiness!—easily form themselves into a mass. This is especially so the longer it is kept together, above all if it is kept together for a long time. Hours turn into days and even into months, depending on the case. At a certain point, a motion needing the group's assent is raised. It's easy to insert in various places in a proposal provisions of tremendous importance when everyone is tired. Most of them won't understand these. The provisions enable those on the inside of the secret scheme to create the pre-established consequences from these motions. These consequences are completely opposite from the expectations of those present. But their later protests can always be answered by saying, 'You wanted it!' Isn't that how it works?"

"I think so," the Pope replied. "As for the impressionableness of the Council Fathers, we Catholics must exclude it when they, unanimously with the Pope, pronounce themselves regarding theological dogma or morality in a rigorously dogmatic Council. By this I mean one that is not purely pastoral, since when it is pastoral it can be contrasted with doctrinal and dogmatic."

"But this opposition, Your Holiness, is unjustified! I am a pastor, and what else should I give to my faithful, if not true doctrine, both theological and moral? Pastoral care that is opposed to true doctrine is nothing but arbitrary and deceptive pragmatism. 'I beg you, do not let this pastoral problem become doctrinal!' a Catholic bishop said when addressing other Catholic bishops in one of the countless meetings that took place at all levels, and which seemed to be exceeding the level of tolerability. What problem? The limitation of births. He was terrified, that Most Eminent bishop, by the rising tide of births! He certainly has traveled little and has no idea of the immensity of deserts, which await man to turn them into gardens. He certainly knows nothing of the results of the sciences that are worthy of the name in terms of greatly increased food production. And this Solomon didn't know then that the terror of the rising population tide is artfully spread by a certain form of racism of people who know what they are doing.

"At the same meeting of Catholic bishops, which was held in a place made famous by the apparitions of Our Lady, they also expressed themselves in trivial terms regarding *Humanae vitae*. Someone noted that mature Christians would not take the encyclical literally.

"Ask your Eminences and Excellencies, Your Holiness, what they mean by maturity, by doctrinal, by pastoral! A *declaratio terminorum*?[3] It's a scandal! Medieval scholasticism! No declarations of terms are given in a romantic climate. What is appropriate for this type of climate is fog, the northern fog that prevents access even to the most dazzling lights of the Middle Ages, when throughout Europe, including on our island, people lived in the same faith and spoke the same language. There were no state barriers. Unparalleled treasures of art came out of the guilds' workshops, Thomas wrote the *Summa*, Dante the *Comedy*, the abbot Gersenio da Cavaglià composed the *De imitatione Christi* in the Benedictine abbey of Vercelli, and the small populace knew theology, the theology of the living God, of course! More than many of today's updated theological unicorns.

"Your Holiness, just ask those individuals who should be the model of their faithful, what they mean by the words maturity, pastoral, and doctrinal. At the most, they will be able to confide

---

[3] "A declaration of terms."

in you the real reason they introduce dynamite sticks smuggled under the label of those words at the right time and place. At the most, they will be able to tell you that those are open statements, used to change everything they want to change, because God's not conservative! And to replace such nonsense, which clashes with the teachings of faith and reason, they will tell you that the Church is also poor in doctrine! They say all this apologetic nonsense, which is based on their know-it-all ignorance, with extreme haughtiness. They spin like tops, so are called compasses!"

"And all this scandalizes you?" the Pope asked him.

"It pains me. How could it scandalize me? What did St. Paul say on the beach of Miletus, in his farewell speech to the presbyters of Ephesus? 'I must warn you in advance that after my departure rapacious wolves will invade the flock, and will not spare the sheep. Not only that, but some of those who will work to pervert others will come out of your own group, and they will try to drag the brothers along with them.' Acts 20:29-30."

"So you know the entire Bible?" the Pope asked him. But after this question, he immediately asked another, non-rhetorical, one which was close to his heart, because it was necessary to examine this extraordinary, highly cultured, and gifted John Power more thoroughly, much more so now that the Pope himself had compromised by quickly placing before him the goal of the episcopate. So he asked him: "In that barrage of aphorisms, haven't you forgotten the most wickedly effective one?"

Intelligence flashed from his blue eyes and his hair shook. Smiling, Power spelled out:

"Irreversibility! How could I forget that? I simply stopped thinking here in front of you, and deep sincerity and frankness that I saw in your eyes moved me. Yes, I interrupted, to repeat to myself: *Ecce vere Israelita, in quo dolus non est!*[4]"

---

4 "Behold an Israelite indeed, in whom there is no guile." (John 1:47)

"Matthew 5:37," the Pope threw at him, smiling, before adding, "*Est? Est! Non? Non! Quod autem his abundantius est, a malo est!*[5] This is the only diplomacy that I think suits me as vicar of the One who left that warning at that moment. But let's return to the irreversibility of those who, like the damned, want only the steps they have taken towards hell to be eternally irreversible."

Power went on, "'Irreversibility?' 'There's no turning back,' these gentlemen say. As if their agitation, which they turn on themselves, were a move forward! With the aphorism of irreversibility, which arose during the Bolshevik revolution, these gentlemen believe they are weakening the resistance of people for their judgment, but people of judgment know, from experience, at least the equivalent of the *Multa renascentur quae iam cecidere, cadentque quae nunc sunt in honore vocabula.*[6] Displaying his artistic criteria on the matter of poetic art, Quintus Horatius Flaccus spoke to the Pisoni about words. But words were born to mean things, and words do not fall and they cannot be reborn, without a correlative falling and rebirth of the things they signify."

"'It's irreversible!' these gentlemen say. 'It is irreversible!' they go on. Returning from a funeral, a friend of mine wittily said to me, '*Ecce vera, universalis et unica irreversibilis progressio populorum omnium! Amen!*'"[7]

Power's humorously solemn pronunciation of "Amen" prompted an outburst of laughter from the Pope.

---

5 "But let your speech be yea, yea: no, no: and that which is over and above these, is of evil."

6 Horace, *Ars poetica* 70-72: "Many things will be reborn which have already fallen...and the words which are now held in honor will fall."

7 "Behold [this is] the truly universal and uniquely irreversible progress of all people! Amen!"—a pun on St. Augustine's oft-repeated "truly... truth," such as in Confessions 7.1: "O eternal truth and true charity and dear eternity," which would be clear to most who have read any Augustine in Latin, together with a reference to Paul VI's encyclical *Populorum progressio*.

"I didn't mean to make you laugh, Your Holiness! It's said that Jesus never laughed..."

"When Jesus turned to Zacchaeus, who thought he was completely hidden and safe among the foliage of the sycamore tree, and told him to come down, do you think the crowd didn't laugh? And that Jesus remained there, totally serious, in the midst of so much laughter? Why should we deny Jesus' divine humanity a sense of humor? And if he didn't laugh, he at least broke out in a smile when Peter showed him the two swords, all ready, and he replied, 'Oh, that's too much!' And Jesus was certainly not an abnormal child, and a normal child laughs at his mother, laughs at the flowers and the beautiful colors. He laughs with the joy and surprise of each new discovery, and a normal child makes some new discovery every day."

Having said this, the Pope returned to the subject by concluding:

"Irreversibility? Even the light of the dawn is irreversible, until the shadows of the evening descend again. Dear reverend, read something by Giovan Battista Vico, if you haven't already done so, and then write something about the ebb and flow of historical irreversibility."

This time they both laughed. Before taking leave, Power got down on one knee and asked for, and faithfully received, the blessing of Our Lady imparted to him by the Pope. Then he left the study, to make way for the Lutheran pastor Thomas Morgenröte.

41

Thomas Morgenröte Searches for the Rock

HE COULD HAVE BEEN THIRTY. HE was known to the Pope for the stir he had caused with one of his articles, in which he reproached Catholics for having resurrected a word that was synonymous with corpse, the word "reform." Many Lutherans had strongly opposed him. A public discussion ensued in Wittenberg, in a hall not far from the tomb of Martin Luther. In this discussion, the Reverend Thomas Morgenröte refuted every one of his opponents with a stream of biblical and historical data, with clear logic, and with refined exposition. He left his opponents with no other argument than insults.

"Traitor to the Reformation! Traitor to Luther!"

They made an uproar like the members of the Sanhedrin did against St. Stephen. He waited for a little silence. Then, a few steps from the tomb of the founder of the Reformation, he raised his forehead and, without betraying the slightest emotion, replied:

"To Luther, faithful to the vows he solemnly made to God, I remain faithful with a clear mind and a pure heart. *Immola Deo sacrificium laudis, et redde Altissimo vota tua,*[1] says the Lord in Psalm 49. But in the First letter to the Corinthians he

---

1 "Offer to God the sacrifice of praise [also a likely reference to Paul VI's document on the recitation of the Choral Divine Office in the document *Sacrificium Laudis*], and render thy vows to the Most High." (Ps. 49:14)

also says: *Animalis autem homo non percipit ea quae Spiritus Dei sunt.*[2] So I cannot remain faithful to whomever breaks his vows to God in order to marry a former nun who is also unfaithful to God, even if his name is Martin Luther!"

It was as if lightning had flashed over the heads of the individuals crowding the room. Stupefied by the astonishing scandal, they were unable to find any words of protest or final insult. Morgenröte took the opportunity to give a half bow before passing undisturbed among them.

Now he was there, seated in a small armchair, almost alongside the Pope, to whom he had "so many things to confide, indeed, to recommend!"

Pius XIV then said to him with a smile, "Reserve some also for my successor, because I am only a pope in transition. Yes, for my successor. My job is only to pave the way for him, and this assignment is now coming to an end. However, I allow you to confide in me at least the first of your recommendations, dear reverend. After the first ones, you can add all those you want them to follow."

They both smiled, and then Morgenröte began.

"I'll start with the Latin scandal. After *Veterum sapientia*[3] a scandal against Latin was unimaginable. The fact that the attack on Latin did happen makes it even more unspeakably scandalous. A Church that so casually bids farewell to her liturgical language also bids farewell to her soul. She abandons not only her own language to the restless waves of linguistic evolution, with all the variations of meaning that this evolution brings about in cultic words, but also to the content of the faith itself, because this content had been faithfully protected by the sacred language. Will that Church be better understood now that she has abandoned that sacred language? Just the opposite!

---

2 "But the sensual man perceiveth not these things that are of the Spirit of God." (1 Cor. 2:14)
3 Pope John XXIII's Apostolic Constitution published in 1962 on Latin and other languages used in the Church.

It won't be anymore. I want to underline this. What for some time now you have parroted as the People of God, whether they understand the Mass or not, is not a question of language. It is a question of catechesis and liturgical formation. Are you surprised, Your Holiness, to hear a Lutheran speak like this?"

"It amazes me, but I'm very happy to hear it"

"Luther himself did not abolish Latin, except for pedagogical reasons. For educational purposes, he prescribed the use of German only for the readings and homily, which was what the Catholics in Germany were already doing. There was no need to go any further. The Lutherans went further, and extended German to the whole mass. However it was a type of German that a short time after became reserved exclusively for religious use. This German language was different from common German. They might as well have kept the Latin!

"I looked over the Catholic translations. Pray and sing those lyrics? Address God with similar terms used when speaking to the butcher or fellow in the garage? It's heart-breaking! The same goes for your *Novus ordo Missae*, not to mention the dogmatic transpositions! In fact, the Canon of your traditional Mass is irreconcilable with the Lutheran faith, while the rite and formulas of your *Novus ordo* can be interpreted without difficulty in the Lutheran sense. Do you think the Lutherans are grateful to you? Or at least happy about it? Maybe one in a hundred thousand, but the others, if they think about it, are scandalized. After all, the immutability of the Catholic Church was a source of comfort for us too, whereas now we see with trepidation that even this cliff has become sand before being carried away and scattered by the waves.

"It goes without saying that, compared to the Catholic ones, the Lutheran translations are much more dignified, and not only from the linguistic point of view. Compare, Your Holiness, even just the German version of the Nicene Creed, as it is in the Lutheran ritual, with what you now have in your new Mass.

Oh, if modern Catholics, reformers four centuries after the fact, were less presumptuous, and humbly dedicated themselves to reading a few pages of the history of the Reformation, they would be frightened, if not completely reckless or wicked, when learning of the very sad experiences of the reformed Churches. I have met some Catholics who have undertaken this effort. It may be that I'm still young... And yet how instructive it would be for them!

"And here also in Catholic churches, on the table of the Last Supper, the Eucharistic Bread is reduced to undetectable crumbs, and the Book dominates, for a more abundant table of the Word! A table that is more abundant than God's Word? I was present this morning at one of your new Masses. The celebrant intruded in the ceremony with his own words five different times, with as many chats at his whim. His chattiness dominated the rest of the rite. It reduced the Eucharistic rite itself from Consecration to Communion, to two fleeting and elusive minutes, which left no impression.

"Among us Lutherans, the most plentiful table of the Word has a whole history. What hasn't been included in all those sermons and in our temples? Who told you that you are doing better than we are? According to what results? If a more abundant table of the Word could have produced all that the best among you today promise from it, our communities should be so well-formed and fervent after four hundred years of this abundant table of the Word, which replaced the sacraments and the ancient mystagogical catechesis. Instead it has dulled the faithful's ability to listen, so that, no matter how hard we try to translate and re-translate it, the same Word of God no longer reaches them.

"I'd like to recommend that Your Holiness read a work which is little known to Protestants and unknown to Catholics. It has a rather lengthy title: "History of the Ancient Forms of the Mass in the Protestant Church of Germany, from the

Reformation to the present day,"[4] by Graff. If you read this work, you might notice with astonishment that your *Novus ordo Missae* already existed in the Age of Enlightenment. You're making exactly the same mistakes that we did in ages past. Of course! This *Novus ordo* is like a piece of furniture at the archives, filled with many drawers. If you pull out certain drawers, you'll still say a Catholic Mass. If you pull out other drawers, you'll say a sort of Protestant Mass or Last Supper. And if you pull at a third type of drawer—the drawer of private inspiration, to which you have opened the doors—you'll say anything, but certainly not a Mass, either Catholic or Lutheran. With the *Novus ordo* in the drawers, you leave the faithful defenseless to the despotic impositions of whoever presides over the divine service on a given day. They are defenseless? Of course, their only defense is that of deserting the services. Who will continue to attend them? Those who, instead of enjoying the freedom given to us by Jesus Christ, are intimidated and slaves of superstition.

"Yes, even in Rome I have seen the tables which so pompously fill many wonderful presbyteries for the celebration *versus populum*, and humiliate the splendor of so many wonderful altars. And so, also for you, what has collapsed is the frontier between time and eternity, between the ephemeral and the eternal, between nothingness and the infinite, which was represented by the balustrade and the altar at which the Catholic priest celebrated *versus Deum*. Do you really believe that looking each other in the face really helps you to penetrate more deeply into the ineffable mystery of transubstantiation, and to adore with more humility God Who really is present in his incarnate Word? This is why I really fear that many Catholics, who started with a four century disadvantage, are

---

4 Paul Graff (1878–1955), *Geschichte der Auflösung der alten gottesdienstlichen Formen in der evangelischen Kirche Deutschlands bis zum Eintritt der Aufklärung und des Rationalismus.*

now overtaking the more casual Protestants themselves who no longer believe in anything."

"Dear reverend, I have already read and meditated on Graff's book," the Pope told him before adding, "many Catholic priests, including the Pope, celebrate again, or as a new thing, *versus Deum*, not *versus populum*. Come to my Mass in the chapel of the Blessed Sacrament of St. Peter's Basilica, and you will see, dear Thomas Morgenröte—Thomas Dawn (or Sunrise), what a beautiful name!—and you will therefore see that the *Novus ordo Missae* has already been archived there. Not only that, but I can assure you that it will be archived throughout the Catholic Church."

"Truly?!" exclaimed Morgenröte. "Because I came in here to tell you so many things, but fearing that I couldn't say much, I'd promised myself to at least inform you of my indignation at seeing that at the same time that I'm beginning to discover the wonders of the Tridentine Mass. Remember, Your Holiness, that I am someone who lived until yesterday in Lutheranism and am speaking to you like this. The Catholics let themselves be torn without caring about the divide they will suffer.

"And then...I would have confided to you all of my heart's intimate bitterness, because I...I am now a stranger in my Church, which no longer has anything to say to me or give me, with all its sermons and symbolic meals. Anyway, I would have found in yours the home I was seeking. And there are so many like me!"

"And if I assure you that the Catholic Counter-Reform will be carried out partly by me and partly by my successor?"

"I think that then I would be left with no choice, and I would become a Catholic, since I no longer feel Lutheran. I no longer want to feel like I am walking on quicksand..."

"...and he came as far as Rome to look for the rock..."

"...Cephas, tu es Petrus!"

42

"Nomen meum Legio"

MONSIGNOR CONSALVE DIDN'T leave the city. Rome was a front line trench. Rome was a wide-ranging observatory. Rome was a unique coordination hub in the world. Rome would have been the Armageddon of the last battle and final victory. Consalve was to remain in Rome, and in Rome he remained, in a much milder climate than the tropical one of his distant homeland. He would think about his diocese later. He would have handed its reins over to another pastor on the assumption that he would certainly remain in Rome at the head of an important ecclesiastical dicastery. Only by renewing the men could one think of renewing the Curia. It was quite a sacrifice to live in exile in Rome, far from one's native land, but humanity's salvation required it. One day, with supersonic air travel he would be able to go home for lunch and be back in Rome for dinner, if he wanted to.

So he stayed in the capital, but didn't rest on his past successes, both because up to then he was still making progress and because it really wasn't the time for him to rest, even on his past. First, he added to the list of charges against Pius XIV. Second, he continued his list of indispensable fellow soldiers for the upcoming great and decisive battle. This second list, much longer and more meticulous than the first, included names, surnames, addresses, professional activities, academic and similar qualifications, positions and assignments, influence and efficiency of the holders of key positions at regional, national, international and ecumenical levels. And more.

Monsignors Quira and Arras finally returned to Rome. They had toured the five continents, looking for names to add to the second list. Monsignor Speakering also arrived, after Consalve had sent him a plane ticket paid for by the president of the international League for Integral Humanism. Though silent, there was always something eloquent about Speakering. Thus the second list was considerably extended. With great satisfaction, Consalve presented its summary, from a variety of perspectives, to the other three monsignors, during a private working dinner for four in the small sitting room of Quira's hotel.

Consalve declared, "More than the quantity, however, is the quality. That's what matters. From the quality standpoint, we have the following groups: psychologists, theologians, experts, sociologists, trade unionists, community activists; mature, responsible and committed lay people; members of the clergy, religious and feminist religious sisters; writers, publicists, publishers, booksellers, lecturers, and journalists in general..."

"...and newsagents?" Speakering asked, breaking his customary silence. "How many publications could end up under the table, if the newsagents they rely on aren't with us!"

The other three looked at him with admiration, thinking that Speakering's word had been as golden as his proverbial silence had been.

Consalve exclaimed, "It's true. We only have the newspapers to help us change the situation. Now we are still in this preliminary phase. How will our messages reach the intended audience?"

Quira exclaimed in turn, "Our messages! Peace, progress, a new earth and new skies, the new era, the redemption of the poor through a multipurpose revolution, the struggle for liberation from all forms of slavery, ecumenism."

Arras exclaimed with even more vigor, "Ecumenism. Ecumenism above all, dear Monsignor Quira! Ecumenism with all the problems that matter: the condemnation of all triumphalism, the prohibition of any fundamentalist and traditionalist apologetics, the end of dogmatism together with the end of Thomism. Pastoral and doctrinal dialogue with non-believers, and the radical change of mentality by believers who do not think like us."

"And that's not even mentioning the progressive and irreversible democratization of the Church, with American democracy as the model, as the infallible Hans Küng proclaimed at Columbia University one fateful Sunday afternoon in November 1971, in front of about a thousand people. I was there. What a speech! Seventy-five minutes! A river of words. He concluded with the message, 'Stay in the Church, but fight!'"

"... as the great Copernicus of theology, our Teilhard, taught us with words and personal example. I am feeding and affirming myself with his letters. Here is what he says on March 21, 1941: 'In keeping with my own principles, I cannot fight Christianity. I can simply work within it to try to transform and convert it. Do you understand, Excellencies? Convert it! A revolutionary attitude would be much easier, and also much more pleasant, but it would be suicide. As a consequence, I have to carry on tenaciously, step by step, and so on.' Here is what the St. Augustine of the Church of tomorrow says!

"The Church of Tomorrow? Listen to what he says about it in a letter dated January 26, 1936: 'What increasingly dominates my spirit is the effort to establish in myself, and to spread around me, a new religion. Do you understand, Excellencies? A new religion! Let's call it a perfected Christianity, if you like, in which a personal God is no longer the great neolithic owner of past times, but the soul of the world.'"

"The soul of the world, the *logos spermatikós* of the Neo-Platonists or something of the sort," Consalve explained. "Magnificent!"

After having deposited the book of Letters by de Chardin, Quira resumed: "But let's get back to the democratization of the Church. Well, the democratization of the Church requires spontaneous groups. These must be carefully prefabricated one by one, that is, in autochthonous cells such as those of the Cathars. They must be governed only by the charisms of the Spirit. Such cells won't presume to possess a ready-made truth transmitted to them, but they will question each other through a permanent collective discussion, in ever new research and experiences. Here is the living Church! This is part of the rising tide of cosmic evolution from the noosphere towards Christ, the omega-point, the reinventing of the primeval virtues of the pre-Constantinian Church. Without evolution, there is no salvation, as our new St. Augustine already said with his prophetic eye in 1955, in *Le Christique*, 'Christ saves, but shall we hesitate to add that Christ himself is saved by evolution?'"

"O most holy Evolution!"

The discussion went on for a long time, like a business dinner that succeeded in increasingly convincing the dinner guests of the sublimity of the cause, and of the contribution that the cause also expected from them—indeed, above all from them. In fact, they were not, like so many unfortunate others, blind and vain instruments in the hands of certain sinister forces, which the fundamentalists and traditionalists called wickedly non-Catholic. It was said that such forces were not always hidden, but always shrewd and fierce. Theirs was not a childish plaything that they had cunningly concocted. The conclusion of the meeting was that it was necessary to hold another one at a higher level, that is, with Cardinal Stolzkamm and the Cardinal Camerlengo himself.

The Camerlengo stalled when Consalve invited him to the meeting via telephone in which Stolzkamm and numerous other high prelates would participate. He told Consalve to call again in the afternoon, because only then would he be able to tell him whether he was free or not. In the meantime he telephoned Stolzkamm, who told him that he had received an identical proposal from Consalve and the assurance that the Camerlengo would be at the meeting. Then he had told him to let him know the time and place.

"Wouldn't it be better to let the dead bury their dead?" the Camerlengo then asked Stolzkamm, who replied:

"For me, I feel obliged to intervene. I have encouraged Consalve's vanity. I have driven him to ruin. Having committed the sin, I must do penance for it, and try to make reparation for it as far as I still can."

The Camerlengo admitted, "In this regard, I too have my remorse. I will therefore reply that I too will come. My part will certainly be easier if you are there to give me a hand."

Cardinal Aurelio Meyerbeer also declared his willingness to lend them a hand, having learned of the matter in one of his by now frequent meetings with the cardinal Camerlengo. Thus it was decided that the meeting would take place in the Camerlengo's office.

The day of the meeting, Consalve and his associates converged on the Vatican. As soon as Romolo realized that the incoming car was driven by Consalve himself, he remembered the crime with the tapes, and ran to hide in a hidden closet of the garage. As soon as Consalve arrived in sight of the Camerlengo's office, he thought he heard the echo of the song that had concluded the meeting of the reels: "The woman is mobile / like a feather in the wind..." and then the echo of Father Viso's uncontainable laughter. This seemed to him a bad omen. As soon as he saw three cardinals lined up in the room, instead of the two summoned, he was even more sinisterly impressed. He quickly recovered by appealing to his sense of duty and responsibility, which was everything in him. He had prepared a brief and succinct report of a dozen pages of the innumerable subjects which he had agreed to set out and debate at that meeting. But when there he preferred to simply read the memo itself:

"... for the sake of both brevity and precision." He then read his pages, with the calmness and decisiveness that is typical of people who are sure of their business, of the good cause, and who are prepared for anything, even martyrdom. After that there was a silence before the others spoke.

Cardinal Aurelio began, "You see, Your Excellency, ecclesiastical democracy, the election of bishops, and therefore also of the pope, by a large stratum of the faithful, the conciliar and synodal parliamentarianism, the senate of theologians, all this was already known by the Church of other times. She suffered from it, and would have died of it, if she were not imperishable. I would say that Your Excellency, during your studies in the history of the Church, lingered too much on the archeology of the catacombs. I read with interest what you wrote about it in your bachelor's degree thesis. You didn't push your investigations to the point of reading the *Constitution civil du Clergé*, voted on July 12, 1790, by an assembly such as the one you wished for, of clergymen and laymen, Catholics, Jansenists, Gallicans, Protestants, deists, atheists, and adventurers—in short, voted by something very close to Your Excellency's assembly of the People of God. Only then the update was called a return to the simplicity of the primitive Church. Is it perhaps by virtue of evolution and progress, to which you have appealed, that you want to go back to those past errors and horrors?

"'Democratize the Church,' Your Excellency said. The Church has its own structure by the will of its Founder. It is a monarchical, non-democratic structure, as the same electors of the pope are elected one by one by the pope himself. You yourself were not elected bishop of your diocese by the People of God. Yet you believe that you have ordinary and indubitable authority over it. It is not lawful for man to change what God has established! But even if lawful, would it be commendable that among the various forms of human government that we could slavishly imitate, we would take after the only one which allows people to go to the polls to decide on questions about which they have no competence, while their wishes are not taken into account in those which directly affect them?

"Your Excellency also asserted that, just as the principle *Omnis potestas a Deo*[1] has been abused for two thousand years, it is now licit to expose oneself to the abuse of the opposite principle, *Omnis potestas a populo*.[2] Well, *nego paritatem*[3]! The use of a false principle is always abusive. The two principles are contrary. At least one of them is false. Which of the two do you think? What would also destroy his current authority as bishop? Tell me?"

Consalve looked at the other two cardinals, and then turned his gaze to his three colleagues, almost seeking support, like an actor on stage waiting and soliciting the prompter's line. Then he quickly flipped through his mental handbook of catchphrases, good for all cases, and found so many that the difficulty of choosing aroused in him a form of literary anguish, which rendered him mute.

Then Aurelio spoke again:

"Your Excellency wants the reform of the current structures of the Church, because they would have been derived, the current ones I mean, arbitrarily from the political system of other times, of the times of Constantine the Great. You would like to remodel the new one on the current structure of the United States of North America. Are you really sure that these correspond to those wanted by Our Lord for His Church?

---

[1] "Every power [is] from God."—a very common remaking of the Scriptural Romans 13:1: *non est potestas nisi a Deo*—there is no power but from God...so not an exact quote, but exactly as many commentators and legislators have used it.
[2] "All power to the people!"
[3] "I deny the equality," i.e., I deny that the two things are equal because there is an "equivocation" in the terms.

"That goes without saying that even these new structures are considered inadequate for the government of that nation. And don't you also think you are arbitrarily imposing something on Church institutions derived from a current and contingent political system, not a divine institution?"

Consalve could not find any response to this question either, and began to feel that he was facing an implacable enemy while flanked by three allies who were like aged corpses.

Aurelio continued: "Your Excellency also said something about ecumenism, that in a world evolving according to the laws of relativity as discovered by Einstein, a world in which two plus two would no longer exactly make four, a world in which the very meaning of words is constantly changing and in which absolute and irrefutable truths can no longer be imposed not only on non-believers, but also on believers of any denomination, will Your Excellency now complain if I also consider your sentence irrefutable, despite the fact that you, contradicting yourself, have uttered it as an absolute and irrefutable truth?

"Now Your Excellency can understand that, given the consequences that you have drawn from the natural instability of words, God himself couldn't reveal to us an absolute truth. Without this, revelation and sacred Scripture would no longer be possible. And then everything that Your Excellency has built, based solely on the Bible—because it is the word of God—doesn't it seem similar to a house built on the sand which falls to ruin at the first gust of wind?"

Consalve wasn't following Aurelio, but frantically formulating in his mind any sentence that could provide an answer, without worrying whether it was appropriate or not. His sole purpose was to demonstrate to himself and the other three that he hadn't yet been conquered or tamed. As soon as Aurelio was silent, Consalve declared:

"I have not been understood. I have been misunderstood.

My words are misunderstood, and you want to nail me to the cross for two words or perhaps even fewer."

Stolzkamm interrupted him: "Your Excellency, how can you say 'two words'? You read from no fewer than twelve pages. I took the liberty of counting them, while you passed them around one at a time."

"In any case, I was still not understood. Revealed truth is indeed revealed, as revealed in the primitive Christian communities thanks to dialogue, ongoing dialogue, and the resulting reflection, done in fraternal charity and in community prayer, under the guidance of the Spirit of Christ. From this were born the Gospels, the Acts of the Apostles, the Letters of the Apostles, and the Apocalypse itself, if it should ever be placed on the same level as the previous writings. Now all this must be reborn in our communities, which had been mortified to the level of silent and passive listeners, by the despotic magisterium of the so-called teaching Church. We do not want to impose our will and Creed on anyone. Much less do we want to disturb the consciences of non-believers. Dialogue at all levels, as discerned by Vatican II, the dynamics of the post-conciliar logic, and the charismatic and prophetic spirit of the new Pentecost, have generated the new Church, the post-conciliar Church. The era of condemnations is over!..."

Aurelio asked him, "What do you say, Excellency? Is the Age of Errors over?"

"*Sat prata biberunt!*"[4] exclaimed Stolzkamm, shaking his head and exchanging a look of commiseration with the other two cardinals. Then, as if they had tacitly agreed to lighten the atmosphere in the hall, they began to converse among

---

4 Reference to the end of Virgil's *Eclogues* III, "The fields have drunk enough [so close the irrigation/rivers!]" Often used for "enough information" or "almost too much of a good thing." or "The meadows have drunk enough."

themselves, but in such a way as to avoid excluding anyone present who wished to take part.

Aurelio asked the Camerlengo, "Your Eminence, do you know the story about ongoing dialogue, which the Soviets disseminated for external use? The art of determining a dichotomy—right and left—even in the most monolithic and concordant systems, such as found in cloistered monasteries—between, say, young and elderly nuns. This dichotomy worked together with the explosive and destructive models of critical sense and personal responsibility. Some bone of contention is thrown into the group. Everyone has to choose between A and B. A possible third solution, which would be the right one, is excluded, so that whatever the majority chooses, it always goes fatally astray. Of course, the group needs sensitization so that no one dares to disengage, no one becomes alienated. Everyone needs to be admonished that mature people do not shirk their responsibilities, and here everyone is mature and committed! In the end, it doesn't matter if some choose one color for the rope and others another color because everyone will be hanged by it, and it will be said to comfort their agony that they have chosen it democratically."

The joke elicited a bellow of laughter and gave a humorous tone to the rest of the conversation, which was brief, because there was no longer any reason to take the intentions of Consalve and his associates seriously even while no one wanted to be cruel to them.

The Camerlengo replied, "I believe I have studied the Holy Scriptures quite well, yet I don't remember reading anywhere that the Lord ever said to His apostles, *'Ite et dialogate*, and don't disturb consciences!' In fact, he commanded just the opposite, which is to disturb the consciences of all men in order to induce them to conversion. And He Himself so disturbed the consciences of His countrymen that, not wanting

His yoke, they crucified Him. Did not the old St. Simeon say of Jesus that he was a sign of contradiction?"

"If the helmsman had to talk to the passengers at each rudder stroke, if he had to stick to the opinion of the majority, where would the boat end up, especially in stormy weather?"

"Here's a very short fable on engaging in dialogue with certain unbelievers: A wolf says in a kind voice to a lamb, which is safely inside an impregnable sheepfold, 'Come out, please, let's have a dialogue!'"

While they were talking to each other, Consalve had time to recover a bit, like Antaeus who, when knocked to the ground, received new energies from Mother Earth. Wasn't the fact that the three old churchmen were rambling on, jumping from branch to branch like three old magpies and falling back on old-school witticisms, a clear sign that they didn't dare to go out into the open field?

"Of course, those two have undergone such a radical change," he muttered to himself, referring to Stolzkamm and the Camerlengo. "No, I couldn't have anticipated it! This bloody Roman air! And that's not even to mention the atmosphere of the Roman Curia! Oh, how right Luther was! Certainly the Pope won over Stolzkamm—such a proud man—by promising to place him at the head of some important dicastery. Judas! For thirty dirty coins! But what could the Pope have promised the Camerlengo? The papal throne, the succession and the triregnum?"

While he was thinking over the answer to this question, the Camerlengo began speaking again:

"Your most reverend Excellencies, I am responsible for having pushed you onto the wrong path, and now I have the duty to tell you: go back! Go back, before you incur the sanctions foreseen by the Code of Canon Law!"

But Consalve, the only one who still had the breath to speak, answered grimly:

"Threats will not stop progress. We march in the direction of history! Can you stop a river with your hands?"

"Leave your progress to Mazzini!" Aurelio replied.

"Our progress has metaphysical, not romantic, foundations! It is the progress of cosmic evolution itself. Whoever is determined to fight proceeds along with it. Whoever lets himself be bought and deserts our cause will be marginalized and overwhelmed," insisted Consalve, trancelike.

Stolzkamm said, "I was where you are going. Go back!"

"We'll keep advancing! We aren't mercenaries! We aren't afraid! We are many, and we grow visibly!"

"*Nomen meum legio*, said the demoniac of Gerasa!" After saying these sad words, Stolzkamm adjourned.

Consalve immediately went to the delegate of the Human Universal Fraternity for Integral Humanism to inform him of the meeting and regain his own spirits. The good president, intelligent and magnanimous, compensated him for every expense incurred up to that moment, plus an additional one thousand dollars that His Excellency had lent to Romolo. But like the good Samaritan, he also gave a few extra little things, in view of rising expenses. He gave him advice that was more valuable than money. The cardinal needed to rely more on the collaboration of married priests, as they were irreversibly engaged in the work of purification and universal spiritual sublimation that was desired by the dynamics of the Second Vatican Council.

"*Optima propositio!*"[5] Consalve exclaimed, putting his wallet back in his pocket. "I hadn't thought of that!"

"And here they are, Your Excellency, the list of married priests, updated to the end of last month."

---

5 "excellent proposal," "great idea!"—a reference to Elijah's idea in 1 Kings 18:24 to have each side call upon God's name and see to which He'd send down fire; to which idea the whole people said "[that's] the best proposition."

The zealous president put a voluminous photocopied file of about five hundred pages into Consalve's hand. But before saying goodbye to his guest, he took the liberty of reminding him:

"It is one of the most integral manifestations of the humanism of every man. It is a phenomenon that must be followed step-by-step in all nations and, with due circumspection, to be intensely promoted."

43

From Wellhausen to Maternalism

"YOU WERE RIGHT TO COME, AND so quickly! Thank you, Monsignor!"

"It is I who must thank you, Your Holiness, for having thought of me," Monsignor Bruno De Gaudenzi replied.

"Well, I would like someone to accompany me to Castel Gandolfo for the next few days. Together with the cardinal Camerlengo, we will see what Professor Amador Moreno of the Mesogaios Institute has already done, *pars magna* of this institution, which has proved to be truly very serious. I would also like you to accompany me to the Monastery of the Passion soon. I feel that it is my duty to pay a last visit to the superior, who is ill and whose days are numbered. We'll go there, as soon as the taxi arrives, which a company in Rome kindly keeps at my disposal for these little incognito trips."

"Like the little boat that Jesus wanted the apostles to keep available for him on Lake Tiberias," De Gaudenzi observed.

"Or something similar. In fact, it is nowhere written that the apostles were forced to change their boat from time to time to protect the privacy of Jesus. Finally, I would like to know if you would like to become cardinal of the Holy Roman Church."

"Of course? But I don't think I deserve it!"

"I think you do, and I promise you the cardinal's hat. But since I don't have much time left, if I can't personally keep my promise, I will bind my successor."

"I hope I can dispose of myself successfully to this honor and burden. Your Holiness hides his years well, and hopefully he will remain in the chair of Peter for a long time to come."

"But my guardian angel is not of this opinion. If St. Pius V or St. Pius X had whispered it in my ear, I would have said, 'sickness!' But since my guardian angel whispered it to me, I say without a doubt, 'accident!' It could also be on the occasion of the planned trip to Castel Gandolfo. Get ready! Are you afraid to travel with me now that I've told you this?"

"Not even in the slightest!"

"You see! You deserve it, the purple. A symbol of martyrdom. To face martyrdom, I believe, requires a little courage. You have to believe in your guardian angel. Do you think, Monsignor, that the Catholic doctrine on the guardian angel can be defined dogmatically?"

"Certainly, certainly, because I've thought about it for a long time. Indeed, I think that such a definition would be very appropriate in our day, in which the Sadducees have so many followers. They denied the resurrection, the immortality of the soul, the spiritual world, and therefore the angels."

"Your opinion, Monsignor, coincides with that of many other prelates, and with the votes of many faithful. I cannot be the Pope who will define the Catholic doctrine on guardian angels as a dogma of faith, but you will see that my successor will also think of this. You remind him of it!"

"It would seem that, instead of going to the monastery of the Passion, Your Holiness is about to go to the Holy Sepulchre, if not directly to Campo Verano! You shouldn't talk like that!"

"Do you remember Leo XIII's last elegy?

> *Extremum radiat, palenti involvitur umbra,*
> *iam iam sol moriens. Mors subit atra, Leo, atra tibi...* [1]

---

[1] Very high poetry, from Pope Leo XIII's personal compositions: "Ultima desiderata" (1897) in *Condita a Christo*. "Let it shine its last, it is covered in pale [death-]shadows, the sun is already dying. Black death draws near, O Leo/Lion, black for thee."

"Leo says black, but Pius hopes and begs for a slightly less classic color perhaps, but more celestial! Let's go back to the purple! You also deserve it for what you continue to do in the biblical field. You have an impact on a few neo-biblists who might be a little biased towards the biblical tradition itself. Do you know that what you wrote in the *Ephemerides Biblico-orientales* of June, regarding Wellhausen and his companions, is quite original?"

De Gaudenzi replied, "I wrote it precisely because it seemed original to me. As far as I know, the hypothesis had not yet been put forward that the Pentateuch, concerning Moses, had not in its substance been written originally in the Hebrew language because that language didn't exist yet. In fact, in the desert the Jews spoke either the new language, learned in Egypt, or the ancient language of Abraham, Proto-Aramaic. Only after their entry into the land of Canaan did the Jews learn Hebrew and how to write it."

The Pope confirmed, "This is beyond any doubt. Hebrew is nothing other than the Canaanite language in the Israelite mouth. However, you present the conclusion you have reached as a mere hypothesis, whereas it is a fact that you have demonstrated flawlessly."

"I present my conclusion as a hypothesis, certain that scholars themselves will accept it as fact."

The Pope nodded, "As is customary in these cases. That way is also more convincing psychologically. Leave it to each individual to take the last step by himself, as if he were himself the discoverer of the treasure, which is placed under his nose."

De Gaudenzi went on, "There's no doubt that during the period of the Judges, practically until Saul, the Israelites lived in Palestine under the cane of the Philistines. Divided into many small tribes, pushed along the central mountainous ridge that was marginally fertile, facing serious economic difficulties, and probably without scribes and the necessary means to draw up copies of the sacred writings, they jealously conversed in Silo, in the Arém-Berit, the Ark of the Covenant.

"Nothing more natural, however, than that a few zealous lovers of the Law, especially from the tribe of Levi, went to Silo to pray. There they lingered to copy at least some sections of the books and translated them into Hebrew, to then read them, from the depths of their hearts, to their tribe or family, especially on the occasion of Passover. Nothing more natural than that the same biblical passage was translated by different scribes in different ways. Nothing more natural, given the great respect of the Jews for the Word of God, than that at least the most worthy of the translations were later absorbed into a complete translation of the entire Pentateuch. This would explain the so-called duplications, the sections in which the name Elohim predominates, and those in which the name Yahwéh predominates. There are many other such details, all of which have offered a specious pretext for the lucubrations of Wellhausen and his disciples, without going into rationalist presuppositions and their imaginative additions."

The Pope said, "In conclusion, the current Pentateuch in Hebrew must be said to be a translation, indeed the result of a work of editing, by divine inspiration, of several translations or remakes of the narration of the same episode, respectfully juxtaposed here and there, as it had been written down during the forty years of permanence of the Jews in the desert. But of the Pentateuch written in the language of the desert—let's call it that—is there nothing left?"

"Nothing, Your Holiness. Everything was lost when Nebukudurra-usur[2] destroyed Solomon's temple. He must have been an art lover like Nebuchadnezzar I, the destroyer of the eighth wonder of the ancient world, perhaps the most wonderful, certainly the most important!"

---

[2] More commonly known as Nebuchadnezzar II.

The Pope said, "It was gone before the other seven. Then it was rebuilt and made more sumptuous by Herod the Great, to be definitively demolished by Titus's men. Now to rebuild it, it would be necessary to demolish the untouchable building which we improperly call the Mosque of Omar, and which the Arabs call Kubbet es-Sékhra, that is the Dome of the Rock. In fact, it protects the rock on which the altar of holocausts once stood. You enter barefoot, but the floor is covered with soft carpets. You are overwhelmed by a soft light of a thousand colors. But at a command from the custodian, a rain of gold and blue descends from the dome and is set on fire with a thousand lights. It is an enchantment. But to describe these marvels in a worthy way, we would need the cardinal Camerlengo here. Not only is he endowed with a very refined artistic sense, but he also possesses a solid metaphysics of art, without which it is impossible to resist the suggestion of today's concerted propaganda. Listen to what he writes here."

At this point, Brother Ambrogio appeared on the threshold of the sitting room in which they were conversing and announced:

"Cincinnato apologizes for the delay. He was not warned in advance and was unavailable as he was on duty. He will arrive as soon as possible."

Ambrogio then disappeared and the Pope resumed his conversation with De Gaudenzi:

"Well, I don't think we're wasting our time. So listen to what he writes here, on this page, which he prepared for our upcoming document, but which, given the nature of the document, we will not be able to include as is: 'Technique conditions artistic expression, that is poetry, and gives the latter entry its broadest and most comprehensive meaning. However, true poetry sublimates the technique in itself and conceals it. A novice pianist-composer cannot fail to show his effort, both in his composition and in the execution of the composition, because his technique is still immature, while the virtuoso pianist performs the compositions, on which he has lavished all the resources of a superior technique, without betraying the slightest effort. He is completely enraptured at this point by the poetry that he expresses. Only at a later time will he discuss the technical effort, but both during the composition and the execution, the poetry in progress, although based on a great amount of technique, sublimates the technique itself by concealing it.' Don't you think what he says is so beautiful, Excellency? And to think that this was not written in the author's mother tongue!"

"Beautiful and true," De Gaudenzi confirmed. Like all long-standing Romans, he also had a solid and innate artistic taste.

"And listen to what he says here: 'There is a *natura perennis*. Therefore, there is also a *natura humana perennis*, and therefore also a *psychologia perennis*, and therefore again an aesthetics, a poetics, and an *ars perennis*. It follows that any philosophy that is not an enrichment of the *philosophia perennis* is aberrant. Any artistic expression that does not flow from, or flow back into, the vein of the *ars perennis* is aberrant, unnecessarily complex, and decadent, if it is still worthy of the name of art. However, even in the artistic field, when everything seems destroyed and knocked down, the myth of the Libyan giant is repeated. He's the son of Neptune and the Earth, who, having not yet fallen to the ground, rises anew.' What do you say, Excellency?"

"I just say, let us hope so! I wouldn't want His Eminence the Camerlengo to be too optimistic, as he was in other matters too, until some time ago. In fact, I fear that the artistic Antaeus has for some time now already found his Hercules who has strangled him and kept him detached a little too long from mother Earth, that is, from the *ars perennis*. I think this way because it is well known that, a few years ago, the cardinal Camerlengo, though he could have prevented it, allowed to appear in a pontifical document the phrase that said something like, 'civilizations are born, grow, and become fixed, but the waves of the rising tide penetrate and advance, each a little further than the last, upon the shore. It is in this way that humanity progresses along the path of history.'

"Now it seems to me that human freedom doesn't justify such a fatally optimistic metaphysics of history, not even if it is limited to the history of art since precisely by virtue of this freedom, man can also regress, so that instead of the rising tide, there is the falling tide.

"Then we would have to define what is meant by progress: the multiplication of machines, of technology, of empirical sciences, of weapons? One can speak of progress or regression only when a certain goal has been set. There is only one supreme goal, God and eternal life. Goodness and progress lead to that goal. All the rest is evil and regression. As for faith, we are assured of only one progress, that of the mustard seed, that is, of the Church, that is, of faith itself. However, even in this progress, it seems to me that winters with frost and cold, like the current ones, are not excluded, even if we are in the middle of summer. And then to dampen our optimism-at-all-costs, there is the Lord's question: 'When the Son of Man returns, do you believe that he will still find faith on earth?'

"I'd say that in the unfortunate sentence quoted above, Teilhardian Gnosticism was heard more than the word of God was. And there's much talk of biblical revival, even while the Bible has never been put underfoot as it is at present! If I weren't afraid of boring you, I would tell Your Holiness about the episode that happened recently in a parish whose name it would be better not to mention.

"A young woman had been assigned to do one of the biblical readings. Very self-confident, she didn't bother to pre-read the passage assigned to her. Don't forget, she was a university student! So it happened that she got the page wrong, and up to a certain point she proclaimed aloud, then read more and more hesitantly, as if waiting to find the correction of what she was reading, the well-known sentence of the first letter to the

Corinthians: 'Let women keep silence in the churches: for it is not permitted them to speak, but to be subject, as also the law saith. But if they would learn anything, let them ask their husbands at home. For it is a shame for a woman to speak in the church.' At this point the university student could no longer contain herself, and ran away, dropping the book to the ground, while all the people of God exclaimed, '"Let us give thanks to the Lord!'

"You, Your Excellency, say that it is a case of the Bible underfoot, but certain modern biblical scholars will tell you that those prescriptions of St. Paul's are not St. Paul's, and that in any case they were valid for his contemporaries, but not for today's women."

De Gaudenzi replied:

"The same can also be said of God's commandments. They were valid for stiff-necked people, but not for the mature Christians of today. What then is contingent and transitory in the Bible, and what is perennial and immutable in it? Everyone decides as he likes, autonomously, thanks to private inspiration!"

"And what about the phrase: the Bible is the history of salvation?" the Pope asked him.

"Your Holiness, forgive me for being frank, but I have to tell you that I don't like that saying. The Bible is above all the book of God, of God's holiness. A Bible-story of man's salvation would end up being a Bible-story of a servant God, and of man as his king and lord."

"You are right," the Pope approved. "Sacred Scripture is not anthropocentric, but essentially theocentric. It's not the story of man's salvation, and of a God who is the instrument of this salvation. It's the story of God's unquestionable supremacy, that is, the story of truth! Of course, to the man who accepts God, God grants salvation, indeed God gives himself. But the accent and primacy must remain on God, and must not be shifted to man."

Finally Brother Ambrogio came to announce that Cincinnato was outside waiting.

"Let's not keep him waiting," the Pope said.

"Indeed!" De Gaudenzi exclaimed: "Even if we've been waiting for him for half an hour!"

On a seat of the taxi they found an issue of *Il focolare cattolico*.

"Excuse me, driver," De Gaudenzi said. "Did you see that someone left this periodical here?"

"I bought it, Excellency," replied Cincinnato, continuing, "For myself, but with the illustrations inside I don't feel like taking it home. We're all a bit old-fashioned!"

"I've received numerous complaints about the doctrinal and moral errors disseminated by this periodical," added the Pope. "Yet the masthead guarantees the product. People buy and read it with confidence that it contains the one true Christian truth. The gnat and the camel are swallowed up."

"I had already promised myself not to waste a penny more, Your Holiness," said Cincinnato, "But what else can I bring into the family that's at least harmless?"

"When I was a boy," the Pope said, "there was the 'Pro familia,' and I didn't understand why 'familia' was written without the 'g.' It was not specified whether it was for a Catholic or a Muslim family, but I found nothing that could offend my naivety. As for this other periodical, someone should rein it in."

"De Gaudenzi said, "It has already been done, Your Holiness. And also to other so-called educative periodicals that are linked to Catholic educational institutes, but what is the result? However, in certain countries, very few edifying publications are sold in the churches themselves!"

"St. Gregory VII didn't hesitate to declare that the faithful were released from obedience to bishops who didn't conform to the doctrine and morals of the Church. Are we getting there soon?"

After a brief pause, the Pope took the Rosary from his pocket, and the three passengers spent the rest of the journey reciting it, until they reached their destination.

The superior of the Passionists immediately expressed the desire to make a confession one last time to the Pope, who had been her ordinary confessor for a very long time. The Pope willingly obliged. He knew he'd been invited there especially for this. De Gaudenzi also went to greet her. He congratulated her on the development of the institute, and found her rather lively, as if she had been revived by the Pope's words. He took a few moments to hear from her directly what had already been told to him by others.

"Why do our novice numbers increase every year? This year, for example, there are four hundred and twelve novices, exactly twenty-four more than last year. In the hundred years of life of our institute—we will celebrate the centenary in three years—the number of our novices has increased by an average of four each year. How come, when other institutes, even more recent ones than ours, are like torrents that fall into the sea leaving their beds dry upstream? How come? Very simple: we haven't updated. We love our Rules as they were given to us by our foundress, who will certainly be canonized one day. If we remade them, we wouldn't like them anymore."

"I think this miracle would be enough to canonize her," said De Gaudenzi.

"Let those institutes that have betrayed their Rules in order to update things be updated by having them return to the precise primitive observance! I don't mean strict observance. I simply say precise observance. Which orders are they? The ones that lack vocations."

"You're all reputed to be highly educated. How do you explain that? I don't think you have any special schools."

"We're not aiming at culture, but at wisdom. We are not going to rummage through the garbage of the modern

Evelys.[3] Hagiographies and St. Thomas are enough for us. For this reason all our sisters ordinarily also study a little Latin. It also suits the mind, and then it should be the language of Holy Mother Church, and the mother tongue of all the children of the Church. Isn't Esperanto advocated to unify peoples? We have our Esperanto, and with what literature! It's the gift of a very special Divine Providence. Denying it multiplies misunderstandings and schisms. Can you imagine the stature of the Indian Church speaking Hindi or Khasi and so on, now that in Indian seminaries everyone remains completely illiterate in terms of Latin? But Your Holiness will be able to tell you more about this, also because now I am short of... breath."

"Excuse me so much, and thank you!"

"Pray for me, and bless me!"

After this the mother superior declared that she was hosting about twenty superiors of various ranks and institutes, who had gathered there for a few days of study. They would be very happy if the Pope could say a few words to them.

"Two words, two words, here on the spot, to so many people, and what people... It's one word!" the Pope said half-jokingly. "You should have told me a little earlier. In any case, I'll go there with Monsignor De Gaudenzi, and if I miss one of the two words requested of me, you'll get him to say the other. He is the Vicar's vicar for the most illustrious audiences. I'm sure you understand!"

The Pope began, "Reverend sisters, the superior of this institute is about to enter eternity, which will immediately be Paradise for her. I assure you that I am not wrong, and don't have the need to appeal to the charisma of papal infallibility. Then you will fully understand all that you owe to those who

---

3 This might be a reference to the Belgian writer and laicized priest Louis Évely (1910-1985), who taught spirituality even after leaving the priesthood and getting married.

have made you work and suffer, who have humiliated you perhaps unjustly, perhaps maliciously. They induced you to pray more often and with more fervor. They made you tremble. They forced you to use up all your strength. Then you will understand how all those people contributed, even unwittingly, to maturing you in the love of God, to putting God first and doing everything for the love of God, to dying a little every day on the cross for the love of He who, before you, wanted to die on the cross for you."

They spoke for quite a long time, touching on various topics, *ex abundantia cordis*[4], with a spontaneity that the Pope found inspiring, with the serene eyes that were looked at him with such respectful trust. He concluded thus:

"A few days ago a postulant from a religious institute—not this one—took a stand in front of her teacher, concluding her protest by saying, 'It's time we opened up to the world, which comes to meet us!' The superior led the postulant to the convent's door, opened it, and said, 'The world is beyond this threshold. Go meet it, if you care so much about it, because I won't let it in here!'

"Worldly life goes to meet the world, and is carried by the current. Religious life goes against the world. It goes against the tide. Against which world? Against people who wish to convert? No! The vices of the world? Yes! Jesus tells you to be perfect, like the heavenly Father. The world tells you to be mature, as the devil told Eve, to get you to make a responsible choice, as he got Eve to do! Mature, authentic, autonomous, open. Enemies of the status quo. In its updated form, it means the enemies of maternalism.

"I knew a superior who said that it was time to put an end to maternalism in the convents, and that in the convents the nuns had to consider themselves as sisters, and equally as sisters of those to whom they addressed their care, such as

---

4   Mt. 12:34, "out of the abundance of the heart."

the sick or students or whomever. Now I don't want to tell you that the word *nun* really means sister, and I don't think it was invented by that superior. Nor do I want to tell you that that same superior, who so opposed maternalism, treated her nuns like experimental guinea pigs, and forbade them from complaining, because complaining was a symptom of pessimism. No, now I want to simply remind you that in every well-ordered family, if the mother passes away, the older sister, older in age or wisdom, automatically takes her place as the mother, and maternalism is reborn. In any case, instead of maternalism, we will have siblingism. Will the superior want to eradicate this too? But then what will remain? Indifferentism! Daughters, be serious! Avoid fashionable neologisms and rhetorical chatter. Souls need rectors, not rhetoricians, and your nuns need directors, not speakers, and a lot of maternalism, which is a reflection of the paternalism that enables us to confidently call God Our Father."

44

Sermons

Every morning, around half past six, Camillo went down to the sacristy of the chapel of the Blessed Sacrament to assist the sacristan so that the Pope could go punctually to the altar at seven o'clock, without any problems or surprises. On their own initiative, Camillo and the sacristan had engaged Monsignor De Gaudenzi to be ready to celebrate at that hour in the Pope's place, if the latter would not be able to celebrate one morning. The disappointment of the faithful of Rome and of the pilgrims would have been mitigated by the Apostolic-Tridentine Mass, all the more so because the Mass itself was what attracted so many people to the Pope's Mass. By now the Pope took care to celebrate it with constant decorum to make himself less and less unworthy of such a great mystery of faith.

The initiatives of the religious sister of the Santi Cosma e Damiano clinic, of the lady of the chalice, of the printer, and of the first group of singers had now passed to a constantly-growing association of the faithful. They prepared songs and lent missals to whomever needed them. The missals had Latin on one side and one of many languages, including modern Greek, Arabic, Hindi, Chinese and Japanese, on the other. It hadn't been difficult because members of "Una Voce," who were found in every country, had contributed enthusiastically. This organization had been founded at the time of the Second Vatican Council for the restoration of the traditional liturgy.

Various *scholae* had their turn in the choir loft. The scholae were always comprised of singers who performed the office as it had to be performed, as a sacred office. It was simpler and more solemn than before, but always devout and without anything showy. This had succeeded to the extent that the idea of obtaining a sacred ordination for these singers, the minor sacred order of the Cantorate, was maturing. The idea didn't seem strange at all, even to the Pope himself. On the contrary! Even the mass of the faithful took part in the singing. They performed the parts of the Ordinary alternately with the schola, including singing before Mass, during Communion, and after Mass. The songs tended to be in Latin, not only out of respect for the cosmopolitan assembly, but also for the very sacredness acquired by this language, which had come about through a very special intervention of Divine Providence.

After the Gospel, the Pope usually said a few words to the faithful, in the manner of a *homilia infra Missam*, which sometimes lasted more than a quarter of an hour. After Mass, with exceptions, the Blessed Sacrament was left exposed for the adoration of the faithful until late in the evening. This new practice, in accord with the aspirations of both the Pope and Monsignor Wong, required more respectful behavior from visitors to the basilica. In a short time, this brought greater discipline from visitors, who needed a free ticket to gain entrance at a specified time, conditional on acceptance of the rules printed in several languages on the back. Sketches of required attire were also drawn there for men and women. As a result, though the basilica was very luminous and festive on the inside, one began to breathe the atmosphere of silence and recollection which suited such a sacred building.

This example was gradually followed by the other major basilicas, and then also by the most important sanctuaries of the entire Catholic Church: *a bove maiore discit arare minor*[1]!

---

1 Proverb: "the younger/littler [ox] learns to plow from the greater/older ox."

As for the regular visitors to the basilica, they were well known to the wardens on duty, and didn't cause concern due to their clothing and demeanor. In any case, they received cards for unlimited entry for themselves and family members.

It was truly edifying, even for the most indifferent tourists, to see a good number of faithful prostrate in adoration in front of the exposed Blessed Sacrament at every hour of the day. They knelt behind the bench reserved for priests. Among these could be spotted high status individuals who didn't disdain being there. They would stay on their knees for a long time, alongside the simplest commoners of Trastevere and on top of the humblest cobblestones.

The Pope carefully prepared his homilies according to a program that he had established, so as to gradually bring into focus the dogmatic, moral, and liturgical points that he believed to require his authoritative word. He discussed them in light of the sacred texts of the day. Sometimes, however, he lingered almost exclusively on some facts from Church history or episodes from the life of the saint of the day. As for the feasts of the Lord and the Madonna, he took care not to let a single one pass by without reliving with reverent affection some episode of their earthly lives in the Holy Land.

Since he liked to deliver his homilies by looking at his listeners, as if to continuously read the impression his words had on them, he didn't want to stand before a lectern. He would think through his notes well and repeat them in his mind a couple of times. This repetition allowed him to establish them perfectly, yet elastically, so he could easily modify them here and there as needed, without fear of losing the thread of the discussion. He always concluded with a topical and significant maxim.

In fact, sometimes the audience demanded some modification, sometimes even the total replacement of the previously-prepared homily, with a nearly improvised homily that contained as its subject a thought that the Pope had retained for a long time and that the constitution of the audience presently offered the opportunity to be formulated and expressed. In these cases of semi-improvisation, having heartily recommended himself to the saints John Chrysostom, Augustine, and Thomas Aquinas, he took the floor. The words flowed together from his mind and heart, without tension or floundering, and always enlightened, at least at the beginning and end of the address. He spoke with a beautiful smile that radiated from all over his face, white and rosy like that of a child.

One morning, having been informed that among the present were members of a brotherhood of the Holy Rosary from Munich, he spoke about the Holy Rosary, albeit more slowly than usual, to give a German priest the opportunity to translate his words, sentence by sentence, into their language. He did this every time there was a large group of non-Italians among the faithful. Sometimes, however, he spoke in Latin, a Latin that those present who spoke a Romance language and were of average culture could understand directly. In one homily, the Pope wanted to recite the first part of the *Ave Maria* in Hebrew, himself translating it sentence by sentence, so that those present could hear it in the language which, he claimed, was the one that the archangel Gabriel had used.

"Of course! Because the Madonna, conforming to the liturgical custom that good manners must be used above all towards God, addressed God in the sacred language, in Hebrew, not Aramaic. Therefore, the archangel also had to address the Madonna in the same language, in sacred Hebrew, and not in vulgar Aramaic. This is justification for the use of Latin in the Catholic liturgy."

Then he explained why: "We are never alone when we address the greeting Peace to You, Mary, that is, *Shalóm lak, Myriám*, because the archangel Gabriel is still with us. Alone? He was ambassador of the Holy Trinity. Therefore, it was the Holy Trinity itself that first greeted the Madonna, and said to her Shalóm, Peace! And with the Holy Trinity, all the other angels, and today the whole mystical Body of the Lord, that is, the Communion of Saints.

"When you pray, no matter how much you enter the *cubiculum suum et clauso ostio*[2], you are never alone, much less when it is celebrated, even without the same servant, in a Siberian mine tunnel. It is never celebrated to the wall, but always in the vast Communion of Saints.

But let's go back to the Hail Mary! Do we avoid praise of the Trinity when we join the Trinity in greeting the creature that the Trinity itself wanted to raise from nothing to the boundless greatness of the Mother of God? *Mater Dei*, an expression that makes the second part of the *Ave* more important than the first, and which modern Nestorians would like to abolish!"

In another homily, he was compelled to touch on the topic of Eucharistic fasting, to justify his refusal to a group of pilgrims who had asked him to celebrate for them in the evening, as the Lord had done at the Last Supper:

"According to St. Augustine, the Eucharistic fast, the most rigorous of all ecclesiastical fasts, began from the very beginning of the Church, in Corinth, on the initiative of St. Paul himself, after he was forced to rebuke the neophytes of Corinth for the abuses which they had committed during the fraternal agape, which took place after the celebration of Holy Mass. This is why St. Cyprian, in Africa, so strongly reproaches those who claimed to continue on with agape meals! This is why in the nascent Church the celebration of Holy Mass took place in the morning, not the evening! Pliny the Younger also lets us know this, in the tenth letter, which he sent to the emperor Trajan: 'Christians usually gather on an appointed day, before the light of the sun, to sing a song to Christ, as their God.'"

---

[2] An allusion to Mt. 6:6: "But thou when thou shalt pray, enter into thy chamber, and having shut the door, pray to thy Father in secret: and thy Father who seeth in secret will repay thee."

In another homily, the Pope addressed an army of nuns who had gathered in Rome to reform their Rules. He warned them against the itch for reform, saying among other things that he had noticed the motto printed at the head of the file of the outlines of their discussions: "Each one has the creativity of the founder herself!"

"Who or what can guarantee that your creativity is exactly that of your foundress? Only the fact that your creativity expresses identical rules that your foundress created for you. But they are already there, beautifully created! Therefore, it's enough for you to practice them faithfully. Otherwise, your creativity, which isn't guaranteed by any law other than your free will, will express other rules, and you'll each be a foundress of your own religious order, but also destroyers of your own order, of the one founded by the creativity of your founder. Therefore, I leave you this new programmatic and demanding motto: 'We take care of the most exact observance of all the precepts of our foundress!'

"Stay rooted in your traditions, in which, and only in which, you find the wisdom, the spirit and the supernatural charism of your foundress. Otherwise, you expose yourself to the danger of acting like the man who, uncomfortable while walking because he put each shoe on the wrong foot, instead of exchanging the two shoes, changes direction and gets lost."

That morning, he spoke more directly to a group of young people who were about to go to Africa on their own initiative to build a bridge paid for entirely by charities and social agencies. Among other things, the Pope told them that it was:

"a work of material charity, if done out of love for God, and in deference to the commandment to love one's neighbor as oneself. If this theological, supernatural motivation were missing, your work would be reduced to simple philanthropy, certainly not reprehensible, but foreign to the Gospel. If, in addition to work, in addition to the example of a life lived in respectful obedience to all the commandments of God and the precepts of the Church, you will also be able to make the natives understand you in words, and you speak to them openly about our Lord, Jesus Christ, the Madonna, the central mysteries of the faith, and eternal life, then, and only then, will you also deserve the glorious title of missionary catechists in your dedication to the primary work of spiritual charity which is the evangelization of the nations.

"You'll then be of help to the missionaries, priests, and lay people, who not only for a relatively short time, as the construction of a bridge requires, but for their entire lives, dedicate themselves to this work. They are true pontiffs of the bridge which, at the end, leads to the open doors of Paradise. They are missionaries who leave economic, health, cultural, and other non-specifically apostolic tasks to others in order to dedicate themselves—like the twelve, transformed from workers into apostles—exclusively to prayer, preaching, the celebration of the Holy Sacrifice, and the administration of the sacraments. You are right to help those missionaries. It will also be good for your health, and perhaps it will provide interesting entertainment. If, once the bridge is built, some of you heard Jesus inviting him, 'Leave your nets and follow me!,' you will be thrice blessed if you answer yes!"

45

Petty Sociology in the Sacristy

AFTER THE MASS, THE LEADERS OF the group were allowed to greet the Pope up close. They had to wait for him to finish his usual thanksgiving at Mass, which that time, by exception, lasted only a quarter of an hour. A friendly conversation ensued, during which he brought up the intention of some of the younger ones to help the natives reform the social structures of their tribes.

The Pope responded, "Marxists call them structures. They only define them vaguely, to include everything in what they want to destroy. We use a more proper term, and call them social institutions. Well, dear young people, do you know these social institutions that you propose to reform?"

One of the youth responded in turn, "It's easy to imagine them. Slavery, imperialism, colonialism. In the name of Christ the liberator and of his Church..."

"First of all, where you are going, I was, and I can assure you that there doesn't exist the form of slavery in which one man is owned as private property by another man, or as public property by the State, as we find in communist countries.

"As for imperialism and colonialism, you won't have much trouble with them if you truly want to be inspired by the examples of the Lord. Do you remember what he said to those who asked him if he should pay tribute to Tiberius Claudius Nero, who was the emperor and absolute monarch of what today would be called the imperialism and colonialism of Rome? 'Give to Caesar what belongs to Caesar!' And St. Paul, in response, says in his letter to the Romans: 'To whom the tribute is due, give the tribute!' And St. John the Baptist, what does he say to the soldiers? 'Be conscientious objectors, throw down your weapons?' No, but, 'Be content with the money that has been set for you, and don't commit robberies!' And he was speaking to those who had volunteered.

"But what does St. Paul say to the slaves themselves? 'Rise up against your masters, and break your chains on their skulls? Gather together in large numbers, so as to establish an anti-slavery legal system? Overthrow the social institutions that oppress you?" Absolutely not! Do you know what St. Paul says about this, writing to the Colossians? 'Slaves, obey your earthly masters in everything. Masters, do not let your slaves lack what is right and convenient, remembering that you too are slaves of the Master who is in Heaven.' But he also writes to Titus in similar terms: 'I recommend that slaves be docile to their masters, so much so as to enter into their good graces, that they don't contradict them, don't steal from them, and show themselves faithful to them, so as to honor the doctrine of God, our Savior, in everything.'"

"St. Peter doesn't think differently: 'Slaves, be submissive and very respectful towards your masters, and not only towards the good and reasonable ones, but also towards those who treat you harshly.' St. Paul himself sends the slave Onesimus back to Philemon, who was his owner according to the law, with an accompanying letter, in which among other things we read: 'Perhaps for this reason Onesimus was taken from you. Remember that he had robbed his master and then fled to Rome from Anatolia! He was taken from you for a short time as a slave, to be returned to you forever as something better than a slave: as a dear brother. St. Paul had baptized him. Dear brother? Certainly to me, but even more to you, to be at your side, to be useful to you—Onesimus means useful—and to be at your side as a brother in the Lord. If you still consider me your friend, welcome him as you would welcome me in person.'

"The Christian truths, the supreme precept of charity, the judgment of God, and eternal punishment, which are preached to everyone, slaves and free, determine these relationships of fatherhood and sonship, these relationships of mutual brotherhood in the common heavenly Father, between master and slave, which anticipate and exceed the benefits of the positive laws of the emancipation of slaves. Without this principle of brotherhood and fatherhood, which Marxists call paternalism and deride because they fear it, no positive law is sufficient to guarantee the weakest from the oppression of the strongest, especially when the latter is left standing in the field and is called the state. In that situation, human relations are reduced to force. They are determined by the prevailing force, even if they result from the revolution brought about by those who, weak until disunited, became a dominant mass with impact when they are reunited.

"The task of directly reforming earthly institutions, including slavery, does not belong to the Church, nor can it be exercised in the name of the Church. Whoever, in the name of the Church, attributes to himself a mandate that the Church cannot give him, because it goes beyond the tasks for which the Church was instituted by the Lord, does not present the divine face of the Church to the people, but a grotesque misrepresentation of it. To those who must represent it by divine mandate, and who are tempted to dedicate themselves to such reforms, the Church simply evokes the words of Jesus: 'Let the dead bury their dead!' Does this come from a contempt for direct social activity? Far from it! It falls within the duties of rigorous justice, but it is up to the laity. So to you too.

"But dear young people, beware of simplistic utopian mirages, and of presenting to the indigenous peoples social institutions as heavy and unbearable. They do not feel the weight and injustice of these institutions at all, thanks to the traditional and innate sense of limitation that they have."

"Sense of limitation?" one of the young men asked.

The Pope replied: "It's the opposite of the sense of *always more*, that is, it's the opposite of the materialist ideal of indefinite progress even after man has conquered the goods of this world. This sense of a limit indicates that the goods of this world provides us with the means to deserve Paradise. When we have enough to lead a modest and dignified Christian life, *sufficit*[1]! A sense of limitation means we are happy with even a little... As for some missionaries, even bishops, they betray the Lord when they put themselves at the head of the so-called proletarians in the class struggle. They work to destroy and replace certain social institutions which they judge as unjust. They become followers of Spartacus or Marx. What does all that lead to? History certifies that they are the first to be overwhelmed by the collapse of the institutions against which they took the open field."

"Strange!" someone said. "The most pacifist priests, opposed to all war, opposed to military service, are the most fanatical in the class struggle! As if the class struggle were not war!"

The joke shifted the conversation to peace.

The Pope said, "Peace on earth is impossible without the faith brought to earth by Our Lord, and without the fear of God. Faith in a Supreme Judge in the Hereafter. It is not enough to desire it, even from everyone and even very ardently!"

A young man declared, "Even Cain craved it very badly! And to obtain it, he had to kill Abel, which made it impossible for him."

From the war, the conversation moved on to the death penalty, and the Pope spoke about it without sentimental pietism, and in no uncertain terms:

---

[1] "enough!" i.e., like "basta"—enough and no more.

"The law must make the crime undesirable through punishment. Punishment has a triple function. First of all, it aims to make the damaged order whole again. For murder, it is no longer possible to do so, since the murdered person cannot be resurrected, not even if his murderer is put to death. Then punishment aims to cure the offender, so as to extinguish his disposition to recidivism. The death penalty radically extinguishes it, don't you think?" asked the Pope, smiling. And then he continued, "Finally the punishment aims to make crime frightening, in order to deter anyone who could otherwise commit it. Death exercises this function to the fullest, and all the more, the sooner it follows from the crime. If, in fact, the punishment were to follow when the subjects had almost forgotten about it, it would easily be mistaken for useless barbarism."

A young man allowed himself to object, "But life is the supreme good. Only God can give it. Only God can take it away!

The Pope corrected him, "Not quite right, although eternal life is the supreme good—the life which continues after death. The murderer who accepts the penalty as a just punishment for his crime prepares himself in a suitable way for eternal life. In any case, he no longer has any right to this life. By putting himself in God's place in killing others, he has also snatched his own life from the hands of God. The authority carries out the death sentence that the unjust murderer has pronounced against himself. By deeming the life of others extinguishable at his own will, he cannot say that his own life is not extinguishable at the will of others. I personally am with Chesterton," concluded the Pope, "who was very much against the death penalty, provided that the murderers first renounced it!"

The group leader asked, "And isn't abortion murder?

"Certainly! The dogma of the Immaculate Conception confirms that with the first moment of conception an innocent, a human person begins to exist and that no one has the right to kill it, much less those who gave it life. But people who lived in those distant lands don't know this. Instead, they get divorced. Now you know that even if a marriage that breaks down is not a sacrament, divorce still violates three commandments of God: the sixth, the ninth and the one that prohibits perjury."

46

BEFORE AND AFTER TREATMENT

"**O**EAR SILENTIUM, SORRY, BUT this is how it went this time!" the Pope exclaimed after raising his eyes to the warning sign "Silentium," under which they had held the out-of-order conversation.

"*Prosit*[1], Your Holiness!" the sacristan kindly said to him as he put the cupboard key in his pocket. It was the end of his first morning's work. The conversation had given him time to put everything in order. "*Prosit*!" he repeated, and then added: "Good young men, but they would like to throw it all away, without knowing what it is they're throwing away. They want to build a bridge of wood and iron, while they tear down a world of spiritual values! You cannot desire what you don't know.[2] Instead, they exchange their fantasies for scientific knowledge. Naive romanticism, or the result of idealism, or of Kantism?"

"However!" the Pope exclaimed. It was the first time that the sacristan had added a few words to the simple "Prosit"! He had been waiting for the opportunity for a long time, since he wanted to make himself better known to the Pope, but he hadn't dared to say anything while the Pope was focused on his *post-Missam* thanksgiving, and much more so because he was always very busy rearranging everything in the sacristy. That morning, however, spotting a favorable opportunity, he seized it.

---

[1] "to thy health," "cheers," "may it benefit"—said as a toast and also at the end of Mass and other ecclesiastical services.
[2] "Incogniti nulla cupido." Ovid, *Ars amatoria*.

"Where did you do your studies?" the Pope asked him.

"In a seminary, but I had to interrupt them due to illness."

"How old are you?"

"Forty, Your Holiness."

"And you have recovered well."

"In practical terms, yes. Not entirely in theoretical terms."

"I don't understand."

"It's a long story, Your Holiness," the sacristan sighed.

The Pope began to feel a few pangs of conscience. For months on a daily basis, he had seen the sacristan with his fine and understated features. For months on a daily basis, he had heard him repeat *Reverentia Cruci... Procedamus in pace* before Mass, and *Prosit* after, and nothing more. He, the Pope, had enjoyed the impeccable and devoted work of the good man, as if the latter had been a vending machine. The Pope hadn't shown the slightest interest towards him, nor asked about his thoughts nor confided in him a little. Never in his life had anything like this happened to him! And it had to happen to him as Pope, right there, in that sacristy, where the Mass itself should have given him a finer intuition, a more delicate charity in his heart. When he felt what he couldn't consider a small fault, something bitter, he tried to repair it as best as possible.

"Did you have breakfast?" he solicitously asked the sacristan. He didn't wait for an answer, given how early it was. "So this morning, you will have a Pope's breakfast with me."

While walking from the sacristy to the Laurini monastery together with Camillo, the Pope tried to get the sacristan, who followed half a step behind, to break the respectful silence.

"What illness did you have?"

"A critical illness, which put me in crisis and brought me down. We had a teacher who repeated to us: 'The so-called critical problem is not a problem. It's a pseudo problem; since it cannot be established without presupposing a resolution. It must be called a critical disease, not a critical problem! A disease that attacks thanks to universal doubt, whether methodical or Cartesian, whatever you want to call it. Once it has attached itself to your cerebellum, it will kill you. It is a mortal disease that is followed by skeptical death.' I believe that teacher would have healed me properly, but one terrible day, he was suspended from teaching and sent elsewhere because, he was told, he wasn't open to the issues of the day. So I ended up in a psychiatric clinic. After fifteen days of hospitalization, the head doctor said to me: 'Don't worry, you are saner than I am. Just study a little less, and get a lot more sleep. And he released me.

"There was no need to go back to the seminary. The rector himself had advised me against returning. I attempted the classical high school diploma, and I got it, in fact with full marks. I opted for the faculty of history and philosophy. I wanted to become a high school teacher. However, I soon dropped out of university because, not having solved my famous problem, I wouldn't have been able to instill certainty in my eventual students of tomorrow, and I didn't feel like acting as a simple repeater of other people's sentences. No, I didn't feel like making my students' heads ring with the thousand different answers given by philosophers down the centuries to the same question, fueling in them distrust in regards to reason, and making them skeptics or pragmatists without valid, true, and certain ideals."

"Well, let's start with breakfast," the Pope said. The papal breakfast consisted of an egg yolk beaten with sugar, and then dissolved in a cup of milk without coffee; and some sweet crust. It therefore lasted only a few minutes; but that morning, to do honor to the guest and to his critical illness, the Pope made it last a little longer, and wanted Camillo to participate too. Ambrogio grumbled about the delay, about the two extra mouths without warning, but in less than no time, he had the necessary service in the refectory, and more garnished than usual. He wanted to make a good impression for the guests. Not only that, but a few minutes later he reappeared and placed a beautiful crystal vase with three roses in the middle of the table. He had picked them fresh from the rose garden outside the guests' entrance, and had also stung his finger with a wicked thistle. In fact, he went back to the kitchen sucking his thumb.

The sacristan said, "I was content with being a tutor, and I started writing stories of educational fiction for children. Even now I keep on with this activity. I have time and the royalties, although modest, allow me to give my mother decent money every six months. As for the critical illness, I have long since recovered from it. As you know, life dissolves the mists. I don't yet clearly possess the theoretical motivations that justify my current objectivist certainty. Yet I'm certainly not guilty of voluntarism. In any case, the disease cut short my career, and instead of becoming a priest, here I am a sacristan! *Et Deo dicamus gratias* for this too!"

"The theoretical motivations of objectivism? They come from the certainty that reality is as we know it, and that knowledge doesn't change if we disguise reality, as for example happens with a twisted lens or a crooked mirror. You remember Latin, right?"

"I delight in St. Augustine, but sometimes I also obsess over Tacitus."

The Pope specified, "The epigraphic! I would call St. Augustine the clearest. Well, the phrase *Si fallor, sum* from St. Augustine: If I am mistaken, I exist! Therefore, when I consider myself to objectively exist, I am not wrong. Now whoever knows how to make a basket can make a hundred thousand. If in that case I have arrived at that true objective, it means that I have the ability to arrive at the true objective. Is that clear?"

Before and After Treatment

"Clear!" Camillo approved, but the sacristan insisted: "I know, Your Holiness. It is the *ad hominem* argument against classical skepticism. But how can we answer Kant, according to whom the real cannot be known, except by being captured by the knower, and therefore itself covered by the characteristics of the knower, that is, disguised?"

"Do you know, dear friend, that you express yourself better than a philosophy teacher of my acquaintance, emeritus for several years, who said that he had become the philosopher he had become through obedience, given that his natural dispositions would have led him to much more. No one doubts this assertion of his."

"An exception to the *Vir oboediens loquetur victorias*?"[3]

"I would say so. But let's go back to Kant. Now do you know why Kant admits the existence of something beyond the knowing subject, the existence of an external world, of a Not-I?"

"Because without that something, the knowing subject wouldn't have the stimulus he needs to put his cognitive faculties into action. The Not-I is admitted by Kant because it stirs something in the ego."

"That is, it is admitted by virtue of the principle of randomness. So let's move on, and you, Camillo, have patience, if our chatter doesn't interest you very much!"

"It interests me very much, Your Holiness, and I wouldn't call it chatter, although I must admit that it isn't exactly the most suitable thing for making breakfast go down!"

"Now in the wardrobe of the Kantian knowing subject, among the various garments that this subject keeps available and, in the act of knowing, makes the object wear and therefore camouflage what is known, we also find what is called the relationship of cause and effect, or the principle of causality. This is the principle by virtue of which where

---

[3] Reference to Proverbs 21:28: "An obedient man shall speak of victory"—i.e., the final victory of the just.

there is something, we are forced to consider it as the effect of a proportionate cause, and consequently to believe that this cause also exists, even though we have not had firsthand contact with it."

"I remember, I remember," confirmed the sacristan. "Among the so-called categories of reason, Kant also places the principle of causality."

"Since it is therefore a subjective activity, it is illicit to infer from this principle the existence of something extra-subjective. It is valid only within the depths of the subject. It is not enough to assure us that in addition to the subject there really exists a world, a non-I, cause of something."

The sacristan added, "This is the conclusion reached by the idealists. They reduce the entire existing universe to the thinking subject—everything, including knowing and manufacturing. They only admit the existence of the ego. They deny the existence of a separate non-I. If then in place of the thinking subject, we put physical matter, we pass without shock from Hegelian idealism to dialectical materialism. It seemed like a short step from dialectical materialism to historical materialism, and Marx took it."

"You remember these things well!" the Pope declared before asking: "But if knowing is reduced to fabricating the object, will knowledge that doesn't correspond to the object ever be possible, that is, will error ever be possible?"

"Of course not! For coherent idealists, error is impossible."

"Therefore, everyone should be in the truth, in full agreement with the idealists. Instead, the idealists themselves accused Kant, their teacher, of error, and they must admit that in the history of philosophy there were countless individuals who did not arrive at the truth, that is, at idealism, and went astray. Error is present. Therefore, error is possible, even if mysterious. Consequently, the idealists are also mistaken, according to whom, if they were right, error cannot exist."

"But then everyone is wrong!" Camillo exclaimed. "And we can't trust anyone anymore."

"The left-wing existentialists logically conclude this: *Ignoramus et ignorabimus*,[4] they are overwhelmed by the wave of an absurd, ephemeral existence, beyond the thresholds of good and evil, in the anxious and desperate expectation of unavoidably falling into the abyss of an even more absurd eternal Nothing."

"And this sort of desperate nihilism," commented the sacristan, "has been called existentialism..."

"...left-wing," added the Pope, "left-wing existentialism, since right-wing existentialism which is spiritualist and theistic, is something completely different. Well, the poisonous root from which idealism, dialectical and historical materialism, and left-wing, immoral and desperate, existentialism all emanate is called Emmanuel Kant, who against the most inescapable experience, wanted to convince himself that knowing was not knowing things as they are, but to disguise them, to cover them with the so-called *a priori* forms of the subject, to synthesize them..."

"Here lies the *busillis*[5]! How does one get out of it?" asked the sacristan.

"But does it really seem that difficult to you? To you, who studied so much?" Camillo asked him before continuing: "Do you remember the advertisement for that famous hair lotion? Two photographs of the same person were compared. In the first, the subject was as bald as a billiard ball, and in the second he had hair that would make Absalom envious. Underneath the photos was written: 'Before and after treatment.' How could they have demonstrated that the lotion was effective, that it modified something or disguised it—to repeat the word used by His Holiness—if they hadn't also published the first

---

4 "We don't know it and we never will know it." Latin aphorism. It was made popular in the late nineteenth century by the German scientist Emil Du Bois-Reymond.
5 Difficult issue.

photograph? So how can Kant say that by knowing things, he alters them, if he does not also know them as they were before the alteration? Just think about it a little. He has to admit that he also knows them as they are before the treatment. Now this first knowledge, which precedes the modifying knowledge that captures and, I would say, surprises reality as it truly is in itself, this, I say, is true knowledge. The other, the modifying or camouflaging one, is the stuff of a sick mind. Sorry, I'm not a philosopher! Please continue..."

"Very good, Camillo!" the Pope approved. "Not much more is needed to unmask the imaginative contradictions of Kantian thought, however disguised they are as vast and profound self-importance. Once the trunk of Kantianism is cut close to the ground, all its branches dry up — dialectical and atheistic idealism and materialism, and left-wing, skeptical, and desperate existentialism. They collapse theoretically, because historically our civilization, wounded to the core by the Enlightenment and the crazed fetishes of the French Revolution, is sick with romantic rationalism and skeptical sepsis. Even after the fall of Pericles, there was a rampage of demagogy in Athens, the amoral skepticism of the Skeptics, and the repugnant protest of the Cynics..."

"...represented today by their belated and shoddy by-product which, in the first appearance, were the hippies. Well, Your Holiness, my former master could not have told me more or more clearly than what Your Holiness yourself just said, and what Commendator Camillo said. The truth is simple; error is multiple and complicated. However, according to Bergson, knowledge is static, while reality is dynamic. Therefore, there remains an irreconcilable non-correspondence between knowledge and the knowable."

"Just a moment! Is reality dynamic? Does the knowable move? Certainly! But even the knower does not stand still, but follows reality with his mental discourse. Henri Bergson figuratively makes metaphysical knowledge a fixed slide when in fact he should make it a continuous film that follows the progress of the knowable step by step, with only the transcendental laws of being remaining in the objective background. These laws are inalienably intrinsic to being itself."

"If I could have my say," Camillo interjected, "I would say that knowing, rather than photographing things at times, is a mirroring of them without interruption no matter how convulsively they shake."

"Very good!" the Pope approved. "And I would add that it's a mirror that moves and orients itself like a radar, and that knowing does not stop at the mirror image it has of things, but through that mirror it reaches them as they are in themselves, outside of the act of knowing itself."

"Therefore," the sacristan concluded, "it is possible to acquire, albeit with difficulty, because the danger of error is always looming, a knowledge that corresponds to the object one wanted to know."

"A knowledge that corresponds to the object?" the Pope asked, smiling and shaking his head doubtfully. "That is, an idea that corresponds to the thing?"

"Exactly," insisted the sacristan. "It's the problem with the bridge."

"Be careful, Camillo! It is a very different bridge from the one they will build in Africa, if they succeed, those good young people we saw this morning."

"I am convinced that it will be made of iron and wood or even concrete, while this other thing could only be made of words. Anyway, it doesn't seem clear to me. Sorry, I'm not a philosopher, but I ask myself, how can I know that a certain knowledge or idea of mine, whatever you want to call it, corresponds to a certain object? By comparing the idea and its object to each other. Only in this way can I see whether they correspond or not. But isn't this realization of mine perhaps a second idea? And will it match its object? Which object? The one constituted by the previous idea considered in tandem with its object. I will therefore have to establish a new comparison between this second idea and its object, constituted by the first idea united with its object. And if I realize that they correspond, it is only thanks to a third idea. But will this third idea correspond to its object? To find out, all I have to do is establish a new comparison between idea and object. But then we're back to the beginning, and we will never finish. Now a road that has no destination is certainly wrong, and we are off the road. Am I right? Sorry, I'm not a philosopher!"

The Pope spoke approvingly, "You have rearranged the bridge. Those on the bridge actually are like the guy who is anxiously looking for his glasses, and doesn't realize that he has them on his nose. So they too are looking for the bridge, and don't realize that they've already passed over it or at least that they are crossing it. In fact, knowledge itself is a bridge, a bridge that connects the knowing subject to the known object. Now these people cannot get busy looking for the bridge between knowledge and the object of knowledge, unless they can see that they are already in possession of this knowledge, that is, without already being in the middle of the bridge."

"That's right!" the sacristan approved in turn. "Knowledge itself is the bridge between the subject and the object, and it no longer has to look for a bridge between knowledge and something else. The error that makes knowledge an object in itself is therefore refuted. The error that makes knowledge an activity that camouflages the object is also refuted. But what is knowledge in a positive sense?"

"What, don't you know?" Camillo asked him scandalized. "You have talked about knowledge so far, without even knowing what you are talking about? But I'm sorry..."

"Don't worry, Commendatore, don't worry," the sacristan responded. "And do you know what knowledge is?"

"Damn!"

"Tell us, then!"

'Knowledge is... Knowing is... In short... Well, putting it in a few words is not easy, especially so because I'm not a philosopher. But I think it happens the same as all the things we know best. Do you know what time is?"

"Of course," replied the sacristan, who understood where Camillo was going.

"So tell me! Tell me, too. I've thought about it a lot, but haven't been able to clarify it as I would like," insisted Camillo.

"Both Aristotle and St. Augustine had a hard time with this question," replied the sacristan. "I don't think you would find my answer very satisfactory, if I told you that time is *numerus motus secundum prius et posterius*[6]."

"In fact, now I know it," Camillo nodded and then resumed: "In any case, I'd say that knowing is like getting out of blindness and loneliness, crossing the famous bridge, thanks to that bridge, which connects me to the rest. While I know something of that rest, I also know myself as a knower. If not, how could I ask myself whether I know anything or not? But then I also know what knowing is. If not, how could I say that I enjoy this knowledge? But then I also know that I have cognitive faculties—intellect, reason, the sensory organs. You know better than I what they are. And I know that reality is constituted in such a way, and is endowed with such characteristics, as to be luminous, that is, knowable. So while I know something, whatever it is that I know, I also include myself and a bunch of other things, which do not exist on their own, and are therefore not knowable as objects in their own right. They are in fact knowable and known only, I would say, a little indirectly, when reality in itself is known directly. They are qualities or characteristics of reality. I don't know if I'm explaining it well.

---

6 Famous definition of motion as an indication of time, as in Aristotle's *Physics* IV: "number[ed] movement according to before and after."

"Now all these objects, even if they are mixed with the coarsest material, in so far as they are known, do not remain placed next to the other, like pieces of stone, but meld together, I would say, dematerialized. So that knowing, even if it collides with something material, is not a material activity, as would be the simple act of touching or eating..."

"...but a spiritual one. It is the declaration in the knower of the existence of an equally spiritual soul," the Pope concluded before declaring, "Dear Camillo, if you were younger, I would entrust you with the chair of philosophy in some pontifical university. I think your pupils would not catch the morbus-criticus."

"Well, Your Holiness, in the meantime let's have another cup of coffee, to help us swallow all these rather indigestible matters." Camillo said. "It keeps very hot for an hour in this container." And without waiting for any order, he poured a cup of coffee for the Pope, another for the sacristan, and a third for himself. He sipped it with satisfaction and then concluded: "It will help us get our feet back on the ground."

"You have a ring finger without a ring," the Pope said to the sacristan.

"I never thought about getting married. Even so, I am useful for something. I can serve God and his vicar. And now, even theoretically, I seem to be calm."

"Add to St. Augustine a bit more of patristics, Scripture, theology, the life of God, of course!"

"Of course, the aspiration for the priesthood has always remained alive at the bottom of my heart, and the esteem for the priesthood has grown in me, as I have been able to see Your Holiness celebrate the Holy Mass."

"Start focusing on the diaconate," insisted the Pope.

"I cannot say no to Your Holiness. On the contrary, I certainly say yes, and thank you from the bottom of my heart!"

"Then you will tell my successor that I promised you the

diaconate, and my successor will keep my word. Then the rest will come."

"Your successor—who knows when, then! I am no longer a young man!"

"You won't have to wait long. Brother Ambrogio is here. He will bear witness." Brother Ambrogio was in fact clearing the table.

"I too can be a witness," Camillo said: "But if you order it, Your Holiness, everything will be done!"

"Dear Camillo, the future is in God's hands. Let us commit ourselves to Him! *Agimus tibi gratias...*" and with this prayer the Pope concluded the convivial conversation on such a critical problem.

47

Drugs are a Serious Problem

ALTHOUGH QUITE ELDERLY, KATE, one of the two clerks at a Genevan pharmacy, felt an attraction for the son of the painter upstairs. He was a well-built young man, although far from an Adonis of beauty. She was very thoughtful in continually coming up with a new excuse to meet him and express her concerns to him. On the morning of the move, she felt obliged to offer her good services to the family. They were all such nice people, even with such unalike faces. Neither the young man nor his sister had anything of their father and mother, and they didn't even look similar. But the young man was very polite, a true gentleman. He energetically defended himself. He didn't want any help, much less from such a kind lady like Kate. The box was light! But there was no way to refuse.

Kate insisted, "Let me give you a hand! I'm familiar with parcels and crates. It's my job, darn it!' While saying that, she took the box from him, while the young man was lifting it to put on his shoulder. The little box fell over and opened. Instead of books, highly crafted silver candlesticks spilled out.

"Oh!" Kate exclaimed.

"Oh!" exclaimed the young man as he hid his displeasure. He knew very well what was inside the box. He had opened the door of Professor Market's warehouse several times, and he and his associates—the girl who passed for his sister, the painter, and the woman who passed for the painter's wife—had repeatedly reviewed the wonders.

It was he, the kind young man employed as a delivery boy at the Housing Office, who sensed the real situation on the day a professor showed up, looking for storage for old books in an out-of-the-way but dry, safe place. He came up with a plan to lighten the professor's library of the most valuable books. Having inspected things in the absence of the professor, he'd been careful not to touch anything. He'd carefully glued back in its place the seal that he had skilfully detached intact from the base of the inner door. Then he'd set up the company which was now moving all the books on its own.

After the second inspection, in fact, the four members of the honored society had decided to wait until the professor had accumulated a greater number of works there. To avoid a surprise from a possible competitor, they rented the long-empty apartment. From there they checked all the comings and goings of the professor and his goods. After the last visit, when the professor had confessed to them that he needed to look for another warehouse that would be larger, less humid, and without so many stairs to climb every time, they decided to carry out the move on their own as soon as possible.

The painter—he really was a painter, at least from time to time, of abstract art, which few were able to duly appreciate, and which none of those few even bought—painted the name of the Velocius moving company, an enterprise of his own invention, on the green tarpaulin of a lorry. On another sepia-colored cloth, of the same size, he painted the name of the agricultural company Cerealia. During the journey from the professor's warehouse to the new house of the painter's family, the Cerealia sheet would descend over the Velocius sheet. In fact, it seemed logical that it was not an agricultural company loading its own truck with books, and that it could not be than an agricultural company dumping chemical fertilizers in an out-of-the-way farmhouse twenty kilometers from Geneva.

Kate's eyes widened when she saw the silver candlesticks. Deceptive in her own right from years as a sales assistant, she became suspicious, but without betraying her thoughts. Why on earth, she wondered, were the four acting as porters themselves?

Stopping the girl, she tried a trick question: "I'm sorry you're leaving! It will once again just be the two of us, Ghita and I, poor women, in such an out-of-the-way building!"

"I'm sorry too," the girl replied, without realizing the importance of her answer. So was it true that they were leaving together with the books? Or was it true that only the books were going away, but that they would stay there, as she had been assured by the young man? Who was telling the truth? The brother or sister? Therefore she consulted with Ghita, who had always shown a certain distrust towards the painter's strange family, which had arrived there some time after the professor.

"Of course!" Ghita confirmed. "They are certified thieves. I can smell them, the thieves. And does it seem possible, logical, and natural to you that the professor authorized them to make such a move, to go so far away and leave this place unoccupied? He's so cautious of every little thing!"

"Notify the police?"

"Good idea! So they start shooting, or take us hostage, and we lose our lives too!"

"But do we really have to wash our hands of all of this?"

"Let them go a little further."

As soon as they heard the truck start moving, the two ladies got on the phone, and the police promptly responded:

"Velocius moving company in Geneva? Ever heard of... Green Tarp Truck? Towards the countryside?...Okay. Thank you!" Police officers checked the Market depot, and saw that it had been carefully emptied of everything. A small undercover police vehicle passed the lorry with the sepia-coloured tarpaulin of the Cerealia company, and then did a u-turn and began to follow it until coming to an old, out-of-the-way farmhouse in the open countryside. A few hours later the Italian police received urgent information from Geneva and immediately set off.

Market was in his Roman depot, intent on photographing a few things for his English-language catalog. He locked himself in, as always, when he had to be engaged in something for any reason, even for a very short time. At one point he noticed that someone was fumbling almost silently at the door. For some reason, he immediately sensed that it was the police. He ran to a safe, and took out a bag filled with jewels and precious stones. Then he went to the window that overlooked the little garden behind the apartment building. Placing the bag on the window sill, he climbed over and jumped into the garden, falling heavily into the undergrowth. He immediately stood up, limping a little, and quickly reached the gate, from where he turned onto the road. Only then did he remember the bag that he had placed on the window sill, and retraced his steps. He reached out to one of the four shrubs that looked like skeletons without a skull with its arms stretched desperately upwards, and broke off a dry branch in fury. But as he was preparing to point the end towards the bag, without even realizing that his right hand was bleeding, he saw before his eyes his most precious bag disappear in the window opening, abruptly withdrawn by an unknown hand. There was nothing left for him to do but disappear too, and quickly.

The police also went to his upstairs apartment and found a second safe there too. It was open and empty. How Market had managed to reach his apartment in the space of a few minutes, open the safe, remove its contents, and disappear like a ghost, no one could ever know. In fact, it appeared to the police, from the analysis of the fingerprints, that the safe had been opened by Market himself a few minutes before the police themselves raided the apartment. There was no trace of him. No one ever heard of him again. Even the newspapers didn't talk about it since the police had justified the visit to the apartment building by saying they had been called there by a passer-by who had smelled gas coming out of the basement, which had been a false alarm or prank.

Meanwhile, Romolo had gotten everything ready. He didn't even think about notifying the commendatore, who was high on the cigarettes given to him by Vassily. That afternoon the Pope would travel by car to Castel Gandolfo. Professor Amador Moreno was waiting for him. He would show him the complete model of the buildings designed by the Mesogaios Institute. The Romanitas Institute had joined the venture. They would also review the works already in progress. It would be a nice trip for the Pope, a little longer than the usual one in the Vatican gardens.

Right up to the last moment, Romolo cleaned and re-cleaned the car that had been chosen for the trip. Then when the driver had taken his seat to drive it to the appointed place, Romolo gave it one last look and arranged the cushions well, because the Pope, of modest build, would certainly need some. He carefully closed the doors, and finally let the driver steer the papal car in front of the Laurini monastery. But immediately afterwards, compelled by an irresistible force, he too had to go there. He walked along Via della Tipografia like a sleepwalker, and stopped a certain distance from the Laurini monastery.

Having misplaced his glasses, the Pope was unusually late. Contrary to most older people, he was not farsighted, but shortsighted, which meant that he didn't clearly see objects that were at a certain distance from him. He rarely used his glasses, because up close he still saw very well for reading and writing, and he thanked Saint Lucia very much for this. But on that beautiful September afternoon, September 12th, the feast of the Holy Name of Mary, he really needed his glasses to enjoy the castle's greenery. After finally locating them, he put them in his pocket and quickly left to take a seat in the car, accompanied by the faithful Camillo and Monsignor Bruno De Gaudenzi.

Romolo had smoked his last cigarette two hours earlier. Afterwards, he had searched his pockets in vain: he had absolutely none left. The lack of drugs made his heart ache and his legs and imagination weak! The pit of his stomach felt so terribly sick! But this lack allowed him to return to himself a little and to start thinking again. In his frantic wait, at the Laurini monastery, he had repeatedly studied the car and, even more, the driver, who was a good man, the father of a family and as prudent as any other. The driver had boasted, and rightly so, that in eighteen years of continuous service, not a single accident had ever happened to him. Then from the car and the driver, Romolo repeatedly brought his eyes back to his wristwatch.

At first it seemed to him that the hands of his watch moved so slowly, so terribly slowly. Slow enough to cause agony! But now it seemed to him that the same hands were moving fast, too fast, and he wanted to slow them down, to have time to reflect and imagine what could happen so that he could come to a decision! But hadn't everything already been decided?

"No! Nothing has been decided! I haven't decided anything!" he screamed inwardly. But then he saw another red hand fixed at sixty minutes. And what were those sixty minutes? Who had set the red hand to sixty minutes? Exactly 3:30 pm. He looked at his watch: 3:25 pm. Five more minutes. At that same moment, the Pope appeared, followed by De Gaudenzi and Camillo. The Pope allowed the photographers to indulge themselves.

"But know this, my dear friends, that this is the first and last time that I'll allow myself to be photographed. I would also be curious to know who tipped you off..."

But right then, one of the photographers, he of the doves, suddenly turned his back on the Pope and towards the car. He stopped a few steps away. He had seen and photographed a young man rushing towards the car, opening a door suddenly, throwing himself in and then coming out with something in his hand. Even Camillo was immediately aware of it. He was upon him with a leap, and tried to snatch the object from his hand.

"Run, idiot!" Romolo shouted at him, but Camillo didn't let go, and snatched the breviary from his hand. The breviary exploded in his hand, with a dull, angry, and powerful detonation. Everyone within five meters was knocked to the ground.

The newspapers and television were able to report an entire slow-motion sequence of the attempt on the Supreme Pontiff Pius XIV. The photographer of the doves was injured, but the filmed reel remained intact. The last frame was a blaze of light.

48

At the Olive Wood Cross

THE POPE WAS IMMEDIATELY TAKEN to his room in the monastery of the Laurini fathers, but it was not suitable. He needed urgent medical attention, including a blood transfusion. He himself was happy to be admitted to the Santi Cosma e Damiano clinic, right in the rather large and very quiet room that had been occupied until recently by the then still simple Father Gregorio. Visits were prohibited. But he wanted his three advisors and De Gaudenzi with him.

"And how is Romolo?" he asked when he felt a little better.

"He died shortly after, but with Father Antonio, he confessed and repented and was absolved."

"Repentant?"

"Yes, Your Holiness. It was he who placed the bomb in the car, but at the last moment he wanted to throw it away. Camillo thought he wanted to throw it at Your Holiness. He tried to snatch it from him. It was hidden in a breviary case. From the analysis of the frames you can see everything exactly, down to the smallest details."

"And Camillo?" asked the Pope, with a tremor in his voice. "How is he?"

"Better, Your Holiness. He's not in pain anymore!"

The Pope was moved, and for some time was unable to utter a word. Finally, he said:

"I will soon go to thank him in Heaven. He preceded me a little, to prepare everything well for my eternal Mass."

He then wished to remain alone with Cardinal Gregorio, his confessor, and Cardinals Aurelio and Norberto also. A few hours later, an urgent telegram was delivered to Monsignor Wong's secretary for the bishop: "Come immediately, on the 9:30 pm supersonic, East-West Company. Seat booked and paid for. Pius XIV."

Thus, on the afternoon of the following day, September 14, Wong would be with the Pope.

The media assumed that the Pope was dying. The progressive forces, lost and disarmed in the face of the simple and straightforward energy of Pius XIV, would certainly have regained their courage and rebuilt their ranks. A conclave in such a threatening climate would have been an inconclusive adventure at best, as the previous conclave had been for a good six months. Depriving the most exalted prelates of the active vote was a drastic and hateful measure at the same time, much more so because Pius XIV had the comfort of the return to the more humble collaboration of characters such as Cardinal Stolzkamm and the Camerlengo. Was it necessary to expand the number of participants in the conclave and bring in numerous prelates of sure faith and guaranteed prudence?

It wouldn't be an easy undertaking, and also required time. And by now, humanly speaking, they couldn't be sure that they would have much time. Therefore, Cardinal Aurelio told the Pope that there was no point in delaying any further, that it was necessary to decide once and for all on the third path, the one that they had discussed together with two, and then with four, as the simplest and safest: the Pope himself would elect his successor.

Sister Rosa was in the hospital room of a sick man. Although she was the director, she also found time for this. The radio softly transmitted the latest news: "... so the supersonic B 24 of the East-West Company, headed towards Europe, left the base at its regular time at 9:30 pm, local time, and crashed half an hour later in the interior of the People's Republic of China. We have no news of the crew and passengers, about sixty people in total."

"How unfortunate!" the nun and sick man commented together. The nun then repeated the same phrase when she ran into Monsignor De Gaudenzi: "How unfortunate! Haven't you heard? A plane from the Far East crashed."

"What plane?"

But the nun couldn't tell him. De Gaudenzi soon came to bring the tragic news to the cardinals who were assisting the Pope. He had to communicate it to the Pope too. The latter listened to Cardinal Gregorio and then closed his eyes, raised his hand with difficulty to smooth his poor beard, without success, and finally said:

"It was airborne. Today, the feast of the Exaltation of the Cross, he will be exalted. Today he will arrive. Tomorrow, I will leave, on the feast of the Seven Sorrows of the Madonna."

Cardinal Gregorio didn't dare contradict him. All the prelates who were present held a council. The two doctors present also consulted each other, and then one of the two reassured the cardinals:

"He's not in imminent danger. His heart has reacted well to the drugs. He can recover."

They decided to wait until the afternoon. That same afternoon, however, they would all meet there, as the cardinal Camerlengo had recommended, though he hadn't needed to say anything. In the afternoon they were all there again, some in the Pope's room, some in the rooms made available to them by the director. Now it happened that the latter, having entered the Pope's chamber to bring something, asked permission to kiss his hand before leaving. As she did so, she couldn't help but take a moment to feel the pulse of the rather cold hand.

"But his pulse is fading!" she exclaimed. The doctor hastened to verify it, and agreed that it was indeed so.

"What can we do?" the prelates wondered. And then Cardinal Aurelio spoke with all frankness to the Camerlengo and prelates whom he had gathered around him:

"His Holiness Pius XIV had decided to elect his own successor himself, personally, so as not to leave the see vacant for even an instant. You can all understand why."

The Camerlengo and the others nodded before Aurelio continued: "His Holiness Pius XIV had decided to elect Monsignor Gabriele Wong as his successor. That's why he had ordered him to come immediately. Now it seems appropriate to ask the Pope what he intends to do, and—" but she interrupted herself. After asking permission, Sister Rosa entered. She approached the cardinal Camerlengo and said a few words to him close to his ear. He immediately hurried to the Pope, followed by Cardinal Aurelio and some other prelates.

And the Pope, in a slow and clear voice, began to say: "Your Eminences, I intend to personally elect my successor..." and he stopped to take a breath.

The Camerlengo took the opportunity to tell him: "Your Holiness, do you know that Monsignor Gabriele Wong..."

The Pope turned his gaze towards him, as if to say: "Let me finish!" and then he added: "Monsignor Wong is coming... by helicopter."

"He's lost his sense of reality!" exclaimed the Pope's sister, who had arrived from her village half an hour earlier. She was now sitting in a corner of the room, with the crown of the Holy Rosary in her hand, and with the briefcase on her lap: "You've lost your sense of things!" she repeated, and burst into tears.

She began looking for her handkerchief, but seemed to have lost it. Then she opened the briefcase, but the rosary crown got caught in the lid of the case, and then the case overturned. Little white sweets jumped onto the waxed floor, and rolled in every direction. Some ended up under fine woolen T-shirts or under soft, warm woolen socks, which had spilled out of the briefcase.

"Sorry, Fathers!" she said between sobs, and began to pick everything up. "They were for him. They are mint sprinkles, from Sulmona. He has always suffered from a sore throat. And I made these socks by hand, because in winter he always suffered from cold feet..." and she started sobbing again.

But the Pope said to her: "Give me at least one of those sprinkles! At least let me see the socks! You can give them to Vito, the blind man. The T-shirts too. He will say a few requiem rosaries for me, while he goes around from house to house looking for alms... They're so soft! You know how to do everything, Angelina! You are truly an angel! And you always did everything right: food, sewing... And those bobbin laces for my first love, the religious vestment? And singing, and painting... And the map of Europe, which you made for me in a hurry, for the test, when I was in the fourth grade? And your eyesight that you ruined while working to support me in my studies... And after the first Mass, celebrated with you there, you told me that I looked like a king to you... And when you went swimming in the sea, as a child, you used to put aside a few pieces of meat for me for a snack... Do my words sound like someone who has lost his sense of reality? Gabriele is arriving by helicopter..."

But he didn't finish the sentence, because the characteristic noise of a helicopter engine filled the room while an urgent phone call begged the director to have everyone clear the park immediately. Shortly afterwards a police helicopter landed in the clinic park.

"See, Angelina?" the Pope said to her: "You have so little faith in Our Lady? And to say that I learned devotion to the Madonna from you! He is coming up in the elevator—" A few moments later, the tall figure of Monsignor Wong appeared noiselessly in the doorway. Then he approached the Pope's bedside.

"Dear Gabriele, everyone here was about to tell you a *De profundis*!" Everyone, including Angelina, smiled at the unexpected exit. "How did it go?" the Pope then asked him.

This is what happened. Wong's secretary had received the urgent telegram, but hadn't dared pass it on to the Monsignor, because the latter was at his mother's bedside, near the very end of her life. He sent it to him a few hours later, when the saintly mother had already passed away. Then the secretary accompanied him to the airport, but the traffic jam at that time delayed their arrival at the airport. Worse, the shape and speed of their car turned it into a tortoise. They arrived at the airport just when the supersonic B-24 had just taken off. What could they do?

Wong's secretary didn't realize the urgency of things, and wanted to advise the Monsignor to postpone everything for another day, until after his mother's funeral, and to return to the episcopate. However, he tried one last solution: a military attaché at the airport. He showed the man Pius XIV's telegram. The military attaché knew that the Pope was dying, so he took the telegram and ran to bring it to the attention of a powerful man, his superior. The powerful man was Irish-American and, naturally, Catholic like his subordinate. He was leaving for New York, and without further ado offered Wong a lift to Rome on the military supersonic which was due to take off at exactly midnight.

Actually the planned route would naturally be eastwards from the Pacific, but given the urgency of the matter, he had the route changed. He flew west to New York with a stopover in Rome. He would arrive two hours before the departure of the connecting flight. While flying, he became an interest of the Italian police. Given the importance of the American, the Pope's grave state, and the usual police intuition, the authorities readied a helicopter for Wong—the same one that was taking off with a roar from the grass of the park of the Santi Cosma e Damiano clinic, its mission accomplished as it blew water and goldfish out of the nearby pond and bent the surrounding foliage towards the outside of the air vortex produced by the rotor.

The Pope helpfully sat upright, with his back supported by numerous pillows. He had the surplice and stole put on. Then he wanted all the prelates present in the clinic to enter his room, and was happy that Sister Rosa had brought a tape recorder. He intoned the *Veni, Creator Spiritus*, which everyone recited until the end, and he himself recited the final *Oremus* in a clear, if tired, voice. Then with a simplicity and solemnity that impressed all the prelates who crowded the room, he uttered the following words:

"In the presence of almighty and everlasting God, Father, Son and Holy Spirit, of the Mother of God, ever virgin Mary Most Holy, of Saints Peter and Paul, and of the whole celestial court, I, Pius XIV, at this moment elect as my successor, as vicar of our Lord, Jesus Christ on earth, Monsignor Gabriele Wong present here, certain that he will meekly accept to succeed me in the supreme pontificate."

The Pope was silent. Everyone's eyes turned towards Wong. He tried to smile even at that moment, but couldn't. His sparkling eyes covered in tears, he simply said:

"Last night my mother, slowly reciting the *Pater noster* with me, uttered the words *Fiat voluntas tua*, and passed away..." He couldn't continue.

After a pause, the cardinal Camerlengo asked him the question: "Monsignor Gabriele Wong, do you agree to become Pope, the legitimate successor of Pius XIV?"

Wong turned his gaze towards the Pope, as if to ask him one last time: "How should I answer?"

The Pope nodded to him to say yes.

Then Wong turned to the Camerlengo and said: "Yes, I accept!"

The Camerlengo, after a short pause, asked him: "What name does Your Holiness wish to assume as the legitimate Pope of the Holy Roman Church?"

The new Pope looked at Father Pio, Pope Pius, and then replied: "The name of my father, the name of Pius."

A long pause of silence followed. Finally in the room a faint yet clear voice arose: "Holiness, Pius XV, would you like to bring the holy Viaticum to this poor sinner as the first gesture of your pontificate?"

Father Pio was immediately granted his wish. Then he asked if he could stay alone for a while. Before they left, all the witnesses to the election of Pius XV signed the documents, duly prepared by the Camerlengo.

Half an hour later Sister Rosa came to Father Pio and said to him: "Holy Father, the parish priest of the Three Holy Brothers is below. He has come to ask your forgiveness."

"If he really wants it, let him come up and get it!" replied Father Pio.

On entering the elevator, the parish priest saw a tall gentleman in a corner. He signaled the priest not to say a word. He was such a noble and distinguished gentleman that the parish priest didn't feel like contradicting him. When they reached the third floor together, the gentleman followed the parish priest and entered with him into Father Pio's room. The Padre recognized him, and greeted him first with a brief wave of his hand before asking him:

"And The Miracle of Lepanto?"

"Here it is, Your Holiness!" Viscount René de Chateaubriand was aware of Pius XIV's resignation, but it seemed respectful to call him simply Father Pio. He showed him a copy of his volume, bound in white leather and decorated with gold, specially prepared for the Pope.

"Give it to Cardinal Aurelio Meyerbeer, who is aware of the matter. I promised him... And what about the adventures?"

"That too is well underway, Your Holiness!"

"Say hello to your mother, and pray for me!"

Then it was the turn of the parish priest of the Three Holy Brothers. The few present in the room learned from him that the police had got their hands on the files of an antique dealer—there was no need to name Osiris Market, and also the police had recommended him not to name names—and that he would place all the recovered sacred furnishings at the disposal of His Holiness, Pius XIV.

"Go ahead and talk about Pius XV," Father Pio corrected him: "I was a pope in transition for a short time. Now I'm back to Father Pio, and I will be until tomorrow, the feast of the Seven Sorrows of Our Lady, but *sacerdos in aeternum*![1] As I wanted for the motto of my first Mass..."

In fact, he died the following morning after the Mass of Our Lady of Sorrows, which was celebrated for him in the hospital room by His Holiness Pius XV, after *Ite, missa est* was declared.

"*Deo gratias!*" he answered. "Iesu, Maria, Ioseph!...Iesu..." and he remained motionless, eyes and mouth half open. His sister Angelina closed his eyes, trying not to hurt him as if he were still alive. She then knelt beside him and bowed her forehead to the bedspread.

Two days later, on 17 September in the afternoon, the feast of the Stigmata of St. Francis of Assisi, he was buried in the little meadow on the outskirts of the Vatican gardens under the shade of a beautiful olive wood cross. Written on the epigraph, a bronze scroll that was fixed almost at the foot of the cross, was:

A HIC IACET Ω
IN PACE DOMINI
PIUS OLIM PAPA XIV
QUI OMNIA UT PONTIFEX BENEFACIENDO
VELOCIUS PERTRANSIIT[2]

With the dates of birth and death.

---

[1] "A priest for eternity."
[2] "A Here lies Ω
In the peace of the Lord
Pius [who was] once [called] Pope XIV
Who as Pontiff by doing good [=blessing] all things
Quite quickly passed [away]."

The prelates and faithful lingered at that cross for a long time. Then gradually the large crowd dispersed. Monsignor Consalve was among the last to leave, and he did so with a thoughtful and troubled mind. Towards sunset, hardly anyone remained. In any case, no one would have dared to push out the few who still lingered. The gardener, the one with the Dutch tulips and the multi-flowering, re-blooming and scented roses, was on the avenue behind the cross, where he was throwing handful after handful of birdseed towards the beautiful white doves.

He advised them:

"These are biscuits, old but fine. Accept them with respect, as if that gentleman there, from Paradise, were throwing them down to you."

A little closer to the cross stood Cincinnato, the taxi driver. He had decisively placed himself at the head of the line of competitors who had rushed to give blood to the Pope:

"I have type-O blood! I'm a universal donor! I was the Pope's first private driver! It's my right! And no one protested. Now he stood there twiddling his cap in his hands. He couldn't make up his mind whether to stay or go. He stood looking at the other two, as if waiting for them, because he would take them back to their home that evening. He had parked the taxi in St. Peter's Square.

The two were on their knees, on either side of the olive cross. Right under the cross, like one of the Marys on Golgotha, was Sister Rosa, the little nun completely transparent with light. A bit further away was the rotund Giorgio Cicibello. They were both crying profusely, trying to hold back their sobbing so as not to annoy each other.

END

Printed in the USA
CPSIA information can be obtained
at www.ICGtesting.com
LVHW052357240524
780940LV00010B/339/J

9 781990 685934